The Austrian Woman

Vinny Stoppia

The Austrian Woman

Published by
Thunderbird Press
P.O. Box 524
Rancho Mirage, CA 92270
www.thunderbirdpress.net
thunderbirdpress@dc.rr.com

This is a work of art. The author values original ideas, procedures, processes, systems, methods of operation, concepts, principles, and discoveries. The purpose of this book is simply to present information and comment on it, criticize it, and even create a parody of it. To the best of the author's knowledge all quoted material is in the public domain.

Cover by Karoline Butler
Book design by Jean Denning

Library of Congress Control Number: 2016961503

Stoppia, Vinny
    The Austrian Woman
    ISBN: 978-1-5369743-0-0 (paperback)

Printed in the United States of America

To Richard Tyler Jordan
Thanks for showing me the way.
Je t'embrasse.

Menu for Reading

Merci Beaucoup

Richard Street—thanks for convincing me that an eight-hundred-page biography was worse than unrelenting halitosis.

Dorys Forray—the nurturing Jewish mother I never had, and my biggest fan ever.

Rhonda and Gary Freeman—whose infinite patience, indispensable insights, and needed corrections saved my *tuckus*.

Thom Bettinger—how many times did you come to my rescue? I've lost count of them, but not of my endless gratitude. *Te agradezco muchisimo.*

Thom Racina—gifted author, you contributed much with your penetrating suggestions, editing advice, and unflagging enthusiasm.

Regina A. Ley—a smart cookie who taught an old goat like me a thing or two.

Eileen Fitzpatrick—my last silent reader whose constructive criticisms were priceless and invariably correct.

Peter Rittenhouse—the Greeks had *deus ex machina;* I fortunately had you.

Bill Bladgett, Peggy Falkenstein, Denise Finch, Judith Franks, Linda Ley, Rich Milner, Ken Remitz, and **Steven Rushefsky**—Her Majesty and I appreciate your valuable input.

Karoline Butler—many thanks for converting the manuscript into InDesign, creating the book cover, e-book and many finishing tasks. *Gott sei Dank fand ich dich.*

And finally, to **Jean Denning**—a veritable *salvatrix*.

The Austrian Woman

WELCOME

*A*ccording to the Internet there are probably a million written publications about Marie Antoinette. Now there are a million and one. Perhaps you are asking yourself whether the world needs another book about this dead woman. Absolutely YES! From the moment the blade of the guillotine severed Antoinette's head, an unquenchable fascination mushroomed about this woman's life.

Do you ever watch trivia game shows? I sheepishly confess that only recently did I catch one of the popular TV staples for the first time. For me it was like watching a magic act. I was mesmerized by the unerring accuracy of the contestants. Serendipitously, as a first-time viewer, one of the categories in the opening round was "The Reign of Terror." I would have jettisoned this writing in shame if I couldn't spit out the correct responses. The first two answers listed were rudimentary, but, the last three were challenging, except for French history crazies.

For the last answer, the current champion tendered a bad guess. The clue read: "This is the first name of a famous woman who narrowly escaped the guillotine, but her husband, Alexandre de Beauharnais, did not," or something like that. The correct response was "Who is Josephine?"—Napoleon's future wife.

The doomed contestant blurted out, "Who is Marie Antoinette?" My jaw dropped open, with a spoon of ice cream suspended in midair. Didn't everyone know that Marie Antoinette was guillotined?

With compassion for this beleaguered man, I murmured, *Gee, I hope this book may be useful for future contestants who appear on quiz shows.*

I acknowledge that this writing is purely a popular account of an unpopular queen. Don't expect academic distinctions, footnotes, appendices, etc. Furthermore, because the parallels between Marie Antoinette's era and our current one are inescapable, I confess to using contemporary references and idioms. My intention is to present a narrative that is informative, interesting, and entertaining. To all readers who were bored to death during history class when it seemed the dismissal bell would never ring, this book beckons you!

Despite the fact that so much has been written about Antoinette, there still persists a perception that she was an unrepentant Valley Girl who minced her way through the palace. These folks feel that she got what was coming to her. Of course, there is a smaller, fervent group of admirers who insist that the title "Saint" should precede her name. Such opposing interpretations are simplified characterizations well treated in other biographies, although they still allow for further reflection.

So, who was Marie Antoinette? A bubbly fourteen-year-old girl hurled into the international spotlight with a platinum credit card shoved into her hand. Originally greeted with enthusiastic thumbs up, the easily-won admiration soon soured. Within fifteen years of arriving at Versailles, Marie Antoinette became the most detested woman in France. How did it happen that this promising debut evaporated so quickly?

Her personal Waterloo unfolded from a shattering quartet of events. First, there was the unsurpassed melodrama of The Affair of the Diamond Necklace in 1785. Actually, the word melodrama is inadequate to describe the swindle that released a trap door, inaugurating the steep plummet of the queen. Second, the calamitous financial crisis of the late 1780s, that from the popular viewpoint, was triggered by the queen's squandering of the national Treasury. Third, came the forced removal of the royal family from Versailles to Paris in October 1789. It's hard to govern confidently with a pike poised at your throat. And lastly, the State assumed control of the Catholic Church in 1790 which provoked the royal family's daring escape from Paris in June 1791. These four pivotal episodes paved the pathway to a nasty ending.

Marie Antoinette's fractured fairy tale brings to mind Thomas Hardy's poem, "The Convergence of the Twain." It was written after the fatal kiss at sea between the dazzling luxury liner, RMS Titanic and its cloaked, floating suitor, The Iceberg. Mr. Hardy steers a relentless course to the inevitable collision of the virginal vessel and phantom iceberg, destined to fulfill their rendezvous like two obsessed lovers. We are left to ponder whether the hand of Fate capriciously ordains the outcome of some tragedies.

Similar to the Titanic, the queen's life resounds with dozens of "what if" or "only if" moments. Throughout her entire adult life, Marie Antoinette felt plagued by a bad luck body patch that I shall refer to as the Lisbon Curse. Thomas Hardy's lyricism reflects Marie Antoinette's inescapable connection with the French Revolution: "Alien they seemed to be, no mortal eye could see, the intimate welding of their later history."

Finally, I wish to cite the legendary authors of The Story of Civilization, Will and Ariel Durant, who summed up their voluminous writings by admitting, "History is mostly guessing; the rest is prejudice." With much enthusiasm and some shpilkes, I offer my two cents' worth of studied prejudice.

Long Live the Queen!

Vinny Stoppia, 2016
Palm Springs, California
www.theaustrianwoman.com

"You know, it's hard work to write a book.
I can't tell you how many times I really get going
on an idea, then the quill breaks.
Or I spill ink all over my writing tunic."
Ellen DeGeneres

An Ending Begets Endless Fascination

A sickly woman of nearly thirty-eight stands in a prison cell as a rat scurries past her feet. She seems immune to the droning of the court-room bureaucrats. She faintly comprehends they speak of her just punish-ment. What do these ruffians know of justice? In the next moment, she is jerked alert with fear. Her linen bonnet is yanked off her head as her neatly arranged hair is brusquely chopped off at the neckline. Against her useless protests, the executioner binds her hands behind her back. Tears trickle down her cheeks as she is led out of the prison to a waiting wagon. She sits on a plank of rough wood for a jolting ride to the place of execution. Floating in and out of her jumbled thoughts, she remains keenly conscious of each sound. She is lulled by the clicking cart wheels on the cobblestones as she oddly recalls a fun-loving girl of six, playing with her toy collection of Noah, his ark, and traveling companions. My God, what ever happened to that once carefree child? How did she, the radiant Queen of France, end up in a dung cart on her way to execution? She knows that she is reviled by the multitude lining the streets. She still wonders what has she done to make them hate her so fervently. Most onlookers peering through the unbroken line of troops are shocked into silence, glimpsing this once mighty monarch reduced to a haggard woman. She struggles to piece together the words rising from thou-sands thronging the route. At last, she comprehends the repeated phrase. It clings to her fleeting moments like a trembling child to its mother. *"Et voilà, l'Autrichienne!*—Look, there goes the Austrian Woman."

"Time flies over us, but leaves its shadow behind."
Nathaniel Hawthorne

Spotlight One

The Days of Intoxicating Youth

Chapter 1

Once upon a time, a Princess ...

*L*ike a classic fairy tale Marie Antoinette's life began in Vienna, Austria on Sunday evening, the second of November, 1755. The babe made an unblemished entrance into the world that even Rousseau would have applauded. The mother, Empress Maria Theresa, barely pulled away from the paperwork clogging her desk to give birth to a small, but healthy, female. It was All Soul's Day, normally a somber holiday to remember the dead sidetracked in Purgatory. It had long been arranged that the godparents for this baby would be the king and queen of Portugal. This happy link between two royal families was shattered by the ultimate lady in charge, Mother Nature.

On the previous day, the Great Lisbon Earthquake occurred while the devout packed the morning mass at Lisbon's cathedral celebrating All Saint's Day. Nowadays, experts estimate that the quake measured a minimum of an 8.5 seismic event. The violent shaking and ensuing tsunami destroyed Lisbon and erased many coastal towns. The official death toll remains unclear, but it is thought to have caused at least sixty thousand deaths. Suddenly, there were thousands of newly dead to be prayed for. A suffocating gloom descended on the Continent when news of the devastation reached foreign capitals. For months, aftershocks of the quake rattled Europe's cities as far away as Munich, gripping the numbed public as they gobbled up the hypnotic front page news.

The celebrations of the child's birth and the safe delivery of her robust mother were forgotten. A newborn with ruined godparents? Something foreboding grasped superstitious souls sensing the presence of the dreaded evil eye as they quickly made the sign of the cross. An unhappy life for this newborn seemed a certainty. Yet, the baby's mother would not permit herself to fall prey to such dark thoughts. She reasoned the disaster was a result of God's displeasure with the sinfulness of the world, and not a frightful foreboding attached to her daughter's destiny. What the mother dismissed as foolery, the fragile infant absorbed like a dormant virus, waiting to be awakened as the Lisbon Curse.

The archduchess, christened Maria Antonia Josepha Johanna, was number fifteen of the sixteen children Maria Theresa delivered during her life. Maria Antonia was the youngest of all the girls. The first name of all but one of the empress' eleven daughters began with Maria, in deference to the Virgin Mary. Inexplicably, one Johanna slipped in. To avoid confusion in the family, all the girls were called by their second name. So the future queen of France was known as Antonia within the palace walls. Considering the size of this armada of children, it was easy to get lost in the bedlam of that household. Although the empress' heavy workload with affairs of State preempted daily maternal supervision, her detailed instructions governed the upbringing of her offspring. Normally, Maria Theresa saw her children together once a week.

Antonia reveled in a rambunctious, sloppily tutored childhood. Her education was spotty at best with huge gaps in learning under the supervision of a well-meaning but indulgent governess. Her insular world centered on a curriculum of being amused and entertained. Boredom was the equivalent of the plague. When she was ten, Antonia could barely read. The sight of a book sparked frowns and pouts. Her compliant governess got the message—less reading! Suddenly, at age twelve, the unstructured days of the archduchess came to a screeching halt. The unthinkable was about to occur. To the shock of all political players, it was decided that Antonia would marry the heir to the French throne.

Only twice over the centuries did a French heir marry an Austrian archduchess. This proposed union carried a huge risk aiming to create allies out of traditional enemies. Six months after Antonia's birth, the unveiling of a treaty of cooperation between France and Austria was announced. King Louis XV resigned himself to the necessity of such an alliance, despite the hostility of his people to forge such a repugnant pact.

Louis XV's indispensable mistress and unofficial prime minister, Madame Pompadour, convincingly tipped the king's hand in favor of a friendship between the Bourbons of France and the Hapsburgs of Austria. The political chessboard of European players had recently reshuffled leaving both France and Austria vulnerable. Louis XV and Maria Theresa could smell the diplomatic coffee demanding an alliance for their mutual benefit. In May 1756 the two countries signed an accord to defend one another against attack. This type of agreement was normally cemented with a dynastic marriage between both parties. With several single daughters at her disposal, the empress would allot one of them to become queen of France. The bossy-pants empress needled the French ambassador, Marquis Durfort, to advance the match. The squeezed ambassador played a delicate game of promise without commitment. Finally, his coy master in Versailles signaled the green light for the nuptials.

Catapulted into the limelight, twelve-year-old Antonia learned of her engagement to the thirteen-year-old grandson of Louis XV. Having two eligible sisters in front of her, Antonia never expected to be in the running for this prestigious match. But the sudden death of one and the quick marriage of the other bumped Antonia to the front of the line. After close inspection, the horrified Empress Maria Theresa exploded when she discovered that Antonia was barely literate. The empress assessed her youngest daughter to be "frivolous, thoughtless, and headstrong." The featherbrained child's indulgent governess was immediately replaced by a more exacting one; but, the damage was done.

Maria Theresa dispatched a distress message to her ambassador at the French court, Count Mercy. She confided that it was a matter of utmost urgency for him to send a tutor to prepare the young princess for her future role. After acknowledging that her daughter was an under-schooled archduchess, the empress expected a miracle worker from France. Count Mercy discreetly asked Louis XV's foreign minister, the Duke of Choiseul, who had negotiated the marriage pact, to suggest someone of impeccable character. Of course, they chose a priest.

With the crack of the whip, Antonia's *zaftig* mother scrutinized the reclamation of her wayward daughter. Maria Theresa's successful reign was characterized by capable leadership along with the knack to never lose touch with the common folk of her realm. Known to have an explosive temper, she could rattle the palace windows and nerves of its residents. Deeply religious, the empress frowned on frivolity and sexual license at her court, spelling a dour court life, especially for the younger set.

But Maria Theresa also exposed a softer image. Daily life in her palace was more relaxed when compared to the exacting etiquette that everyone goose-stepped to at Versailles. The empress knew how to roll out the imperial pomp when required for State occasions. But, most often, she and her consort, Francis of Lorraine, had little patience for court etiquette that the Austrians deemed a waste of time and money. Being more informal, the large royal family presented musical and theatrical entertainments for their enjoyment, in which most of the children participated as principal performers. The entire family sang and played a musical instrument, forerunners of the talented Von Trapp clan. These familial socials remained part of the DNA of the youngest daughter of Maria Theresa and future queen of France.

The empress realized that her daughter's intended foreign home was not a Viennese look-alike. She needed to prepare Antonia for the huge shift that awaited her, the glittering snake pit of Versailles. Now it was the French ambassador's turn to push the empress' buttons. The French viewed Vienna as a marginally civilized outpost in Europe and insisted upon certain conditions to upgrade the unrefined archduchess. Aware of her daughter's shortcomings, Maria Theresa agreed to the laundry list of requirements.

So began the parade of French-imported experts. The first to arrive in the autumn of 1768 was the tutor, Reverend Vermond, a thirty-three-year-old priest, who was formerly employed as a librarian.

What a shock awaited Vermond. After his introduction to Antonia, he gulped hard at the scope of his task. He quickly discovered that his pupil was easily bored and detested reading. He posed as an older friend to gain Antonia's confidence and to rein in her drifting attention. Lessons were presented with a coating of fun. Vermond sent Count Mercy the preliminary report card of the archduchess: "A bit of laziness, and a great deal of giddiness have made my instruction difficult; however, she has a good memory. In the end, I came to recognize that she would only learn so long as she was being amused." Vermond's first goal was to improve Antonia's French which could never pass muster at Versailles. After a year, her French improved and was nearly flawless. And then there was her penmanship. It was a barbaric scrawl, hardly suited to a future queen. This was another challenging task, but Vermond knew he had to succeed because the clock was ticking fast.

The priest drilled Antonia in the lineage of French kings, including the names and backgrounds of the king's close relatives, known as the princes of the Blood, and other major personages at court. She eventually knew more about French history than she did of her own native Austria. The indispensable Vermond, with the prompting of his superiors at Versailles, cautioned Antonia that the French did not embrace warmly any foreign princess who did not put France's interests first. The upshot was that she had to remain politically disengaged, a valuable red flag warning that flew right over her naive head. Politics proved even more tiresome than reading! The highlight of these cram sessions cum entertainment was a connection between teacher and student that would endure for many years.

"People will pay more to be entertained than educated."
Johnny Carson

Chapter 2

Finishing Touches

A dentist imported from France arrived to fix Antonia's crooked teeth. For three months she sucked up the pain of the primitive braces as a price for her illustrious marriage. Next came Monsieur Larsenneur, the A-list hairdresser tasked with transforming Antonia's hair that was considered too curly and wild for French taste. Monsieur Larsenneur excelled at his job but lacked imagination. Arranging the hair of a girl not yet fourteen in the style of a middle-aged woman did not exactly flatter the young teen. Although Antonia looked more acceptable to pass muster at Versailles, the resulting hairdo appeared stiff and frumpy.

Additionally, proficient stage actors and the celebrated dance master, Jean-Georges Noverre, arrived to teach Antoinette some vital social skills. She practiced the art of speaking politely with an authoritative tone. And most importantly, she learned to walk as though she were not touching the floor. This was known as the Versailles glide, a difficult feat to achieve considering the weighty gowns that imprisoned the female body. But Antonia met this challenge with ease. Being a natural on the dance floor, she impressed her tutors by learning the court dances to perfection. They unanimously agreed that she exhibited a natural grace to her walk and a charming social demeanor. Most of all, the tutors remarked about the high manner with which she carried her head. It was impressive but came across as a bit haughty. This unique carriage would become Antonia's signature trademark as queen.

During her personal overhaul, the future bride received several portraits of her fiancé. There remains no record of her response but, judging from the empress' subsequent sermonizing, the young girl's dreams of a dashing prince evaporated. The empress went on the offensive lecturing her daughter, "that passionate love soon disappears, whereas domestic happiness consists of mutual trust and kindness." Excellent advice for sure, but for a teenage girl, such words smacked more of adult cynicism than the romanticized future envisioned by most adolescents.

Squeezed in between the accelerated instruction, Maria Theresa drilled Antonia on the importance of the alliance between France and Austria, stressing her daughter's responsibility to make it succeed. Distracted by the daydreams of the life that awaited her, Antonia registered next to zero comprehension of her mother's sales pitch. But she paid rapt attention to the trousseau that was ordered from Paris which made her Austrian apparel resemble thrift-store merchandise. The budget conscious empress spent a bundle (about two million dollars in today's money) on her daughter's trousseau. Of course, she expected a big political return on her investment. With a dreamy wardrobe like this, Antonia must have asked, "What could possibly go wrong, mother dear?"

While Maria Theresa bombarded Antonia with advice on being a successful queen and wife, the empress was impatiently tapping her foot for THE sign. Without it, the marriage could not proceed. That signal sprang to life on February 7, 1770, when Antonia began menstruating for the first time, confirming her readiness for the conjugal bed. The news whisked its way to Versailles accelerating the marriage plans. Louis XV relayed his delight of Antonia's womanhood as he indelicately pestered the empress to know the size of her daughter's breasts. The irritated Maria Theresa conceded that her daughter was still maturing, yet showed promising signs of an ample bosom.

Besides a dizzying whirlwind of pre-nuptial festivities, Maria Theresa conducted an intense week of bedtime harangues, instructing her daughter on how to behave in her new role. These maternal sermons required Antonia to sleep in her mother's bedroom, where the windows remained open no matter what season of the year. All too soon, the day arrived for the young queen-to-be to leave Vienna. On the eve of her departure, Maria Theresa gave Antonia a delicate gold watch, a cherished keepsake she would revere always.

Besides this sentimental memento, the pragmatic empress included a how-to manual regarding her conduct. Her mother made her promise to recite religiously, "Regulations to Read Every Month." Upon reading them, it was natural to conclude that the young archduchess was about to take the veil in a convent. The first third of the rules governed her daughter's daily prayers and religious practices. The remainder of the maternal epistle dealt with stern recommendations for Antonia's behavior away from Vienna. It was a catalog of "do this," and "don't do that." One prescient sentence warned, "All eyes will be fixed on you."

Louis XV sent an impressive set of wheels to Vienna to convey the future bride to France. Everyone marveled at its grandeur which resembled a glass jewel box with an interior depicting the four seasons. On Saturday morning, April 21, 1770, with unabashed tears, Antonia slowly rode off to a questionable future. The anguished archduchess kept looking back at her receding family until they disappeared from view. An impressive caravan of fifty-seven coaches, each drawn by six horses, captivated all eyes throughout the long progress. The trail of horse manure alone from the more than three hundred horses must have been overwhelming.

> "Parents can only give children good advice
> or put them on the right paths,
> but the final forming of a person's character
> lies in their own hands."
> *Anne Frank*

Chapter 3

Frenchies, Here I Come!

Once Antonia's carriage disappeared from view, Maria Theresa headed for her desk to write a heartfelt letter to her new son-in-law. Royal progeny knew from birth that their marriage partner would not be someone of their choice; or in the words of the empress, "They are born to obey." But being a protective mother, the empress tried to pave the way for her daughter's marital harmony. The opening lines read like a slippery prophesy from the priestess at Delphi, "Your bride, my dear Dauphin, has just left me. I do hope that she will be the cause of your happiness. I have brought her up with the design that she should do so because I have foreseen for some time that she would share your destiny."

The caravan of carriages progressed its way toward Versailles, traveling eight or nine hours each day for three weeks. Continually on display, the bride-to-be waved at the well-wishers who hailed her as she floated by in her heavenly coach. She was regaled with receptions wherever she stopped for the night. She came down with a nasty cold during the trip, but her schedule did not cut her any slack in her public duties. She was learning fast that the demands of royalty exacted a personal cost.

On an island in the center of the Rhine, between the borders of France and Austria, stood a hastily built wooden pavilion where Antonia was handed over on May 7, 1770. In the room on the Austrian side, Maria Antonia experienced a rite of passage that a foreign bride endured on entering

France. Although the clothes she was wearing came from Paris, they were deemed "soiled by Austria." It was as though the French were symbolically delousing the bride of foreign contamination. Antonia was stripped of each stitch of clothing, shoes, hair ornaments, jewels, and anything on her person. Buck naked, she stood shivering in the drafty room with rain beating down on the cardboard thin roof. She felt humiliated with all the eyes glued to her. And she was dumbfounded that her attending ladies began arguing over the castoffs, which they snatched as souvenirs. Antonia was redressed from head to toe with every piece from Paris, and touched only by French hands. Arrayed in the sanctioned apparel, the archduchess could be presented as authentically French.

After this ordeal, Antonia exchanged a wrenching goodbye with her Viennese attendants. The final shock before she crossed the pavilion to the French side was the seizure of her dog, Mops. This confiscation almost precipitated a princess meltdown. In a distressed state, Antonia almost had to be dragged to a room where the handover would take place.

As Maria Antonia passed from the Austrian to the French side of the pavilion, she became forevermore, Marie Antoinette. She was greeted by the encyclopedic mistress of court etiquette, the imposing Countess Noailles. She would serve as Antoinette's Lady of Honor, the most senior of the ladies in Marie Antoinette's service. Although a demanding job, it rated as a lucrative and coveted post at Versailles.

Antoinette, who had behaved perfectly up to this point, visibly faltered. Overcome by the strain of the journey and separation from all that was familiar, she sobbed as she ran to embrace Madame Noailles. Instead of comforting the bewildered girl, the stiff countess reprimanded her about the impropriety of her emotional outburst. Like a slap in the face, she got her first taste of court expectations. No surprise that Antoinette would never warm up to this French version of Nurse Ratched.

The French entourage rested the night at Strasbourg. The following morning Antoinette met Bishop Louis Rohan, the appealing officiant of the mass she attended. They exchanged brief pleasantries, never imaging the turbulent destiny that would one day entwine them. While the traveling party of two hundred persons meandered toward Versailles, folks along the route paid homage to the future queen of France. Antoinette delighted the cheering admirers with her effervescent attention and smiles. In the opulent coach, Madame Noailles bombarded Antoinette with endless instructions regarding the etiquette to be observed once she arrived at Versailles. Most importantly, the countess drilled the bride-to-be on how to greet Louis XV, demanding that her first impression be flawlessly correct.

Before reaching her final destination, a courier from Vienna caught up with Antoinette's carriage delivering a letter from her mother that she excitedly tore open: "Here you are where Providence has decreed you should live. Remember a wife must submit to her husband and have no business other than to please him and obey him." The empress enclosed two more letters, instructing Antoinette to give the first to Louis XV and the second to his daughters, her new aunts. In these respective notes, Maria Theresa urged the recipients to guide her inexperienced offspring.

On May 14 at a sylvan location near the chateau of Compiègne, Louis XV waited with his three daughters and the shuffling bridegroom to meet the new bride. Antoinette's coach came to a halt at three in the afternoon. She was greeted by the Duke of Choiseul, who had negotiated the marriage. Forgetting Madame Noailles' instructions, Antoinette bolted toward the still comely man, King Louis XV, and dropped to a spot-on curtsey.

The king was delighted with this spontaneous greeting, refreshingly contrary to the rulebook of Versailles. Remembering her mother's admonition to make everyone like her, Antoinette gushed with a girlish eagerness to please. The king kissed the new addition to the family, expressing his delight. He presented her to his husky grandson, her chosen husband. Stiff as a board, the klutzy heir lurched forward, planted a stingy peck on Antoinette's neck, and receded into the background, avoiding her gaze. If she was disappointed, Antoinette concealed it well. She had to make this fellow like her because the success of this political gamble hinged on these two inexperienced teenagers.

While Antoinette was being graciously welcomed, hovering in attendance stood members of the royal entourage, resembling costumed vultures sniffing out their prey. The intimidating crowd kept their eyes scrupulously trained on Antoinette. This fourteen-year-old girl would now become the most senior female at court, requiring unpleasant adjustments from some in the crowd. Most considered Antoinette as a minor-league player from the B Team Vienna. Could she step up to the exigencies of Versailles, the major leagues? Before Antoinette got the chance to utter her first bonjour, there already existed a clique of courtiers who resented the juvenile import. If the Austrian presented problems for them, they would pounce to crush her.

After the meet and greet, the royal party drove to the chateau of Compiègne for a family dinner. Here Antoinette met her husband's two younger brothers: the porky brains of the family, Count Provence; and the dashing wastrel, Count Artois. Finally, she was introduced to the princes of the Blood. It was also at Compiègne that Antoinette met the recently widowed Princess Lamballe, who would become a lifelong friend.

The following day the royal party made its way to the chateau of La Muette where the bride would spend the night as the royals gathered for the wedding rehearsal dinner. Among the ladies dining with the gentlemen, Antoinette spotted a gregarious and impressively jeweled woman sitting next to the king. Her physical beauty was inescapable, and her speech was colored with an appealing lisp. She definitely stood out in the crowd.

Antoinette whispered in Madame Noailles' ear to identify this divine creation. The countess replied that the breathtaking lady was Madame du Barry. Antoinette curiously asked what role the countess performed at court. The diners in the immediate vicinity stopped chewing in unison, anticipating the response. In her deadpan voice, the countess informed Antoinette that the lady's purpose was "to amuse the King." Ever the charmer, Antoinette coquettishly challenged the king's enchantress, "Well, then, I shall be her rival." Her playful retort sparked forks to falter as fans snapped open in a flutter.

Louis XV had chosen this gathering of the clan to include his low-class mistress, Madame du Barry, at a family affair. It was a shock to all present, except to the unaware Antoinette. At the end of the dinner, one grizzled veteran of the court asked the new bride what her impressions were of the stunning beauty at the table. All ears were attuned when Antoinette simply replied, "Charming."

Everyone was betting that this initial estimation would undergo a radical recalculation.

> "It's not easy to come somewhere
> And have to find your place."
> *Fernando Torres*

Chapter 4

Going to the Chapel

*A*t nine in the morning on Wednesday, May 16, 1770, Antoinette pulled up to Versailles for the first time. OMG! She gawked like a tourist. It was hard to digest all at once the endless wonder of the edifice. As grand as it appeared, the palace was not the brilliant gem it used to be. A lot of deferred maintenance was needed but always postponed for reasons of economy. The most recent improvement within the palace was the addition of the Opera House, a beautiful theater surrounded by magnificent balconies. It was where the wedding reception would be showcased.

Antoinette waltzed into a vast ground floor apartment reserved for the Dauphine of France, the wife of the heir. In France, the male heir was called the dauphin, and his consort was known as the dauphine. Upon her arrival, Louis XV entered to welcome Antoinette. He introduced her to the groom's two youngest sisters: nine-year-old Clotilde, already more wide than she was tall; and, the baby of the family, six-year-old, sweet Elisabeth.

After the introductions came the big surprise. The king presented Antoinette with a treasure chest of jewels. The bride gasped at the countless gems and diamonds suddenly at her disposal. Antoinette also received an exquisite necklace of large, matched pearls that was brought to France by Anne, the daughter of the king of Spain, when she married Louis XIII in 1615. This coveted necklace had been worn exclusively by the queens and dauphines of France; Antoinette pinched herself to be the latest recipient. But she didn't have time to try on these glittering trinkets because three hours of bridal preparations beckoned. It was going to be a long day for everybody.

Perhaps nothing would strike more terror in a bride's heart than to discover a tailoring disaster as she slipped into her wedding gown before floating down the aisle. Believe it or not, that is what happened to Marie Antoinette. Three months before she left Vienna, her measurements were sent to Versailles to insure a fitted dress for her wedding day. The gown was a shimmering silver design, loaded with glittering diamonds and pearls. But it didn't fit. One of the seamstresses had misread the measurements and the resulting gown was too small in the bodice, preventing the dress from being laced up in the rear, exposing the bride's lush undergarments. The initial horror gave way to emergency bridal triage. The attending ladies brainstormed possible quick fixes, but time did not permit any useful adjustments. Louis XV was leading the wedding procession at one o'clock sharp, and Antoinette had to be in that lineup, no matter what she was wearing. In this exquisitely flawed garment Antoinette looked runway perfect from the front, but the rear view failed Versailles' exacting standards.

Antoinette went up to the king's rooms where her fidgeting fiancé took her hand. The doors swung open and the couple entered the Hall of Mirrors. They walked toward the chapel under the intense gaze of a discerning crowd. The radiant bride sailed across the parquet floors like a swan, with her head held high. The groom splendidly dressed in a suit of gold fabric, encrusted with diamonds, wished he were anyplace else but there.

Wishful thinking that the dress business would be overlooked. The wedding venue was Versailles where nothing escaped criticism. Some of the five thousand guests commented disapprovingly in gossipy letters home, reporting on the shame of the bride's visible unmentionables. But with youthful optimism, a radiant smile, and perfect poise, Antoinette didn't allow this defective gown to mar her day. As for the erring seamstress, no credible sources mention what befell her. But it's a good guess that she passed the remainder of her career sewing nothing more elaborate than prison uniforms.

Antoinette commanded all eyes with her appearance and ready smile. The groom, on the other hand, was ill at ease in his wedding finery, blushing deep red during the ceremony especially during the exchange of vows. The archbishop of Rheims officiated at the altar imploring bountiful blessings on the couple. The marriage contract, signed by the entire royal family, began with the king's signature; second came the groom; and third was the bride's signature. Her name stood out unfavorably among all others due to a sizable blotch of ink on the first "J" of her four given names, Marie Antoinette

Josèphe Jeanne. Maybe she was nervous, but the blot on the document was an eyesore for all to point fingers.

A sumptuous wedding dinner followed in the newly-constructed Opera House. This venue had been in the works since the reign of Louis XIV. The postponed construction became urgent when Louis XV demanded a wow factor to showcase the weddings of his three grandsons. The gifted architect, Ange-Jacques Gabriel, labored twenty-one months to complete this masterpiece. This showroom would be the crowning destination for concerts, stage productions, operas, balls, and other festivities for the pleasure of the courtiers. Even the most jaded denizens of Versailles raved about its opulence. Sadly, it failed to be used to the extent intended by its visionary designer. The prickly problem of the high cost to mount productions limited its use.

During the wedding dinner, Louis XV eyed his grandson, who stuffed his face with each successive entrée. The king playfully elbowed his grandson, suggesting that he go easy on the second helpings; after all, he winked, it was his wedding night. The obtuse heir assured his grandfather that he always slept better on a full stomach. A despairing Louis XV visibly winced and turned away.

According to custom, the court escorted the newlyweds to their bedchamber with appropriate pomp. Once dressed in their night clothes, the newlyweds sat up together in bed. The archbishop prayed for a fruitful union as everyone solemnly bowed and withdrew with their fingers crossed. After the last courtier disappeared, the nervous couple was alone for the first time. Without even a miserly kiss, the groom mumbled goodnight to his bride and promptly fell asleep. Wide awake, Antoinette felt bewildered as her husband slept soundly beside her. She knew that something was wrong with this setup. Her mother had drummed it into her head that the primary purpose of her life in France was to produce heirs. But her mother did not prepare her for the possibility of an unresponsive partner. Antoinette knew she was in a jam, and she was sure her mother was going to pitch an imperial-size hissy fit.

"I blame my mother for my poor sex life.
All she told me was 'the man goes on top,
and the woman underneath.' For three years
my husband and I slept in bunk beds."
Joan Rivers

Chapter 5

Who Can Resist Gossip?

$\mathcal{A}$ntoinette's world changed dramatically when she awoke the following morning. Overnight she left behind the life of an unobserved girl with a handful of attendants. At Versailles, she faced over three hundred servants employed to fulfill her needs. And spy on her. In addition, scores of courtiers milled around in constant attendance. The requirement of being under microscopic display around the clock was a huge shock. For the rest of her life, Antoinette struggled to circumvent this lack of privacy.

The day after the wedding, everyone knew the marriage had not been consummated. Ambassadors and well-placed courtiers had bribed servants to disclose the condition of the bed linens. The verdict: unstained sheets resembling fresh laundry. The news raced across France and all of Europe like a tabloid headline screaming "No Consummation on Wedding Night!" The dauphine was also bursting to tell someone about the unsettling news.

Antoinette spilled her guts to Reverend Vermond at her first opportunity to speak to him privately. Vermond soothed her distress, assuring her that nature would take its natural course in the bedroom. Once Vermond left Antoinette, he tracked down Count Mercy and reported the bride's angst.

Vermond was not just Antoinette's confidant but also the primary mole who kept Mercy and Maria Theresa inside the loop. Antoinette remained unaware that Vermond was both pal and spy. But Mercy did not rely exclusively on Vermond's word. The Austrian ambassador maintained on his payroll three of Antoinette's servants to divulge every bitty detail that they witnessed. Mercy conveyed the discouraging outcome to the empress.

Any hope for privacy within the palace walls was futile. Imagine the harm of this daily scrutiny on the couple's love making attempts. The newlyweds cringed that they were the source of juicy gossip. This humiliation would shadow the couple for seven frustrating years with damaging consequences for the monarchical system and them personally. The Lisbon Curse had begun to cast its dark sinister shadow.

The reaction of the empress arrived like a thud on the virgin wife's desk. Maria Theresa did not hit the ceiling as Antoinette had feared, but the empress pelted her daughter with reproductive advice. The empress' tone was supportive, yet unequivocal. Antoinette's responsibility required that she excite her husband to fulfill his dynastic duties: "The only real happiness in this world is that which comes from a happy marriage. I can speak from experience. Everything depends on the wife—if she is obliging, amiable, and amusing." That word "amusing" meant you were not to lie there passively. The empress had been an eager lover in her own dynastic bed. But she had the advantage of being blessed with an equally enthusiastic partner.

On each night that Louis chose to share his wife's bed, the young bride must have wondered who was this indifferent groom lying next to her in a deep slumber. Antoinette speculated how her future might unfold disastrously if her new husband didn't perform his conjugal duties. She had to win the confidence of the man sharing her bed. As her mother often preached, success depended on the wife. This was no way to spend a honeymoon.

"Niagara Falls is the bride's second great disappointment."
Oscar Wilde

Chapter 6

The Boy Who Didn't Want to be King

*A*ntoinette didn't have a clue when she married that Louis was repulsed to have an Austrian archduchess for a wife. Both his parents, had they still been alive, would have vigorously opposed such a union. To further understand the young Louis' cool response to his wife, a peek at his upbringing should be helpful.

Antoinette's husband, Louis Auguste, known as the Duke of Berry, was born on Friday, August 23, 1754. He was the third of five sons born to the heir of the throne, the Dauphin Louis Ferdinand, and his wife, the Dauphine Marie-Josèphe of Saxony, affectionately called Pepa. (What a chore to keep track of all those guys named Louis!) Since Antoinette's husband was not son number one, he was ignored by the adults in charge, a natural response given the boy's oafish appearance and drab personality. So, how did this hapless lad find himself center stage in such a brief time? Perhaps call it a compelling case for "if only" circumstances, but his career prospects changed radically within a few years.

Louis Ferdinand differed radically from his father, Louis XV. The dauphin was devoutly religious, well educated, and politically the polar opposite. Louis Ferdinand admired Rousseau and some of the heavyweights of the Enlightenment, grasping the need for reform. He believed that, "Ignorance produces almost as many tyrants in monarchies, as does ambition in republics." With thoughts like these it's no surprise that relations between him and his father were frayed.

Most unconventional of all, Louis Ferdinand remained strictly faithful in his marriage. He and Pepa madly loved one another, nothing short of miraculous for an arranged marriage in those days. They happily fulfilled their marital vows by becoming a dependable baby factory during their marriage of eighteen years. The couple's first son died during his infancy, but their second son thrived. He was a precocious child, smart, quick-witted, and imperious, captivating even the most cynical of courtiers. All observers remarked that the charismatic child would usher in a golden age of monarchy, prosperity, and glory for France. Aware of the budding royal prodigy, Louis XV, the boy's parents, and the entire court doted on him. The couple's younger offspring were unintentionally shoved to the sidelines, overshadowed by their elder brother. Sadly, this rising star of the dynasty died at age nine in 1761.

The disconsolate Louis Ferdinand and Pepa were forced to take a belated interest in the education of their surviving children. Not long before he died, Louis Ferdinand requisitioned the baptismal registry from the parish church in Versailles where the names of his children were inscribed along with ordinary kids. The father pointed out, "My dear children, see your names written here alongside those who are poor and destitute. Religion and nature have made all men equal; it is only personal virtue that establishes any difference among all of you listed here. Perhaps even the most unfortunate child's name that precedes your own on this list will achieve more greatness in the eyes of God than you ever will in the eyes of the people." This fatherly admonition had a lasting effect on the eldest son, Duke of Berry, who would one day reign as Louis XVI.

On December 10, 1765, Louis Ferdinand died of tuberculosis. His death dealt a blow to the hopes of the common people for a better future. The inconsolable Pepa sank into an irreversible depression, and followed her husband to the grave fifteen months later. With the consecutive deaths of the future monarchs, a gloom descended on the court as well as the country, mourning for what the future could have brought if the couple had lived to reign. The promise of an entire generation had been effaced in less than two years, exposing a bleak reality. An aging, debauched Louis XV manned the helm, and an eleven-year-old grandson, quivering in his shiny shoes, stood on the top deck. Not a rosy forecast for smooth sailing.

Louis Auguste, Duke of Berry, became the dauphin at age eleven. Courtiers groaned in unison at the prospect of his becoming king one day. Called Berry in his family, the lonely boy suffered from the cruel jabs of his younger brothers. Bombarded with so much disapproval, he felt insecure about his future inheritance. Fortunately, his unmarried aunts provided familial warmth, encouraging him to be a normal kid in their private apartments. In a nutshell, this tween suddenly propelled into the spotlight, sensed that most people wrote him off as a *schlemiel*.

Painfully shy, physically bland, stocky, taciturn, socially unskilled, and always squinting thanks to myopia, the dauphin appeared eminently out of place during public events, seeming gruff and rude. He was the despair of his valet with his princely garments perpetually rumpled. His tutor drilled into Louis' head that women were tainted harlots, citing the examples of Louis XV's mistresses and their harmful intrigues. The tutor also stoked a hatred for all things Austrian.

The dauphin's interests focused on hunting, making locks, studying maps, naval matters, and the unspeakable habit of lending a hand to laborers making repairs around Versailles. He took particular interest in the care of his horses and cherished his hunting dogs. He hated cats and occasionally shot at them from the roof of Versailles. Nearly two centuries later, after eying intently a portrait of Louis XVI, Winston Churchill concluded, "Now I understand why there was a French Revolution."

But Louis Auguste was neither a fool nor a loser. His education was thorough and well-grounded. He read voraciously, subscribing to the major newspapers of his time. Besides French, he knew Italian, German, English and Latin. Louis' greatest passion in life was the sport of hunting. All through his life he maintained a diary of his exploits in this escape from the palace grind. The hunt afforded the heir one of the few occasions where he could bond with his grandfather in an activity that both enjoyed. However, Louis XV failed disgracefully to provide his heir with a blueprint on governing.

Antoinette would have to adjust her expectations and find a way to succeed in relating to this complex husband and future king. It definitely was not the image she had dreamt about in Vienna. Nor what her mother had led her to expect. What do you do with a man who does not want to be a husband or a king?

"He looks as though he was weaned on a pickle."
Alice Roosevelt Longworth

Chapter 7

Trapped in a Straight-Jacket

A rigid schedule caged in Antoinette's daily life with a routine that rarely varied. Her day was orchestrated by Madame Noailles and her attendants with military precision. Every minute was metered out for a specific purpose with little wiggle room for spontaneity. Hailed as the undisputed guardian of court etiquette, even the king deferred to Madame Noailles on matters of precedence. Everyone's success at court hinged on the observance of these endless procedures, so numerous that they would equal the size of a ponderous coffee table book.

Madame Noailles lacked the maternal affection needed to guide a fourteen-year-old high-spirited girl. She was mostly starch with sparse sugar, torpedoing a valuable opportunity to groom this future queen. One countess described Madame Noailles' success at Versailles as owing to "a certain reserve and a great social grace which compensated for the lack of a mind." In short order, the exasperated teen, who loved to bestow nicknames, hit upon the perfect one for Madame Noailles: Antoinette christened her "Madame Etiquette."

Antoinette provided a snapshot of her daily grind in a letter to her mother:

> I rise between half past nine and ten o'clock. And after dressing I
> say my prayers. Then I have breakfast and go to my aunts where
> I usually meet the King. At eleven I have my hair dressed. I put
> on my rouge and wash my hands before everybody. Then the
> gentlemen go out and the ladies stay; I dress before them. At

twelve is mass. After mass, we dine together before everyone, but it is over by half-past one, as we all eat quickly. I then go to Monsieur the Dauphin. If he is busy I return to my own apartments where I read, write or work, for I am embroidering a vest for the King which does not get on quickly, but with God's help, it will be finished in a few years. At three I go to my aunts, and at four the Abbé comes to me; at five the master for the harpsichord or the singing master until six. At half-past six, I generally go to my aunts when I do not go out. My husband always comes with me to my aunts. At seven, card playing till nine; but when the weather is fine, I go out. At nine we have supper. When the King is absent my aunts come to dine with us; when the King is there we wait for the King who comes usually at a quarter to eleven, but I lie on a large sofa and sleep till his arrival. When he is not expected, I go to bed at eleven. Such is my day.

The exasperation in Antoinette's tone is hard to miss. If she were lucky, she was tucked in bed by midnight, pooped out from another meaningless day. A sure recipe for rebellion was brewing within a bored teenager who dreamed of a radical readjustment to etiquette once she achieved a more independent status.

Antoinette received little genuine warmth from her new family. She longed for a set of friends who were not imposed on her, such as her cherished companions back in Vienna, Charlotte and Louise. (These two sisters would correspond faithfully with Antoinette for the rest of her life.) To assuage her loneliness, Antoinette consoled herself with her spoiled dogs, none of whom ever saw an elegant chair leg that they didn't chew or pee on. Besides her dogs, the young mistress of the chateau amused herself with children, including her husband's sister, Elisabeth. The spontaneous company of the children cheered her, dispelling some of her melancholy. Naturally, Madame Noailles reprimanded Antoinette on the inappropriateness of such unbecoming comportment—what else was new?

In her early years at Versailles, Antoinette spent a lot of time with her husband's three spinster aunts: Mesdames Adélaïde, Victoire, and Sophie. Imagine them as once promising princesses, now reduced to soured has-beens. There was a fourth sister, but she had entered a Carmelite convent, devoting her days to atoning for her father's scandalous life; such a celestial goal would have required an entire fleet of nuns praying non-stop.

Being the eldest, Adélaïde orchestrated the daily proceedings for her sisters. In her youth, Adélaïde was appealing, intelligent, witty, haughty, and temperamental—all sterling qualities for a princess. An accomplished musician, she excelled especially on the violin. Adélaïde cursed destiny for cheating her out of being the heir, convinced she would have made the best ruler for the kingdom. Adélaïde and her sisters exemplified the shallow existence of many courtiers, engrossed in satisfying their self-serving ends. When Antoinette arrived on the scene, Louis XV instructed Adélaïde to include the dauphine into her circle of activities.

Maria Theresa expressed her satisfaction that these respectable ladies acted as chaperones for her capricious daughter. Following her mother's advice and the king's orders, Antoinette spent hours each day with these ladies. The highlight of the dauphin's day was to play cards with three middle-aged spinsters—yippee! But Antoinette felt nurtured in the family circle the aunts provided, even if it were not apparently sincere. Auntie Adélaïde's game plan was to snare Antoinette in her web of intrigue by pretending to soothe Antoinette's homesickness for faraway Vienna. Even though she was a newcomer, Antoinette knew that her husband was fond of these middle-aged biddies. By winning their approval and affection she hoped to spark some conjugal attention from her unresponsive husband.

Before Antoinette's arrival at Versailles, Adélaïde presided as first lady of the land after the death of her mother in 1768. Adélaïde loved the spotlight and hated to cede her place to this childish teen, especially an Austrian archduchess forced on France by the policies of Louis XV's previous mistress, Madame Pompadour. Since the death of her adored brother in 1765, Adélaïde and her circle of likeminded courtiers felt unfairly robbed of their influence as her three nephews were perched for their grab at power. But if Adélaïde plotted her next move carefully, she might achieve a slice of the recognition she craved.

Adélaïde's immediate goal was to get rid of her father's slutty mistress. It was no secret that all three sisters harmonized in their loathing of Madame du Barry, snubbing the king's mistress at every opportunity. The street-smart mistress ignored the jabs of Adélaïde and her flunkies, taking her cue from the king. She figured out fast that the royal daughters were sidelined players at court. Ignored, Adélaïde and her sisters fumed from their quarters in the chateau. But luckily their dream patsy, the unseasoned Antoinette, appeared on the scene. They saw the struggle with the Du Barry woman as the first big test of their influence on the pliable teen. Cagey Adélaïde intended to use Antoinette to dislodge the king's favorite.

cᗺ cᗺ cᗺ

Antoinette's teenage rebelliousness blossomed after she turned fifteen. Her first act of defiance surfaced when she balked at wearing a corset. Madame Noailles' OCD kicked in big time, alerting the entire palace of this grave infraction. The French court was outraged that this budding first lady would flout wearing this mandatory staple of female dress. Even Count Mercy and Reverend Vermond chastised Antoinette for thumbing her nose at royal decorum. Of course, mama bear in Vienna warned Antoinette about every misfortune, short of death itself, that would befall her if she abandoned wearing a corset. Eventually, Louis XV chimed in expressing his displeasure, prompting the dauphine to resume wearing corsets.

Next followed the tug of war regarding the dauphine's passion for horseback riding. Maria Theresa, who learned that her daughter was riding out to the hunt, demanded that all riding end immediately. With threats of a ruined figure and certain sterility, the empress' insistence ultimately carried the argument. A compromise was reached between Vienna and Versailles whereby Antoinette would be allowed to ride a donkey. This arrangement did not satisfy the teenager one bit, but she was obliged to follow the orders of Louis XV.

Antoinette formed her first close friendship with Princess Lamballe, whom she had met on her arrival in France. Both young women soon became inseparable. Lamballe was the widow of a wealthy self-destructive party-boy. At the age of nineteen, Lamballe attracted a lot of male attention because of her cha-ching wealth. Lamballe exuded the innocence of a child that partly accounted for Antoinette's delight in her company. Also, like Antoinette, she was a foreigner, imported from Turin. Lamballe was famed for her swooning fits that could last for hours. Initially moved by these expressions of sensitivity, Antoinette would eventually find them tiresome. Within a few years, Antoinette came to feel that Madame Lamballe's cloying sweetness was something of a bore. Yet the bond between these two women, with all its ups and downs, would last a lifetime.

> "You have to learn the rules of the game.
> And then you have to play better than anyone else."
> *Albert Einstein*

Chapter 8

Two Competitors Arrive

The social event of 1771 highlighted the nuptials of the king's grandson Count Provence, addressed by the court as "Monsieur." Unlike his brother's fair looks, Provence took after his Bourbon predecessors, with dark hair and eyes, and more attractive facial features than his elder brother. By his teens, Provence was already bursting his breeches, inching his way to obesity. His visible flaw was his manner of walking, an ungainly waddle due to his vast size. Realizing this drawback triggered an unfavorable impression, Monsieur moved as little as possible in public. He was the sharpest mind of the three brothers but also the craftiest. He prided himself on delivering witty comebacks and preened when listeners applauded his quips. He hated the hunt and any physical activity. His manners and adherence to court etiquette were impeccable. He lived on a grand scale ever mindful of his esteemed ancestors. Sincerity, though, would never be remotely counted as one of Monsieur's princely virtues.

Count Provence married a princess from the House of Savoy, Marie Josèphe, the Italian daughter of the King of Sardinia in 1771. When she arrived at Versailles, the entire court recoiled at her exceptional dumpiness. Madame du Barry summed up everyone's unspoken thoughts: "She's ugly and she smells." Countess Provence was neither a fan of bathing nor of cleaning her teeth. She was short with a swarthy complexion, unruly bushy eyebrows, and a large nose climaxing above a lip with wispy traces of a mustache.

The embarrassment of such a grand-daughter-in-law offended Louis XV who contacted Marie Josèphe's father, urging him to instruct his daughter to wash her neck. In accordance with the customs of the French court, when you embraced a lady you did not kiss her on the cheek, lest you smeared the makeup application. Instead you kissed her on her neck, and who wanted to kiss a raunchy one? Besides her offensive physical presentation, there was the matter of her fondness for swigging back the vino. The countess could create unbecoming "scenes" when she was hitting the bottle. She would have improved her position at court immensely with a month-long intensive at a beauty spa, as well as daily meetings for substance abusers.

The marriage of Provence spiked a jolt of concern for Antoinette. If the couple produced an heir, Antoinette's significance at court would be undermined. The day after his wedding, Provence bragged to his skeptical grandfather that he had celebrated his manhood four times with his new wife. Given his enormous girth, even one try at reproduction would have been a feat worthy of Hercules. But an anxious Antoinette relaxed when her network of snoops assured her that she had nothing to fear from that passionless love nest. Husband and wife succeeded in harmoniously hating one another until death parted them.

The next of Louis XV's grandsons to marry was the youngest of the three brothers, Count Artois. He was the cocky, handsome prince of the family and the only slender one. He lived life lavishly, progressing from one good time to another. Although dashing and entertaining, he was the most superficial sibling. He was a spoiled brat who solidified that behavior in adulthood. He liked to shout out "Good Morning, Grand-papa" whenever he passed Louis XIV's statue in the royal garden, an irreverence that delighted some courtiers.

Artois married Marie Louise from the House of Savoy in 1773. She was the younger sister of Countess Provence, minus the mustache. While no beauty, she was an olfactory improvement over her older sister. Her new husband didn't conceal his disappointment with his lackluster bride. Count Artois deemed the marriage a bust when his bride displayed no grace as they opened the ball for their wedding. Marie Louise, dismissed as a ninny, attracted ridicule from everybody at court. But the marriage was a rushed Hail Mary maneuver in light of the inability of Artois' two senior brothers to produce an heir. In contrast to his male siblings, Count Artois performed his conjugal duties without hesitation, proud to be the one in the family to keep the dynasty in business.

The three married couples got together for social pastimes that Adélaïde arranged for the younger set. But the ever-sharp Count Mercy alerted Antoinette that it was her duty as first lady of the court to lead the way. Antoinette took on the chore and emceed many of the evening activities for the three couples. She hoped to create a family camaraderie similar to the one she had enjoyed in Vienna.

Disappointingly, the attempt to establish a close bond deteriorated into a shallow connection among the three married couples. Anytime Antoinette and the two sisters from Savoy gathered in joint company, the visual was almost humorous, recalling a beauty queen trailed by two charwomen. Not exactly a comparison to encourage sisterly affection.

> "Like the best families, we have our share
> of eccentricities, of impetuous and wayward
> youth and of family disagreements."
> *Queen Elizabeth II*

Chapter 9

Clash of the Crinolines

*A*fter months of swelling anticipation, the time ripened for the bout between two powerful rivals. The reigning champion was Madame du Barry, the king's confident royal mistress, pitted against the challenging newcomer and future queen, Marie Antoinette. Both were determined to deliver a knockout punch.

Two weeks after the marriage of Louis and Antoinette, Madame du Barry paid a courtesy visit to the dauphine. Being cordially received, the satisfied mistress smiled her way out of the room but the facade of civility quickly disintegrated. Within two months, the rivalry between the two women took shape as the residents at Versailles prepped themselves for a diverting stage show. In her first letter to her mother, Antoinette mentions the king's favorite with a hint of the ruckus to come:

> The King is infinitely kind to me and I love him dearly, but his
> weakness for Madame du Barry is pitiful. She is the most stupid
> and impertinent creature imaginable. Twice I found myself next to
> her at Marly, but she did not speak to me, and I did not exactly try
> to talk to her, although when it was necessary, I did say a word or
> two. I shall always treat her as she deserves.

Antoinette's appraisal of Du Barry presaged the stormy relations that lay ahead. Like two queen bees vying for sole ownership of the hive, the conflict cruised to a climax in 1771. Everyone at court fussed with frenzied anticipation at the inevitable take-down. Who was going to blink first—the brassy mistress, or the feisty future queen?

Where did Madame du Barry come from and why did Antoinette find her so loathsome? It all began with King Louis XV, who like most male monarchs in Europe kept a mistress that his queen tolerated in martyred silence. But a king of France couldn't just *shtup* any woman he liked. Etiquette dictated the terms. The paramount consideration demanded that the chosen lady be high born. If that were not the case, then an arrangement would be designed for a marriage to occur between the lady and an obliging nobleman. Of course, all of that effort came with a hefty price tag.

The later years of Louis XV's reign had not been kind to him. The king suffered humiliating military losses to the British. The finances of the State bordered close to insolvency. And the inequitable tax system forced an unfair burden on the lower classes. Formerly, Louis' subjects hailed him as the "Well Loved." Now they prayed for his death. He became reluctant to show his face in public beyond his circuit of palaces. Within several years, death snatched his favorite grandson, the indispensable Madame Pompadour, his heir Louis Ferdinand, his likeable daughter-in-law, and finally, his queen. Confronted with an avalanche of loss, the king felt old, vulnerable, and worst of all, mortal. He sought distraction from an impressive elixir to rouse his spirits and body parts. And a striking beauty such as Du Barry was just the remedy; with a pinup figure, luxuriant blonde hair, and buoyant breasts—all weaknesses of the king.

Marie Jeanne Bécu was born out of wedlock on August 19, 1743, to a pretty maid and a randy friar. Educated in a convent, she held menial jobs in dress shops and hairdressers' establishments. But beyond the customer counter she dispensed more than sales help. She entranced all who met her with her lovely, languid violet eyes, encircled by a radiant complexion sprinkled with a few freckles. Being quite the looker, she became quite the hooker to a dissolute nobleman, Jean-Baptiste du Barry, who had earned his fortune as a war contractor. Always short on cash, her paramour would pimp out Jeanne to some of his bored rich pals. She found herself thrust into the spotlight, delighting in the renown that her natural gifts inspired. Her head buzzed with dreams of jewels, carriages, servants, and a secure social status. She fixed her sights on the biggest prize of all, the king.

Mere weeks after the death of Louis XV's wife in 1768, this shopgirl on a mission caught the king's wandering eye. She employed the standard gimmick of positioning herself in the king's path. Her ruse produced the desired effect. The smitten king instructed his valet to invite the lady to be introduced to His Most Willing Majesty. Louis XV zoomed into testosterone overdrive with this knockout beauty. Her exceptionally stained past, compounded by her bottom-of-the-barrel social background, stamped her unworthy of a king's attentions. But her bewitching beauty and big boobs forged the way to bypass the insuperable odds of becoming the royal main squeeze.

In record time, Jeanne Bécu sealed the deal and became Louis XV's official mistress. Holding this title signified she was not just an occasional one-night stand. After the king, the official mistress normally wielded the most clout at court. Few folks in France begrudged their king some frolicking amusement on the side. But to elevate a former call girl, no matter how attractive, to the status of official mistress was too much for almost everyone. Jeanne Bécu polluted the esteemed title of official mistress with her shocking inferiority.

Louis XV's approval ratings nosedived, but the king no longer gave a damn about public opinion. One official at court asked the king why he chose Jeanne. Louis XV explained, "Well, first she's beautiful and more importantly, she allows me to forget that I will soon be sixty." What the king omitted to reveal was that at his age he knew Death was closing in on him. Mademoiselle Bécu was just the sorceress he desired to distract Death from claiming him as its next victim.

To overcome the inconvenient details of her inferiority, a suitable marriage needed to be arranged to a compliant gentleman with a title. In this case, Jean-Baptiste du Barry, the lady's lowlife protector, suggested his bachelor brother, Count Guillaume du Barry, as the bridegroom. The rube of a brother resided in provincial obscurity with his mother and spinster sisters. You couldn't find a bunch of better titled hillbillies, whose prosperity and social standing would billow with such a marriage.

In an indecent hurry, the unwitting Guillaume married Jeanne. The bewildered groom was bundled off to his provincial estate with a comfortable pension in exchange for a title for his wife, the newly minted Countess du Barry.

On April 22, 1769, at age twenty-six, with her passport of titled credentials in hand, a bejeweled and tardy Madame du Barry swept into the palace of Versailles as Louis XV's official mistress. Upon seeing her, the king forgot his keen displeasure at being kept waiting, preening like a young buck. Her spectacular white dress and beauty blindsided the stupefied upper crust gathered to greet her. Her abundant physical charms loaded with a blaze of diamonds contrasted sharply with her trashy pedigree. Eager to shake things up at Versailles, the countess took over the palace with long term plans to keep the king entranced. The "lady" Du Barry had just landed the best gig in town.

Marie Antoinette caught on fast to what it meant "to amuse the king." After coming from the tight moral ship her mother ran in Vienna, Antoinette cringed that Louis XV debased himself with a prostitute. The dauphine fronted a frosty demeanor toward the glamour puss whenever she was within spitting distance.

This behavior did not go unnoticed by the delighted inhabitants of the chateau. To further poison the well, Duke of Choiseul, who had successfully negotiated Antoinette's marriage and shared bad blood with Du Barry, was dismissed from his post in December 1770. His replacement as foreign minister happened to be a buddy of Du Barry—Duke Aiguillon. A distraught Antoinette considered the ouster of Choiseul as a personal loss and an affront to Austria. But there was nothing she could do to alter the outcome. Her husband did not offer the slightest comfort either. His late father had detested Choiseul, and Antoinette's husband rarely second-guessed the opinion of his esteemed father. While the venomous aunts cheered Choiseul's disgrace, they carefully nursed Antoinette's hostility toward the king's mistress. They convinced Antoinette that the floozy undermined her position at court. More importantly, the mistress' downfall would guarantee the salvation of the king's soul. The aunts declared a holy war to save the monarch from the clutches of hell, with Antoinette willingly signing on to the crusade.

In truth, Countess du Barry was not a bad sort. Mercy described her in a dispatch to Vienna, "She has a fine enough appearance, but her conversation smacks of her former condition." Considering her negligible origins, she was thrilled to be where she was. Snubbed repeatedly by Antoinette, Du Barry knew that Antoinette's smartass behavior made her look bad. She surmised that the flames of loathing were being fanned in other quarters.

According to the meticulous rules of etiquette, a person on the lower pecking order, such as Madame du Barry, could not speak first to someone higher up the aristo food chain. And Antoinette was at the top of the female social pyramid. Oftentimes, the king's mistress approached the dauphine in the hope of securing an indifferent greeting in the presence of the assembled court. Antoinette repeatedly froze out the royal favorite. After numerous public rejections, Madame du Barry, who referred to Antoinette as "the little redhead," was determined to show her who was the real boss at Versailles, at least temporarily.

Countess du Barry and her clique spread rumors that the Austrian's marriage could be voided since she had failed to conceive an heir. This particular barb struck the dauphine in her most vulnerable spot. But at age fifteen, Antoinette proved that she was no spongy marshmallow, further intensifying the tensions between the royal mistress and herself. Madame du Barry, who liked to call Louis XV, "France," didn't need a degree in royal affairs to remind him between kisses that an insult to her was also an affront to him. She cooed and pouted to be accorded the respect due to her as official mistress.

Louis XV detested face-to-face confrontations, preferring to communicate his desires through intermediaries. First summoned to learn of the king's discomfort was the pillar of court rectitude, Madame Noailles. Louis XV expressed his annoyance with the dauphine's attitude toward his mistress, "She is unfortunate in her advice. I am aware of the source of such advice, and it strongly displeases me." Quick on the uptake, Madame Etiquette knew the king was referring to his three daughters. The king requested her to disclose his distress regarding this matter close to his crotch.

Madame Noailles sped off like a roadrunner to the apartments of the aunts. She alerted them of the king's disquiet regarding their influence on the dauphine. Instead of hyperventilating in their corsets, the aunts danced a jig, elated at the success of their strategy. They redoubled their efforts to sustain the dauphine's cold shoulder tactic toward the king's favorite. Antoinette needed little encouragement to give up the struggle.

But soon an imperial grenade exploded. Empress Maria Theresa did a sharp one-eighty when she learned through Mercy that these old maids were using Antoinette for their own political purposes. The empress sounded the alarm bells in letters warning her daughter that the aunts planned to undermine her position at court:

> I respect them [the aunts], I like them, but they have never known
> how to win the admiration or affection of their family or the public,
> and you want to go the same way—that fear and embarrassment
> about talking to the King, the best of fathers, or to people to
> whom you are advised to speak! You made such a good start.
> Your appearance, your judgment, when not directed by others, are

always true and for the best. Let yourself be guided by Mercy; what interest do we, he and I, have other than your particular happiness and the good of the State? You must not be ruled like a child when you wish to speak. Admit this embarrassment to the King. Your refusal to merely offer a greeting, or compliment a pretty dress is worse than self-indulgence. I demand that you convince the King by your every action of your respect and your love. You have one goal only, and that it is to please the King and obey him.

Antoinette wavered after this letter from the empress, but not enough to break her silence with Du Barry. Her mother had to ramp up the pressure.

Disappointed by the failure of Madame Noailles' efforts, Louis XV enlisted the help of Count Mercy. He alerted the count that the dauphine's obstinacy was highly disturbing to His Majesty. Oops! Not the message that anyone wanted to receive from the king. Louis XV used polished speech but the subtext was a definite warning, "Until now you have been the Ambassador of the Empress. Now I beg you to be mine, at least for a short time. I love Madame the Dauphine dearly. I think she is charming, but as she is lively and has a husband who is not in a position to guide her, she cannot possibly avoid the traps set for her by intrigue." The king got it right. An unchecked wife and future queen of France was a potential danger at Versailles. Mercy assured His Majesty that he would handle the matter.

Count Mercy darted off to the dauphine's apartments insisting to see Antoinette alone. He raised the alarm about her snubs to the king's favorite. Antoinette would not budge, refusing to utter one syllable of recognition to the royal whore. Antoinette felt that she was morally correct, and that any concessions would be contrary to her principles. She blithely reminded Mercy that Louis XV, whom she called Papa, was always so sweet to her; how could it be true that he was displeased with her?

Wow, was Antoinette misinformed! Louis XV was famously predictable for being charming in the morning to an unsuspecting soul and then banishing the victim by dusk. A dreaded letter from the king, known as a *lettre de cachet,* was a notice of banishment from the royal court with orders to await the king's pleasure. Normally that translated into the equivalent of a life sentence in provincial Sing Sing, where you slowly decayed through intentional neglect. Absolutely nothing was worse than being kicked out of Versailles. You might as well have bubonic plague. Nobody dared to venture near you, for fear of rousing the king's displeasure. You simply ceased to exist.

Mercy bluntly spelled out to Antoinette the king's manner of dealing with unpleasantness by using surrogates to deliver bad news. He warned her that the Franco-Austrian alliance was possibly at risk, especially since she was not yet pregnant after eighteen months of marriage. Although uneasy with this news, Antoinette petulantly remained non-committal to speak to Du Barry whom she referred to as "that creature." Vexed, Mercy dashed off an SOS to the empress, knowing the escalating feud had to end.

Maria Theresa's next missive tore into Antoinette:

> I can no longer keep silent. After Mercy told you what the King
> desired and your duty demanded, you have dared to fail him!
> What reason can you give for such conduct? None at all. You are
> the King's first subject and you owe him submission. You ought
> to set a good example to show the courtiers at Versailles that you
> are ready to do your Master's will. The aunts have reduced you
> to dependence by treating you as a child. They will make you
> unloved and disrespected. Does my love deserve less reciprocation
> than theirs? I must admit that this thought wounds my heart.

After the onslaught of maternal reprimands, Antoinette submitted to the imperial pressure from Vienna, recognizing the risk of alienating the king. In a face-saving justification, Antoinette explained to her mother, "I do not say that I will never speak to Du Barry anymore, but I cannot consent to do so at an agreed time so that she can talk about it in advance and act triumphantly." But, in the end, Antoinette buckled to an arranged rendezvous, glumly promising to say a few words to "the creature."

With negotiations hashed out by Count Mercy, the public greeting would occur at the dauphine's Sunday evening card games. Word leaked out, and it seemed that most of Versailles wanted to play cards that night. As Antoinette approached the table where the expectant Du Barry sat, an attendant to the aunts swooped down and exhorted the dauphine to make haste, shouting that the king was impatiently waiting for her at Adélaïde's apartments. Flushed with uncertainty, Antoinette folded to the command and fled. Without the arranged greeting in a packed public setting, the jilted mistress stood openly humiliated. Now the standoff was at a breaking point. The unamused sovereign summoned Count Mercy, blasting him, "Well, Monsieur Mercy, your advice hardly bears any fruit. I shall have to come to your assistance." The chastised ambassador left the king's presence to tongue-lash the dauphine, demanding that the next attempt succeed, lest the wrath of God and the empress crash down on her head.

Another meeting of the two rivals was hammered out. On this occasion, tight discretion was exercised to keep everyone, especially the vigilant aunts, out of the loop. A high noon face-off was secretly scheduled for a public reception on New Year's Day 1772 in the dauphine's apartments.

When a radiant Du Barry appeared at the entrance to Antoinette's suite, the mood in the room flipped instantly, as bets flew back and forth on the outcome. The suspense sucked the air out of the room as the royal mistress slowly advanced, enjoying each step and every stare. Would Antoinette engage the favorite, or gaze above her with the usual ice maiden pose, signifying, "Really, I don't care if you drop dead"?

As Madame du Barry stood before Antoinette, the crowd resembled Tussaud figures while the ticking mantle clocks seemed suddenly loud. The dauphine purposely locked eyes with the concubine, nonchalantly remarking, "There are a lot of people at Versailles today." The wound-up crowd went ballistic. News that the dauphine waved the flag of surrender went viral in minutes throughout the seven-hundred-room chateau. The favorite savored her triumph as she curtsied to the dauphine; the king glowed with affection for Antoinette; Mercy could at last relax; and Maria Theresa rejoiced that a crisis was averted. As for the aunts, they stewed in their lair feeling betrayed. Adélaïde was probably the first individual to refer to Antoinette as *l'Autrichienne,* the Austrian Woman.

Later that day, when Antoinette managed a few minutes alone with Count Mercy, she exploded: "I followed your advice. I spoke to her once, but I am determined to go no farther, and that woman will never again hear the sound of my voice." But she couldn't keep this vow lest she risk angering the king. From time to time she would allow "the creature" a tidbit of recognition or a morsel of a few words. Even though she lost this battle, Antoinette nursed her wounded pride. She swore to even the score, unaware that the payback day was not far off.

After her capitulation to Du Barry, Antoinette paid her a left-handed compliment. One day, one of the ladies from the dauphine's circle shared a bit of juicy gossip. The tattler spoke with gleeful disgust of a distraught mother who had implored the mistress to intervene in the pardoning of her son who had fought in a duel. Antoinette ignored the spiteful sentiments, expressing her concern for the young man's mother, sighing, "If I had been in her place, I would have done the same, and if necessary I would have thrown myself at the feet of Zamore himself." (Zamore was the diminutive black page whom the king had gifted to his mistress.) Although Versailles could be a harsh environment, Antoinette revealed a hint of the protective mother she would be one day, including a glimpse of a tender heart that resided beneath her proud exterior.

How did Antoinette's husband react to this melodrama played out within the family? He reminded her that obedience to the king was paramount. Louis related that his own saintly mother exhibited civility to the former mistress, Madame Pompadour, thereby winning the affection of Louis XV, an unfair comparison, indeed. Madame Pompadour had arranged the marriage of Louis' parents in 1747. His mother may have been pious, but she was not a political nitwit. Louis encouraged Antoinette to emulate his mother's example, instead of ordering her to do so. The dauphine respectfully disagreed. She swore to have the last word because she was the legitimate lady of the land.

> "Be the kind of woman that when your feet
> hit the floor every morning, the Devil says,
> 'Oh crap! She's up.'"
> *Untraced Author*

Chapter 10

A Menace Seals His Fate

*I*n June 1771 Antoinette casually mentioned to her mother, "I hear it is the future bishop of Strasbourg who is being sent to Vienna [France's new ambassador]. He comes from a very great family, but the life he has led is more that of a soldier than that of a bishop." Antoinette had met Bishop Louis Rohan on her arrival in France at the cathedral of Strasbourg. His lifestyle hinted at nothing priestly. Maria Theresa balked to have an ambassador at her court who conducted himself more like a sailor on shore leave. When Rohan introduced salacious silk stockings at her court that he smuggled into Austria through diplomatic pouch bags, the empress condemned the gesture as the path to moral perdition. This forbidden luxury delighted the younger ladies in Vienna who adored Ambassador Rohan. His aim was to please them and not a frumpy empress. But worst of all, Maria Theresa abhorred Rohan for hunting on Sundays, instead of saying mass, proving there was an acolyte of Satan in her midst. Rohan basked in the satisfaction that his behavior bugged the empress and by extension, her daughter Marie Antoinette. Solid proof of this emerged with the Polish affair.

After Rohan's posting to Vienna, a sinister event unfolded, diminishing the sovereignty of Poland with its elected King Stanislaw Poniatowski. Poland, engaged in a civil war, became a sitting duck ripe for the plucking by its covetous neighbor, Russia. But accomplices were required to make Poland's rape palatable. Greedy Russia, guided by Catherine the Great, convinced the surrounding neighbors, Prussia and Austria, to partake in a land grab, thereby reducing the likelihood of foreign intervention. In September 1772 the three countries partially partitioned Poland among themselves. Louis XV's recently deceased queen was Polish, a fact that could have triggered France to declare war over the incident.

Antoinette found herself in an unenviable bind, married to the French heir and the daughter to one of the belligerent parties. Publicly she remained neutral, avoiding the appearance of supporting Austria's interests. Fortunately for Antoinette, the French king barely squawked about the violation of Poland. Outside of teasing Antoinette about Austria's nasty behavior, Louis XV did not lift a finger to save Poland. In his senior years, Louis neither exhibited a zest for war nor was he capable of paying for one. Sadly, no foreign powers intervened beyond the perfunctory diplomatic protests, allowing chunks of Poland to be kissed goodbye.

The reliable palace grapevine buzzed with news that Du Barry regaled her chums in the king's presence with a stinging letter from Ambassador Rohan decimating Antoinette's mother. As a consequence, Antoinette's loathing for "the creature" became more personal, extending beyond a battle for female hegemony at Versailles.

Rohan knew that the empress had voiced her intense displeasure about his scandalous behavior in letters to Versailles. With the Polish heist, he could sling some mud of his own. The prince exacted a snippet of spite by exposing the uneven piety of the empress. His scathing portrayal of Maria Theresa as a holy hypocrite while she carved out her slice of Poland with her rosary beads clutched in her hands, titillated the French court. Outraged by Rohan's remarks about her revered mother, Antoinette held her tongue and feigned indifference. But prone to holding a grudge, she would never forgive him for staining her mother's honor. Maria Theresa might often upbraid Antoinette, but no one was going to badmouth her mother. Reconciliation would never be an option with Rohan.

"He's like a snake in the grass.
Hey, if you chop its head off,
it'll still bite you—See!"
Duck Dynasty

Chapter 11

No Babies, No Respect

*I*n the early 1770s the scuttlebutt that ranked number one centered on the impasse in the bedroom of the dauphin and dauphine. Unflattering rumors circulated in comic-book style throughout France. A typical damning headline blared, "The Coquette and the Impotent One." Some speculated that Louis was incapable of getting an erection while others joked about malformed genitals. It was universal news that he didn't keep a mistress, proving that he lacked the virile enthusiasm of his ancestors.

For Antoinette, it was more complicated. Natural prejudice signaled her as the culprit, since she was perceived as an infertile foreigner. Others blamed Antoinette for rejecting a husband she considered repulsive in the sack. The dauphine's non-pregnant condition became the story that left Antoinette skating on thin dynastic ice, overshadowing the Du Barry imbroglio. With each passing month, everyone demanded that the royal couple get with the program.

In a letter to Count Mercy, the empress unloaded her frustration: "Van Swieten [the empress' physician] feels that if a young woman as attractive as the Dauphine cannot wake up the Dauphin, all remedy would be useless; that therefore, it is better not to try any and to allow time to change so strange a way of behaving." Practically every letter exchanged between the empress and Antoinette made reference to the stalemate.

Maria Theresa knew that Versailles was driven by factions, and the virulent anti-Austrian clique warranted her fears of a possible annulment. Like a drill sergeant, the empress stressed Antoinette's duty to charm her husband, "to use caresses, cajolings, but without too much urgency, which would spoil everything. Sweetness and patience are the only means you must use." Ultimately, it was Antoinette's job to arouse her husband's reproductive functions. Every month the dauphine reported to her mother the arrival date of her periods that they euphemistically referred to as "General Krottendorf." Nothing like a military metaphor to instill disciplined copulation!

Marie Antoinette keenly felt the despair of her situation. Antoinette poignantly revealed the depth of her distress to her mother while relating a sad tale:

> You will have surely heard, my dear Mama, about the tragedy of Madame the Duchess of Chartres, who was just delivered of a dead child; even though it is terrible, I still wish it had happened to me, but there is still no hope of it, even though Monsieur the Dauphin always sleeps with me and treats me in the friendliest way.

What a disclosure of her predicament! The dynastic bed was not intended for being "friendly," but, rather, an arena that demanded focused friskiness. This letter from Antoinette contained a fib, as well. Louis did not sleep with his wife every night. That may have been the homey custom in Vienna but not at Versailles where it was standard practice for the royal couple to maintain separate beds. A husband would have to visit his wife's bedroom to perform his duty to maintain the line of succession. When the empress learned of the actual sleeping practices at Versailles, she raised the alarm about such a haphazard arrangement at procreative intimacy. In every letter to her daughter, Maria Theresa insisted that Antoinette sleep every night with her husband to achieve the desired pregnancy.

Louis XV, apprised of the pristine state of the marital bed, spoke to his grandson about this sensitive matter, suspecting that the dauphin was largely responsible. The king had once confided to a courtier his disappointment regarding his grandson, grumbling, "He's not a normal boy." Some Frenchmen wondered aloud if the royal couple couldn't get the lovemaking right, then what were their chances of being capable rulers? The king ordered the couple to appear before him in October 1772 and explain themselves. He ordered his personal physician to examine the prince. The doctor did his best to offend no one with his conclusions. He diagnosed that the lad was genetically well formed. He believed that the heir did not suffer from phimosis, an abnormally tight foreskin of the penis. The physician counseled patience as the most effective remedy. The doctor hinted that the bashful teen needed more time to embrace his reproductive prowess.

The groom's reticence in the marriage bed came with an acquired history. When the dauphin was a boy, his tutor brainwashed him that women were conniving sluts. With no shortage of visual confirmation of this dictum at his grandfather's court, the prince agreed. Antoinette's wooing attentions, instigated by maternal orders from Vienna, made him uneasy and caused him to suspect the sincerity of Antoinette's motives. Observers often remarked that the dauphin moved with a glazed, listless lethargy that hinted at a late onset of puberty or a possible hormonal imbalance. He would have much preferred to hunt or do manual labor instead of playing the role of a Romeo.

A year after his marriage, Louis did begin to warm up to Antoinette and expressed his growing affection for her. He whispered in her ear that he knew the mechanics required to produce a baby, filling his young wife with hope. Reverend Vermond was the first to hear this news from Antoinette's excited lips, heralding a big leap forward under the sheets. But still no pregnancy. Apparently, some fine-tuning was still required.

In the spring of 1773 an impatient Louis XV intervened again and requested the dauphine's physician to counsel the couple to overcome "their mutual awkwardness and ignorance." The frustrated king questioned what could be more natural than lovemaking. Despite physical exams and a review of the basics of the birds and the bees, Antoinette and Louis were still incapable of producing an heir. Their mutual frustration fostered strains in their relationship that didn't improve the chances of conception.

"If sex is such a natural phenomenon,
how come there are so many books on how to do it?"
Bette Midler

Chapter 12

A Taste of Future Glory

Antoinette's body began to noticeably mature as her figure became a source of admiration. Her emerging personality also became more apparent. In the plus column, she was, gracious, eager to please, spontaneously warm, self-assured, and irresistibly charismatic. On the minus side, she liked to loll around whenever possible, to read as little as possible, to exhibit a more mercurial temper, and to hang out with a hip crowd who partied nightly in Paris. She longed to join them in the tempting capital. Antoinette also began to embrace an active interest in her personal appearance and wardrobe. She was on the cusp of becoming a fashion template to be copied by women throughout Europe. She just needed a helpful guru.

In the early 1770s the epitome of the Parisian fashion goddess reposed in the person of the chic Duchess of Chartres. She resided in Paris in the opulent Palais Royal, surrounded by many pricey retail opportunities. With a bountiful expense account, she set the standard for the latest must haves in fashion. Women quickly copied her example. Antoinette noticed her stunning appearance and asked for some tips regarding her own wardrobe. The duchess revealed her secret to fashion success—a dressmaker in Paris.

The genie who embodied the source of fashion fantasies, Mademoiselle Rose Bertin, appeared in early 1774. She was a twenty-four-year-old commoner with a messianic drive to succeed. This talented lady with needle and thread was introduced to Antoinette by her high-profile customer, the Duchess of Chartres. A unique bond formed between this commoner and the style-hungry royal. Never before did a social nobody have direct access to the first lady of the land. The calculating seamstress predicted to Antoinette, "There are no new fashions, yet just a word from you is all that is needed to create them. You do not follow fashion; it will follow you." Together Antoinette and Rose re-branded European fashion to the art of haute couture. Marie Antoinette soon became Mademoiselle's premier client. And the dressmaker made sure everyone knew it.

As fashion took center stage in Antoinette's life, she yearned for the delights beyond the confines of the palace. The dauphin and dauphine had been married for three years and had not yet gone to Paris. Being heirs to the throne, an official reception in the capital was their due. Antoinette sensed that she and her husband were getting the royal runaround with a series of lame excuses. One day the dauphine ambushed Louis XV for a date to be allowed their postponed debut to the good people of Paris. Caught off guard by her bluntness, the king consented to her request. This approval was a vital concession for it signaled that after the official presentation, the couple could go together or solo to Paris whenever they wished, without needing any further permission.

On June 8, 1773, the heirs made their official appearance to overjoyed Parisians. Both were deeply moved by the universal affection. However, they didn't grasp that their rapturous reception was more of a rebuke to the unpopular king and his trampy mistress than a blanket endorsement of them personally. This young couple represented the hopes of an impatient populace who expected way too much from them.

After the triumphant couple returned to Versailles, Antoinette wisely sought out the king. She gushed to Louis XV, "Oh, Sire, Your Majesty must be well loved by the people of Paris, for they have given us such a fine welcome." The old king was not fooled by the compliment. He knew that all of Paris prayed earnestly every night that he would croak before daybreak. The soured populace longed for the day when his heirs would rule in his place. A few days later, a still floating dauphine wrote to her mother:

> Last Tuesday I had a day that I shall remember as long as I live;
> we made our official entry into Paris. As far as honors go, we
> were given every possible one; what touched me the most was
> the love and enthusiasm of the poor people who, in spite of taxes
> which weigh heavily upon them, were besides themselves with
> joy because they could see us. Something else which pleased me
> greatly during that fine day was the behavior of my husband. He

answered all the speeches admirably, noticed everything that was
being done for him, and he showed the people much kindness. I
realize every day more and more what my dear Mama has done for
me. I was the youngest, and you have treated me as the eldest. My
heart is filled with tender gratitude.

For a sixteen-year-old girl this letter promises greatness once she ascends
the throne. Too bad Antoinette did not keep a copy of this letter for future
reflection.

One positive outcome of the visit to Paris for the royal couple resulted in
a deepening of their mutual affection. The court normally spent the summer
at the more intimate setting of Compiègne. From there Antoinette informed
her mother of her mating rituals. In July 1773 Antoinette disclosed, "I can
tell you, my dear Mama, and only to you that since we arrived here my
situation has improved dramatically, and I believe that my marriage is now
consummated." A month later she excitedly informed her mother, "Two days
after writing to you, Monsieur the Dauphin and I believed it was our duty
to tell the King of our happy state. The King hugged me tenderly and called
me his dear daughter. Since that time, there is still no sign of pregnancy,
because my period returned last month a few days early as usual in my case."
Apparently there existed a gap between believing a marriage is consummated
and the real deal. As the couple would soon comprehend with unrelenting
disappointment, they were still missing the mark.

Being allowed to visit Paris at will, the young couple indulged themselves.
Antoinette thrilled with the choices this new liberty offered. Count Mercy
recorded her every visit to Paris to his boss in Vienna. "Madame the
Dauphine goes every week to Paris; she has visited the salon of paintings,
the gallery of maps, some shops, and the fair of Saint-Ovide. She has gone
back to three performances at the Opéra, the Comédie-Française, and the
Comédie-Italienne." The dauphine was putting those stable horses through
their paces.

Several months later, on January 30, 1774, Louis and Antoinette,
attended their first masked ball. Like the legendary club, Studio 54 in New
York, the masked balls in Paris were the "in-place" for the beautiful people
to party the night away. It was on this memorable evening that Antoinette
made the acquaintance of a handsome Swede, Axel von Fersen. For both
young adults, it would prove to be a life-altering moment.

Antoinette made many dashes to Paris to revel in the masked balls and
theater productions. Normally she went out unaccompanied by her husband,
who preferred to be in bed by eleven. Often her fun-loving brother-in-law
Count Artois served as her cavalier chaperone. For the unleashed Antoinette,

Paris provided amusement and escape from the stifling etiquette of Versailles. Antoinette loved the unstructured freedom of these nights out on the town, but it was disapprovingly noted how familiar she behaved with fellow partygoers.

During her first years in France, Marie Antoinette was generally welcomed by the public with enthusiasm, despite her Austrian roots. She jumped to the mistaken conclusion that all this adulation was about her personally. The oblivious teenager figured that she merited the applause by showing up in a gorgeous gown, with a flashing smile, and with her perfectly executed curtsies. This queen business was going to be a piece of cake. (Oops, did I use the "C" word?)

But an unexpected event in May 1774 would turn up the heat significantly on this couple to fulfill the demands of a dissatisfied nation for an heir. The unexpected event was a situation both were ill prepared to face.

"Young people are in a condition like permanent intoxication, because youth is sweet and they are growing."
Aristotle

Chapter 13

The King is Dead, Thank God!

On April 27, 1774, Louis XV woke up feeling lousy. He complained of a headache, chills, and a backache. He was spending a few stolen days at the Petit Trianon with Madame du Barry. A day later his condition had not improved. By the next evening, the king's doctor, Monsieur La Martinière, was summoned to examine the king. The physician demanded an immediate return to the palace. He ruled it unthinkable that the king should be cared for by his valet and a flashy mistress. But Louis and Du Barry wished to remain in the solitude of the Petit Trianon. Doctor Martinière sternly reminded the king, "It is at Versailles, Sire, that Your Majesty must be sick." The ever-powerful force of etiquette governed the actions of the monarch. Knowing what was expected of him, the king grumbled his consent to be transferred to Versailles. Now all of the courtiers could witness the king's illness in accordance with their duty and privilege.

Louis XV's indisposition quickly spread throughout Versailles. Given his age of sixty-four, the denizens of Versailles perked up even if the king just got the sniffles. In his majestic bed, the fourteen members of the faculty of medicine could not agree on the king's diagnosis. Their safest consensus prescribed the king to be given enemas and to be bled, both staple remedies of the times—the contemporary equivalent of "take two aspirins, and call me in the morning."

Louis XV's three daughters insisted on tending their father during the day. After they departed in the early evening, Madame du Barry slipped into the room via a concealed door. She passed the night at the king's bedside holding his hand and soothing him. The mistress and the dauphin had their respective physicians examine the king. Both intoned the same remedy: more bleeding. The king's condition deteriorated quickly (ah, duh ... all that loss of blood). To facilitate his care, Louis XV was moved from his ornate bed to a smaller, more practical one.

Throughout his illness, the king's bedroom resembled a rush-hour train platform. Courtiers with the right of entry kept jockeying for the best location nearest His Majesty in the gilded sickroom. Typical of the petty behavior at Versailles, scuffles broke out over who had more right to be in the room at a given time. The king's eldest daughter, the bossy Madame Adélaïde, played referee, imposing an orderly flow in and out of the bed chamber.

During a courtesy call by the dauphin and dauphine, a servant brought a candle quite close to the king's face. The attendant froze in disbelief on the spot. His terrified reaction alerted the doctors who approached the bed, stunned to recognize the unmistakable signs of smallpox. Louis XV, sensing a sudden shift in the mood, requested a mirror. He beheld his disfigured face, alarmed at the small sores filled with puss. Fear gripped his gut. He blinked several times incredulously and moaned aloud, "It's smallpox!" At his age, the shattered king knew the diagnosis signified zero chance of recovery.

Smallpox, the most dreaded disease of that time, cared nothing for social rank. Rich or poor, smallpox did not discriminate. On average during the eighteenth century, four hundred thousand Europeans died each year of this viral infection. If you were fortunate to survive the disease, you would likely be disfigured for life. If you were a young lady, smallpox guaranteed spinsterhood, unless you were a wealthy heiress whose tempting bank account could compensate for a disagreeable countenance.

Like a brush fire sparked during a drought, the news of the king's diagnosis consumed the palace. The throngs of courtiers, once elbowing each other for a coveted spot in the king's bedroom, melted away. All who had found themselves in close proximity to the sovereign now ran the risk of contagion. Confronted with the highly infectious smallpox, even the unbending rules of court etiquette buckled as daily attendance on His Majesty nosedived.

Outside the sick room, unseemly arguments erupted. Madame du Barry's clique, in the person of the foreign minister, Aiguillon, already locked horns with other notables including the allies of the former foreign minister, Choiseul, a favorite of Marie Antoinette. Everybody was jockeying to wield power in the new reign. Tempers flared over the sensitive timing of getting the king to agree to take the holy sacraments. Open hostilities for a power grab would shift into high gear once Louis resigned himself to taking that step.

The dauphin and dauphine, along with others in the line of succession, were barred from the sick room. Versailles was one of the few royal courts that had not yet embraced the medical novelty of being vaccinated against smallpox. Madame du Barry refused to abandon the king, signaling that she and Louis were a package deal. To their brave credit, the king's three crone daughters put their broomsticks aside and comforted their father. Antoinette requested to assist the aunts in caring for the king. Fortunately, she was immune to infection having been exposed to a mild form of smallpox when she was two years old. The request was flatly denied by the attending doctors as too risky. And Adélaïde would never have allowed Antoinette to cross the king's threshold and rain on her parade.

As rumors swirled about the king's condition, Countess du Barry had the most at stake. The king would probably die, spelling a rapid adieu to her sweet services. Worst of all, if she caught smallpox, her famous beauty would be ruined, providing she were lucky enough to survive. Luckily for her, Du Barry escaped the smallpox.

With each passing hour, Louis XV trembled that his soul was in grave jeopardy. It had been almost four decades since the king last confessed his sins and received the sacred host. Petrified that the gates of hell were being greased for his arrival, Louis braced himself to accept the inevitable. During her evening visit on May 4, the king broke the news to Madame du Barry that she would have to vacate the palace. He promised her that he had made provisions for a rosy future. The mistress knew damn well that a dead king's wishes counted for nothing. Early the next morning, the distraught mistress sneaked out of Versailles for the nearby chateau of Ruel that belonged to her buddy, Foreign Minister Aiguillon. The nervous countess was probably one of three persons in France praying for an unlikely cure. Most Parisians were thrilled at the king's rapid decline, and some traveled to Versailles to await the outcome. A carnival atmosphere prevailed outside the palace. This royal death would be celebrated and not mourned.

A decaying Louis XV made his confession on May 7 for the first time in thirty-eight years. Whew, now he was assured of his place in heaven. He gratefully received absolution and took holy communion before the reluctant courtiers kneeling outside his bedroom. Nobody wanted to be anywhere near Louis XV, but they knew this ceremony was an all-hands-on-deck appearance. If the king recovered, their absence would be hard to explain. The king insisted that the tottering Cardinal Roche-Aymon read aloud, "Gentlemen, the King has asked me to tell you that he begs God's forgiveness for having offended Him, and for the scandal that he caused his people. If God grants him health, he will look to penitence, to sustaining our religion, and to relieving his people." If a miracle did happen, the smart money was on the quick return of an avenging Du Barry.

On Tuesday, May 10, 1774, Louis XV was closing in on his last breath. The king was unrecognizable, with his swollen features, copper colored face, and stench of oozing sores. He remained fairly alert despite his suffering. He uttered at one point, "How I pity my poor successor." It was a bit too late for those sentiments. His failure to prepare his grandson for the difficult job ahead must have spiked the king's misery. As for the trembling heir about to rule France, his grandfather's apprehensions were justified. The dauphin, faced with the terrifying responsibility of governing, didn't know whether he was on foot or horseback.

All eyes stayed glued to a candle burning in Louis XV's bedroom window. Crowds of varying sizes huddled together under the window, hoping to witness the confirmation of death. Messengers on horseback would take off at a gallop in scattered directions once the candle was extinguished. Shortly after three in the afternoon, a figure was spotted at the window solemnly putting out the flame of the candle. The demise of the old king was now official as messengers took off in a frenzy to reach their respective clients. Within the chateau, the doors of the king's bedroom swung open, and the tense crowd standing at a safe distance was officially informed, "The King is dead. Long live the King."

Mimicking the messengers outside the palace, the assembled courtiers bolted in a stampede to the apartment of the heirs. No matter what their private feelings of the new king might be, everyone at Versailles recognized him to be the new dispenser of the royal cookie jar. Antoinette and Louis were gathered with Louis' brothers and their wives in Antoinette's apartments. With them were Louis' younger sisters, Clotilde and Elisabeth. The mood in the room was subdued, dreading the expected announcement.

From afar the dauphin along with his sequestered intimates heard a noise that sounded like an approaching avalanche. It turned out to be the galloping feet of courtiers on the parquet floors rushing to hail the new king. As scores of courtiers burst into the stillness of the dauphine's suite, the only words heard were chants of "Long Live the King." Overcome with emotion, Louis and Antoinette sobbed as they clung to one another, bewailing they were too young to reign. The new king, now Louis XVI, blurted out, "I feel as though the universe is falling upon me." It was a touching scene to all present as power peacefully passed to a virtuous prince.

Madame Noailles appeared first on the scene to offer her allegiance, slipping instantly into her role as the guardian of etiquette. She firmly cued the jostling crowd as to their appropriate conduct for the given circumstances. This was one supervision that Antoinette welcomed due to her own emotionally charged condition. As each courtier pledged his or her loyalty, the royal couple slowly grasped that they were now the center of the French world. At the prodding of Madame Noailles, Marie Antoinette gave her first orders as queen, commanding the carriages to convey the court to the chateau at Choisy. Court etiquette stipulated that a new king temporarily reside in a different royal residence from where a former king died.

Within an hour of Louis XV's death, the palace of Versailles resembled a ghost town. With indelicate speed the dead king's pustulant corpse was sealed in a lead coffin without the ritual embalming. Fear of contracting the dreaded smallpox overrode that stipulation of etiquette. They hurried Louis XV's corpse off to the burial crypt at St. Denis at night. Those who had gathered to witness the coffin being transported to its resting place raucously shouted, "There goes the ladies' pleasure." Louis XV would neither be remembered nor missed. A mere three masses for the repose of the king's soul were recorded in Notre Dame Cathedral's register—not an encouraging endorsement for a glorious arrival into heaven.

But back to the living. The new king and his queen sped from the noxious air of Versailles for the more sanitary royal residence at Choisy, about five miles from Paris. Louis, Antoinette, and the king's brothers and wives rode in uneasy silence. Yet within minutes they were all laughing and joking with one another. Once they arrived at Choisy, Louis XVI ordered a seven-month period of mourning for his grandfather. Although black attire and somber draperies were ubiquitous, the general mood was one of giddy gaiety. The confident new crew in charge felt certain that there would be only Bourbon blue skies from now on.

> "In the naïveté of their youth, they believed Fate
> to be a kind mistress. None of them were prepared
> for the beast that was about to pick them up by the throats
> and shake them until their teeth rattled."
> *Melodie Ramone*

Spotlight Two

The Days of Living in High Cotton

Chapter 14

Guess Who Gets the Boot?

$\mathcal{W}$hen nineteen-year-old Louis XVI inherited the crown, France could not have been blessed with a more honest and well intentioned king. And rarely had a reign in France been inaugurated with a man who possessed almost zero executive and political abilities.

The new king's first task was to establish his council of ministers. Would he retain his grandfather's choices or strike out on his own with new blood in the council? More significantly, would he appoint a prime minister to oversee the council, or would he continue the practice of his two predecessors by shepherding the council himself? These vital questions would soon shape the course of the new reign. Louis believed that his sterling intentions and moral rectitude would illuminate his pathway to governing success. His lack of self-confidence and chronic indecisiveness would prove otherwise.

On one issue Louis XVI did not hesitate to flex some muscle. Hoping to restore a firmer morality to the court of Versailles, the new king ordered that the royal favorite, Countess du Barry, get the royal heave-ho. By banishing Du Barry, Louis signaled that the era of meddling mistresses was caput. In May 1774 he instructed the minister of the royal household to send her a *lettre de cachet* [a letter of banishment] "to enter a provincial convent and command her to see nobody. I leave to you the choice of the place and the pension which I am giving her, so that she may live like an honest woman out of consideration to the memory of my grandfather."

In a flash "the creature" was forced to enter a convent about twenty-five miles from Paris, the Abbaye du Pont aux Dames, operated by a group of Cistercian nuns. These nuns dedicated their lives to prayer, silence, and contemplation. God only knows what the twenty sheltered sisters thought about the new guest forced on them. The street savvy mistress readily adapted to her new circumstances and managed to charm the stern mother abbess and community of religious women in no time at all. When you think of what could have been her punishment, the mistress got off relatively easy.

In October 1776 Madame du Barry got a lucky break when she received permission to return to her cherished residence, the chateau at Louveciennes. More importantly, all of her booty that she had amassed during her five years as official mistress was released to her. Marie Antoinette could have been vindictive by pressuring the king to prevent the release of the former favorite's treasures, mothballed at Versailles. Antoinette had little to say regarding Du Barry's fate. The queen tersely mentioned in a letter to her mother, "The creature has been placed in a convent and all who bore this scandalous name have been driven from Court." Antoinette seemed content that her former rival was forever branded an outcast. As for the discarded countess, she led a charmed life at Louveciennes.

"She's the kind of girl who climbed the ladder of success,
wrong by wrong."
Mae West

Chapter 15

Louis' First Days on the Job

From 1643 until 1774 France had been ruled by two kings, Louis XIV and Louis XV. Imagine having one of these two figures dominate your entire existence. Some background on these previous kings should help to understand Louis XVI's course for ruling France.

First, Louis XIV ranks as the big daddy of absolute monarchy. The eye-popping portrait of Louis XIV, painted by Hyacinthe Rigaud, seems almost comical by today's standards. But don't be fooled by the frills, ribbons, silk stockings, and the red heels. In its time, the portrait aimed to impress and intimidate. The towering wig and heels allowed Louis to stand out in a crowd, convincing the viewer that Louis XIV was virile, all powerful, and monitoring everyone's day-to-day life.

But it didn't start out that way. As a child, Louis XIV lived through uncertain times as powerful lords vied for power. As a young adult, he grasped that the threat to his authority came from these scheming nobles whose ambitions Louis XIV would systematically alter. First, Louis purged them from his council of ministers. Second, the king orchestrated petty squabbles among his nobles to perpetuate their reliance on his favor. He perfected a rigorous code of duties to be performed as a distinction in service to the king. This catechism of court etiquette micromanaged all behavior at court. If you messed up, you could become permanently "invisible" in the king's presence. At the height of his glory, Louis XIV explained to his only brother, the role of etiquette in sustaining the divine right of kings:

Before God, you and I are exactly the same as other creatures that
live and breathe; but before men we are seemingly extraordinary
beings, greater, more refined, and more perfect. The day that
people shall abandon their respect and veneration, which is the
mainstay of monarchies—on the day that they regard us as their
equals, then all the prestige of our position will be destroyed.

Louis XIV submitted to the exacting etiquette, aware that it was the
mechanism that kept the incense wafting his way. By sacrificing his privacy,
he remained the eternal principal at center stage, perpetuating his fame as
The Sun King.

As Louis XIV consolidated power to himself, he ditched Paris as his
capital, a slight that Parisians never forgave. He moved the seat of government
twelve miles away to what had once been a hunting lodge for his father,
Louis XIII. There he embarked on a building project that became the palace
of Versailles. In this jaw-dropping stunning edifice the king allotted coveted
apartments for the cream of the nobility.

Unlike other European royal courts, powerful nobles in France did not
occasionally attend the king and pass the bulk of their time supervising their
estates. At Versailles, the king oversaw their lives as they hovered near him
in the hope of receiving royal favors. The ideal opportunity for attracting
the king's eye occurred as he paraded to mass each day. Expectant courtiers
grovelingly petitioned him with written requests. The king would dispense
the same noncommittal response: "We shall see." This guy knew how to
work a crowd.

In old age, Louis XIV provided his heirs with a three-step formula for
autocratic rule: listen to the concerns of the people; weigh the advice of your
ministers; and make your decisions alone. Sound instructions to maintain
an iron grip. The success of a one-man dynastic operation required a Louis
XIV clone to succeed him upon his death. In 1715 Louis XIV's ultimate
successor was his five-year-old great-grandson, Louis XV.

Louis XV was a handsome boy admired by all, but his surface appeal could
not shield forever his mediocre ability to govern. On the surface, Louis XV
looked every silk inch the autocrat. But he lacked the genius of his predecessor.
He slowly led France into a series of wars that weakened its image abroad
and at home. The inefficient and unfair tax system never seemed to meet the
requirements of the Crown's needs. The endless maintenance of Versailles
and other royal residences required vast sums. Eventually the palace of

Versailles resembled a bejeweled dowager—impressive from afar, but a fraying disappointment up close.

Worst of all, Louis XV allowed his weakness for the ladies to influence his conduct in State affairs. His lengthy liaison with the refined Madame Pompadour led to disastrous results. For a period of almost twenty years, she was a shadow prime minister, dictating the rise and fall of ministers. She urged the king to adopt a foreign policy that most Frenchmen abhorred, namely an alliance with Austria. His people despised his weakness for being browbeaten by a mistress. The older Louis XV became, the faster popular devotion evaporated, leaving no room in any heart for redemption.

During Louis XV's reign, some intellectuals and philosophers, such as Voltaire, Rousseau, Diderot, and Raynal began to question the validity of an absolute monarchy. By the 1750s a movement known as The Enlightenment manifested itself primarily in the writings of men who espoused individual liberty and advocated limiting the powers of the Church and Crown—not a secure occupation to pursue under autocratic rule.

With Louis XVI's accession, hope for change surged across France. The new king guaranteed a thumbs up response from his subjects when he announced that he would forego his traditional right of a customary tax granted every new king. Antoinette likewise renounced her similar tax privilege known as the Queen's Girdle. The public was impressed with this modest salvo, raising the hopes of the oppressed throughout the realm. They expected more magnanimous interventions, imagining swift relief was just a royal signature away.

Louis XVI felt bewildered by the responsibilities staring him in the face. On his first night as king, devious Aunt Adélaïde came to his rescue with a document. Waiting for this opportunity, she had kept the text hidden for nine years. Hoping to gain influence over her nephew, she produced a written guide from his late father, Louis Ferdinand, for choosing competent ministers to govern France. It was entitled "List of various persons recommended by the Dauphin to that one of his children who shall succeed Louis XV."

The novice king exhaled a sigh of relief as he studied his father's memo. The suggestions provided a needed road map for Louis XVI to appoint ministers who would serve with merit and distinction. Louis experienced a boost in confidence with the list of candidates provided by his father's foresight. Louis asked his aunt to advise him from the proposed candidates— just what auntie was hoping for. Adélaïde felt relevant again.

The king's council consisted of six officials: the Keeper of the Seals (aka the Minister of Justice); the Minister of Finance; the Minister of War; the Minister of the Navy; the Minister of Foreign Affairs; and lastly, the Minister of the King's Household (who was also responsible for the security of Paris).

In the tradition of his recent ancestors, the new king convinced himself that he could govern France on his own with no prime minister. Louis XVI believed that he required only a temporary guide until he got the hang of governing. Following Aunt Adélaïde's suggestion, the king settled on Count Maurepas. With a flicker of confidence, Louis felt he was off to a good start that would spark success. Louis wrote in haste to Maurepas:

I am now the King and I have not yet acquired all the necessary knowledge. Moreover, I cannot see any minister, all of them having been with the King during his last illness. I have always heard of your integrity, as well as the reputation that your deep knowledge of affairs has so rightly won you. It is this that induces me to beg you to be so kind as to help me with your advice and understanding. Come then as soon as possible, and you will make me most pleased.

"The only place where success comes
before work is in a dictionary."
Vidal Sassoon

Chapter 16

Uncorking a Vintage Bottle

The seventy-three-year-old Count Maurepas once served as the naval minister until he ran afoul of Madame Pompadour who sank his ambitions with exile in 1749. Now he would serve as the training wheels for the early years of Louis' reign.

Resurrected after decades of oblivion, the spry septuagenarian and his wife packed their trunks and jauntily rode off to the center of the universe, Versailles. The count assumed he was being tapped to serve as prime minister. What a triumph for him! His former enemies (at least, those still alive) would now have to kowtow before him. But the novice king punctured that fantasy, appointing Maurepas as a "minister at large," with the task of advising the king—Louis planned on running the government himself. Maurepas may have been out of circulation for decades, but his wits were as sharp as ever: "Well then, Sire, I shall teach you how to rule without a prime minister."

The nature of their relationship was more like a father and a son. Maurepas did not shrink from lecturing the king on what type of behavior was appropriate for a monarch, as well as which policies to pursue. Yet his words oozed support and encouragement. In reality, he became a de facto prime minister, with a mixed record of success. He projected amiability, having learned not to rock the boat of the established order. He seriously weighed every change with an eye to offending the least number of people. He and his wife were allotted the choice suite of rooms that had been vacated by the discarded Du Barry. With the secret stairway linking Maurepas' apartment to that of the king, a close bond formed between these two men. For the next seven years, Louis would consistently rely on Maurepas to chart the best course of action. The court soon baptized him "The Mentor."

All eyes at Versailles focused on Louis XVI's early moves. Would he command the nobles at Versailles to reform their idle lifestyle and their pursuit of political mischief? These early months would end most speculation. The wily British ambassador, Lord Stormont, sent an insightful analysis of the new monarch to his king, George III:

> His Majesty wishes to place himself out of the reach of all intrigue. This however is a vain expectation, and the foolish fancy of a young, inexperienced mind. The throne he fills, far from distancing him from intrigue, places him in the center of it. Great and eminent superiority of talents might indeed crush these cabals, but as there is no reason to believe the King possessed of that superiority, I think that he will be prey to them and find himself more entangled every day.

Benched on the sidelines, Louis XV's former ministers nervously contacted the new king. Because of Louis' nine-day quarantine at Choisy, he was not allowed to come into physical contact with anyone who had shared proximity with his departed grandfather. The immediate concern of the ministers was whether they still had a job. The king responded that for the present there would be no changes. He informed the ministers that he would sign all documents as "Louis" and not "Louis Auguste." The king closed his message, "If anything important were to arise, then the matter should be sent to me." Louis was grateful for the nine days of sequestration, needing time to pick Maurepas' brain.

Ten days after becoming king, Louis met with his council ministers for the first time. Now their boss, Louis stiffly read a prepared speech with Maurepas' input, hinting at what lay ahead: "I want each of you to hold himself in readiness for the time that I shall indicate to render a clear and exact account of his department. Since I wish only to occupy myself with my kingdom and the happiness of my people, it is only by your conformity to those principles that your work will have my approbation." These words left little doubt that the king planned to clean house. But the impediment for that radical step was Louis himself: he felt intimidated by these experienced ministers and kept devising excuses to delay their dismissal. Maurepas' immediate mission was to squash the hesitation of the king.

But just when Maurepas and the king were midstream reconstituting the cabinet, a roadblock popped up, signaling a threat to the royal succession. Within a month of Louis XV's grotesque death, about fifty persons at court, including the three royal aunts, became stricken with smallpox. Ten of these unlucky souls died. The king decided that he and his brothers would be inoculated against smallpox. Antoinette heartily encouraged him but his doctors and some clergymen opposed the procedure; such remedies smacked of sorcery in their eyes. The memory of the late king's agonizing death overruled the naysayers and Louis was inoculated. After a month of isolation, the king emerged feeling quite well, knowing he would not suffer the scourge of this feared illness. But for the rest of his life his face bore the pimply blotches as a souvenir of the inoculation. As for the aunts, they all recovered. Aunt Adélaïde suffered the most and it was feared she might die. But being a tough old bird, she bounced back proving the doctors wrong.

One of Maurepas' first innovations was to install a suggestion box at the palace entrance. It swiftly bulged with demands for reform, prompting its removal late one night. Next came the moment that Maurepas had been planning since late May. With the minister's prodding, Louis issued a pile of pink slips, relieving all of his grandfather's ministers of their posts. Louis reasoned that these ministers were either complicit in, or tainted by, the late king's dissolute life. He wanted to restore a sense of morality to the Crown and reestablish the honor of the Bourbon family in the eyes of the people.

With Maurepas' guidance, Louis chose six men who above all were known for their integrity. These men would frame the governmental policy of the first two years of the reign. The list of new ministers surprised many because it included persons perceived as a threat to the interests of the powerful. The most radical of the new ministers was Monsieur Turgot for the post of finance minister; he would soon ignite an upheaval in the court and the nation. The longest serving would be the cautious workaholic, Count Vergennes, as foreign minister. He and Louis would develop a close working relationship built on mutual trust. Finally, Lamoignon Malesherbes became minister of the king's household. Known as a man opposed to the abuses of privilege, he would be the unlucky chap to keep a lid on the gimme, gimme habits of the courtiers. Malesherbes' term in office would last a mere nine months, but his attachment to the king endured a lifetime.

Cynical observers discounted the king's efforts to rectify bureaucratic abuses that plagued the nation. They wagered that the youthful inexperience of the king would work against him. Besides, most insiders predicted his early zeal to govern would peter out, given his listless disposition. But the common people viewed events in an uncomplicated manner: they expected greatness from this king.

The king and his council normally met twice a week. Absolutely no one—not a prince, not an heir, not a queen—gained admission to this elite gathering. Without a prime minister, the king had to set the agenda for the nation and guide his ministers to implement his wishes. Here, Louis failed miserably. At every opportunity, vested interests attacked his broad agenda to "guarantee the happiness of my people." His heart beat with the best of intentions but his executive ability lacked direction. If Louis had appointed a prime minister, it would have fallen to that official to conduct the council meetings and implement policies. But without such an overseer, Louis vacillated on most issues, torn as to which path to take, often agreeing with the last voice to be heard. Luckily for him, his capable ministers in the early years of his reign set the course of the government. And the king followed along, hesitantly.

> "He who wishes to be obeyed,
> must know how to command."
> *Machiavelli*

Chapter 17

Mama, I'm a Big Queen Now

*W*hile Louis buried himself in the business of operating a complicated kingdom, Antoinette kept pinching herself. What a thrill—she was now the queen! In a letter to her mother, Antoinette basked in her delight: "Although from birth God intended that I should hold this exalted position today, I cannot but be amazed that Providence should have reserved for me, the youngest of your daughters, the most beautiful kingdom in all of Europe." At age eighteen and with no tether, Antoinette skipped off to a reign of boundless brilliance.

After reading her daughter's triumphal letter, Maria Theresa harbored ambivalent emotions, dousing cold water on Antoinette's dewy visions. She warned Louis and Antoinette of the pitfalls awaiting them:

> You are both very young, and the burden is heavy; I worry, really worry about it. All I can say and wish is that you rush nothing; see with your own eyes and change nothing; and allow everything to continue as it is. Otherwise, there would be insurmountable chaos and intrigues, and you my dear children would be so confused that you could never manage.

Maria Theresa confessed to Count Mercy her nagging apprehensions regarding Antoinette's new role:

I tell you frankly that I cannot wish that my daughter be too
influential in affairs. I know only too well from my own experience
what a grievous load government and monarchy can be. Moreover,
I know the youth and volatility of my daughter, which joined
to her lack of application, makes me fear for the success of the
government of a monarchy as rotten as that of France is at present.

As for her daughter's influence on governing, the empress conveniently overruled any misgivings of meddling whenever Austria's political interests surfaced; the empress never perceived that tactic to be disingenuous on her part.

But Louis made it clear to his wife that he would not tolerate petticoat interference in the council chamber. To their sour surprise, Adélaïde and her sisters returned to court after their bout of smallpox only to learn that their nephew no longer required their assistance either. To reinforce the new playing field at Versailles, the queen, at the prompting of Count Mercy, let it be known that she served as the mistress of the maison. She received the returned spinsters kindly, but they got the message. Once again they became bit players on the royal stage.

Within days of the accession, Antoinette got an unpleasant jolt that being a queen was a tricky job. Unintentionally, Antoinette created a breach of etiquette. It was the custom in France that after a dauphine became queen, titled ladies would make their way to Versailles to pay homage to the new queen. Some of these ladies, at great personal expense, made this journey expecting to be greeted by an appreciative monarch. As the ceremony dragged on for hours, Antoinette caused a stir by what was interpreted as rude behavior.

Did you ever have to behave solemnly in public for hours? Almost anything can trigger a fit of the giggles. One of the queen's attendants grew weary of standing during the ceremony. She plopped down on the floor hidden by the wide dresses in front of her. She kept cracking comments about the procession of solemn ladies. Antoinette hid her face behind her fan laughing at the biting one-liners. She was reported to have whispered, "When one has passed thirty, I cannot understand how one dares to appear at Court." Whether she said this is not certain, but gossip made it Gospel.

But Antoinette did refer to the dowager ladies as "the centuries," confirming that she needed to put a muzzle on her immature chatter. These offended ladies returned to their distant castles with an unfavorable opinion of the snotty foreign queen. It didn't take long for a stinging bit of verse to meander its way across the land with a threat attached, "Little queen of twenty years, you treat people so badly, you will be sent back across the border."

"I'm not a princess, I don't need saving."
I am a queen, I got this shit handled."
Harriet Morgan

Chapter 18

First Impressions

This is the perfect moment to describe the expected role of a French queen. France was a nation ruled by the Salic Law—only legitimately-born males could inherit the throne. The king wielded the scepter as the alpha male at court, and the queen followed in his shadow. If the king displayed weakness or became incapacitated, then an opportunity would arise for a queen to exercise clout, but at the risk of strong public censure. Being a queen of France was rarely an enviable job choice.

The search for a suitable consort to the king normally centered on the political advantages to the bachelor monarch. It helped if the chosen lady was physically appealing to motivate the king to perform his conjugal duties to assure healthy sons. Most queens were foreigners, whose loyalty was often questioned. To foster compliance, reminders were plastered above the queen's magnificent bed, adorned with ravishing paintings executed by François Boucher. The artist allegorically depicted the virtues of a French queen: Charity, Abundance, Fidelity, and Prudence—more stringent than the vows of a nun.

Besides being an obedient wife, an admirable queen was religiously pregnant. She regularly provided charitable assistance to the less fortunate, especially in times of famine. When required, the queen would be trotted out for court functions as an ornament of the king and his court. Afterward, she would dutifully retrace her steps to her quarters while the king kicked back with his cronies and mistress du jour. Other than these duties, the queen was expected to live a pious, modest existence, never meddle in politics, keep her mouth shut, die without causing a fuss for the king, and soon be forgotten. This image was what everyone expected of an exemplary French queen. A semi-cloistered existence did not jive with the vision that Marie Antoinette pictured for herself. Given her strong personality, she would not willingly consign herself to a corner of the chateau. She would rewrite the job description to accommodate the "modern" life she chose to lead. Antoinette envisioned a future of bloated splendor.

Since Antoinette's arrival at Versailles, she had submitted to the demands of those who micromanaged her activities from dawn to dusk. And from Vienna, she had endured her mother's sermons about her behavior every time the mail arrived. No one ever seemed satisfied with her. Despite her efforts to please—it was a steady stream of criticism: she should do better or she should know better. Now her moment of liberation beckoned. She could burn her corset in the chapel if she so desired. Antoinette had nobody to please but herself, and no one to obey except the king.

Louis could have imposed limits on his wife's activities. But after four years of marriage, Antoinette was confident her husband would not clip her wings. Unlike his brothers who wore the pants in their respective marriages, Louis often allowed Antoinette's whims because of his embarrassment at not satisfactorily fulfilling his stud services to produce an heir. Plus, he had grown genuinely fond of his high-spirited wife. Antoinette, for her part, liked Louis, but she could barely conceal her disappointment regarding his physical appearance, his lack of royal panache, and his inability to make decisions.

Ascending the throne came with a one-shot chance for Antoinette to consolidate the widespread approval that she enjoyed. Instead of capitalizing on the significance of her ceremonial appeal, she chose a different path. Her epiphany of exalted status laid the foundation for years of self-indulgent behavior and occasional political interference, usually sparked by her Austrian relatives. Antoinette charted a new role for herself as a dynamic, unconventional queen with a slightly naughty edge. There would never be a chance that the public would swallow this unorthodox arrangement.

As expected, the queen's early years on the throne received close scrutiny. Her public report card soon reflected her sinking grades. She rebelled against the strict observance of the crippling court etiquette. More importantly, she craved private time away from the prying eyes of the court, pining for the more relaxed atmosphere she had enjoyed in Vienna. Without a commanding husband to reign in her non-conforming style as queen, Antoinette tweaked her daily schedule to skirt some of the traditional requirements. In the process, she successfully offended persons of rank at court. From the nobles on down the social scale, they did not approve of the self-absorbed conduct of this foreign queen.

Along with the title of queen came a firm sense of entitlement. Almost overnight, Marie Antoinette blossomed, revealing a woman who could be highly strung while requiring high maintenance. She bewildered ministers and courtiers alike. Whenever she wanted something, she first oozed charm. If that failed, she imperiously stomped her foot. When expressing her wishes to uncooperative ministers, she often prefaced her remarks with "I desire and demand." No room for ambiguity with those requests.

However, Antoinette failed to consider the blowback to her reputation as a result of her demands. The owl-like Mercy wrote to Empress Maria Theresa to express his reservations regarding the queen's sudden power, "Whenever the Queen desires something firmly, she will obtain it; but if in the long run she only uses her influence to satisfy her momentary whims, then nothing will remain of the brilliant perspective now open to her."

Antoinette embarked on a pursuit of costly upgrades to several royal residences frequented by the court to reflect her refined aesthetic sensibilities. She first tackled her grand bedroom at Versailles. The queen's apartments had been stripped bare at the death of Louis XV's consort, Marie Leszczynska in 1768. According to the oftentimes inexplicable etiquette, the queen's lady of honor, Countess Noailles in this case, was entitled to all of the queen's furniture on the monarch's death. Overall Antoinette admired the exquisite style of the room, adding furniture and some personal touches, such as tapestry portraits of her mother and brother. Antoinette also installed a device that with the simple tug on a chord allowed her to lock all four doors of her bedroom at will. Courtiers considered this an assault on their accessibility to the monarch. Why did the queen need to lock doors that previously had remained open to all?

Antoinette's thrifty husband, who noted every sou that he spent, was admired throughout France for living within his means. The queen, on the other hand, dependably exceeded her allowance. As the nation's hostess and trendsetter with the responsibility to impress, she expected a dependable blank check for her many projects. This perception was not exactly unfounded when successive finance ministers consented to her requests. Louis and his ministers learned not to make a fuss regarding her list of expenditures during the early years of the reign. Most ministers had experienced her scrotum shrinking stare whenever they objected to one of her requirements. But they valued the tradeoff of a queen preoccupied with shopping and decorating, rather than having her stick her nose into politics.

Alarm bells sounded in Vienna when Maria Theresa read damaging remarks from her spy in residence at Versailles, Count Mercy. Other sources also volunteered observations that did not fill the empress with maternal pride. The edgy empress weighed in with corrective advice to her daughter:

> They also speak of millions to be spent on palaces. They say
> you cannot tell the Queen from the other Princes, that they are
> extremely familiar with you. God prevent me from wanting you
> to make them feel how superior you are to them—God made
> you so—but you have already been compromised many times by
> their like. The Count Artois, they say, is bold to excess, you must
> not tolerate that—in time it could do you real harm. You must
> stay in your place and play your own role; that will put you and
> everyone else at their ease. Be kind and attentive to all but show
> no familiarity; do not play at being their friend. A firm character
> in which justice is blended with kindness and the right sort of
> economizing will make both friends and enemies respect the
> Monarch.

As usual, Maria Theresa not only knew her daughter, the empress was a seasoned pro at identifying the pitfalls of life at court. Was her daughter listening to any of this? Antoinette did not completely absolve herself of the list of shortcomings outlined by her mother. In reply, the queen sought to soothe her mother:

> The King is not about to spend millions on palaces—that is an
> exaggeration. It is true that the Count Artois is very lively and
> thoughtless, but I know how to make him feel that he is wrong.
> As for the aunts, they no longer rule me, and I am very far from
> confiding in Count Provence and his wife. I must admit I am lazy
> and dissipated when it comes to serious things. I want and hope
> to improve little by little, and without being party to any intrigue,
> make myself such as to justify the King's trust, for he still treats
> me as his friend.

Antoinette knew what was expected of her to be a traditional queen. But the temptation to succumb to the fast lane was too appealing to resist.

The early favorable impressions of Antoinette on her subjects slowly chipped away after 1774. As rumors of her runaway spending and promoting intimate friends to lucrative posts circulated the land, Antoinette's popularity listed downward. Convincing stories were whispered that she advanced the interests of Austria to the king whenever the bed curtains were drawn. In addition, there was the paramount issue that she still had not provided the nation with an heir. Determined to ignore the sniping of the sore losers who berated her, Antoinette flitted willfully from one amusement to another.

"I don't mean to be a diva,
but some days you wake up
and you're Barbra Streisand."
Courtney Love

Chapter 19

The Queen's Private Getaway

*T*he court resumed residing at the sanitized Versailles in the fall of 1774. Same palace, different monarchs.

Remember when you could walk anywhere in public without being observed by a camera? Nowadays for security reasons, everyone is resigned to being recorded almost everywhere in public. It seems the only remaining private sanctuaries are restrooms and fitting rooms in clothing stores.

A similar scenario operated at the palace of Versailles, minus the cameras. Without exception, the royal personages lived under the perpetual scrutiny of anyone who sauntered through the palace, whether a high born office holder, ubiquitous serving staff, or purely pedestrian visitor. Think of the palace as an amusement park with free admission where the royals headlined as the main attraction. And security rated as benign at best—such a situation would be unthinkable today.

The palace grounds and vestibule mimicked a modern-day flea market. Near the palace gates, food vendors satisfied the hunger of the swarm of daily visitors with the fried fast food of its day. The booths of merchants even crept onto the landings of interior staircases, selling a variety of goods to visitors. A popular concession allowed a male sightseer to rent a sword and hat, two articles that were mandatory if you wished to see the royals up close. Adorned with these two prerequisites, a fellow could gawk to his heart's content and venture wherever he wished through the palace. Tourists accounted for most visitors who came in hopes of catching a glimpse of the king and his family parade off to mass, or the more popular diversion of checking out the royals as they dined in public. Since the schedule at court was set in marble, a day-tripper knew exactly where and when to show up for a good view.

On an average day, the palace teemed with professional pickpockets; ladies for hire luring their next client; street urchins dashing about delivering messages while snatching food from public buffet tables; someone unloading his bladder in a stairwell; gaping provincial and foreign tourists; preoccupied servants scurrying around; street performers; petitioners seeking the appropriate ear; ambassadors with their attendants; and ever hopeful courtiers plotting their advancement. Some visitors could not resist the temptation of slipping into their pockets any tchotchke that wasn't nailed down. Imagine Grand Central Station in New York at five on a Friday evening and you will have a sense for the setting inside Versailles on a typical day. It was controlled bedlam at best—no wonder the queen wanted out.

At heart, Antoinette was a private person who loved a cozy, homey atmosphere. Although her inner apartments at Versailles offered refuge, they usually lacked sunlight. She yearned for bright sun-splashed rooms with a garden view. She just had to have her own home where her every gesture or word was not scrutinized by a thousand eyes. Antoinette dropped hints to Madame Noailles, who in turn tipped off Louis that his wife desired a residence that would be her private domain. Not only did the queen crave privacy, she was also instinctively suspicious; her desk was always kept locked, she burned most correspondence, and no one was allowed to enter her apartments without her permission.

In June 1774 Louis XVI gifted Antoinette the Petit Trianon, a cream puff mini-palace of seven rooms, and a parcel of the Versailles grounds surrounding it. With a written note, the king thrilled the queen: "Madame, this pleasure house is now yours." Louis included a key fit for a queen, encrusted with 531 diamonds. With the acquisition of the Petit Trianon, Antoinette would occasionally escape the life-draining schedule of Versailles.

Antoinette gratefully accepted her husband's offer, but promptly set her conditions. No one, not even the king, would gain admission without her permission. Posted signs announced that entrance to the grounds was *"de par la reine"*—by order of the queen. Louis accepted this stipulation without a peep of protest. The king could violate this injunction whenever he wished, but he permitted the queen to rule exclusively in her private domain. At the Petit Trianon, she requested her guests to not rise when she entered a room, but at the palace this would count as a mortal sin. This alternating behavior sent mixed signals to her intimate circle.

The court and country judged Antoinette's ownership of the Petit Trianon a disgrace. A queen of France claiming autonomy of her person in her own dwelling—absolutely scandalous! Her behavior flaunted her disregard for the public's accustomed access to all royal homes. From the public's perspective, they had paid for this impressive property and merited entry.

The off-limits venue sparked a universal question. What was Antoinette doing when she was cocooning unobserved in her private realm? Aunt Adélaïde, envious courtiers, and the uninvited wondered aloud what shenanigans were afoot in that secretive enclave. They sarcastically referred to the queen's lair as "Little Vienna." Antoinette dismissed the petty criticism countering that she wished to be a "modern" monarch with fewer restraints.

Once Antoinette became queen, etiquette's grasp tightened even more. Attendants pounced on the queen as soon as she awoke. A serving lady presented her with an assortment of delicate undergarments and handkerchiefs needed for the day. Next, a lady of the wardrobe would appear with an elaborate fashion handbook, corresponding to the season of the year, containing drawings and fabric samples of her dresses. Using pins, Antoinette selected three dresses to be worn that day, appropriate for the schedule. Then the queen would take a bath wearing a flannel gown that buttoned to her neck. After a light breakfast, the onslaught of morning visitors got underway as members of the immediate family appeared, including a drop-in visit by the king. Intimate friends wandered in and out, as well as the physician, reader, and other people in her service.

By late morning, the mega entrée commenced when the queen dressed according to strict rules. There's a well recorded moment in Antoinette's life that exposed the mindless rigidity of court etiquette. Women did not wear panties at that time; instead, a linen chemise sufficed. Etiquette dictated that the highest-ranking lady present would have the honor of handing the undergarment to the queen. One winter morning Antoinette stood shivering in her drafty bedroom waiting for her undergarments. Unexpectedly, several ladies, each of higher rank than the previous one, announced their arrival by scratching at the door. (At Versailles you never knocked on the door of a member of the royal family; you always scratched the door with the long nail of your left pinky finger—don't ask why—just chalk it up to one of the thousands of regulations governing palace procedures.) As each higher born lady entered the room, she claimed the honor of handing the undergarment to the queen. Did anyone in attendance ever shout out "To hell with the rules; give her the damn undies already!"? A naked Antoinette put up with the tedious delay, but she muttered through chattering teeth, "This is just intolerable." And she was right.

After the ritual of dressing, the queen's hair was arranged, and the finale came as she applied her mandatory rouge. Meanwhile, dignitaries, princes of the Blood, and other highly-placed persons entered the room and were accorded greetings by the queen depending on their rank. The higher up the social ladder, the more expressive the compensatory recognition required by the queen.

Once Antoinette looked regally presentable, she exited her chambers to meet the king for the procession to mass, sometimes followed by a public luncheon. Sundays always promised a splendid spectacle as the royal family dined in public with ambassadors and visitors paying rapt attention. Observed by all present, the king inhaled every course while the queen picked at her plate. Many felt cheated by the queen's reticence to eat. After all, they got dressed in their best finery and came to Versailles to witness the chowdown. Antoinette would eat later, unobserved in the privacy of her intimate apartments. She never drank wine with her meals, only Ville d' Avray mineral water. In the afternoons she would snatch some quiet time whenever possible. Most evenings her job as hostess dictated that the courtiers would be entertained by her or her surrogates. The daily ceremonies governed by the inflexible rules of court etiquette would make anyone's life seem monotonously rehearsed.

Marie Antoinette's flouting of the traditions of the sacred past reflected the chasm of a huge generation gap. When Louis XV died in his mid-sixties, power and influence passed to a generation in their late teens, reinforcing the saying, "Out with the old, in with the new." Among the young crowd was the hip Count Ségur, who would later recount the fashion to look cool during the early years of the new reign, "We, the young French nobility, who had neither regret for the past nor anxiety for the future, stepped gaily on a carpet of flowers that concealed an abyss. Happy to scoff at the outmoded ways, of the feudal pride and solemn manners of our fathers, everything that was established seemed to us tiresome and ridiculous." This recollection sounds familiar to any younger generation pushing the boundaries of adult solidity.

However, the over-thirty crowd at Versailles who expected to wait upon Antoinette resented this new arrangement that deprived them of their hard-won prerogatives. An unflattering image of Antoinette fermented from the upper crust of Versailles' society. In less than a decade, an unfavorable perception of Marie Antoinette coalesced, condemning her as a disliked foreigner who would never be one of them.

The Petit Trianon would always be Antoinette's Arcadian sanctuary where she could banish all unpleasantness. As she once exclaimed about the Petit Trianon, "Here I am no longer Queen. I can be myself."

"It's tangible, it's solid, it's beautiful.
It's artistic from my standpoint, and
I just love real estate."
Donald Trump

Chapter 20

Louis Lays an Egg

*B*efore Louis comfortably adjusted his ample derriere to the seat of his throne in 1774, he got dragged into a contentious domestic matter. Everyone had a pigheaded opinion about the hot button issue of the Parlements.

The Parlements were not a legislative body as their name may suggest, but more of a court of justice. It consisted of thirteen courts scattered across France, with the one in Paris being the most important. The best reference for today is to think of SCOTUS as a comparable body for the Paris Parlement and the U.S. Courts of Appeal for the provincial Parlements dotting the rest of France. The common people revered these legal bodies as a protection against unfair taxation by the Crown. In reality, these courts nurtured their own selfish interests, preserving the prerogatives of their class. They promoted themselves as victims of the Crown when necessary to curry favor with the disaffected.

The Paris Parlement registered new laws and taxes prescribed by the king. But sometimes they defied the king's wishes. The monarch could force approval by holding what was termed a *lit de justice* (literally, a bed of justice), a ceremony demanding compliance to the king. If the Paris Parlement remained obstinate then the king would exile them to the boonies and proceed with his proposed decrees. When the nation was ruled by an assertive king, Parlement played nice. When it detected weakness, it sprouted fangs to claw at the Crown.

Under Louis XV this entity emerged as the main obstacle to autocratic power. In early 1771 a stymied Louis XV had suffered enough of their lip.

In a radical move, Louis XV revamped the French legal system, dismantling the Paris Parlement and reconfiguring the twelve remaining courts. This unprecedented change during the reign of Louis XV could have altered French history if left undisturbed. Even Voltaire applauded this bold move by Louis XV: "Better to be ruled by a great lion than by two hundred rats of their kind." But with a new king, the chance to undo the ground-breaking deeds of 1771 loomed large.

Weeks into his new job, Louis XVI was bombarded with appeals to resurrect the Parlements that had been dissolved during the final years of Louis XV's reign. Equally passionate proponents insisted on the permanent abolition of the Parlements. Which side would prevail in this first tug of war for the king's ear?

The uncertain Louis canvassed the opinions of his council members, including his brother Count Provence. Some ministers urged Louis not to recall the Parlements. Provence predicted that the king would be reduced to an emasculated figurehead. He reminded Louis that their late father had detested the Parlements, an argument that usually scored an emotional home run with the king. Even his mother-in-law in Vienna exhorted him to resist any recall. One adviser warned the king that, "the magistrates would return gentle as lambs, and once on their benches become lions."

On the other hand, nobles who had links to the Parlements clamored for their reinstatement. Another voice in favor of the recall came from Antoinette who entered the fracas believing this action would boost the Crown's popularity among the common people. It seemed like an even split by those closest to the king. Just the recipe for paralyzing the king's response.

Ultimately, the last word apparently lay with Maurepas who sided with the restoration of the Parlements. Maurepas eased Louis XVI's anxieties, emphasizing the long tradition of the institution. Maurepas mistakenly warned the king that, "without Parlement, there is no monarchy." He ignored that France had survived nicely for almost four years without the meddling of the Parlements. Louis, a sucker for upholding tradition, fell for the bait of Maurepas' argument and revived the Parlements in November 1774.

Louis' ambivalence about his decision for the return of the magistrates surfaced in a reinstatement ceremony: "I recall you today to your functions. Appreciate my goodness, and never forget it. Do not occupy yourselves with anything but the response to my wishes." This first blockbuster decision by Louis XVI proved to be the most disastrous of his entire reign. The tough words of admonishment would have worked under Louis XIV, but these judges of the Parlements knew that the times and king were different.

Within a few years, Louis and Antoinette would personally suffer the ferocious side of these justices. Once again, Voltaire penned the best appraisal of the decision to recall the Parlements with his inimitable sparkle of satin sarcasm:

At last all the Parlements were reformed and it was hoped that we would see the reform of the laws likewise. We were mistaken; nothing has been reformed. Louis XVI in his wisdom reestablished the Parlements that Louis XV with justice destroyed. The people witnessed their return with transports of joy.

"I never speak ill of dead people or live judges."
Edwin Edwards

Chapter 21

Show Us the Money

Once the matter of the Parlements seemed settled, Louis faced two other front burner issues. The first centered on the precarious finances of the nation. The second concerned the enthusiasm for intervening in the war of independence by the colonists in America rebelling against England. In France, the American patriots were called "insurgents."

Louis rightly prioritized the money issue as the more pressing problem. He expected his new Finance Minister Turgot to perform a financial miracle worthy of biblical admiration. Turgot confidently took charge of taming the spending habits of the government. What a brilliant coup if he succeeded, and what a steep descent if he failed!

Turgot, a pragmatic visionary, was the smartest and most focused man to serve a king in ages. He aimed to modernize an ossified system of government. Turgot saw the bigger picture and came armed with the solutions. In a memo to Louis, he bluntly spelled it out, "Your nation has no constitution. It is a society composed of different orders, imperfectly united, and of a people whose members have very few social links among themselves, with the result that each one is concerned exclusively with his own interests." Although Louis grew uneasy when anyone mentioned that profane word constitution, he yielded to Turgot's convincing sales pitch for reform.

The prickly minister pledged to keep a tight lid on the Crown's treasure chest. His mantra for economic reform relied on three imperatives: No Bankruptcy, No Increase of Taxes, and No Borrowing. Louis' thrifty side easily related to such a policy. Louis fondly recalled his late father's admonition that: "A King is the steward of the nation's finances." The optimistic king rejoiced prematurely in the improvements that Turgot predicted; it all sounded so attainable. As an example of economizing, Turgot insisted that his own salary be slashed, prompting Louis to reduce the expenses of his own household. At this early stage of Turgot's ministry, Louis remained firmly on the same page as his minister.

Turgot's policy envisioned a single tax on land and a drastic retrenchment in benefits enjoyed by the clergy, the nobility, the members of the Parlements, the powerful guilds, and all those who collected individual tolls and fees for commercial transactions. These folks represented the powerful interest groups that controlled the wealth. These forces quickly protested and aligned themselves to disgrace this minister who dared to tamper with their perks.

Turgot might have fared better if he had gradually instituted his reforms. The wise Malesherbes, Turgot's friend and fellow minister, begged Turgot to slow the pace of the reforms lest he face a crushing opposition. Maurepas counseled the same advice. And none knew better than Maurepas how the pernicious forces at Versailles could sabotage one's career. The forty-eight-year-old Turgot dismissed these warnings saying he needed to hurry because the men in his family died by their fiftieth birthday. Turgot's ESP factor was almost on target; he died at age fifty-three.

The major hurdle with the plan for unprecedented reform was the minister himself. As one witty observer quipped, "Monsieur Turgot does good things badly." A social Neanderthal, the minister dismissed the importance of schmoozing the grandees at court, and, in particular, the titled ladies who flourished with flattering compliments. Finance and social reform were Turgot's strengths, not fawning gallantry. He offended everyone with his less than servile responses for favors, such as dispensing pensions or desired appointments. The stung courtiers schemed to topple this unspeakable Mr. Scrooge from their midst.

In the end, the unified chorus from Louis' council of ministers mattered most. Turgot failed to be a team player with his fellow ministers, behaving like a bully in their midst. Maurepas, in particular, took personal offense at this power grab. Even Louis voiced his unhappiness with Turgot, noting, "Only his friends have merit, and only his ideas are good."

From the start, several bad breaks from Mother Nature hobbled the success of Turgot's reforms. First, an infectious disease decimated many cattle. Then worst of all, the pitiful grain harvest of the autumn of 1774 caused the price of bread to skyrocket. Rumors flew about France that grain merchants and wealthy farmers were hoarding grain to reap a huge profit. By April 1775 riots popped up throughout the country—known as The Flour War. Most of the unrest occurred in the area surrounding Paris, including angry demonstrators besieging the gates of Versailles. With Turgot's firm prodding, Louis ordered troops to restore order. By mid-May a tentative tranquility returned with the use of force. Meanwhile the king instructed grain merchants to sell grain at a fair price, and he urged local clergy to foster calm among their flock. This was one of the few occasions during his reign when Louis responded decisively to a crisis.

In January 1776 Turgot submitted his package of reforms to the Paris Parlement. As predicted, the recently recalled Parlement of Paris morphed from Dr. Jekyll to Mr. Hyde, refusing to register the edicts. What a blow to Turgot's grand scheme. And he had championed Parlement's recall!

Turgot hounded Louis to support these reform measures, or else face a financial calamity. The king accepted Turgot's demands by forcing the Parlement of Paris to register the reforms in March 1776. But within weeks Turgot could not count one friend standing in his corner at court. Even the queen, who mostly approved of Turgot, chimed in, demanding that Turgot get the trapdoor. Turgot had miffed Antoinette when he had engineered the recall of one of her pals from his diplomatic post in England.

The fatal blow came when Turgot's biggest fan, Malesherbes, resigned his council seat. With Malesherbes' departure, all of the remaining ministers turned a cold shoulder against Turgot. The frightened king withdrew his support of Turgot overnight, declaring, "Turgot wants to me be me; I will not allow it." Abandoned and isolated, Turgot continued to resist the scuttling of his reforms. In a seven-page letter to Louis, Turgot served notice that it was up to the king to save the day:

> Sire, I am profoundly hurt at the cruel silence with which you listened to me last Sunday after I have pointed out to you in detail my position, your own, and the dangers facing your authority. It will be impossible for me to continue to serve you if you do not aid me. You have not deigned to reply. I cannot believe, Sire, that you would light-heartedly consent to sacrifice your reign and the welfare of your people. You are too young to judge men, and you have said so yourself, Sire, that you lack experience and need a guide. Some people say that you are weak and indeed on occasion I have seen this defect in your character. Never forget, Sire, that weakness put the head of Charles I on the chopping block.

The tactless letter continued in the same vein, echoing the voice of a demanding father describing an underachieving son. To phrase his concerns in a more palatable manner for a royal ego to stomach, Turgot should have first submitted this letter to his pal, Malesherbes. He might have won over the inexperienced monarch and the outcome could have rescued his plan.

Louis imploded after reading this numbing letter. Turgot had hit him where it hurt most, his fragile self-confidence. The king bristled at its harsh personal assessment. And how dare Turgot compare Louis' prospects with a beheaded English king! Louis ignored all attempts by the minister to see him, hoping that Turgot would get the message and slink away. But Turgot stayed resolutely at his desk, plugging away for the implementation of his policies. After Maurepas goosed the king to act, Louis sent a blunt order on May 12, 1776, ordering Turgot to immediately relinquish his post. A defeated Turgot departed for his country estate far from the tinsel of Versailles while unbridled merriment erupted in the hearts of the courtiers he left behind. The temporarily derailed gravy train once again chugged along dispensing goodies.

"Once he makes up his mind, he is full of indecision."
Oscar Levant

Chapter 22

The Original One Percenters

*A*lthough Louis XVI considered himself an absolute monarch, his real world proved otherwise. There were two tiny segments of the population that on paper worked in harmonious submission to the king's wishes. But in practice, these powerful entities often upstaged the king and proved daringly confrontational during Louis' reign.

For centuries, the two groups were known as the First Estate (the clergy), and the Second Estate (the nobility). These two powerful forces accounted for approximately one percent of the twenty-eight million French population in 1780. Both estates can lay claim as the original title holders of The One Percent. Their financial perks came at the expense of the remaining ninety-nine percent, known as the Third Estate.

The First Estate numbered about 170,000 clerics spread among a few mighty archbishops, bishops, and abbots (mostly from noble families); and they were augmented by the numerous local priests, monks, and nuns. The Church in France controlled vast wealth, owning ten percent of the land and raking in a yearly tithe of ten percent of the annual harvest. With ninety-seven percent of the population identifying as Catholic, the Church exerted great influence on the daily lives of the common people, providing an array of social services.

The Second Estate—the nobility—estimated to be 125,000 persons during Louis XVI's reign, owned thirty percent of the land. Who made up this elite class that wielded unbreachable power? They consisted of a two-tiered group: the nobility of the sword and the nobility of the robe.

The nobility of the sword constituted the venerable names of France whose ancestors had fought alongside French kings in time of war. Their wealth derived from their holdings of land with a customary chateau serving as their official seat of power. They enhanced their income with a collection of fees imposed on the peasants within their jurisdiction. The nobility of the sword generally snickered at the pretensions of the new kids on the block, the nobility of the robe.

The nobility of the robe's increasing numbers challenged the nobility of the sword's superior perch. Some of these lower ranking aristos received their titles as a reward from a grateful monarch for services rendered the Crown. However, most of this ennobled group had purchased their titles thanks to their wealth. This practice to elevate one's status gained prominence during the reign of the calculating Louis XIV. He smoothly endorsed this technique of raising revenue required to finance his wars and ceaseless construction projects. This newer breed of nobleman often held hereditary government positions, such as serving as judges of the Crown's courts. These nobles actually had a job to perform, unlike most of their top bunk "cousins."

By today's standards, it's not difficult to grasp the influence wielded by these privileged, entrenched entities. Their status of entitlement was sanctified by the belief that this natural order of society was ordained by God, and that tree-loving radical, Jean-Jacques Rousseau, could go to hell. Most nobles ruthlessly safeguarded their platinum benefits while disdaining the miserable plight of the vast majority. By the late 1780s the gross imbalance would trigger a corresponding retribution.

"We don't pay taxes. Only the little people pay taxes."
Leona Helmsley

Chapter 23

Branded an Illegal Alien

*D*uring the seventeenth and eighteenth centuries in France, if someone had a beef, he expressed it in pamphlets that made the rounds from the salons in Paris to the remotest provincial towns. Think of it as a primitive form of electronic messaging. The most popular writings were rhymed ditties that both entertained and criticized at the same time. By the 1750s the quantity of pamphlets exploded, becoming increasingly incendiary. Some writers included soft-porn imagery to seduce the viewer's opinion. Most of the public enjoyed a belly laugh, yet digested the information presented as reliable. Many pamphlets were printed abroad and smuggled into France. Like drug trafficking nowadays, the crown censors could barely make a dent in stemming the flood of seedy writings.

Until the 1770s most pamphlets were written by disgruntled members of the nobility, undermining the very structure that made their privileged life possible. And the image of Louis XVI's queen was always at the center of the dartboard of these scriveners. The best sellers religiously slammed Antoinette as a bloodsucking foreigner, predicting she would spell the ruin of France. They tagged her the "Austrian Woman," a title that stuck.

At first the name was meant as a dismissive putdown. But it gradually evolved into a more pejorative label. In French, *"l'Autrichienne,"* the Austrian Woman, roughly corresponded to English words meaning "the bitch." It did not require a big grammatical leap for Antoinette's detractors to rally around the earthier translation. From the blue-bloods at Versailles, to the peasants toiling in the fields, most royal subjects began referring to

Antoinette as the Austrian Woman, discrediting the alien queen at every opportunity. The offensive title was commonplace in less than a decade.

The Austrian Woman referenced the unpopular alliance between France and Austria. Many suspected that the queen manipulated the king to pursue policies advantageous to her native Austria. But the French were unaware that Empress Maria Theresa hounded her daughter to further the interests of Austria, "Don't be ashamed to be German, even to the point of awkwardness." And Antoinette never missed the chance to promote the recognition of visiting Austrian luminaries which truly bugged the French.

Empress Maria Theresa took fright at the spread of these libels and their rabid message. Antoinette tried to calm her mother as she made light of the fraudulent exaggerations: "My dear Mama is perfectly right to denounce the frivolity of the French, but I am really pained that she has conceived a dislike for the entire nation. The character of the French is very flighty, but it is not evil; pens and tongues say many things which the hearts don't believe." Dismissing her mother's fears regarding the harmful writings, one day Antoinette would be forced to revise that generous assessment.

It may be the ultimate justice that the ruin of the One Percenters of Louis XVI's reign, found its origins in the toxic couplets, songs, and pamphlets they penned and circulated.

"My dog is half pit-bull, half poodle.
Not much of a watchdog, but a vicious gossip."
Craig Shoemaker

Chapter 24

Fleeting Magic of Coronation

On Sunday, June 11, 1775, Louis XVI was crowned in accord with the centuries-old ceremony in the Cathedral of Rheims. Turgot, who was still finance minister at the time, pushed hard to stage the gala event in Paris, hoping to save a lot of money. Turgot teased Louis with the carrot that the economy of Paris would receive a big boost, thereby earning the king the kudos of the hard-to-please Parisians. Ever the waffler, Louis agonized over which choice was best. Given the recent food riots he felt reluctant to spend a bundle and risk intensifying the grumblings of the people; but Louis also was a stickler for the tradition of his ancestors. He just could not make up his mind. Then the queen intervened.

Antoinette reasoned with justification that this rite of passage was a once-in-a-lifetime expense. This was one time where economizing ought to take a back seat to the divine right of kings, requiring an expenditure that preserved the mystique of the monarchy. Privately, Antoinette hoped that the ceremony might provide just the lift in confidence that Louis sorely needed. After hearing his wife's arguments, Louis the Unsure, suggested that Antoinette approach Turgot. For once Turgot bit his tongue, promising the queen to somehow scrape together the needed funds for the ritual.

The elaborate coronation took place on a boiling hot day. The cathedral opened its doors at four in the morning for the invited guests and for anyone else who could squeeze in. The crowd gasped in unison when at daybreak the radiant queen entered the cathedral, taking her seat in an exclusive grandstand. Surrounded by the ladies of her household, Antoinette dazzled everyone. Louis entered the cathedral at seven in the morning wearing a white satin suit and sporting red heeled boots. One witness who elbowed himself into the cathedral was a sixteen-year-old lad who had walked sixty miles from Troyes to witness the pageantry. Fifteen years later, Louis would come to dread this anonymous face in the immense crowd, Georges Danton, who would emerge as a bombastic revolutionary.

With the crown affixed to his head, Louis XVI became the sixty-sixth man to be King of France. Antoinette, overcome with fits of sobbing during the rite, withdrew from public view to regain her composure. The crowd cheered loudly at the loving glances exchanged between king and queen. Antoinette described the memorable day to her mother:

> The coronation was in every way perfect; it seems that everyone
> was pleased with the King. The ceremony in the cathedral was
> interrupted at the moment of coronation with the most touching
> acclamations. I could not control myself. It is surprising to be
> so well received two months after the uprising, in spite of the
> high cost of bread, which unfortunately still continues. It is a
> prodigious thing in the French character that they let themselves be
> transported by bad advice and then forget it in a moment and return
> to good. It is certain that seeing people in their misery treat us so
> well, we are more obliged to work for their benefit. As for myself,
> I will never in my life—should it last a hundred years—forget the
> day of the coronation.

These are touching sentiments from a young woman who is overwhelmed by the historic occasion. What pops out in the letter is Antoinette's observation of the mercurial French temperament of which one day she would be the target.

After returning to Versailles following the coronation, Louis and Antoinette buried themselves in their respective roles. The lack of an heir created a wedge between them that left them intimately adrift, magnifying their personal humiliation. Antoinette escaped the shame of bearing no children by immersing herself in distractions that did not erase her emptiness. Every day she behaved more like a bossy mistress of a king than that of a docile queen. But before the dilemma of the marriage bed's resolution, an incident occurred prompting an explosive exchange of letters between Maria Theresa and Antoinette.

A month after the coronation, Antoinette wrote a letter to an old friend of her family in Vienna, Count Rosenberg, an urbane man who had recently visited France. The fond contact with someone from her hometown prompted Antoinette to confide her latest exploits to the count, delighting in the foamy intoxication of queenhood.

Antoinette breathlessly rattled off her achievements. With a loose tongue, she did a victory lap on how she instigated the exclusion of a former minister, Duke Aiguillion, from the coronation ceremony, as well as his exile from court, "I had put up with enough. This evil man is full of calumnies and espionage, thus I asked the King to remove him. We are also getting rid of Monsieur de la Vrillière [minister of the king's household]. Although he is hard of hearing, he realized it was time to leave before the door was slammed in his face."

Without reflection, Antoinette recounted an incident to Rosenberg about getting the king to do her bidding, chuckling at her success:

> You may have heard about the audience that I gave the Duke of
> Choiseul at Rheims. People have talked about it so much that I
> wouldn't be surprised if old Maurepas was afraid he was going
> to be sent home for a rest. You may well believe that I didn't
> see him without first telling the King, but you will never guess
> the stratagem that I used not to look as if I were asking for his
> permission. I told him that I felt like seeing Monsieur Choiseul,
> and that I was only puzzled about the day. I managed it so well
> that the poor man settled himself the hour at which I would see
> Choiseul. I think I used my prerogative as a woman to the full. I
> have quite another project in mind. The old Maréchale de Mouchy
> [Madame Etiquette] will be leaving I am told. I will request that
> the King take advantage of this circumstance to appoint Madame
> Lamballe as my Superintendant of Household. Imagine my joy! By
> rendering my intimate friend happy, I will enjoy it even more than
> her. This is a secret; I am not yet telling the Empress.

This is the not so pretty side of Marie Antoinette. She waved her regal wand settling old scores and advancing the careers of her chums. She obviously forgot about the destitute people she fretted over just a month earlier.

Count Rosenberg was troubled by Antoinette's disregard for someone of Madame Etiquette's standing at court. And openly treating the king as her patsy was the most shocking of all. The count had no choice but to show the letter to Antoinette's mother. Then all hell broke loose and Maria Theresa went postal. In a fury, her mother fired off a memorable letter:

> I cannot hide from you that a letter you sent to Rosenberg upset me most dreadfully. What style! What frivolity! Where is the kind and generous heart of the Archduchess Antoinette? All I see is intrigue, low hatred, a persecuting spirit, and cheap wit—intrigue of a sort that a Pompadour or a Du Barry would have indulged in so as to play a great role. It is utterly unfitting for a Queen, a great Princess of the House of Lorraine and Austria, who should be full of kindness and decency. Your too early success and entourage of flatterers have always made me fear for you, ever since last winter when you wallowed in pleasures and ridiculous fashions. And what a tone! 'The Poor Man!' Where is the respect and gratitude you owe him for all his kindness? I leave you to your own thoughts and say no more, although there would be much more to say. Your happiness can vanish all too fast, and you may be plunged by your own doing, into the greatest calamities. That is the result of your terrible dissipation, which prevents you from being assiduous about anything serious. What have you read? And, after that, you dare to opine on the greatest State matters, on the choice of Ministers? What does the Abbé Vermond do? And Count Mercy? It seems to me that you dislike them because instead of behaving like low flatterers, they want you to be happy and do not amuse you or take advantage of your weaknesses. You will realize this all one day, but it will be too late. I hope not to survive that dreadful time, and I pray to God that He end my days sooner, since I can no longer help you, but cannot bear to lose or watch the sufferings of my dear child, whom I will love dearly to my last breath.

The letter ended with no smiley faces attached. What a letter from a mother to a daughter! And, besides the forecast of a rotten future, the empress zeroed in on the comparison of Antoinette's behavior to that of a king's mistress. This admission had to be painful for the empress to express, yet she was right on message. Her maternal judgment would soon parallel the views of most French people regarding the Austrian Woman.

Antoinette's response was not dripping with filial remorse. She was now accustomed to issuing orders and expected to be obeyed. Being a queen, she considered herself a peer to her mother and exempt from such a dressing down. Antoinette testily replied to her mother's stink-bomb letter:

I could never write to my august Mother if I felt half as guilty as
she thinks me. To be compared to a Pompadour, to a Du Barry,
to be covered with the most dreadful epithets, does not fit your
daughter. I wrote a letter to a man I trust, whom you trust, and
to whom on so respectable precedent, I felt I could give my own
trust. Since he has been in France, he knows the value of certain
sentences and I could therefore fear no ill effect from their use. My
dear Mama feels otherwise; I can only bow my head and hope that
in other circumstances she will judge me more favorably and, I
dare say it, as I deserve to be.

With this letter, Antoinette issued herself a free pass, taking no responsibility
for her actions. Most of all, she was fuming that her mother compared her, of
all people, to Madame du Barry. This pivotal exchange of letters would color
the remainder of their correspondence for the next five years. The empress
sadly resigned herself that her valuable advice was tossed in the trash basket.
From Versailles, Antoinette would often omit mentioning circumstances that
might rile her mother. She began to tell fibs to minimize the flow of nasty
reprimands from Vienna. Yet, all the while, Count Mercy kept the empress
au courant of her daughter's missteps. No wonder that the king's sister,
Madame Elisabeth, would describe Count Mercy in years to come as "the
old fox."

"Being ready isn't enough;
you have to be prepared for a promotion
or any other significant change."
Pat Riley

Chapter 25

Shakeup in Personnel

$\mathcal{M}$arie Antoinette's reputation took a big hit when the queen embarked on making staff changes in her household, guaranteeing the creation of an enemies list.

Antoinette purged some of the primary ladies who had been imposed upon her when she arrived in France. She wanted younger, amusing, less critical, and more trustworthy faces attending her. She needed the king to sign off on these changes. Louis understood Antoinette's desire for replacing some veteran courtiers among her staff; he agreed to her list of newcomers. It would take a few years, but Antoinette eventually surrounded herself with handpicked key attendants, most of whom became her confidantes. This shift in personnel both earned new friends and created foes with axes to grind.

The very top of the expulsion list targeted Countess Noailles—Madame Etiquette. For five years Countess Noailles had failed to win the affection of the dauphine and now confident queen. There was no question that she had served Antoinette well, but she saw Antoinette exclusively through the lens of her rigid role. The queen desired warm and gossipy people around her to match her own personal tastes. There was nothing remotely fuzzy about Madame Noailles.

In the summer of 1775 Antoinette hatched a scheme to dump Madame Noailles. The queen requested Louis to bestow on her bosom buddy, Princess Lamballe, the office of superintendent of the queen's household. This was the most powerful post in the queen's service and it had been vacant since 1741. If the king agreed to such a request, Madame Noailles would have a superior and be forced to report to the Princess Lamballe and not the queen. In effect, she would no longer run the show on the queen's behalf—a major putdown for such a proud lady.

The tight-fisted Turgot was still the finance minister in 1775. He sat on Louis to scrub the revival of this expensive court post. Turgot even pleaded with Count Mercy and Reverend Vermond to reason with the queen. Antoinette initially agreed to the terms of the minister, meaning that Madame Lamballe would receive a diminished salary for the post. The contract also set limitations on Lamballe's powers in order to minimize friction with the ladies directly below her in the queen's service, a diplomatic effort to console Madame Noailles. This arrangement was agreed to by all parties and seemed a done deal. But the Princess Lamballe's family goaded her to appeal to the queen that a paltry paycheck and diminished authority would also minimize her dignity. Seeing her friend in tears and unwilling to accept the post, the agitated queen insisted on the original terms. A beleaguered Louis agreed to his wife's wishes and poor Turgot passed another sleepless night figuring out how to pay for these expenses.

If Louis XVI had behaved as the man in charge, he would have refused to revive the superintendent of the queen's household, if for no other reason than for exigencies of economy. In turn, he would have sent a stern message to the entire royal family to get on board with his desire to trim expenses. Antoinette, among others, would have been forced to comply. But Louis failed to demand that his family emulate his thrifty habits. Anytime his wife, brothers, or aunts showed up begging for money to pay their debts, Louis always wrote the check. Any serious in-house measures at belt tightening had to fail with such a flimflam policy.

A humiliated Madame Noailles submitted her resignation to the queen's delight. However, Antoinette created in the process a formidable foe. The spurned Madame Etiquette defected to the growing camp of court castoffs that were itching to even the score with the Austrian Woman. Most disaffected rejects received a warm welcome at the nearby chateau of Bellevue, the residence of the royal aunts who set a tart tone against the queen.

After the shakeup in her personal household, Marie Antoinette next wanted to oust another formidable lady. She maneuvered the retirement of Madame Marsan from her position as governess to the Children of France. This crusty lady had held this influential position for twenty-one years, and she was furious to forego this plum job. Several years earlier while Antoinette was still dauphine, she had remarked to her attendants of her displeasure at how Madame Marsan handled the rearing of her husband's youngest sister, Madame Elisabeth. Before sundown, the criticism reached the governess' ears, who took the slight personally. In her mind, what did an inexperienced teenager know about child rearing?

Afterward, a frosty glaze coated the relationship between Antoinette and Madame Marsan.

Antoinette delighted in the replacement governess, Princess Guéméné, a live wire who kept the queen in stitches; besides, the queen felt sure that Princess Guéméné would be perfect for the job of royal governess once the queen had children of her own. Even though the position remained in Madame Marsan's family with the appointment handed to her gregarious niece, Princess Guéméné, Madame Marsan would not be placated. The discarded Marsan became another outspoken critic of the queen.

"If you live long enough,
you'll see that every victory turns into a defeat."
Simone de Beauvoir

Chapter 26

Living Like a Rebel

The five years after the coronation exemplified the queen's throwaway years. During this period of her reign, Antoinette reveled in a non-stop flurry of social events. Depending on the season, the queen hosted two balls a week at Versailles, and on occasion she organized theatricals or musical concerts. The king hit the hay early whereas the queen came alive when all the palace candles blazed. If Louis did attend entertainments, he invariably left first, signaling the start of the real fun. Besides the galas at Versailles, the queen was a frequent party girl at the hottest spots in Paris. Her outings on the town set many tongues wagging as Antoinette partied *sans mari*. The added bonus of these late nights allowed Antoinette to sleep in and avoid the morning rituals.

Antoinette cringed at being bored. Even though she had an exquisite personal library, it remained mostly decorative. Her reading tastes rarely strayed from sentimental romances and adventure sagas. She would have preferred a visit to the dentist than to endure a tiresome treatise on history.

Horse racing, a sport imported from England, swept the trendsetters in Paris. Antoinette became an immediate fan, attending the races in the company of her rakish brother-in-law Count Artois. A grandstand had been erected especially for the queen's viewing pleasure, allowing gossips to observe the raucous joking between the two royals. Conclusions were drawn that less innocent fun was being conducted away from the track. This nasty talk reached Louis' ears, causing him to order the dismantling of the grandstand. But the tsk, tsk, tsks did not abate one bit. Reverend Vermond and Count Mercy tried without success to squelch this edgy diversion. Mercy tattled to the empress, "The races often take place on Tuesdays, and the queen then fails to receive the Ambassadors, whose audience day it is. And recently, the Ambassadors were prevented from paying court to the Queen for three entire weeks." On cue, Maria Theresa sighed, grabbed her pen, and shot off another motherly dressing-down.

Antoinette's addiction to the gaming tables further sank her reputation. Most European courts regarded gambling as acceptable evening entertainment, but it escalated into a ruinous habit for Antoinette. At Versailles anyone, irrespective of rank, could mingle at the gaming tables. The queen mixed with all sorts of people, some not so savory, as she dared Lady Luck for a big win. Antoinette's preferred game of chance was faro, a popular card game requiring players to bet on the order in which the cards appeared. Most times Antoinette lost vast sums, and Louis dutifully picked up the tab.

Count Mercy clued in the empress about the queen's gambling obsession. After a few years with no change in Antoinette's habits, the empress let it rip in December 1777:

> You are not doing your duty, which is to adapt yourself to your husband. If he is too kind, that is no excuse for you and only makes you more wrong. I tremble for your future. Have no illusions that gambling brings with it the worst company and actions everywhere in the world. I know the consequences only too well. You are losing much of your popularity, especially abroad which I feel terribly because I love you so dearly.

Once again, big mama in Vienna knew the real deal, warning her daughter that she was stacking the deck against herself. Antoinette read the letter, grimaced for a moment, and then primped herself for the nighttime fun.

Next came the costly surrender to the dictates of fashion. The queen pioneered the way for a style that would be copied throughout Europe. Even Antoinette's enemies admitted all eyes followed her when she walked into a room. Along with her stunning wardrobe, Antoinette had a manner of walk that riveted attention.

Antoinette ordered one hundred to one hundred fifty dresses per year, stored in three large rooms in the palace. During her reign, fashion underwent radical changes in quick succession. Keeping up with the latest trends required a hefty bank account and a husband's steady sense of humor. It was considered cheesy if the queen wore the same court dress twice. Occasionally, dresses would be reborn with accessories to provide a fresh look. Part of the queen's role was to spur the economy with the hum of the

French silk factories. Antoinette's wardrobe kept many a fashion enterprise working overtime to satisfy demand from both home and abroad.

The staid John Adams, the diplomatic envoy from the American colonies, used superlatives to describe Antoinette's allure in a letter to his wife, Abigail, in June 1778. From a front row seat, Adams observed the spectacle of the queen dining in public at Versailles. Despite his starchy roots, the future U.S. president ogled the splendor of the setting. Never one to hold back with his opinion, Adams raved about Antoinette:

> She is an object too sublime and beautiful for my dull pen to describe; her dress was everything that art and wealth could make it. One of her maids of honor told me that she had diamonds upon her person to the value of eighteen million livres, and I always thought Her Majesty much beholden to her dress. She had a fine complexion indicating her perfect health, and she was a handsome woman in her face and figure. Not a feature of her face, nor a motion of any part of her person, especially her arms and hands, could be criticized for being out of order.

Next came the towering hairdos that defined hairstyles at the time of Louis XVI's accession to the throne. Monsieur Léonard Autie, the high priest of coiffure, pontificated as the queen's hairdresser, erecting ever higher hair edifices. The style became known as the pouf and rose on average three feet above the forehead, dusted with a starch-based powder infused with a light-scented oil. Elaborate poufs sported miniature figurines expressing a lady's sentiments. The pouf became the rage throughout Europe for the younger set. Antoinette took the lead in this fad of ever higher, ornamented hair that she crowned with a fluttering bunch of ostrich feathers.

The downside of towering and elaborate hairstyles was the time it took to construct and the peril of spontaneous physical movement. Travel presented challenges since most ladies had to kneel in their carriages on their way to an event if they hoped to preserve the integrity of their up-do. At court dances, an attendant was on call to repair any hair malfunctions. And, at bedtime, most female heads looked like a securely wrapped delivery package. Even the humblest gals tried to copy the ascent of the hairline. With the exception of the young, sensible adults frowned on the foolish fad. And guess who got blamed for promoting its popularity? Antoinette, of course.

The motherly voice of disapproval chimed in from Vienna as expected. Having received a portrait of her daughter, the empress caustically responded, "No, this is not the portrait of a Queen of France; there must be an error.

It is the portrait of an actress." And in another reprimand, Maria Theresa chastised her daughter:

> I can't prevent myself raising a point which many gazettes repeat all too often: it is the coiffure you use; they say that from the forehead up, it is thirty-six inches high, and with so many feathers and ribbons to adorn it! You know that I have always thought that fashion should be followed moderately, without ever exaggerating them. A young and pretty Queen, who is full of attractions, doesn't need all of these follies; on the contrary, the simplicity of your adornment will show you off better, and is more suitable to your rank as Queen.

Antoinette must have rolled her eyes, and thought to herself "how not with it" the empress appeared. Antoinette couldn't resist the last word, hoping to silence her mother, "It is true that I take some care of the way I dress; and as for feathers, everyone wears them, and it would seem ridiculous not to wear them." A pleasant rebuke to advise dear mama to MYOB on this one.

Mention must also be made of Antoinette's cache of jewelry. She owned plenty of jewels and diamonds in addition to the precious pieces comprising the Crown Jewels. The queen patronized the celebrated jewelers, Boehmer and Bassenge. Although she did not buy a lot from them, her purchases were always top shelf. Antoinette bought a pair of magnificent diamond chandelier earrings, originally intended for Madame du Barry's ears, followed by sticker-shock bracelets. The jewelers always made an enviable profit when selling to the queen, agreeing to be remunerated through an installment plan. Like a trusted timepiece, Louis always came to Antoinette's rescue when she fell behind on the payments.

Besides these diversions, tongues wagged about some of the questionable company Antoinette had invited into her circle. It was noticed that some "close" friendships were formed between the queen and several young beauties at court. No wonder she remained childless when she squandered her lust among these women. At least that was the buzz. Besides Madame Lamballe, the record holding swooner of all time, a supreme girlfriend appeared, Gabrielle Polignac, a dazzling brunette with alabaster skin and violet eyes. With her greedy retinue of deadbeat relatives, the easy-going Gabrielle enthralled Antoinette. Gabrielle's clique became fixtures of the queen's inner circle, some acquiring key court posts through her intervention. Antoinette closeted herself with these successful sycophants who became her surrogate family. In their company, tedious etiquette melted away.

Count Mercy alerted Maria Theresa, "It is reckoned that the Polignac family, without any claim upon the State and by pure favor, has obtained through public appointments and other beneficial gifts, nearly five hundred thousand livres of annual revenue." The empress moaned to heaven that her youngest daughter would hasten her death. Even Reverend Vermond, always watching from the sidelines, admonished Antoinette about her worthless pals, "You are not strict enough regarding the morality and the reputation of your friends, both male and female. A tarnished or a lost reputation, immorality, misconduct of all kinds seem to constitute title for admission to your society." Although attached to Vermond, the queen dismissed his rebukes as petty; after all, he was old enough to be her father. Vermond planned to resign his post in disgust, but the empress begged him to hang on.

Antoinette incurred further expenses on improvements to her private enclave of the Petit Trianon and other royal residences frequented by the court. Soon anonymous authors were penning unflattering pamphlets about these follies of the queen, pamphlets that filtered down the social pyramid. Like a dormant volcano, these trashy tracts to sully Antoinette's reputation gathered steam, threatening to erupt with a cataclysmic fury. But Antoinette ignored the negative press, rationalizing the expenses as necessary to maintain her sanity for putting up with the rulebook of Versailles. She knew she was a rebel to shocked observers, but she had a cause—to be the hippest queen yet!

"People say I am extravagant because
I want to be surrounded by beauty. But tell me,
who wants to be surrounded by garbage?"
Imelda Marcos

Chapter 27

A Brother Rides to the Rescue

*D*uring the first seven years of Antoinette's marriage, hardly a letter exchanged between the daughter queen and her mother empress that did not address the vacant bassinet. In every letter Antoinette described her predicament, often referring to the king's possible need for minor surgery.

Maria Theresa relentlessly upbraided her daughter for not sleeping with her husband every night. Antoinette explained that was not the custom at Versailles. The empress had little tolerance for such stupidities that lessened the opportunities for bawling offspring. With the king's permission, Antoinette had a secret passageway built between their rooms in the spring of 1775 to allow unobserved conjugal visits. This news did little to revise Maria Theresa's disapproval on the sleeping arrangements of the French monarchs.

In January 1776 Antoinette sent a mixed message updating her mother on the king's condition:

> The King sent for Moreau, the surgeon of the Hôtel-Dieu [hospital] of Paris. He said about the same as the others that the operation was not necessary and that there was every hope without it. It is true that there is a considerable change in the King and that his body seems to gain in consistency. He has promised me that if nothing changes within the next few months, then he would decide to have the operation on his own accord.

Circumstances remained unchanged, and no operation transpired. In fact, Antoinette informed her mother a few months later, "I have ever greater hopes and am convinced that an operation is no longer necessary." These conflicting exchanges confirmed how the queen herself discussed an operation as being both a necessity and a rejected option, depending on the outcome of the most current baby-making attempts.

Meanwhile Louis and Antoinette dreaded a forthcoming event. Antoinette's sister-in-law, Countess Artois, was the first of the three royal wives to become pregnant. Excitement swirled through the palace weeks before the expected due date. In August 1775 the countess delivered a healthy boy. Louis XVI behaved magnanimously, bestowing on his first nephew, the title of Duke of Angoulême.

Antoinette, required to attend the birth, applauded the gender of the newborn child like everyone else. But on a gut level, her exasperation at not being a mother was painful. The queen relayed her anguish to the empress, "I need not tell my dear Mama how I suffered in seeing an heir who isn't mine. But I still managed not to forget any attention due to the mother and child."

After congratulating her sister-in-law, Marie Antoinette left the bedroom to nurse her humiliation. She was unprepared for what she encountered in the hallways. She was cornered by the foul-mouthed market women of Paris who had come to Versailles to witness the royal birth. Over the course of many decades these tough working class females had established an oddly accepted tradition of peppering the royals with their unvarnished opinions. Never censoring their words, they shamed the queen, "to open your legs and get on with it." Outwardly calm, Antoinette bore their taunts as she inched her way to her apartments. Once safely inside the confines of her own rooms, the distraught Antoinette broke down into sobs, aware of the harsh truth of their stinging remarks.

Everybody had an opinion on the stalemate to produce an heir, most of them unflattering. Blame was equally allotted to both parties, but Louis bore the brunt of it. A popular rhyme circulated throughout France at the time, declaring: "It is well known that poor Sire, three or four times condemned for complete impotence, cannot satisfy Antoinette. Of this misfortune, we are sure given that his 'match' is no fatter than a straw, always soft and always curved." Censors tried to intercept these disrespectful writings, but the story proved too juicy to be suppressed. Put on the spot, the police chief of Paris admitted defeat: "If I started making arrests for the things people say, I would have to arrest all of Paris." Even Antoinette commented on the libels in a letter to her mother:

> We are in the midst of satirical songs. They are being written about
> everyone at Court, men and women alike, and the frivolity of the
> French did not spare the King. The need for the operation has been
> the main theme against the King. As for me, I haven't been spared;
> I have liberally been gratified with both tastes, those for male and
> female lovers. Although nasty writings are quite successful here,
> these are so dull and so gross that they have been taken up neither
> in the public nor in society.

This was wishful thinking on Antoinette's part, especially the charge of lesbianism that in France was called the "German Vice." Everyone repeated these trashy lyrics and absorbed the message. The damage to the couple's integrity piled up with every new ditty being cranked out.

Apparently, the Spanish Ambassador, Count Aranda, who employed a network of informants, seemed the best informed or the most voyeuristic. Aranda spilled this scoop to his bosses in Madrid:

> It is said that the foreskin is so tight that it does not pull back
> when the member is introduced and so causes a sharp pain which
> prevents His Majesty from giving the necessary impulsion to the
> act. Others say that the foreskin is so tight that it prevents the
> head or point of the member from emerging and so His Majesty's
> erections cannot attain the requisite degree of elasticity.

The Spanish ambassador also hinted that the king's brother, Provence, suffered the same impediment. This Castilian guy sure had a firm hold on his sources. Thank God for the Count Artois' well-made reproductive parts.

By the fall of 1776, an exasperated Maria Theresa concluded that her daughter was diminished by the lack of an heir and ruled for an intervention in the bedroom of the floundering spouses. The universal guffawing could not be allowed to continue. The empress dispatched her eldest son and co-ruler, Joseph II, to resolve the marital quagmire. Joseph was tasked to fulfill the role of a how-to emissary, embodying a last-ditch effort to ensure successful copulation.

Before Joseph's arrival, the hot topic of the day was not the royal nest, but royal revenge. The entire French court and nation were glued to the drama unfolding across the Atlantic. National sentiments lock-stepped in agreement that Louis should aid the American rebels fighting against the forces of the English King George III. Soon, Louis would need to take a firm stand—always a herculean challenge for him. Joseph appreciated the distraction from across the ocean that served as an ideal smokescreen to mask the true intention of his visit. Furthermore, the rumor mill churned that the twice widowed Joseph's aim in visiting France was to check out the king's thirteen-year-old sister, Madame Elisabeth, as a potential wife number three.

Joseph arrived in Paris on April 18, 1777, traveling under an assumed name, Count Falkenstein, to avoid the hoopla and expense that plagued an emperor's travels. Like a respectable tourist, Joseph checked in at the Hôtel Tréville near the Luxembourg Palace. The following morning, his carriage took him to Versailles where Reverend Vermond whisked him off to his sister's suite. The meeting between brother and sister was an emotionally charged moment. All who witnessed it remarked on the touching reactions of the sobbing siblings. Antoinette and Joseph happily sequestered themselves for more than two hours, reveling in their reunion. Joseph avoided the delicate matter of bedroom intimacy, wishing to first win the confidence of his brother-in-law before tackling the touchy subject with his sister.

Joseph busied himself with discovering Paris and Versailles. He visited Parisian institutions, including hospitals and prisons where he asked a lot of questions, a practice that Louis XVI should have emulated. From the Frenchman's viewpoint, the emperor seemed to be an engaged monarch without the superficial frills.

Joseph agreed with his sister about the absurdity of the rigid formalities that governed life at Versailles. The queen's brother castigated the groaning court etiquette, especially the king's *lever*, the morning ceremony observed as the king got out of bed. The extravagance of the French court shocked Joseph, and much to his sister's embarrassment, he broadcasted his opinion.

He observed Antoinette's routines and the behavior of her favorites. He chastised his sister for her superficial pastimes and pals, ridiculing her outrageous hairdos, makeup, and unbridled gambling in the evenings. But, deep down, he loved his sister and he knew she possessed sterling qualities, including a solid intuition and a warm heart. Regardless of his many reproaches, Antoinette accepted them without making a scene, idolizing this cherished brother.

Joseph charmed all he met, but his private thoughts concealed some wry observations that he divulged to his brother Leopold, Grand Duke of

Tuscany. First, he provided a snapshot of Louis XVI that was coolly candid: "His appearance is against him but he is honorable, yet he is weak in the presence of those who know how to intimidate him and therefore lead him by the nose; he has ideas and sound judgment, but his mind and body are apathetic."

Next, Joseph sketched an unflattering, but accurate description of his sister's in-laws. With regard to the king's brother Count Provence, Joseph described him as "an undefinable being, better looking than the king, but mortally cold, and his enormous girth prevents him from walking properly." He pulverized Provence's Savoyard wife with the withering remark, "She is coarse, ugly, and full of intrigues." He contemptuously dismissed the youngest brother, Count Artois, as "A thoroughgoing fop, and his wife, the only one to produce children is a complete imbecile." As for the king's sister, Madame Elisabeth, Joseph remained non-committal: "Madame Elisabeth is neither pretty nor ugly; I seldom see her, as I am determined to remain unmarried." He decorously disposed of the meddlesome aunts with, "Mesdames the Aunts are kindly women who no longer matter."

Most importantly, he judged the day-to-day function of the government, "The King is but an absolute lord in order to succeed from one slavery to another. He can always change ministers but he can never become master of his own business. Petty intrigues are treated with the utmost care, but important affairs are completely neglected." This was perhaps the sharpest assessment written about the everyday Bourbon heavyweights, describing the dysfunction that stemmed from the top.

Joseph reserved his lengthier observations for Antoinette's behavior. His remarks depicted a solid portrait of his sister:

> The Queen is a very pretty and amiable young woman, and could
> be seen as such anywhere, but she thinks only of having fun. She
> feels nothing for the King. She makes him do what she wants,
> more through her authority than in any other way. She is drunk
> with the dissipation typical of this country. She fulfills neither
> her function as a woman nor as a Queen as she should. As a
> woman, she completely neglects the King. She spends time with
> him neither during the day nor the night. As Queen, she is tied
> down by no etiquette. She goes out, runs around alone or with a
> few people without the outward signs of her position. She is not
> doing her job, and that may well have consequences in the future.
> Her virtue is intact, even strict, but less through forethought than
> inborn disposition. In a word, it has been all right until now, but
> in the long run she will find herself resourceless, and things may

go badly. That is what I have been telling her, but although I am perfectly satisfied with her friendship and her sincerity, she listens, she agrees, and then the whirlwind of dissipation which surrounds her prevents her from thinking of anything but going from pleasure to pleasure. All the people who surround her entourage are steeped in this same frenzy. How could I alone prevent it? Still, I have made some progress, especially about her gambling, which is dreadful.

Joseph got down to the business of his visit none too soon. A palace bulletin announced that Count Artois' wife was pregnant again, mortifying the royal couple. The emperor questioned his sister and brother-in-law, both separately and jointly, regarding the state of their marriage bed, an arena where activity on a good night resembled the Dead Sea. They described their plight, admitting they were desperate for a remedy. Joseph observed that one of the main obstacles to producing a baby revolved around their schedules. The king shined as a morning person whereas the queen perked up at dusk. When Louis turned in for the night, Antoinette was often on the road to Paris for a night of partying. Among other suggestions, the pragmatic Joseph urged the couple to put aside an hour every afternoon for love making—an excellent idea that the couple promised to practice.

Joseph provided a tantalizing peek at what transpired in the bedroom in a letter to his brother Leopold. He recounted a description of Louis' sexual interactions with his wife:

> In the conjugal bed, here is the secret. The King has excellent erections, inserts his organ, remains there without stirring for perhaps two minutes, then withdraws without ever discharging; still erect, he bids his wife goodnight. It is incomprehensible, all the more so since he sometimes has nocturnal emissions. He is quite satisfied and admits that he performs the act from duty alone and takes no pleasure in it. Ah! If I could only have been in there once, I should have put things right. He ought to be whipped, to make him ejaculate, as one whips donkeys. As for my sister, she is not amorously inclined, and they are a couple of incompetents put together.

This letter either supported the diagnosis of the king's phimosis, or outed the incredulous ignorance of the couple concerning copulation. While Joseph confirmed that the king did not thrust his penis rhythmically, he never mentioned that it was a painful process; the king only acknowledged that he did not enjoy it. This begs the question: *why didn't he enjoy it?* When you read between the lines of Joseph's letter, it appeared that the king and queen were both killjoys under the sheets.

On the last day of May, Joseph left his sister amid tearful goodbyes. Notwithstanding his criticisms, Antoinette was crestfallen at her brother's departure. Joseph left a document for Antoinette's contemplation, entitled, "The Reflections." He minced no words; he may have loved his sister, but he chastised her for falling short in her role as wife and queen. In the lengthy document scrutinizing the personal interactions between husband and wife, Joseph chides his sister for her indifferent behavior toward the king, "Do you try to make yourself necessary to him, do you sacrifice any of your own pleasures for his sake, do you keep silent on the subject of his failings and mistakes, and do you refuse to allow others to comment on them?"

Joseph reserved the most shocking words of his message for the end of his reflections. Like a biblical prophet, he echoed the same fears his mother had wailed about two years earlier in her letter to her daughter after the king's coronation: "Truly I tremble for your happiness, because in the long run things cannot go on like this. The revolution will be a cruel one, perhaps one of your own making." The emperor was referencing his sister's capricious behavior, the corrupt court system, and the shape of the government. Antoinette would have plenty of time to ponder these words in the years to come.

Antoinette took Joseph's exhortations to heart, revealing to her mother:

> I must tell my dear Mama that he gave me a thing that I asked
> for repeatedly and which pleases me greatly; he has left me with
> written advice. This is my main reading now and if ever, which
> I doubt, I could forget what he told me, I would have this paper
> always before me, which would soon bring me back to my duty.

Maria Theresa felt buoyed by Antoinette's resolve, praying that her scattered daughter would relinquish her vacuous lifestyle and step up to the role of an exemplary queen. Although Antoinette genuinely promised personal reform, the lure of available amusements would prove too hard to resist.

Joseph also felt distress on leaving his sister. Following his departure, he wrote to his mother describing his sister's genuine warmth when she was not fending off the slings and arrows of court life:

I left Versailles with difficulty because I was really fond of my
sister. I found in her a sweetness of life which I had given up,
but the taste for which I now see that I retain. She is amiable and
charming. I spent hours and hours with her without realizing
that time was passing. Her emotions when I left were great, but
she admirably held herself in check; I found that I needed all my
strength to walk away.

During his road trip home, Joseph wrote to his brother Leopold revealing
more details about his sister's life. Joseph inherited his mother's skill for
accurate observation:

I have become very fond of my sister, and I saw her sorrow at our
parting which made mine worse. She is an amiable and honest
woman, a little young, thoughtless, but at bottom with feelings
of honesty and virtue, an understanding of her position and really
respectable. She is clever and sees things so clearly that I have
often been surprised. Her first reaction is always the best, if she
stayed with it and thought about it a little more, and if she listened
less to the people who urge her on, of which there are armies, and
in different camps, she would be perfect. The desire to have fun is
very powerful in her, and since people are aware of it, they prey
upon that weakness, and those who give her the largest amount
of it and the most varied pleasure are treated well. Her situation
with the King is very odd; he is only two thirds of a husband, and
although he loves her, he fears her more; our sister has the kind
of power to be expected of a royal mistress, not the kind a wife
should have, for she forces him to do things he doesn't wish to do.
He is weak, but not stupid. He has ideas, he is able to judge, but is
apathetic in mind and body; he has no desire to learn, no curiosity,
and is impotent neither in body nor mind, but the *fiat lux* [the
spark] hasn't come. That is about how things are except that the
government which depends on an octogenarian minister [Maurepas
was seventy-six in 1777] goes as best it can and is devoid of a real
system. In a word, they try to move forward without worrying
about what happens on the left or the right.

"Advice is seldom welcome;
and those who want it the most, like it the least."
George Chapman

Chapter 28

Bullseye!

*A*ntoinette wrote to her mother regarding her brother's reproductive advice: "I am not without hope of becoming pregnant, my brother will tell my dear Mama all about it. The King talked to him on this point in a friendly and trusting way." It would not be long until the queen's hopes would become manifest.

In August 1777 Antoinette dropped some encouraging hints of a progress in the king's amorous attempts: "I do not despair of becoming pregnant; there is a slight improvement in that the King is more eager than before in his marital duties, which for him is saying quite a bit. Otherwise he is in good health, and I have only reasons to be pleased with him." She neglected to mention if she was contributing the mandatory "cajoling and caressing."

Within days of this letter Louis XVI proved to be exceptionally eager— the couple finally mastered the baby-making formula. So, did Louis have the surgery? The two-month period since Joseph's departure from Versailles provides some evidence that the king did submit to the minor snip of foreskin. The healing time sounds just right for him to resume his marital duties. But there is no written proof that the surgery transpired. Furthermore, Louis continued to hunt as usual—such an operation would have made any time in the saddle painfully uncomfortable. Surgery or not, Louis and Antoinette could pop the champagne cork.

On the verge of delirium, Antoinette wrote to her mother, announcing that her marriage was consummated for real this time:

I am in a state of the most profound happiness. Eight days ago, my marriage was perfectly consummated, the practice was reiterated and more completely than the first time. I wanted to send the news to my dear mother at once, but I was afraid it might be premature. And I wanted to be absolutely convinced. I do not think that I am already pregnant, but at least I have the hope that I may be at any moment. What will be my dear mother's joy, I know it will be as great as my own.

Even taciturn Louis confided in his virgin aunts that he regretted it took him so long to know the pleasures of the marriage bed. His personal confidence swelled along with his vigorous ejaculations. But it would require an international crisis to get the queen pregnant.

In January 1778 Joseph II decided to annex a portion of lower Bavaria, sparking an exchange of war threats between Prussia and Austria. Maria Theresa and Joseph lobbied Antoinette to support her Hapsburg family by getting Louis to hop on board their side of the war wagon. The empress used a dose of motherly guilt in one letter to Antoinette: "A change in our alliance would be my death." This line got the queen's immediate attention.

Antoinette rushed to the king, urging him to come to Austria's defense. The queen got the shock of her life when Louis turned her down. Louis told his wife, "Your relatives' ambition will upset everything. They began with Poland, and now they covet Bavaria. I feel sorry for you." Louis may have felt pity, but Antoinette was seeing red. She summoned Maurepas and Vergennes, the ministers she held responsible for leading the king by the nose. She staged a diva scene, insisting they come to her family's aid. The ministers calmly offered vague assurances, and they politely withdrew. Soon the entire court heard about Antoinette's interference, casting doubts on the queen's loyalties.

Mercy advised Antoinette to win her battle with the king's ministers with an assault of wifely attentions. The queen purposely slept with her husband almost daily in March 1778. Irrespective of all the lovemaking, Louis remained firm in his refusal to help Austria. The politically focused Antoinette lost sight of the fact that she might get pregnant from these bedroom negotiating sessions. And that is exactly what happened.

Antoinette missed her period in early April and suddenly became hopeful that something good might have popped up from her sexual charm offensive.

By mid-April, her physician confirmed that she was pregnant. On April 19
Antoinette could finally give her mother the news she longed for:

> I have never been late, on the contrary always a little early; I had
> my period on the third of March; today is the nineteenth of April
> and nothing has happened. Other than that, I feel perfectly well,
> my appetite and the time I sleep have increased; I must also soothe
> my dear Mama's alarms by giving her a faithful account of the way
> I live. I stopped all riding in carriages and have limited myself to
> short walks. I am told that when the second missed period is past, it
> will be healthier not to stay in so much. My dear Mama can count
> on my being very moderate and careful about all my movements.

Antoinette figured that this miraculous news would swing the king to her
family's side in the conflict with Prussia. Still, Louis would not budge from
his non-interventionist stance. Antoinette lamented her helplessness to her
mother, "It is the ministers' weakness and the King's extreme lack of self-
confidence that are the cause of the problem." Her family in Austria let
her know that she let them down. Ultimately, the flare-up between Austria
and Prussia was settled with everyone getting something to salvage their
wounded egos, except for Antoinette. She emerged from the conflict as a less
than trustworthy queen in the minds of many— just the unpleasantness that
Louis feared would result for his wife.

After swallowing her defeat on the international stage, Antoinette became
engrossed about the baby growing within her. The royal couple could at last
discard seven years of public humiliation. She and the king delighted in
the progress of her pregnancy, mending any hurt feelings on Antoinette's
part. They walked arm in arm those summer nights in 1778 in the gardens
at Versailles so all could see the growing baby bump. Everyone rapturously
anticipated a royal birth before the end of the year; of course, counting on a
boy. As a bonus for Antoinette, Louis suspended any further conjugal visits
for the remainder of her pregnancy.

The whole country anticipated the royal birth by the end of the year.
Some nobles not residing at Versailles filled the town along with a host of
expectant visitors. At the birth of a male heir there would be a one-hundred-
and-one cannon salute, while a female baby merited only twenty-one.

On the evening of December 18, Marie Antoinette went to bed sensing
her delivery was near. During the night labor pains commenced, and the
king hurried to the queen's bedside. Since Antoinette could not be attended

to properly in her ornate bed, she moved to a small bed near the fireplace designed especially for birthing. After eleven exhausting hours of labor, the moment approached, and the male midwife, called the *accoucher,* shouted out the imminent birth. A rush of people swarmed into the room, their voices and excitement overtaking the chamber. One hundred thirty persons from all ranks of life jammed into the queen's bedroom and strained to get a better view of her suffering. It was all too much for the queen's head honcho, the delicate Lamballe, who on cue dropped into a dead faint.

A new life entered the world at half past eleven in the morning on December 19, 1778. At the moment of birth, Antoinette panicked, thinking that the child was stillborn. She began hyperventilating, and she lost consciousness. The man delivering the baby, yelled out that the unresponsive queen needed air in the suffocatingly hot room. Tradition required that all two thousand windows at Versailles be taped shut from late October to the end of April to minimize nasty drafts. The quick-thinking Louis and several gentlemen broke the nearest windows for fresh air to circulate quickly.

As the queen lay unconscious, fear gripped those present that she was dying. Having a baby in that era was risky business for mother and child. It was possible that the *accoucher* might have inflicted some minor injury to the queen. Several letters dispatched from witnesses to the birth mentioned that the queen had been "wounded" during her delivery. Although this could have been spiteful gossip because the male midwife was the brother of Reverend Vermond, the queen's close adviser. But Antoinette had carefully chosen who would deliver her baby after consulting with her physician and recent mothers, all of whom recommended Monsieur Vermond's services.

Thankfully, Antoinette revived, only to behold glum faces surrounding her. When the queen learned she had delivered a girl, she wept, painfully aware that she had failed to give the nation the desired heir. Even though the newborn was a female, the infant was accorded a staff of eighty persons to wait on her. No wonder France was going broke.

Louis XVI was tickled pink. At last, he had sired a child of his own, with boys surely to follow. When the newborn was brought to her mother, Antoinette's tears evaporated, holding this longed-for child lying in her arms. She cradled the infant, cooing to her, "Poor little one, you were not wanted; but you will be all the dearer to me." Yet, that is not how this mother-daughter relationship would ultimately play out; the naturally haughty child would fear more than love her disciplinarian mother and would instead idolize her indulgent father. This was the mirror image of Marie Antoinette's own bonding with her parents.

The baby was named Marie Thérèse Charlotte in honor of her maternal grandmother in Vienna. But during her young life everyone called her Madame Royale. And what a life it would be!

After the difficult birth of her daughter, Antoinette let Louis know that she desired a temporary timeout from the requirements of child rearing. So, there may be some truth about a "wound." More likely, she dreaded to become pregnant so soon after a birth that nearly killed her. Several months would elapse before the royal couple resumed conjugal relations. Antoinette was lucky to have an understanding king for a husband. But the nation was not so indulgent; they demanded male heirs now. And her Austrian family echoed similar appeals in every letter.

> "Family—that dear octopus from whose
> tentacles we never quite escape, nor
> in our inmost hearts, ever quite wish to."
> *Dodie Smith*

Chapter 29

Oh, La Publicité!

Antoinette may have taken a breather from being a breeder but not from being a party girl. The thrill of Paris soon beckoned. The queen resumed her after-dark junkets to Paris, although with less frequency. During one night out on the town, her carriage broke down in the streets of Paris. She decided to hail a cab to reach her party venue. Once at the ball, the queen giddily confessed to her intimates what naughty fun it had been, "Imagine, me in a hackney coach—how amusing." This was just the type of impropriety that her brother had warned her of. Next day word snaked through Paris exposing the brazen behavior of the new mother. Ordinary Parisians did not find it amusing at all.

In February 1779 Antoinette followed the tradition of going to Notre Dame Cathedral for a religious ceremony to give thanks for the safe delivery of her baby. This event was always a big deal for it required generous offerings by the queen to the people of Paris. Dowries were provided for one hundred couples, and parish priests were supplied with alms for the neediest. There were fireworks, free food and wine, and complimentary admission to performances at the Comédie-Française. A royal birth brought many perks for the masses—no surprise the French liked to see their queens pregnant.

To complicate conjugal relations, Antoinette came down with the measles in April 1779. She decided to quarantine herself at the Petit Trianon to protect the king from contagion. This was one isolation that the queen orchestrated to her advantage. She could finally justify spending the night sleeping in her deluxe single bed in her enchanting bedroom, free of the restraints of the palace.

Tempers flared when word leaked out that the queen requested four gentlemen of her circle to keep her company as she mended. Apparently, Her Majesty was not concerned about her male companions catching the measles. The four fellows arrived in the morning and remained until eleven in the evening. Of course, Antoinette needed Louis' permission, which being the good *schlemiel* that he was, he granted. But poor Louis felt swept aside. A deluge of disgrace showered down on Antoinette.

Even though two ladies were always present with the four guys, this was considered outrageously unbecoming for a queen of France. Antoinette, wishing to be amused with these handpicked male companions, petulantly dismissed any suggestion about the impropriety of her convalescence companions. But the pamphleteers worked overtime, proving once again that Antoinette was an easy meal ticket. Count Mercy recognized the catastrophic effect this whim of the queen would inflict on her reputation. He castigated her conduct in an urgent letter to the empress:

> The Queen has failed to see the consequences of these male
> companions. The result has been some deplorable rumors, bad
> jokes in which the courtiers tried to decide which four ladies
> would be chosen to keep the King company if he should also be
> ill. Besides the bad effect produced by so unusual an arrangement,
> I must also worry about the dangerous ideas suggested to the
> Queen during her conversations with these persons. The Queen
> had demanded out of concern for the King that he refrain from
> seeing her. Her companions dared to criticize the King's obedience
> to the Queen's wishes, so that she became angry at her husband.
> I trembled when I thought of the consequences that this might
> have, and on the tenth day of the illness, together with the Abbé
> Vermond, I asked the Queen to write a few pleasant words to the
> King. That proposal was rejected with much anger. I owe it to
> Vermond, that it was he alone who brought the Queen back to her
> senses.

Her anguished mother took to her bed when she learned of this latest indiscretion, bemoaning her daughter's "thoughtless act." Reverend Vermond, Antoinette's steadfast confidant since she was thirteen, shamed Antoinette into writing a tender message to the king, telling him that she missed him. This forced *billet doux* spurred Louis to appear below the balcony of the queen's window at the Petit Trianon, bidding her a speedy return to Versailles. The scene may have seemed romantic, but the public raged that the Austrian Woman would allow King Louis XVI to implore her return. A different king would have locked her away in a convent to atone for such outrageous behavior. One can't fault the French for calling her a bitch on this occasion.

Expecting that her mother's displeasure would descend on her at full throttle rage, Antoinette dashed off a note to the empress portraying a different account:

> The measles I have just had were more painful than usual. My eyes were not affected, and there are no fears for my chest. I am moving to Trianon today to have a change of air until the end of my three weeks, at which time I will be able to see the King again. I stopped him from closing himself in with me; he has never had measles, and especially in a moment when he has so much business, it would have been unfortunate if he had caught the disease. We write each other every day; I saw him yesterday from a balcony outside. May I kiss my dear mother? I am not strong enough to write more.

After three weeks, Antoinette knew the escapade had run its course and returned to Versailles. She had to get down to business and provide a male heir. If not, the French would never regard her as an authentic queen.

After resuming conjugal relations, Antoinette became pregnant but, she miscarried early in her pregnancy. She tried to conceal this loss from her mother. She knew too well the sermon she would endure from the empress about not safeguarding her health—any indulgence in physical exertions during early pregnancy was viewed as irresponsible. When the empress learned of the miscarriage, Antoinette braced herself for a finger-wagging tirade. Instead, she received words of comfort: "Your letter of 16 July afflicted me greatly because all our fine hopes were gone; and I must admit that I really counted upon them. Nothing is lost; you are both young, in good health, and love one another, so it will easily be made up, but it is better to have than to hope. Thank God you had no hemorrhage, inconvenience, or weakness."

On the evening of December 6, 1780, word reached Louis that his mother-in-law had died. The empress had been in poor health since October, suffering from severe rheumatism. By the end of November, the sinking empress, stricken with pneumonia, sensed her death was at hand. Ever the organizer, she sewed the shroud that would cover her body. On November 29, 1780, just hours before her death, Maria Theresa sat hunched over her desk, struggling to tackle some State papers. She then corralled those of her children in Vienna, made her farewells, and at age sixty-three she died in the arms of her son, Joseph II.

Several weeks prior to her death, the empress had dispatched her last letter to Antoinette. Reflecting on her worn-out condition, the failing empress gently advised her daughter one last time. In her final letter, Maria Theresa was pitch perfect in her message to Antoinette. What a great lady!

> I am very glad that you intend to resume a full Court life at
> Versailles. I know how dull and empty it is; but believe me,
> without it the drawbacks are far more important than the little
> inconveniences of public ceremonies, especially in your country,
> with such a lively people. For a month, I have suffered a
> rheumatism in the right arm, which is why this letter is less well
> written than usual, and it makes me end, assuring you of all my
> love.

Louis had never addressed a word to Reverend Vermond since his arrival at Versailles in 1770. The king considered the man an odious sycophant because of his ties to the detested former minister, Choiseul. However, the king now required his services. Through an intermediary, the king instructed Vermond to break the news of the empress' death to Antoinette.

After Vermond's unpleasant task was fulfilled, the king sought out his wife and comforted her as best he could. Antoinette was devastated. Even though the exchange of letters over the past ten years had been bumpy at times, her mother's death packed a wallop. The queen revered the empress as an invincible Minerva. People like her just didn't die. The loss marked the passing of a significant link to her native country, making the queen feel vulnerable. In desperation, she poured her heart out to her brother:

> Crushed by the most dreadful misfortune, I cannot stop crying as I
> write to you. Oh my brother, oh my friend! You alone are now left
> to me in a country which is, and always will be dear to me! Take
> care of yourself, watch over yourself, you owe it to all. Adieu. I
> no longer see what I am writing. Remember we are friends, allies;
> love me. I embrace you.

The queen appreciated the king's kind attentions during her grief, which fostered a deeper bond between them. The palace announced that the queen was pregnant in February 1781. The late empress had to be slapping high fives in heaven by the effect her death had on the couple. Despite the queen's joy of a possible heir, it took a long time for Antoinette to accept that the courier from Vienna would never deliver another letter from her dear mama.

"By the time a woman realizes her mother was right,
she has a daughter who thinks she is wrong."
Untraced Author

Chapter 30

The Gamble Across the Atlantic

For nearly a decade spanning the mid-1770s and early 1780s, all of France thrilled to the revolt of the English colonies in America. Imagine ordinary people defying their king. In May 1776 Louis forced Finance Minister Turgot to resign his post, but not before Turgot heatedly opposed France's involvement in this overseas adventure. He spelled it out to Louis, "The first gunshot will drive the State into bankruptcy." He pitched to the king that eventually England would have to concede the loss of the American colonies without costing France one U.S. penny. Louis' gut instincts told him that Turgot was right. Being a king, Louis fretted about aiding rebels fighting against their lawful monarch.

After Turgot got the axe, Foreign Minister Vergennes assumed the alpha male ranking in the king's council. Vergennes nudged Louis in the direction of French intervention in the conflict. The minister stoked the smoldering sore feelings of the French against the British over the French losses of Canada and commercial outposts in India and Africa in the 1760s. All of France yearned to see the hated English humbled. With Vergennes' consistent prodding, Louis engaged a maverick named Beaumarchais to operate a fictitious company with the aim of providing clandestine assistance to the American patriots—an ageless, murky means of doing political business. Louis temporarily adopted a two-track policy: for international ears Louis professed a firm neutrality; but in secret, Louis supported the rebels in America. So began France's effort to foster American independence, to secure England's defeat, and to out the French public's thirst for liberty.

The English ambassador to France, Lord Stormont sniffed out the real deal through a network of spies that he employed to eavesdrop on the conversations of the rebel envoys in Paris. Stormont howled to Vergennes, "In the history of the world there is no example of aid given to the rebels of a country that one professes to be friendly with." Yet, the ultimate victory of the fledgling nation in America would hinge largely on the genius of one man—Benjamin Franklin.

After four weeks of vomiting at sea, the shrewdy from Philadelphia gratefully hugged terra firma in Brittany on December 3, 1776. His assignment was to coax the French government to supply more support for the colonists. Franklin meandered toward Versailles, where, at the end of December he met Vergennes in a hush-hush tryst. Vergennes assured him of France's assistance, albeit secretive for the time being. To demonstrate the minister's sincerity, Vergennes provided Franklin with funds to establish himself in a household in the delightful village of Passy, on the doorstep of Paris. Addressed as Doctor Franklin wherever he went, he got the nickname "The Electrical Ambassador" after delighting his neighbors by installing on his house one of his lightning conductors.

Franklin's arrival in France mimicked the Beatles' reception at JFK airport in New York in 1964. Franklin's fans kept screaming, "I want to hold your hand." He was world famous for his many scientific investigations, catchy adages, and affable republican views. His pragmatic innovations benefitting the American colonists were legendary. His image could be found on a variety of items briskly sold throughout Paris, crowning him as the first international superstar. Who needed a calling card with such renowned fame?

With his white stringy hair, folksy demeanor, and ubiquitous plain brown suit, Franklin embodied Rousseau's portrait of the ideal natural man. His celebrity sparked daily invitations for dinners, lectures, and entertainments. He recognized that business was best conducted amidst food, wine, and witty chatter. His beaver fur hat alone made ladies swoon. He was a refreshing contrast to the multitude of colorful peacocks who crowded around him at social gatherings. But beneath that rustic fur hat pulsed one of the sharpest brains of all time. Like the Pied Piper, Franklin bewitched everyone from the lowliest chambermaid to the frostiest aristocrat. For the French to unequivocally revere a foreigner was unprecedented. Perhaps no American ever caused such a sensation in France as Ben Franklin. His fame was no mere flash of lightning.

Within weeks of his arrival, Doctor Franklin conveyed to Congress his diagnosis of the disposition of France as an ally to America, noting Louis XVI's enthusiasm hovered below room temperature. Franklin explained, "The cry of this nation is for us, but the Court views an approaching war with reluctance." He prescribed that it would be his duty, above all, "to please the Court." And wow them he did.

Louis XVI was not so smitten with Doctor Franklin. Countess Diane Polignac, the sister-in-law of the queen's bosom buddy, Gabrielle Polignac, was one of the few ladies at court with whom the king shared a friendly camaraderie. Diane sang the American envoy's praises one time too many for the king's taste. Louis ordered an exquisite porcelain chamber pot from the Sèvres factory and presented it to Diane. On the outside was Turgot's stirring accolade of Franklin: "He seized fire from the heavens and the scepter from tyrants." On the bottom of the inside of the chamber pot appeared a much-admired portrait of Mr. Franklin, atop of which bodily excrement would be plopped with regular frequency. Diane shared a good laugh with Louis, but she also got the message—she ceased extolling the virtues of the man from Philadelphia.

For most of 1777 the war in the colonies proved to be a bad investment for France; then a stunning victory was reported. The English General Burgoyne, along with his entire army, surrendered at Saratoga, New York. This was just the victory that Vergennes needed to prod Louis to overcome his ambivalence about the insurgents.

Except for Finance Minister Necker, the king's council hopped on board to recognize the new republic. Like his predecessor Turgot, Necker wrung his hands about the huge cost of financing a victory over England, but his jitters were pooh-poohed. Petrified to levy any taxes to fund the war, Necker instead raised loans dreading the day when they would come due.

To convince Louis to support the insurgents, Vergennes arm-twisted Spain and the Dutch Republic to join as allies against the British. Most young French officers, aching to cross the Atlantic to avenge France's honor, squawked the most for the king to intervene. Louis felt he had little choice but to swallow his queasiness about supporting a revolt against a fellow monarch. At last, the king tilted in Vergennes' direction and announced France's recognition of the American republic. Vergennes promised Louis that the commercial advantages of a victory would compensate for the cost of the war. In retrospect, Vergennes would have failed as a qualified CFO.

On February 6, 1778, France signed a treaty assuring military support and commercial trade links with the Thirteen United States of America. Louis received in his grand apartments the rebel ambassador, Benjamin Franklin, and his American cohorts, Silas Deane, and Arthur Lee. While the three representatives of the American colonies drove up to Versailles in their carriage, the British ambassador left France in a fury to board the first ship to England.

As always, all eyes followed the fascinating Franklin during the presentation. The king greeted the gentlemen with a terse welcome, reflecting his lingering apprehensions regarding the alliance: "Pray assure Congress of my friendship. I hope this will be for the good of both of our nations." Later that same evening, the good doctor stood behind Antoinette's chair as she played cards, a considerable distinction. Franklin reigned as the feted monarch of French society.

Marie Antoinette allowed herself to get caught up in the fuss over the rebels' conflict. Her chums at Countess Polignac's evening entertainments were absolutely gaga over the struggle of the American colonists. But like Louis, the idea of supporting the revolt of subjects against their king instinctively unsettled Antoinette. Her public embrace for a successful conflict against the British was not exactly patriotic. A gentleman of particular importance, Axel von Fersen, had signed up to serve in the American Revolutionary War. He sailed to America in May 1780 and, for the next three years, Antoinette nourished a vested interest in the outcome across the sea.

With significant French aid, the Americans eventually prevailed in the war against England. When a final treaty was inked in September 1783, France netted only minor gains, primarily due to Doctor Franklin's sly negotiations for peace terms that he had worked out in advance with England. Vergennes, who thought he held Franklin in his back pocket, emerged as the one to be outfoxed by the crafty American. In the final agreement, France scored a few islands in the Caribbean, a toehold in India and Africa, and the right to fortify its naval port of Dunkirk. Despite these paltry prizes, the French government rationalized the expensive foray by touting that the terms of the treaty provided optimistic trade opportunities that, to its sour surprise, never materialized.

The outpouring of public joy in France at defeating the English boosted national pride. Louis XVI's popularity soared with the restoration of French honor. An exhausted Vergennes crowed that England had been shamed during his tenure in office. Eventually, French pride in defeating the British would disintegrate once the tab for the conflict came due. The stratospheric debt, that purchased a victory for a far-off revolution, would spawn a second one in France itself. Years later, in a confession to his naval minister, Louis would sadly lament, "I never think of the American affair without regrets; in those days my youth was taken advantage of, and now we are suffering the consequence."

His mission accomplished, Doctor Franklin reluctantly departed France in July 1784. He enjoyed the French way of living, a style that complemented his own tastes. As he tendered his adieux and boarded ship for America, the seventy-eight-year-old Franklin wrote a farewell note to Vergennes:

> Sir, express respectfully for me to His Majesty the deep sense I have of all the inestimable Benefits his Goodness has conferred on my country; a sentiment that it will be the business of the little remainder of life now left me, to impress equally on the minds of all my countrymen. My sincere prayers are that God may shower down his blessings on the King, the Queen, their Children, and all the royal family to the latest generations.

By the time Benjamin Franklin died in Philadelphia on April 17, 1790, the Revolution in France was already in high gear. The news of the good Doctor's death devastated most Frenchmen, prompting the French National Assembly to vote unanimously for a three-day mourning period as though Franklin were a national hero of France. And he was.

"When good Americans die, they go to Paris."
Oscar Wilde

Chapter 31

A Minuet or a Tango?

For devotees enthralled by the life of Marie Antoinette, one issue always elicits volatile opinions: the poop on the relationship between the French queen and the Swedish Count Axel von Fersen. Were they platonic, close friends or did they share physical intimacies? And who was this Scandinavian hunk with close ties to the French royal couple? These questions excite scholars and enthusiasts, alike.

Axel von Fersen, born on September 4, 1755, came from a powerful Swedish family. As a young boy, he was groomed to be a soldier, complementing his precision-minded personality. Like many a young man from a privileged background, he made the customary Grand Tour through Europe to complete his education. Normally such an undertaking would take several years. In Fersen's experience, he spent four years on the road, with an attending tutor.

While polishing his military skills at various academies, Fersen met crowned heads and celebrities, such as when he visited Voltaire in Switzerland. During his stay in France, he stopped at Versailles where he paid court to Louis XV and his mistress, Countess du Barry.

Several weeks later Axel and Antoinette's paths intersected for the first time. On January 30, 1774, Axel von Fersen met Marie Antoinette while she was still dauphine at a masked ball in Paris. Louis and his brother Provence were also in attendance that evening. Antoinette, emboldened by the security of her mask, saucily approached the handsome partygoer. Each unaware of the other's identity, they easily chatted and teased one another. The youthful

Swede dispassionately recorded their first meeting, "The Dauphine talked to me for a long time without me knowing who she was; at last when she was recognized, everybody pressed around her and she retired into a box at three o'clock: I left the ball." A born army guy for sure, he instinctively noted the time. The Swede melted away into the crowd, but the spark ignited that evening would never be extinguished.

A few weeks later in mid-February 1774, Fersen attended a ball at Versailles where Antoinette dominated the setting. With no opportunity to chat, they both exchanged lingering glances, containing all the ingredients of a promising romance for a Jane Austen novel.

Axel hung out in Paris until the end of April. He then resumed his Grand Tour with its final destination of London. He took in the sights and met the elite of the social register, including the royal family. Everywhere he went he was much admired; people commented on his handsomeness. The society moguls aptly nicknamed him, "The Picture." While Fersen was in England, Louis XV died and Antoinette became queen; Axel's emotions must have stirred when he heard this news. By the end of the year he was back in gloomy Sweden where he had to placate a difficult father and enter into the service of his king, Gustavus III. The delights of Paris seemed like a distant idyll.

Fersen's dour father pressured his twenty-two-year-old son and heir to marry a wealthy catch and begin producing sons of his own. The young Fersen buoyed his father's hopes, hinting at a promising candidate. He disclosed that during his travels he had been introduced to Miss Catherine Lyell. Axel described his potential bride as "charming, talented, and sweet-tempered." Miss Lyell's family hailed from Sweden, but had relocated to England to make a killing in international commerce. Although aligned to the merchant class, the young lady was the only child and heiress to an eye-popping fortune. That news alone won the senior Fersen's enthusiastic approval. The Fersen family would provide the lady with the title of countess and she, in turn, would bankroll her new family.

In April 1778 Axel returned to England to secure the heart and purse strings of Miss Lyell, who warmed to the physical charms of her suitor. For two months Axel laid siege to her family's home, determined to win the young heiress' hand. Axel seemed confident of his conquest. But ultimately the lady Lyell declined the proposal, shattering Fersen's ego. While Catherine professed her love for Axel, she dreaded leaving her parents for a faraway life. She dangled the slim hope that her domestic responsibilities might alter in a few years, paving the way for a possible future with Axel.

Writing from London, Fersen felt ashamed to explain the courtship debacle to his father. The hardened senior Fersen could not accept that a virile prize like Axel proved to be a blank shot in the wooing game. The dejected Axel wrote to his sister, Sophie, "I am in despair at the thought that I did everything in my power to please him and win the girl's consent."

Fersen resolved to salvage his manly honor by seducing every attractive lady who threw herself at him. Besides his appealing appearance, Fersen projected a subtle brooding disposition that each damsel felt she alone could dispel. All those who tried to win his heart were disappointed, no matter how persuasive their charms. That was one organ of his body that remained consistently untouchable. Meanwhile, Fersen raised his father's sunken dynastic hopes, hinting at still roping Miss Lyell. Both son and father allowed themselves to be lulled by this fantasy:

> I mustn't entirely abandon the project therefore. Let us allow
> matters to take their course. If she loves me I can always pick up
> where I left off, and I am certain that four or five or even six years
> will be time enough to start thinking seriously about the matter.
> Papa Lyell is old, and he's sick. When he dies the objections from
> his side will die with him. All the money would then come to me
> directly.

With no nuptials on the horizon, Fersen shifted his focus to his career with his father's approval. Axel shopped around for the best available military opportunity, submitting a request for a slot in Frederick the Great's much admired army. Gladly abandoning London, the scene of his matchmaking humiliation, Axel scampered off to Paris for some diversion while awaiting a response from the Prussians.

The dashing count reappeared at the French court in August 1778 when Antoinette was pregnant with her first child. Fersen confided in his journal, "Last Tuesday I went to Versailles to be presented to the royal family. The Queen, who is charming, said when she saw me, 'Ah! Here is an old acquaintance.' The rest of the family did not say a word to me." Marie Antoinette instantly recognized the man who had electrified her heart three years previously. Knowing that his father had a weakness for all things French, Fersen described his success at Versailles:

> The Queen, who is the loveliest and most amiable princess that can
> be imagined, has had the goodness to inquire more than once about
> me. The Queen treats me with great kindness; I often pay her my
> respects at her card games on Sunday evenings, and each time she

makes to me little speeches that are full of good will. As someone
had told her of my Swedish uniform, she expressed an interest to
see me in it. I am to go this Thursday thus dressed not to court, but
to the queen's apartments.

Fersen glowed, knowing that he had attracted the queen's particular attention
when she requested he appear in his officer's uniform that consisted of a
blue doublet, white tunic, and sprayed on chamois breeches—what a visual!
Nothing more hormonally intoxicating than a man in uniform.

Throughout 1779 Fersen became a fixture of Antoinette's inner circle and
a regular of the handpicked group whom she included at the Petit Trianon,
with its relaxed rules of etiquette. On several occasions, both Axel and
Antoinette were spotted at the raucous masked balls in Paris, sitting alone
for hours in a private box. Axel behaved stiff-upper-lip correct in public
while Antoinette strove to contain her feelings. Diehard gossips salivated
about the possible interactions between the two. The Swedish Ambassador
to France, Count Creutz, informed Gustavus III in April 1779 of the buzz
about the French queen and the Swedish beefcake:

> I must inform Your Majesty in confidence that the young Count
> Fersen has been so warmly received by the Queen that some
> people here have taken umbrage. I must admit that I cannot help
> believing that she has an inclination for him. I have seen signs that
> are too clear to be doubted. Young Count Fersen's behavior on this
> occasion was admirable in its modesty and reserve.

Axel wasn't just ripped eye-candy. He remained fixated on securing a military
assignment. When he got the news that Prussia had rejected his application,
he shifted gears to serving in America. By early 1780 France was assembling
an armed force to assist the rebel colonies. Foreign Minister Vergennes who
was an admirer of the elder Fersen in Sweden, pulled a few strings and got
Axel appointed to the dream posting as an assistant to Marshall Rochambeau,
the commander of the French Expeditionary Force fighting in America. Like
all young warriors, Fersen was bursting with readiness to taste the dreamed
of military glory: "I am in a state of joy that cannot be expressed." Courtiers
noted that Antoinette appeared visibly shaken at Fersen's imminent departure
that would span three long years.

In May 1780 an enthusiastic Axel sailed from Brest for Newport, Rhode
Island. Fersen recorded his impressions of Americans and their fledgling
republic: "They are happy with the little necessities of life that in other
countries would only satisfy the lower classes. Their clothing is plain but

good, and their customs have not been spoiled by European luxury. Money is the first motive of all their actions. They have been robbing us blind." Later in 1782, when he witnessed the shameful abyss between master and slave, Fersen revised his opinion of the republican virtues of the new nation: "I shouldn't be surprised to see Virginia to cede from the other states." Always alert to female charms, he described the women as "pretty, friendly, and coquettes"—guy talk for his conquests beyond the battlefield. Having a prominent place in Rochambeau's service, Fersen got to rub shoulders with everyone of importance, including George Washington, whom he described: "He has the air of a hero; he is very cold and speaks very little, but he is polite and a gentleman."

Returning to France in June 1783, Fersen headed straight to Versailles. He and the queen were overjoyed to see one another. Courtiers remarked that Fersen's looks had taken a hit due to an illness he suffered in America. Yet, in the queen's eyes, he was all the more gallant.

Still on message, Fersen's father in Sweden pestered his heir to marry. Father and son were jolted when they learned that Miss Lyell had tied the knot with an English lord. Suddenly, a replacement bride became a top priority. Earnest talk circulated about Fersen marrying the fabulously wealthy Mademoiselle Germaine Necker. Sixteen years old and definitely no prom queen, she compensated for her looks with her sharp intellect and buxom dowry. The nuptial negotiations fell through when Gustavus III overruled Fersen's plans. The Swedish king commanded that Missy Necker be snatched up by a fellow Swede, Baron Erik Staël von Holstein. To sweeten the contract for the bride's parents, the bridegroom was appointed the Swedish Ambassador to France. This union would be a big step up for the commoner's daughter, but a disaster for the incompatible couple. While her husband dithered as a minor nobody, Germaine would mooch the limelight, becoming one of the most famous women in Europe.

After this second rejection, Fersen defied his father—*Basta*, no more marriage proposals. Axel breathed a sigh of relief not to win the hand of Mademoiselle Necker. He confided to a pal, "Don't feel bad for me, my friend, for I am convinced that this marriage will suit him better than it would have suited me. Just between us, I never thought of it except to please my father, and I am not at all sorry that it cannot be." Axel nurtured another reason for remaining unattached. He was smitten with Antoinette. Axel shared his true feelings with his sister, Sophie: "I have made up my mind. I have decided never to marry. It would be too unnatural. I cannot belong to the one woman whom I should like to belong, and who alone truly loves me, so I will belong to no other." Sophie knew of her brother's attachment to the queen and shared her concerns about this potentially dangerous liaison.

With Fersen back in her life, Antoinette devised a legitimate reason to keep him as a regular at Versailles. Fersen plotted for the same outcome. The Swedish king, Antoinette, and Louis XVI arranged for Fersen to purchase the command of a French Regiment, composed of foreigners, called the *Royal Suédois.* This assignment guaranteed that Fersen would never be far from the queen. Part of the deal to secure this post required Fersen to spend about half of each year in his king's service, whether in Sweden or elsewhere. But, by the late 1780s and until June 1791, Axel remained almost exclusively in France.

During this period, Antoinette asked her perfumer, Jean-Louis Fargeon to create a toilet water "for an elegant gentleman who is as virile as a man can be." Delicate alterations began in the spring of 1787 in the queen's interior apartments, considered the Holy of Holies. It was whispered that a room was prepared for Fersen's particular use. Perhaps true, but unnecessary since Fersen had a house and stables in the town of Versailles. Antoinette's closest friends likely knew or suspected the nature of the alliance between the two admirers, but kept their mouths shut. Both queen and count were discreet in public, but passed most afternoons alone at the Petit Trianon where they escaped prying eyes.

So, back to the enigma that intrigues everyone. Were Fersen and Antoinette sexually intimate—yes or no? There are passionate arguments for both possibilities. Much of their personal correspondence has been lost or purposely destroyed by Fersen's family in the late nineteenth century. What scraps remain point to an unbreakable link between them. Ultimately, whether they slept together matters little. If I had to take a game show guess, I would wager that they were doing it. Turbulent events of the time would have probably drawn these two lovers close together, culminating in their physical union. Sex or no sex, this couple loved each other ardently, and that part of the story is undeniable. They vowed to be the other's beloved.

"Soul meets soul in lovers' lips."
Percy Shelley

Chapter 32

Curtains Up, Revolt's in Sight

*I*t's difficult to grasp that a theatrical production could sway the course of history but that is what occurred with Pierre Augustin Caron's satirical play, *The Marriage of Figaro.*

The playwright, who went by the name of Beaumarchais, figured as one of the most unique men of the age. Born in Paris in 1732, the only son among five sisters, he was apprenticed to his father's business of making time pieces. The precocious lad forged technological improvements by designing an escapement that took up less space and improved the accuracy of clocks. Louis XV was impressed and designated him the royal watchmaker. The promising Beaumarchais married a wealthy widow whose dowry allowed him to purchase a nobleman's title. Next, he became a music teacher giving harp lessons to Louis XV's daughters. Soon, Monsieur Beaumarchais switched gears and served as a secret agent for Louis XV and, later, for Louis XVI. These achievements bolstered Beaumarchais' reputation as a man of unlimited talents. In between his gigs as spymaster, he wrote several popular plays and published the complete works of Voltaire. With the exception of a fitness video, this guy did it all.

Beaumarchais wrote the controversial play *The Marriage of Figaro* in 1778. It was the second of a trilogy of plays. The first in the series of plays was *The Barber of Seville* that premiered in February 1774. The plot was a staple of French comedy: A Spanish count, unsure of the pretty maiden whom he loves, engages the cunning services of a servant to win his prize. The production bombed on opening night. Undaunted, Beaumarchais rewrote it within forty-eight hours. The revised version had the audience begging for more—it was a smash hit! As Madame Deffand, the witty society matron par excellence recounted, "At the first night the comedy was soundly hissed, but its second performance scored an extravagant success." An overnight resurrection of a stage production seemed impossible in theater history, but Beaumarchais also excelled as a magician.

However, the playwright's supernatural powers faltered at the doorstep of the Crown's censors. They denied approval to mount his second play in the series, *The Marriage of Figaro*. Despite his persistent efforts, for six years Beaumarchais encountered solid opposition. On the surface, the plot dealt with a married nobleman who desired to bed a young maiden but is thwarted in his efforts by a young servant in his employ.

The playwright appealed to the king, and at Antoinette's suggestion, Louis had the play read to him. The king considered the play to be an attack on the ruling class system and an affront to the State prisons: "It is detestable! It must never be performed. To allow it would be the same as destroying the Bastille. The man ridicules everything that should be respected in government." It was hard to fault the king's judgment with lines spoken by Figaro in Act V: "What is it to be a courtier? To receive, to take, to ask. Because you are a great lord, you think you are a great genius. Nobility, fortune, rank, positions, it all makes a man so proud. You gave yourselves the trouble to be born, and nothing more; for the rest, you are simply ordinary." On the playwright's manuscript, Louis scribbled a note to the minister of justice, "The censor must permit neither its performance nor its publication."

Louis XVI correctly feared that the play would provoke chants for reform, or, even worse, revolt. But Beaumarchais was no groveling subject. He clung to his dialogue of stinging satire aimed at the ruling hierarchy. Ironically, the fatuous upper crust pestered Louis to grant his approval for Beaumarchais to stage the play. As the famous Euripides warned centuries before, "Whom the gods would destroy, they first make mad." And the top-tiered aristos were mad about Figaro.

After prolonged wrangling, Beaumarchais edited the script. He switched the setting of the play from France to the less threatening Spain. He erased both the nasty references to the Bastille and the biting criticisms of the Catholic clergy. Everything seemed ready for the production to be presented in June 1783. Then the police showed up during final rehearsals, closing the show on orders of the king. Theater-goers cried foul. Beaumarchais fumed, angrily scolding the police, "Well, Messieurs, the King does not wish it to be performed here, yet I trust that it will be performed, and perhaps in the choir of Notre Dame." That kind of defiant comeback could warrant a prolonged stay in the Bastille.

Luckily Beaumarchais scored a crack in the barrier of royal refusal. The queen's jaded set of intimates managed to wrangle Louis' consent to permit a private performance of the taboo play at the home of Count Vaudreuil, a friend of Beaumarchais, and a fixture of Gabrielle Polignac's crowd. The son of a West Indian plantation owner, Vaudreuil came to Paris to spend his sugar fortune. Vaudreuil invited fifty privileged guests, including Count Artois and Gabrielle Polignac. Beaumarchais was betting that this audience would rave about the play, thus coercing Louis to consent to public performances. Antoinette was dying to attend the hush-hush show, but Louis gave her an ambiguous consent. She wisely interpreted the king's approval as disapproval, and so announced that she felt poorly and would stay in that evening. The private performance gained fifty instant fans who spread the word that the play was riotously funny and a must-see production. Just the effect that Beaumarchais intended.

Private readings became the rage at the poshest Parisian townhouses at which Beaumarchais showcased sections of the text behind gilded doors. The teasing worked. Soon everyone clamored to swallow the entire forbidden fruit. The more Louis tried to prevent the public production of the play, the louder became the demands to allow it. Cries of "tyranny" bombarded the king. Louis appointed Baron Breteuil, a trusted adviser, to head a committee in March 1784 to make a final decision. With the committee's lukewarm "yes," Louis, against his better judgment, surrendered his disapproval. He announced that the play could be performed in public; privately he hoped that the play would be a colossal flop. Beaumarchais agreed to some tepid concessions in the script, but the dialogue retained its explosive impact.

Opening night took place on April 27, 1784, at the Comédie-Française in Paris. The curtain was scheduled to rise at six in the evening, a bit later than the customary time of five in the afternoon. Outside the theater, near riot conditions prevailed the entire day. The play heralded such an exceptional premiere that every seat in the theater was jealously occupied more than an hour before the curtain rose. Scanning the excited audience, there in a choice seat sat Princess Lamballe, one of many A-listers present that evening. The playwright chose to see his work from a private box behind a lattice screen in the company of two priests, just in case he needed divine intercession. Not even a wrathful god would dare to jeopardize the play's success.

As Beaumarchais suspected, the crowd went wild for Figaro. Almost every line was greeted with applause causing the play to deliciously drag on for more than four hours. The evening climaxed with an unprecedented twelve curtain calls. Louis' initial reservations proved to be correct: nothing good could come from entertainment in which the servants usurped the master's role, and the lords proved to be no more than useless ornaments.

The political impact of the stage production was inescapable. A few years later, the revolutionary, Georges Danton, would hail it as "The play that killed off the nobility." And a generation later, Napoleon deemed it "The Revolution already put into action."

Trouble erupted after several performances, spoiling Beaumarchais' triumph. Peevish Church officials condemned the play as immoral. The religious king tortured himself with second thoughts and suspended further performances. Beaumarchais struck back at the prejudiced prelates with stinging barbs, determined to expose the corrupting stranglehold of these hypocrites who dominated French life.

To cure Beaumarchais of his criticisms, Louis XVI confined the fifty-two-year-old author to Saint Lazare prison for five nights of attitude adjustment. The playwright's supporters assailed the king, who relented and ordered Beaumarchais' release. Louis thought that he had proved his point to Beaumarchais that both Church and Crown could alter the destiny of one's life. To the glee of many, Beaumarchais refused to budge from prison without an apology from the Crown. How cheeky can you get! Unfathomably, the king agreed.

The performances resumed the day after Beaumarchais' release from prison, with the king's entire cabinet sitting in the audience. Almost one hundred performances followed to packed houses for the next eight months. Marie Antoinette got to see the stage show in June 1784 and thought it hilariously entertaining. Antoinette kept a copy of *The Marriage of Figaro* in her library at the Petit Trianon for her reading pleasure.

The ultimate irony unfolded that same summer. One of the conditions for Beaumarchais' release from prison stipulated that he be the invited guest at a performance of his play *The Barber of Seville* in the queen's boutique theater at the Petit Trianon. No surprise, Marie Antoinette played the starring role of the heroine, Rosine, accompanied by her brother-in-law Artois as Figaro— an image that must have cheered Beaumarchais' liberal sensibilities. The vindicated playwright sat on the king's right throughout the performance, no doubt smiling to himself about how he had subdued both a monarch and the bigoted Church fathers. Times were definitely changing.

> "I do not care how the Word of God applies here.
> This is a courtroom, not a church, so don't preach to me"
> *Judge Judy Sheindlin*

Chapter 33

The Good, Sweet Years

From 1780 through mid-1785, Louis and Antoinette would have rated their reign as a success. Without doubt, the crowning highlight of those years was the birth of an heir. In early 1781 national hopes took flight when the palace confirmed that Antoinette was pregnant. Everyone in France, except for the queen, was convinced that this time the child would be a boy.

On October 22, 1781, Marie Antoinette gave birth. In contrast to the queen's first delivery in 1778, the birth of her second child was significantly easier. Further, the king strictly limited those invited to witness the birth. Antoinette, unaware of the child's gender, feared that she had produced another girl. Upon the king's orders, he alone would disclose the baby's gender.

Growing anxious at the ciphered faces surrounding her, Antoinette implored, "You see how reasonable I am; I am saying nothing."

At that moment, a tearful king approached the queen, announcing, "Madame, you have fulfilled my wishes and those of France; Monsieur the Dauphin begs to meet you."

Both the king and queen, oblivious of the crowd around them, sobbed for joy in each other's embrace. After cradling her son for the first time, custom dictated that the queen hand over the newborn to the beaming royal governess, Princess Guéméné, for he belonged to the State. The long-awaited child was named Louis Joseph, the Dauphin; Louis, after his father, and Joseph after his godfather and uncle in Vienna.

Halleluiah, they had provided what the country demanded. At last, a hundred and one cannon salute announced the birth of a dauphin. The entire nation erupted in delirious cheers at the news of an heir. Louis, normally untalkative and poker-faced in social settings, gushed freely to anyone about his heir, boasting of more boys to follow. Louis made reference "to my son, the Dauphin," at every opportunity.

Others in the king's family were not so enthusiastic about the new heir. When the eldest boy of Count Artois saw the baby, he whispered to his father, "How small my cousin is, Papa."

The count dryly quipped, "The day will come when you will find him big enough."

The king's other brother, Provence, barely concealed his sour response to the birth that effectively snuffed out his hopes for the throne.

A euphoria swept France following the birth of the dauphin, relieved that governing stability was now assured. An incandescent Antoinette glowed at finally fulfilling her primary role as queen. With the birth of her son, she felt that she had cemented her link to the French nation. For a brief flash, her popularity rose with all segments of society. Even the king sensed this shift in appreciation for the queen remarking, "Even those who cared least for the Queen, were carried away by the general rejoicing." But the French people were more interested in the heir than his mother. Still perceived by many as a meddling foreigner, Antoinette would be tolerated as long as she continued pumping out a string of healthy boys.

Dampening the king's joy, Louis XVI suffered a personal shock four weeks after the birth of his son. His dependable upstairs neighbor, Count Maurepas, died on November 21, 1781. The eighty-year-old count had been Louis' chief adviser for seven years. The king spilled his distress to the queen over the loss of The Mentor with tears trickling down his cheeks: "I shall never again hear my friend in the morning pacing overhead." Everyone at Versailles wondered whom Louis would choose to replace Maurepas. Louis surprised everybody when he decided to leave the post vacant. He felt his days of using training wheels were over. Oh, boy!

After her son's birth, a change took hold in the queen's habits. Her late nights sampling the delights of Paris faded along with her pursuit of gambling. Her fashion choices became more classically sophisticated with less ostentatious ornamentation. The queen embraced needlepoint, which both calmed her and provided the silk covers for many chairs in the royal residences. Antoinette, devoted to the care of her children, passed delightful hours with them at the

Petit Trianon, picnicking outside when the weather was agreeable; when possible, the king would join them. Antoinette was finally getting the cozy family that she had dreamed about. Unfortunately, Antoinette's reformed lifestyle was perceived as window dressing and barely altered public opinion.

The happy news of the arrival of the French heir floated across the Atlantic Ocean to the new republic, the United States of America. In honor of the birth of Louis' son, a county in Pennsylvania (which included the state capital, Harrisburg) was named Dauphin County. The people of Pennsylvania wished to express their admiration and thanks to Louis XVI for his support in their war of independence from England. A republic's honor bestowed on the son of a king. What irony!

An unexpected shakeup in the queen's household occurred in 1782. Prince Guéméné and his wife, the royal governess of the king's children, were admired as the dream couple among their contemporaries. They had it all: youth, looks, money, and status at court. In the fall of 1782 their enviable world disintegrated overnight, plunging them into bankruptcy, owing the equivalent nowadays of a quarter billion dollars.

Like many prominent persons at Versailles, the prince lived beyond his ample means. He borrowed from bankers, financial investors, courtiers, tradesmen, even servants, always promising to repay. And many critics blamed the out-of-control gambling of the princess as a further cause of the couple's ruin. Since the prince was also related to the influential Rohan family, the financial repercussions convulsed the spread sheets of many powerful people. The bluebloods blanched that a couple so close to the throne could lose it all.

Under the shameful circumstances, and coincidentally on the first birthday of the dauphin, Princess Guéméné resigned her post as royal governess. The disgraced couple's close connection to the royals insulated them from an austere fate; overnight they slinked off to a country estate. The king's council ordered the prince's assets to be liquidated in a puerile effort to satisfy the host of creditors. Both Louis and Antoinette provided monetary assistance to the ruined couple—not the most politically correct gesture, considering the scope of the prince's abuse of his status.

The financial collapse of this golden couple spread goose bumps to courtiers throughout Versailles, aware that the same nightmare could engulf them, as well. Living at court remained an expensive challenge. To maintain a respectable façade, most courtiers survived on credit. Each courtier strived to be impeccably dressed, coiffed, capable of delivering a memorably witty phrase, and vigilant to catch the attention of a receptive royal. It looked like a glamorous life, but up close it was a grueling job. As one crusty veteran of the court advised an optimistic newcomer, "You have only three things to do. Say nice things about everyone, ask for any income providing position that is available, and sit down when you can." Useful, practical advice. Many a courtier passed tedious hours, hoping for the royal recognition that could instantly alter one's prospects.

Upon the resignation of Princess Guémené, a successor had to be appointed for the care of the royal children. The position went to Antoinette's bosom buddy, Gabrielle Polignac. She was not exactly thrilled to get the job. Even though she was a natural with kids, the new responsibilities would force the duchess to rein in her mostly carefree existence. Yet, her family pushed so hard for the appointment that she felt obligated to accept. The job came with a lot of perks including a grand suite of rooms in Versailles.

Louis XVI heartily approved of Gabrielle's promotion for the care of his children. Not only did the king like Gabrielle, he appreciated her knack of diffusing Antoinette's occasional temper outbursts. Gabrielle knew how to cope with the queen's disagreeable moods when tensions would surface between the women regarding the children. For this reason alone, Louis was grateful that Gabrielle got the job. While most of the nobility at Versailles judged the selection of Gabrielle to be a stain on the office and an overreach of privilege, Louis saw in Gabrielle a godsend to promote familial harmony.

The imagination of the country soared in 1783 with the spectacle of air flight. Balloons, made of paper and cloth inflated by the gassy smoke of a burning fire, floated high above Paris. The Montgolfier brothers, paper-makers by trade, engineered this majestic flying vessel. A demonstration financed by the king took place before the court and thousands of spectators at Versailles on September 19, 1783. The idea that the French beat the British with such a leap skyward thrilled the nation and the king. First the defeat of England in America, and now conquering the skies. Louis felt his reign was flying high, cruising toward a memorable legacy.

Flush with the achievements of 1783, Louis XVI rewarded himself and purchased Rambouillet, a chateau located about thirty miles south of Paris. Although normally thrifty, Louis, rarely penny-pinched when it came to his passion for the hunt, and the forest surrounding the chateau was reputed to be the best for the king's sport. When he brought the queen to see the property in November of 1783, she did not conceal her disappointment. She chided Louis, "How can I be asked to stay in that Gothic dive meant for toads?" She used the word *crapaudière* to describe the castle, a genteel term for calling it a "shitbox." To overcome the queen's harsh opinion, Louis secretly constructed a fancy dairy for her use—a society lady's must-have. Antoinette softened her earlier criticism of Rambouillet on seeing the deluxe dairy, proving that she would always be an uptown kind of girl.

During the summer of 1783, Antoinette precipitated an unforeseen wave of criticism, all because of a dress. The queen, like so many other upscale ladies, had grown weary of the elaborate clothing she wore daily. Chic women yearned for something simpler and more comfortable to wear. The queen heralded a radical trend in ladies' wear and was painted wearing the new fashion, called *la chemise à la reine.* And it was not meant as a compliment. A chemise was an undergarment similar to a slip or nightgown. The dress, simulating a nightgown's simplicity, was usually white muslin, and used drawstrings instead of being perfectly fitted. It was finished off with a broad sash, frilly sleeves and neckline, and was often worn with a feather festooned straw hat. A painting of the queen in her new fashion nearly touched off a riot when it was exhibited at the art salon in Paris. What a disgrace that a queen of France should demean her office by sporting such an offensive garment! The liberating fashion scored a hit with most ladies, but it was the queen who was condemned. The public believed that no respectable queen should wear what appeared to be underwear. They blamed Antoinette for ruining the livelihood of the silk manufacturers. No matter what Antoinette did, the public faulted her.

Marital harmony was once again tested in 1784 by Antoinette's Austrian connection. Her brother Emperor Joseph II wanted the Dutch to expand the port of Antwerp to allow the Austrian Netherlands a better outlet to the North Sea. Holland refused to accommodate Joseph, and France stood solidly behind Holland.

Joseph bombarded Antoinette with demands to persuade Louis to support the emperor's cause. He accused his sister of letting him down when he needed her most. Upset, the queen knew the first person with whom she had to buck horns with was Foreign Minister Vergennes. A stormy interview transpired between them. In so many courteous words, Vergennes told the queen to mind her own business. The queen was furious, threatening the minister with dismissal between her sobs. Vergennes held his ground, reminding the queen, "Madame, I am speaking to the mother of the Dauphin and not the sister of the Emperor Joseph." This zinger set the queen off, as she made a scene worthy of the stage. Vergennes, fed up with her interference and her personal dislike of him, offered his resignation to the king. Louis could not bear the loss of the man he trusted most. He assured Vergennes that no troops would be sent to aid the emperor's schemes in the Netherlands. The king mollified his wife, but stood firm with Vergennes. No French help for Austria.

Short-lived hostilities did erupt between Austria and Holland. When no country sided with Joseph II, the embarrassed emperor had to accept Louis XVI's offer to arbitrate a peace. What a coup for Louis! The arranged peace stipulated that Austria would receive financial compensation in exchange for renouncing its aims of expansion of the port of Antwerp. The snarly Dutch paid Joseph only eighty percent of the sum he demanded. In a gesture of friendship to Joseph, and a desire to close the deal, Louis offered to pay Joseph the outstanding twenty percent. Once the French public got wind of the terms, they accused the Austrian Woman of forcing the king to send wagons of French gold to her brother. The queen was even worse than a Madame Pompadour.

Antoinette wrote to her brother after the Dutch-Austrian flare-up, providing an insight regarding her involvement in affairs of State. Antoinette described her interactions with Louis: "He responds to me when I speak to him, but he hardly can be said to keep me informed. And when I learn about some small portion of business, I have to be cunning in getting the ministers to tell me the rest of it, letting them believe that the King has told me everything." This was the very behavior that the French detested in their queen; she did not know how to keep her foreign nose out of policy making. The French did not empathize for one moment with the constant nagging their queen endured from Vienna. With pragmatic exasperation, Antoinette rhetorically asked her brother, "Would it be wise of me to have scenes with his ministers over matters in which it is practically certain the King would not support me?"

From the viewpoint of the king's ministers, caution never prevented the queen from making a scene when she was prodded by her Hapsburg relatives. Even the queen's Polignac crew questioned Antoinette's loyalties. Wounded by their cutting remarks, especially after all she had done for them, Antoinette sounded off to Gabrielle Polignac, expecting her support. Surprisingly, Gabrielle took the side of her chums, retorting, "Because Your Majesty honors my rooms with your presence, it is no reason why I should be expected to exclude all others for whom I care." After years of fostering relaxed rules of etiquette with her friends, Polignac's crowd had grown accustomed to respond to Antoinette not as their sovereign but as a peer. Stung, Antoinette gradually drifted from their caustic company. Antoinette never imagined such an outcome. Sensing the queen's coolness, Gabrielle opted for a change of scenery with an extended stay in England.

After the international incident and its palace fallout, Marie Antoinette consoled herself by spending more time at her hideaway, the Petit Trianon. During these years, the queen, like other wealthy ladies, oversaw the fabrication of what amounted to a small theme park based on an idyllic Norman village, known as *L'Hameau*, the Hamlet. It boasted of a make-believe world dotted with cottages, two dairies, a mill, a barn, a working farm, and, as the centerpiece, the queen's two-story house resting at the edge of a tranquil lake. Here Antoinette delighted her children and selected guests, far from the poisonous gossip of nearby Versailles. The queen was happiest in this cocoon of engineered bliss where life seemed perfect, just like in the storybooks she read to her children.

Antoinette also constructed an exquisite theater with a hundred seats on the grounds of the Petit Trianon. This invitation-only venue offered another confirmation that Antoinette snubbed the great families of France living at Versailles. Only the royal family, the queen's favorite companions, and some of her servants snagged the limited tickets; Antoinette felt unbound to the laws of Versailles' etiquette in her private domain. Yet, those excluded felt cheated and disrespected.

Antoinette handpicked a cast of players and staged popular frothy comedies. The repertoire company included the king's siblings Count Artois, Madame Elisabeth, and select members of Antoinette's inner circle. The queen usually nabbed the starring roles for herself. The king enjoyed these productions, contributing the loudest applause.

One memorable evening in June 1784, the guest of honor at Antoinette's theater was Gustavus III, the King of Sweden. After the performance, the Swedish king marveled at the unforgettable evening Antoinette had created. The outdoor entertainment was backlit with bewitching lighting where the invited ladies wore white gowns, creating a Garden of Eden fantasy.

It was around this time that Antoinette realized she was pregnant again. The queen was quite large during the pregnancy, and some speculated that she might be carrying twins. Instead, one large healthy boy named Louis Charles arrived on Easter Sunday, March 27, 1785. While her first son was frail and sickly, the second boy was robust and spunky. The little chap would charm all who met him with his fair looks and gregarious personality.

With this second son, the queen felt that she had secured the line of succession. She expected that the French would finally accept her as one of their own. To her panicked dismay, an eerie silence greeted her when she made the ritual ride to Notre Dame to give thanks for the successful delivery. The new child might be welcomed, but the mother was not. Upon returning to Versailles, the queen dissolved into tears, not comprehending the public's cold shoulder. She moaned, "What have I done to them?"

By 1784 the queen set her sights on the delightful chateau of Saint Cloud. With persuasive reasoning, Antoinette got Louis to see the need for acquiring this perfect home for their expanding family. Like many husbands, Louis appreciated the value of the mantra, "Happy wife, happy life."

The idea of owning this blue-chip property delighted Antoinette. Versailles was scheduled for an overdue renovation, expected to take five years, as soon as the funds were available. The queen envisioned Saint Cloud as an ideal residence to serve as a temporary home for her family while repairs engulfed Versailles. Due to its smaller size, Saint Cloud could only accommodate the royal family and their intimates. Finally, Antoinette would be able to lead the more relaxed court life that she remembered from her youth in Vienna.

A new finance minister, Charles Alexander Calonne, had replaced Jacques Necker in November 1783. Antoinette had opposed his appointment, only to be outwitted once again by the influence of Vergennes. Calonne cheerfully assured investors that the finances of France were sound. Despite his rosy forecast, Calonne was trying hard to economize. Not long after his appointment, Calonne learned of Louis' plans to purchase the chateau of Saint Cloud near Paris. The minister audibly gasped when he learned of the asking price; the purchase of this prime real estate might derail his belt tightening plans. He petitioned the queen to withdraw her request. As Antoinette heard Calonne's entreaty, her gaze alone froze him to solid ice. She imperiously threatened him, "If I do not have it, I will forbid your presence before me, and your presence at Madame Polignac's, whenever I am there." Calonne, no social ascetic, dreaded being excluded from the social swirl of Versailles. Accustomed to getting what she asked for, Antoinette got her chateau. But Calonne never forgave her bullying, and he became another earnest enemy of Her Majesty.

The transaction for the purchase of Saint Cloud closed in February 1785. When the acquisition became public knowledge, Antoinette triggered another spasm of public censure. She brushed aside the criticisms and buried herself in the decorating plans for her new acquisition.

On Sundays, Parisians picnicked in the queen's gardens at Saint Cloud of which Antoinette had magnanimously opened to them on that day alone. The queen often appeared with her children, mingling with the crowds from Paris. Antoinette failed to win the approval of a colicky public by allowing them admission to her private estate. Although the public came in droves to enjoy the park, they were not at all appreciative toward the Austrian Woman.

Most people considered it a scandal that a queen of France would have two properties in her own name. Antoinette rationalized that she had earned this residence by providing the nation with a spare heir. Antoinette tried to put a sensible spin on the purchase citing the money to be saved with a substantially reduced household staff. The French dismissed this lame explanation. They were itching for an excuse to permanently yank the Austrian from her place on the royal stage. This pent-up frustration was about to find its voice in August 1785.

"They are not long, the days of wine and roses:
Out of a misty dream
Our path emerges for a while, then closes
Within a dream."
Ernest Dowson

Intermission

I feel the readers of this book deserve a moment to brace for what follows—the endless turbulence that overturned the world of late eighteenth century France. Until now, Marie Antoinette's life was mostly a cushy appointment, enjoying the best of everything and expecting the best of everything. From this point forward, a trail of bitter disappointments and undreamed of shocks would dismantle her world. Life would not be fair, and the payback would be brutal.

"Anyone who has lost something they thought was theirs forever,
finally comes to realize that nothing really belongs to them."
Paulo Coelho

Spotlight Three

The Days of Shifting Fortunes

Chapter 34

Diamonds: A Girl's Best Friend?

Before there was a Watergate, Irangate, Monicagate, Weinergate, or Bridgegate, there was the ultimate progenitor of all "gates" ever—Diamondgate—a scandal that set the bar for every sleazy scam to follow in its wake. This once in an epoch event signaled the beginning of the queen's personal apocalypse.

Imagine a dime store thriller with a cast of these unlikely characters: two jewelers in a financial bind; an unpopular foreign queen; an epicurean cardinal; a delusional countess with a twin loser for a husband; a charlatan posing as a gifted seer; a flunky petty nobleman; and the obligatory streetwalker. Finally, toss in the most extravagant necklace ever assembled. If this swindle sounds preposterous, that is understandable. Sadly, it was all too real in France in 1785. This saga would hold all of Europe spellbound for nearly a year as it achieved iconic notoriety as "The Affair of the Diamond Necklace." The unparalleled event would serve as an indictment of everything that provoked resentment with autocratic rule, igniting the opening salvo for what would become known as the French Revolution.

Personally, for Marie Antoinette, life would never be the same. Her entire narrative can be neatly demarcated by this singular catastrophe. There was her life before the necklace affair and her life after it—period. The carefree, pampered existence she once led sank forever from view. In its place a harsher reality popped to the surface. All because of a necklace that became a passport to infamy for the strangest assortment of bedfellows ever assembled.

❧ ❧ ❧

The melodrama starts with a pair of jewelers in the early 1770s. Charles Boehmer managed the enterprise as the salesman of the team. His partner, Paul Bassenge, complemented him on the design end with tempting creations. Renowned for their upscale merchandise, they were sought after by the wealthy from Paris to St. Petersburg.

Perhaps blinded by fame, the jewelers took a huge financial risk. They borrowed heavily to finance a one-of-a-kind diamond doozy known as The Slave Collar—the name alone was ominous in its implications. The eye-popping adornment would be the most unique showstopper ever seen, more worthy of a flashy social climber than a pedigreed princess. The necklace consisted of 647 diamonds, weighing 2,800 carats. The bling impact was blinding. In today's market it might fetch about ten million dollars. Imagine the security required to retain possession of such a walking jewelry store.

The ostentation of the necklace could complement only the tastes of a woman like Madame du Barry. During one of the jeweler's visits to Du Barry's apartments, they let her peek at the paste design. As hoped for, she oohed with delight, picturing herself wearing this unsurpassed extravagance. The jewelers interpreted her enthusiasm as a signal that the transaction was a done deal.

Finding the perfect diamonds for this trophy required patience. The jewelers traversed the continent to amass flawless stones, some of which came from as far as Brazil. Before the necklace was completely assembled, the overly confident jewelers suffered a huge jolt of business reality. Louis XV died, convulsing the jeweler's financial empire, swallowing it into a huge sinkhole, and taking Madame du Barry with it. No longer having a sure bet for a purchase, the desperate fellows had to seduce another customer.

As an obvious back-up, Boehmer tried to entice the new king, Louis XVI, to purchase it for Antoinette. The jewelers timed their offer with the birth of Antoinette's first child in 1778. The king was tempted, but he didn't bite. Pooh on him! Despite their best efforts, no other big spenders stepped up to the purchase counter. Finally, the jewelers were convinced Louis would consent to anything on the birth of his heir in 1781. On this occasion, Louis did approach his wife about the necklace, but she declined the gift. Antoinette's taste veered toward sophisticated jewels, and this piece was too gaudy for her jewelry box.

With bankruptcy beckoning, the jewelers redoubled their efforts to lure the royal couple to purchase the mega-trinket. On one occasion, Monsieur Boehmer threw himself at Antoinette's feet, imploring her to rescue him lest he hurl himself into the Seine. Shocked that a merchant would behave in such an offensive manner, the queen ordered him to rise and to never mention the necklace again. She sensibly suggested that he break up the necklace and sell the stones individually. He would lose money, but at least remain solvent. In Boehmer's eyes such an option bordered on sacrilege; he stubbornly kept the necklace intact. After the jeweler exited, Antoinette informed her attending ladies that Monsieur Boehmer was no longer to be granted an audience unless she herself requested his presence. Like overpriced real estate that has been on the market too long, the necklace became stale goods.

"Big girls deserve big diamonds."
Elizabeth Taylor

Chapter 35

A Necklace Wreaks Devastation

None of this soap opera would have sprung to life without the daydreamer, Prince Louis Rohan. Who was this man of the Church who provided the ammunition for the first cannon shot to destroy the ruling class structure? At his core, Rohan mirrored a well-heeled playboy, not uncommon at that time for an upper crust churchman. Every member of the Rohan clan learned from birth to view himself as a contributing partner of a corporation. His family had decided that he would wear the red *zucchetto* of a cardinal; and with a bit of luck, become the king's prime minister like Cardinals Richelieu and Mazarin before him.

Louis XVI had promised the Rohan family at his coronation in 1775 that Prince Rohan would claim the post of Grand Almoner, the top churchman at the court of Versailles, once the current holder, Cardinal Roche-Aymon croaked. Even the most irreligious clergyman would have made a pilgrimage to Jerusalem to land a job that guaranteed frequent contact with the royal family.

In the intervening time, Antoinette tried unsuccessfully to convince Louis to appoint Rohan's younger brother, the archbishop of Bordeaux, to the post; as compensation, Rohan would receive a cardinal's hat to salve his ego. Antoinette figured that this arrangement should satisfy everyone—perhaps a good compromise someplace more rational, but not at Versailles. Louis agreed with his wife, but dared not to renege on his promise to the Rohan clan. The queen sounded off her displeasure in a letter to Vienna: "The Grand Almoner is at death's door; Prince Louis of Rohan will replace him in that office. I am really annoyed by this, and it will be much against his own inclination that the King will appoint him. If Rohan behaves as he always did, then we will have many intrigues."

When the eighty-year-old Cardinal Roche-Aymon died in October 1777, Prince Rohan got his dream job, the Grand Almoner of France. Rohan embraced his prestigious post with exuberance, expecting to be in everyone's good graces. Not so. Louis behaved cordially but remained distant, while the queen froze Rohan out of her daily life. After a year in his new job, the Vatican elevated Rohan to the cardinalate. Unable to prevent the Vatican's decision, the king held his nose in disgust.

Recognizing the queen was his key to becoming prime minister, the now Cardinal Rohan launched a charm offensive—it didn't make a dent. He repeatedly failed to attract Antoinette's attention; she glided by him as though he were a curtain of cellophane. How could he, a Rohan, be invisible? He prayed to find a way to patch things up with the queen. Behold Madame La Motte, the devil's answer to Rohan's prayers.

Madame Jeanne La Motte-Valois could trace her lineage to the Baron Saint-Rémy, a bastard son of King Henry II of the Valois dynasty. The illegitimate son and his offspring never achieved star status. The dirt-poor Jeanne luckily acquired a benefactress who verified Jeanne's heritage and petitioned Louis XVI to bestow on her a small pension.

Then, in 1780 Jeanne Valois, eight months pregnant with twin boys, resigned herself to marry the father, a penniless charmer, who styled himself Count Nicolas La Motte. In eighteenth century France, it was not uncommon for obscure gentlemen to adjust their titles upward to add extra oomph. After their twin boys died within days of their birth, the newlyweds accepted that their mutual avarice would be the only glue to hold together their cardboard marriage.

Jeanne was introduced to Cardinal Rohan while on a visit to her provincial roots in September of 1781. She filed a mental note that the prelate could serve as a prospect for future fleecing.

Soon after meeting the cardinal, the countess, with her hubby in tow, took the road to Paris. The count nabbed a commission in the regiment of the bodyguards of the Count Artois. With her husband's new posting, Madame La Motte wedged her high-heeled foot into the back door of the royal palace, determined to secure a position from the Crown in alignment with her Valois background. Resorting to a familiar trick at court, Jeanne fainted twice as the queen passed on the way to mass. Rats—the queen didn't even notice! But the same ploy worked on the king's sister Elisabeth who proved to be more responsive. Elisabeth advocated on Jeanne's behalf, resulting in a doubling of her pension. But to Jeanne, it was still peanuts; she set her sights on bigger prizes.

Like most scam artists, Madame La Motte convinced her victims of her sincerity. She stitched together a credible lie of being an insider of the queen's circle. She would be spotted walking from the Petit Trianon, confiding to those nearby that she had just departed the queen. Some gullible courtiers slipped money to the well-placed Jeanne, dreaming of gaining entrée to this off-limits enclave. At the French court, someone like Jeanne was known as a "facilitator," a go-to person to make desired contacts.

Jeanne's husband introduced her to a former army buddy and bottom-rung aristocrat, Rétaux Villette. The countess instantly clicked with the tall, handsome, and blue-eyed blond. The two miscreants shared a mutual passion for easy money. Jeanne was thrilled to learn of Rétaux's forgery skills. She engaged him to serve as her secretary, and so much more. Monsieur Villette soon shared the countess' bed, no doubt enhancing the dictation sessions.

In 1784 Jeanne renewed her acquaintance with Rohan. Bingo! The scheming countess recognized the cardinal as the big catch she dreamed of trapping in her net. She spent many evenings at Rohan's palace, and they were not saying the rosary. During pillow talk, the cardinal bemoaned the cold shoulder of the queen, thwarting his hopes of becoming prime minister. On cue, Jeanne soothed the cardinal and promised to put in a good word for him when she next saw the queen. Elated, Rohan envisioned his advancement to be in the bag.

Within days, the wily countess hinted to Rohan that Antoinette might be inclined to revise her poor opinion of him if he were to write the queen a *mea culpa* for his past transgressions. Rohan penned the required contrition, hoping for royal absolution. Soon afterward, Jeanne delivered to Rohan a note, supposedly from the queen, "I have read your letter. I am delighted to find you are not guilty. I am not yet able to grant you the audience you desire. When circumstances permit it, I will let you know. Be discreet." At last, a hoped-for reconciliation! So began an imaginary correspondence from Antoinette on perfumed stationery that caused the cardinal's hopes to soar and his common sense to fold.

Now about those fragrant letters. After receipt of the first note, a steady trickle of messages arrived from the queen, through the kind facilitator, Countess La Motte. The dainty notes on blue paper with gilded edges, written in pretty script, were not penned by the queen (whose penmanship could never be described as pretty). Jeanne dictated the letters to her sex-toy secretary, Villette. Everything seemed to be proceeding nicely. But then Rohan began pestering Jeanne for an audience with the queen. Jeanne had to devise a ruse.

The first step to success warranted a shopping trip. Jeanne sent her husband to the Palais Royal in Paris with specific buying instructions—a pretty hooker. The Palais Royal complex bankrolled the lavish lifestyle of the Duke of Orléans; he rented out the grounds of his palace as an upscale strip-mall with a naughty flavor. Shops and cafés attracted big crowds, while seditious conversations and banned publications flourished. So did ladies of easy virtue. The venue was off-limits to police because Orléans was a prince of the Blood.

Nicolas found just the girl for hire, sampling the merits of his purchase before bringing her home. The attractive twenty-four-year-old Nicole Leguay delighted Jeanne, who remarked that Nicole bore a resemblance to the queen. Jeanne sweetly, but deceptively, explained to Nicole that the queen requested her services for which she would be rewarded. Jeanne told Nicole she would be known as the Baroness Oliva for so long as she served the queen. Goodness, a noble lady's title! Nicole's head was swimming.

With her queen stand-in solidly on board, Jeanne informed the cardinal that the queen had consented to meet him in a midnight rendezvous in the park of Versailles. Any doubts of the cardinal concerning Jeanne's sincerity fizzled in a flash.

On the appointed evening a nervous Rohan approached a female figure who then handed him a rose. He recognized the style of the dress favored by Antoinette. And, in the darkness, her height and visage seemed to be that of the queen. The overwhelmed cardinal knelt before her and kissed the hem of her dress. The veiled lady whispered to let bygones be bygones. But poof, she vanished when Madame La Motte swooped down, warning the parties of approaching footsteps. As the cardinal floated all the way home with his cherished rose, Jeanne exulted that Rohan was now putty in her hands. Afterward, she and her fellow conspirators split their sides with laughter at the cardinal's gullibility. Picture it, the Grand Almoner of France kissing the hem of a whore!

A few days after the midnight tryst, Jeanne let it slip to Rohan that Antoinette, a bit short on pin money, wished to help an esteemed noble family down on their luck. She wondered if he could advance her the money to rescue this family. And it wasn't a small sum either. Although vastly wealthy, the cardinal was eternally short of cash. Yet, he obliged the request, securing a loan to cover the amount.

Several months later in November 1784, Jeanne approached the cardinal with a similar sob story, only this time for a larger amount. Incredibly, the cardinal forked over the money. But, in return, he insisted Jeanne arrange another meeting with the queen. As Jeanne counseled the cardinal to be patient, she celebrated. She splurged on a jumbo shopping binge with her pocketed alms, buying a country estate, pretty clothes, flashy jewelry, plush furnishings, and a gourmet stocked kitchen. But at her rate of spending, Jeanne calculated that she needed a bigger payday to permanently secure the good life.

Countess La Motte hosted a soirée in November 1784. Among her guests was a friend of the jeweler Boehmer, an attorney named Laporte. The lawyer cornered the countess and asked her to use chumminess with the queen to advance the purchase of the diamond necklace, and thereby rescue poor Boehmer from financial ruin. La Motte's instinctual greed shifted into overdrive, asking pointed questions about the value of the necklace. My God, she had found the meal ticket that could set her up for life. The jeweler brought the necklace to Jeanne's residence for examination. He harped on his need to unload it. Jeanne sighed sympathetically, promising to help him ink a deal. After the jeweler left, she cooked up a plan.

On January 5, 1785, Rohan was in Alsace when a fictitious message arrived from the queen, urging him to return to Paris and call on Madame La Motte for further instructions. Rohan rushed back to hear Jeanne tell him that Antoinette wished him to act as an intermediary to purchase a necklace without the king's knowledge. Jeanne explained that Antoinette feared her husband's disapproval. Rohan knew through the court grapevine that the queen had a reputation for being less than forthcoming with the king; Rohan could understand how such a purchase had to be kept hush-hush. Rohan spontaneously replied in the affirmative to the request. Obviously not one of his sharpest days.

Soon after the cardinal inspected the necklace. Rohan was floored at the armada of jewels. He was surprised that the queen desired such an ostentatious acquisition. But if this monstrosity set the price for becoming prime minister, then so be it. The cardinal drew up the contract in his own hand, setting the terms and payment schedules, whispering to the jewelers that he was acting on behalf of an anonymous lady.

The next day, Jeanne related that Antoinette expressed satisfaction with the terms, but the queen preferred to not sign the document. Jeanne also disclosed that the queen wished to wear the jewel on February 2, Candlemas

Day, a religious feast day. The entire transaction nearly unraveled as the cardinal applied the emergency brake, for once experiencing a glimmer of practicality. He wouldn't budge: either the queen signed the contract, or he would pull out of the deal. Acting fast, Jeanne got Villette to forge a hand written "Approved" next to each paragraph of the contract. Having never seen the queen's signature, La Motte instructed Rétaux to sign the contract as "Marie Antoinette of France."

A victorious Jeanne scampered off to the cardinal's residence with the signed contract. She explained to Rohan that the queen wanted him, and not the jewelers, to retain the agreement. Later, while the cardinal finalized the purchase, Madame La Motte was jumping up and down at home.

On the first of February, the relieved jewelers handed over the costly necklace to the scammed cardinal. At this moment, Rohan identified the great lady for whom the necklace was destined, declaring, "The Queen has made known her intentions to me." The jewelers were thunderstruck but had to feign ignorance until the queen wore the stunner in public.

That evening, the cardinal hurried to Jeanne's residence with the prized case. The slimy Villette, impersonating a valet of the queen's household, appeared at the countess' door to receive the necklace. While the cardinal hid in an alcove to observe the transfer, Villette presented a note authorizing him to accept the jewelry case on the queen's behalf. The countess graciously relinquished the necklace to the phony valet.

At this juncture, a comic-opera figure entered the mix, Count Alessandro Cagliostro. Of Sicilian origin, Cagliostro ranked as one of the most gifted charlatans of the century. Even though he looked like a dumpy troll, he could cast a charismatic spell on both the gullible and the skeptical. Being a card-carrying member of the Masonic Lodge reserved a spot for him on the Church's bad boys list. Like most shysters, he profited handsomely from the sale of his curative elixirs. His ability to read minds and induce hypnotic trances was legendary. Nowadays, he would be a TV preacher, saving souls as he fondled the Sunday collection in the plush seat of his private jet.

Rohan first encountered Cagliostro in Strasbourg in 1780, instantly becoming one of his fans. The cardinal's dealings with the fraud proved that the churchman excelled at placing his confidence in con artists. Rohan extolled the quack count as "his oracle, his guide, his compass." Cagliostro became an indispensable member of Rohan's entourage.

In January 1785 Cagliostro and his wife, Serafina, joined the cardinal in Paris, generating a huge buzz. Jeanne saw an opportunity to use the fake's talents to solidify her hold on Rohan. In February 1785 the queen was eight months' pregnant with her third child. Jeanne falsely claimed that the queen feared her pregnancy would end badly. Would Rohan implore his seer to peer into the queen's future? The charlatan staged a séance of smoke and mirrors, offering a message from the spirit world: the queen's delivery would be routine and problem free. Rohan clapped for joy. The countess expressed her eagerness to convey the rosy prediction to Antoinette. And it did prove to be an easy delivery for the queen at the end of March.

Candlemas Day came and went but Antoinette did not wear her new acquisition, disappointing the cardinal. To keep him on message, another scented letter arrived, ordering Rohan to temporarily leave Versailles because, "Your absence is necessary to afford me the opportunity to make my final preparations for your appointment to that high post to which you rightly aspire." With Rohan out of the way, the countess banished any misgivings with some serious retail therapy.

"I always say shopping is cheaper than a psychiatrist."
Tammy Faye Baker

Chapter 36

If It's Too Good to Be True ...

*A*fter Jeanne got her claws on the necklace, she broke up the diamond wonder—an ignoble au revoir to Boehmer's masterpiece. Soon thereafter, the Paris police received a report that a shady guy was trying to sell diamonds for a distressed compensation. The police collared the seller, Rétaux Villette, who protested that he was acting on orders of Countess La Motte-Valois, relative to the royal family. The police wisely backed off. To avoid further close calls with the law, Jeanne dispatched her husband to London with a satchel of diamonds to sell in a safer setting.

Jeanne realized that within months Rohan would discover that he had been conned. She wagered that the repercussions of such a scandal would paralyze Rohan's urge to scream foul, forcing him to pay for the necklace. Rohan would undoubtedly hate her forever, but she figured that her significant wealth would insulate her from harm.

The Grand Almoner was already getting antsy. It had been five months since he had forked over the necklace, and Antoinette had never worn it. He confronted the countess, suspecting that something seemed fishy. La Motte blurted out that a snag had popped up. The queen was experiencing buyer's remorse; she demanded a discount, or she would return the necklace.

Rohan sprang into action which was a lucky break for Jeanne who lacked a Plan B. If the jewelers had balked and demanded the return of the necklace, she would have been running for the border. Fortunately for Jeanne, on July 10 the cardinal convinced the hard-nosed Boehmer to accept the revised terms. A note to the queen, composed by Rohan but signed by Boehmer, cooed:

Your Majesty, it is with the utmost gratification, we venture
to think that the last arrangement proposed to us, to which we
have agreed with zeal and respect, affords a new proof of our
submission and devotion to Your Majesty's orders, and it gives us
great satisfaction that the most beautiful set of diamonds in the
world were about to adorn the greatest and best of queens.

Antoinette received this puzzling plaudit on July 12, not having a clue as to
its meaning. She mentioned it to her first lady of the bedchamber, Madame
Campan. Dismissing it as foolish dribble, she burned the note thinking
that Boehmer had finally gone bonkers. If Antoinette had read the note
carefully, she would have uncovered some serious hijinks. But the queen
was preoccupied with learning lines for her role as Rosine in Beaumarchais'
play *The Barber of Seville*. She would present this production in just a few
days at her theater at the Petit Trianon for a chosen few, and she could not be
bothered with such pettiness. She would later regret her haste to destroy this
warning buzzer of worse to come.

The entire heist began to unravel at alarming speed. Knowing that the first
payment was due on the first of August, the countess tipped off the cardinal
that the queen could not make the first payment until early October. But La
Motte claimed the queen would pay the accrued interest payments, money
that Jeanne had scraped together and gave to the cardinal. Rohan sped to the
jewelers with the paltry sum and unsettling news.

The apoplectic merchants hovered near emotional meltdown as they
rebuffed the cardinal, threatening to approach the queen directly. Knowing
he would not be granted an audience by the queen, Boehmer paid Madame
Campan an unannounced visit. He unloaded his story, insisting that the queen
owed him a lot of money for his necklace. At the same time, Madame La
Motte dropped a bomb on Bassenge. She coolly disclosed that the jewelers
had been deceived, admitting the contract was a forgery. She insisted that
Rohan would pay the tab rather than risk disgrace.

After dismissing the dazed Bassenge, Jeanne got busy packing up her
treasures. On August 6, after curtly telling the cardinal she and Antoinette
had a nasty spat, Jeanne left her flat in Paris for the false security of her
chateau in Bar-sur-Aube.

Matters verged on the breaking point when Madame Campan spilled
the beans to Antoinette of Boehmer's house call. At first, the queen was
speechless. But then, Antoinette grew alarmed and summoned Boehmer.

On August 9 Boehmer appeared at Trianon, informing Antoinette that he was aware of her dealings with Rohan to purchase the prized necklace. The queen vehemently denied Boehmer's story. But the jeweler held his ground, insisting, "Madame, there is no longer time for pretending. Condescend to admit that you have my necklace, and let some help be given to me, or my bankruptcy will bring the whole business to light." Stunned, the queen ordered the jeweler to write down everything that he knew about the transaction.

Antoinette exploded in a fury after she read Boehmer's declaration. How could Rohan dare to believe that she would employ him to act on her behalf? The queen huddled with the minister she trusted most, Baron Breteuil. The baron, who shared a long history of animosity with the cardinal, convinced Antoinette that the cardinal stole the necklace to pay his debts and allow the blame to fall on her. The queen trembled as she rushed off to inform Louis. The king was equally incredulous hearing the sketchy details. He knew that the cardinal led less than a saintly life, but this sordid activity seemed beneath even Rohan himself. Since the cardinal would be at court in two days to perform his priestly duties, the royal couple decided to summon him on that day to provide his account of the shameful business.

Monday, August 15, 1785, was a big day at Versailles and all over France. First, it was a religious holiday, celebrating the Assumption of the Virgin Mary; and second, it marked the name day of the queen. Versailles swarmed with courtiers, ambassadors, Parisians, and provincial visitors, all decked out in their Sunday best. Eager for the onset of festivities, guests jostled one another for the best position to glimpse the royals. This holiday intended to honor the queen's name would become the occasion that forever tarnished it.

The kick-off event would begin with mass in the royal chapel. In the overflowing crowd filling the Hall of Mirrors, the impressively robed Cardinal Louis Rohan stood first in line, awaiting the appearance of the sovereigns at ten in the morning. The idling attendees noticed the agenda of the day was not proceeding according to the immutable schedule of Versailles. To everyone's surprise, the chief valet summoned the cardinal to attend the king in his study.

Once inside the room, Rohan faced the king and queen, Foreign Minister Vergennes, and two other ministers, Baron Breteuil and Marquis Miromesnil, not exactly drinking buddies of the cardinal. With this group icily glaring at him, Rohan felt the frostbite setting in.

Louis bluntly asked the cardinal if he had purchased a necklace for the queen. The ashen prelate replied in the affirmative. The king handed Boehmer's report to Rohan, asking him to read it. As he grasped the king's desk to steady himself, the trembling cardinal admitted that a lady, Countess La Motte, engaged his services to purchase the necklace for the queen. Louis instructed Rohan to write a summary of his conduct in the adjoining room. The cardinal returned fifteen minutes later with a jumble of words that reflected his considerable agitation.

No longer able to retain her rage, Antoinette berated Rohan for believing that she would ever employ his services. She reminded him that she had never even glanced in his direction for the past eight years. The spastic Rohan became a puddle on the parquet as he protested that there was a signed contract bearing the queen's signature, Marie Antoinette of France. The queen angrily declared that such a contract was a forgery; she signed all documents as Marie Antoinette. The king scolded Rohan, reminding him that Their Majesties signed all documents with their baptismal names only, with no reference to nation; the cardinal of all people should have known that. With the room swirling, the cardinal confessed that he must have been hoodwinked. He offered to pay the jewelers the full sum for the necklace, imploring Louis not to expose his misdeed and bring shame on himself and his family. The king ordered Rohan to leave the room and await his orders; the unsteady cardinal resumed his place in the line of procession.

Louis had to make a decision fast. Most of all, he was suspicious of the cardinal's motives. Rohan himself had drafted the contract. And, Louis wasn't buying the cardinal's line about being ignorant of how the royals signed their names. The wounded countenance of the queen, the convincing arguments of Breteuil for arrest, as well as the cardinal's erring deeds, tipped the king's hand.

The doors to the king's study burst open. The incredulous courtiers heard Baron Breteuil bark out to the guards, "By orders of the King, arrest Monsieur the Cardinal." The hyperventilating crowd wildly convulsed, tinkling the palace chandeliers. Holiday celebrations no longer mattered.

As bedlam erupted among the spectators, the cardinal recollected himself to scribble a few lines in German. He slipped the note to his valet, who rushed to Rohan's palace in Paris. The note directed Rohan's secretary to burn the contents of a red portfolio in his desk that contained the forged letters from the queen. At the same time, Louis also wrote a note directing the Governor of the Bastille, Monsieur Launay, to house Cardinal Rohan until further notice. Once the cardinal's papers and the fraudulent contract were seized, he was hauled off to the Bastille. Rohan couldn't believe this was happening to him, the Grand Almoner of France.

The mind-blowing moment reverberated throughout the realm like an earthquake. The legal aftershocks in the months that followed would inflict even more havoc.

"Life resembles a novel more often
than novels resemble life."
George Sand

Chapter 37

The Juiciest Trial Ever

*I*mmediately an APB was issued for Madame La Motte. On August 17 the countess figured prominently at a dinner in an abbey near her chateau. During the meal, a tardy guest burst in, exploding a news grenade. He breathlessly recounted how Cardinal Rohan had been arrested at Versailles on the Feast of the Assumption. La Motte's appetite abruptly faded as she made her apologies and darted home. She began burning all letters written by the cardinal to the queen, along with any other indelicate messages. Feeling secure, she tucked herself into bed for a good sleep.

Early the next morning, Jeanne's sunny disposition got a nasty jolt. Officers of the Crown woke her with orders to escort her to Paris for several days of questioning. The officers seized her remaining papers as Jeanne dressed and packed some necessities for the trip. But before the countess walked out the door, her husband, home from London for a brief visit, removed every piece of jewelry she wore, lest her investigators sniffed any possible evidence. Monsieur La Motte promised to follow Jeanne to Paris

In truth, Nicolas correctly surmised if they took his wife into custody for "friendly" questioning, they would surely finger him. He packed his bags and took off to the French border from where he made a dash for England. He resumed selling jewels in London while living the life of a randy bachelor. French agents pursued Nicolas hoping to kidnap him but he cleverly eluded their grasp.

Jeanne was not so fortunate. She was plopped into the Bastille as soon as she reached Paris. Nicole Leguay and Rétaux Villette had discretely left town when news of Jeanne's arrest grabbed the headlines.

A week after the scandal broke, the queen wrote to her brother in Vienna relating the skimpy details. In this letter the queen speaks of courtiers who already perceived her as a party to the scandal. This suspicion alone should have been a warning to her to quietly bury the matter:

> No doubt, you have already heard, my dear brother, of the catastrophe involving the Cardinal Rohan. The Cardinal admits to having purchased, in my name and through the use of a signature he believed to be mine, a diamond necklace valued at 1,600,000 livres. He claims that he has been tricked by a Lady Valois of La Motte. This common adventuress has no standing at Court and has never had access to my company. She has been in the Bastille for two days, and although in her first interrogation she admits to intimate relations with the Cardinal, she denies having played any part in the necklace transaction. It should be noted that the terms of the contract are written in the Cardinal's hand. In the margin alongside each paragraph, the word, "Approved" appears in the same handwriting as that of the signature below "Marie Antoinette of France." Presumably this signature and the "Approved" notations were written by the aforesaid Valois of La Motte. Comparison is being made with specimens of her handwriting. It is also noteworthy that no attempt was made to imitate my script, and of course I never sign myself "of France." To all the Court here it is indeed a mystifying tale, in which I am supposed to have confided in the Cardinal a secret mission. All decisions relative to the handling of the matter were made by the King and me. The King sent for the Cardinal and questioned him in the presence of the Minister of the King's Household and the Minister of Justice. I was present at that meeting and was touched by the reason and firmness the King displayed in so trying a session. I hope that this affair can be wound up shortly, but I am determined that the whole horrid business be clarified before the eyes of the world.

A month later in September, the scandal still monopolized the queen's waking hours. Writing to her sister Maria Christina in the Austrian Netherlands, Antoinette described the female culprit:

> I have never so much as laid eyes on the La Motte woman, who is apparently an intriguer of the basest order, although not without a measure of attraction and flare, a dashing sort of creature. People say they have encountered her more than once on the secret back

stairway leading to my private apartments—obviously, a strategy on her part (and not new among intriguers here) to trick her dupes into believing she is on terms of intimacy with me.

Antoinette gave vent to her cynical feelings of having lived at Versailles for fifteen years. By now, the queen sized up most denizens of the palace, lumping them into three categories: the flakes, the fakes, and the snakes. No wonder she spent most of her time at Petit Trianon.

The Bastille under Governor Launay's tenure resembled a detention facility more than the mythical house of horrors. But the desolate isolation endured by the captives eroded anyone's hopes of deliverance from this outpost of hell. The cardinal received every consideration for a man of his rank, occupying a comfy suite of rooms. In addition, a chef and staff were engaged for his personal use, generously paid for with a per diem from the king. Rohan, who always sported elegant court clothes, converted to wearing strictly religious attire. He consoled himself with a steady stream of sympathetic visitors sometimes entertaining twenty guests at his dinner table. The only chains the cardinal wore were the solid gold ones that bore his pectoral cross.

Louis appointed two ministers, the trusty Vergennes and Army Marshall Castries, to conduct an investigation of the suspects in the Bastille. They commenced with Rohan who consistently stuck to his story of being duped. He admitted he had instructed his secretary to burn the forged letters he had received from the queen. Both ministers found him to be credible despite his foolish behavior. The king's investigators moved on to the Valois guest in the prison.

From the get-go Jeanne pinned all blame on the cardinal and especially, Count Cagliostro. The countess fingered the slithery Sicilian as the brains behind the scheme. She ranted how the count had ensnared the cardinal with his predictions. She denied any friendship with the queen, insisting Rohan concocted that tale to give himself a cover when dealing with the jewelers. She protested that she was a victim of the cardinal's lust for power. She never uttered the names Nicole Leguay or Rétaux Villette. She pointedly reminded her inquisitors that she hailed from the House of Valois, and as kin to the king, she deserved more respect and upscale prison frills.

When questioned about the remarkable rise in her standard of living, Jeanne's lies flowed easily. She asserted that the cardinal had engaged her and her husband to sell some diamonds on his behalf. She revealed that Rohan had occasionally given her generous sums, and she delicately confided that she and the cardinal shared physical intimacies. Furthermore, she pouted that she would have fled the country if she were a criminal. The ministers remained skeptical of her story, convinced she wasn't coming clean. However, they did visit Cagliostro in light of Jeanne's allegations relating to his participation in the hoax. During the search of his home, a quantity of diamonds and questionable papers were found among Serafina's personal effects that triggered the police to cart the couple off to the Bastille.

The questioning of Cagliostro proved to be more comical than relevant. He befriended his interrogators, absolving himself of any crimes regarding the sale of the necklace. He professed that he remained the staunchest of Catholics and regaled his listeners with stories of his upbringing in ancient Egypt. After a couple of hours, the investigators wondered aloud whether Cagliostro belonged in prison. Perhaps he'd be better placed in a benign asylum or on the stage of a theater.

While these key figures underwent interrogation, the royals at Versailles met with council ministers to strategize. The royal couple reminded those present that the cardinal's immense debts would be erased with the sale of the necklace. The queen voiced her outrage as the victim in this scam. Fed up with being maligned for years in outrageous pamphlets, Antoinette insisted that a public trial would exonerate her. She begged the king to salvage her honor and convince the people that she was not the devious witch they imagined her to be.

Some ministers predicted an unfriendly response to the Crown if the Parlement got involved. They argued that Louis, as the supreme arbiter in the kingdom, should settle the matter himself. The queen countered by suggesting the king allow the cardinal to choose his form of justice: Parlement or Louis. Antoinette felt confident that Rohan would opt for a public trial, fearing Louis' punishment. While Louis' gut nudged him to resolve the matter unilaterally, he agreed to this arrangement to placate the queen.

The Rohan capos felt that Louis XVI had overstepped his authority by shaming their family at the prodding of his foreign wife. They hired the best lawyer in the kingdom, the mega rotund Guy-Jean-Baptiste Target. The courtroom superstar laid out their options: "If the means of showing your innocence can be found, then the Parlement is preferable, even if it means being subjected to the lengthy humiliations of a criminal investigation. If measures taken by your enemies will prevent you from making your defense, you must choose the smaller of the two evils; in that case, it's worth placing yourself at the mercy of the King." On September 5 Rohan announced that he would seek a public trial—a gamble that he prayed would work to his advantage.

Meanwhile, handwriting experts reported their preliminary findings to investigators. Based on the samples of the then suspects and accomplices, the experts concluded that a close buddy to the cardinal was the likely forger. Since the contract was written by the cardinal, evidence implied that Rohan got his pal to forge the queen's authorizations and signature. The case against the cardinal grew credible legs.

The affair of the necklace dominated conversations in France and abroad. The cardinal and Jeanne seemed the guilty parties, but suspicions encircled the queen. Popular opinion already speculated that Antoinette staged the scam to permanently discredit Rohan. Thanks to the nasty pamphlets that wallpapered the kingdom, it wasn't a stretch to believe that Antoinette could have behaved like a low class shopgirl, cavorting in the bushes late at night.

Louis' family did not exactly have the king's back. The king's brother Count Provence, no fan of Antoinette, perceived the danger of a trial. He later assessed the situation commenting, "The Queen wished for a judgment which would publish the truth. She was wrong, because in such affairs it is better to let them die quietly of themselves. The Queen, however, only listened to her wounded heart."

The royals seemed abandoned by just about everyone, including the international community. On September 27, 1785, the Amsterdam Gazette recorded the public pulse: "Everyone is outraged at such a blatant act of absolute despotism as the seizure of His Eminence Prince Rohan, an act attributed by many people to the personal animosity of a vengeful Cabinet minister." Even the queen's brother Joseph II seemed ambivalent, confiding in a letter to Count Mercy: "I have always known the Grand Almoner to be inconceivably light-minded and hopelessly extravagant; but I must avow that I hesitate to believe him capable of such a piece of rascality, of so black a crime as that of which he is now accused." With Antoinette's brother not firmly in her corner, perhaps the queen should have rethought her demand for public exoneration.

The queen's ardent admirer, Count Fersen, also chimed in, informing King Gustavus III: "The tales about the Cardinal especially in the provinces are fantastic. Most people seem to think that the necklace transaction and the forgery of the Queen's name are not the real reasons for his imprisonment; instead they attribute it to secret motives, which is certainly not the case. The most popular theory is that it was all an intrigue between the Queen and the Cardinal, that she pretended to dislike him, the better to conceal their little game, that actually he was very much in her good graces, and that she did commission him to arrange the necklace purchase for her."

The seismic shift in public opinion pulverized the Crown's image. To underscore this public perception, a little ditty was hummed on nearly every street corner in Paris:

> Our Holy Father reddened him,
> The King and Queen blackened him,
> Madame La Motte has smeared him,
> but the Parlement will whiten him.

The public's verdict already seemed fixed—the cardinal was being framed. The British ambassador, the Duke of Dorset, pinpointed the feelings of the French, weighing in, "The people in general, unaccustomed to events of such extraordinary nature, have imagined that there must be some intrigue of State at the bottom, and that very great personages are implicated in it." This was the price for demanding a public trial. And Louis and Antoinette would be flying this trial solo.

> "For every man there exists a bait
> which he cannot resist swallowing."
> *Friedrich Nietzsche*

Chapter 38

The Case Comes to Life

The Crown presented to the Paris Parlement the preliminary interrogations of the three detainees in the Bastille in September 1785. The focus of the Crown's charges did not revolve around the forgery. Rather, their argument emphasized the crime of *lèse-majesté*, a major disrespect to the queen's honor—a far more serious offense than forgery. The Parlement appointed two of its own investigators, Messieurs Titon and Dupuis, to compile a file of evidence. Once completed, this report would be presented to the Paris Parlement for its consideration. All defendants would now be required to engage the services of a lawyer.

Target and three additional hotshot attorneys already represented Cardinal Rohan. Madame La Motte recruited Monsieur Doillot, an experienced attorney, who gallantly defended his bewitching client. Count Cagliostro hired Messieurs Brazon and Thilorier to serve as his legal advisers, but he proved to be his own best defense.

In a tedious process stretching from September to December 1785, a long list of witnesses, uncovered during the preliminary investigation, faced Parlement's two investigators.

Luckily for Rohan, his devoted secretary, Reverend Georgel, worked fast digging up dirt on Jeanne. He got a tip to chat up Friar Nicolas Loth, Jeanne's neighbor, confessor, and general gofer. As a frequent visitor to Jeanne's home, Loth had witnessed numerous irregular activities. But he refused to squeal on the countess, prompting Rohan's lead attorney, Monsieur Target, to join the conversation. After being threatened with a prolonged stay in the Bastille, the uncooperative friar blabbed non-stop.

Loth unveiled the following smoking guns: Jeanne kept for herself the money the cardinal had given her on behalf of the queen's charities; the evening when a woman named D'Oliva did a credible job of impersonating the queen; occasions when Jeanne closeted herself with Rétaux Villette forging letters; the jewelers remunerating the countess for finding a buyer for the necklace; and, most damning of all, Monsieur La Motte taking lots of diamonds to London. According to Loth, hubby La Motte, loverboy Villette, and the D'Oliva woman left France in August. Friar Loth proved to be the mother lode of crucial information that sparked an international dragnet to track down the outstanding suspects. The scope of the scandal became more unbelievable with each passing day. And Loth provided a life jacket for the cardinal's defense.

Rohan's prospects got another boost when he learned that Jeanne had burned his steamy letters to the queen. Rohan's immediate concern centered on the jewelers. The cardinal learned in early November that the king had refused to compensate the jewelers, judging the purchase a fraud. Rohan had to quickly come to terms with the jewelers lest they sought justice through the legal system. A compromise deal was brokered with the king's assistance. The cost of the necklace and accruing interest payments would be amortized from the annual revenues the cardinal received from his Abbey of Saint Vast. With extra belt tightening, the colossal debt of the necklace would be paid off. The creditors signed on to this arrangement. The jewelers avoided bankruptcy, and the cardinal escaped their damaging testimony.

Another break in the case happened on October 19, 1785, when authorities in Brussels nailed Nicole Leguay and her worthless boyfriend, Toussaint Beausire. Both were hustled back to Paris, but Nicole's boyfriend was released when investigators discovered that his sole transgression was impregnating Nicole. The two outstanding suspects, Nicolas La Motte and Rétaux Villette, continued to elude capture. They would prove more difficult to collar, thereby prolonging the beginning of the trial. All the parties involved groaned at the delay.

Titillation stirred the starchy Parlement with the uncensored revelations of Jeanne's domestic staff, particularly from her personal maid, Rosalie Briffault. This pert coquette described a household in financial chaos that overnight went from sparse kitchen cupboards to the best champagne. She described the visits of the cardinal to Madame's boudoir, conceding that the door was kept slightly ajar. The dishy maid also confirmed that her boss entertained an array of male admirers. Finally, she thrilled about the night she had assisted the countess in dressing up Nicole Leguay for a risky rendezvous—just the racy stories that the newspapers loved to print. Overnight saucy Rosalie's portrait became the hottest item for sale.

One evening, a lady entered the Palace of Justice causing a commotion. It was Countess du Barry, the woman for whom the necklace was originally intended. Out of the limelight for ten years, the spectators took in her still smoldering charms. When asked her age, the cougar countess teasingly scolded the examining magistrate, saying no gentleman would ask that question of a lady. The humorless official replied that he would list her age as fifty. The sex siren did not take offense but playfully countered that the prickly magistrate should enter sixty because "that would add some fun to the proceedings." Everyone in the courtroom laughed, and the transcripts championed Du Barry; Madame was listed as being thirty-five. (Du Barry was actually forty-two at the time of the trial.)

During her interrogation, the former mistress testified that Madame La Motte had approached her for employment as a lady's companion several years past and, not long after, Jeanne appealed to Du Barry to intercede on her behalf for an increase in her pension. This testimony poked holes into La Motte's version of how she pulled off such a lavish lifestyle.

By December 1785 the last of the witnesses had testified. The new year would begin with the interrogation of the suspects by the Parlement's investigators. Meanwhile, everyone at Versailles and beyond its bubble spoke of nothing but the impending trial. Vergennes, the workaholic foreign minister, sighed how weary he felt by the trial hoopla. He expressed the frustrations of many in a note to an ambassador: "Happy are they whose occupations shelter them from hearing from morning until evening, arguments for and against the same matter which makes everyone feel imprisoned, for no reason and no useful purpose."

Even Antoinette was not immune to the persistent hype stoked by the scandal. All through the proceedings, the queen followed the process closely. In a letter in December, she vented to her brother:

> From the moment of the Cardinal's arrest, I was sure that he
> would never appear again at our Court, but the trial, which will
> last several months, may have consequences even more serious.
> The judicial procedure of the Parlement began with the issuance of
> writs of arrest suspending all of his civil rights and functions until
> the pronouncement of judgment in the case. Writs were also issued
> for the charlatan Cagliostro and his wife, for the La Motte woman,
> and for Oliva, a streetwalker. What company for a Grand Almoner
> of France, a cardinal of the house of Rohan!

⚜   ⚜   ⚜

The formal investigation of the suspects commenced in January 1786 and would not wrap up until May. The defendants were prohibited any outside visitors once the official interrogations began. This was particularly punishing for the cardinal—no more dinner parties for his supporters. Rohan sank into a depression, feeling cut off from his fan base. The two investigators reported their findings to the members of the Parlement in February 1786. At this juncture, the judges could have released some or all of the suspects, but they ruled that the evidence against all four suspects pointed to serious criminal action. The defendants would be summoned again to offer any amendments to their testimony. After that review, they would face witnesses individually and finally each other.

Lawyers were not permitted to accompany the accused in the courtroom, forcing them to advise their clients privately before any hearings. An attorney's big moment would come when he presented his trial brief. These highly-anticipated documents presented a defense plea for the consideration of the Parlement. Once the magistrates of the Parlement acknowledged receipt of the trial brief, custom allowed the contents to be published, which could make or break a lawyer's career. The attorney's most critical decision hinged on the date to publish, hoping to corral the largest favorable response. In this sensational case, the merits of each trial brief were passionately debated in sales shops, swanky salons, and the eighteen hundred coffee houses dotting Paris. Often, briefs were distributed free of charge. When each attorney's office announced the release of a brief, a stampede arose to snag a copy.

On December 4, 1785, Monsieur Doillot, Jeanne's attorney, took the plunge first. The brief sparked a sensation; Doillot distributed free of charge more than four thousand copies to the feisty crowd besieging his office. As expected, Jeanne's emotional brief tilted the pendulum in her direction, momentarily stoking sympathy for her and exposing the cardinal to the derision of the masses. Target counseled the cardinal not to fret; Madame La Motte would get her payback. As the Christmas and New Year holidays approached, the other lawyers waited for a less distracting moment to lure the attention of the public.

Cagliostro's lawyers published his brief in February 1786. Three thousand copies were snapped up within hours. Most of Cagliostro's defense read like a tale out of the *Arabian Nights*. But cleverly sandwiched between these stories were remarks by Cagliostro that would incite the public and offend the Crown. One portion, in particular, electrified the masses who dreamed of a future assault on the hateful Bastille:

On the subject of Madame La Motte, I am convinced that the
grave harm she has done me, she has done less out of hatred than
out of desperation to shift the blame from her shoulders to those
of another. Indeed, once I am assured that my own innocence has
been recognized, I shall petition His Majesty the King to grant
clemency to the unfortunate La Motte. Nor would clemency
constitute an offense to justice. For, no matter the Countess' guilt,
she has already been punished. Ah, you may take my word for it,
there is no crime in the world which is not expiated by six months
in the Bastille.

One immediate benefit of Cagliostro's brief concerned the fate of his
wife, Serafina, who had been scooped up with him in the same dragnet
that hurled him into prison. He insisted that she be freed immediately. The
public vehemently agreed and the Parlement felt forced to release Madame
Cagliostro who played no part in the scheme. For more than a week after her
return home, Serafina patiently dealt with the stream of carriages jamming
her street with well-wishers dropping by to congratulate her.

Of all the trial briefs, Nicole Leguay's achieved the most notoriety. More
than twenty thousand copies disappeared in a jiffy. Her attorney, Maître
Blondel, depicted her as an innocent, who was abused by the chief architect
of the scandal, Madame La Motte. The narrative proved an easy sell to the
public who nodded in agreement at how the aristos always held the advantage
over the lower classes. Her attorney rhapsodically repackaged the image of
his client from stained whore to unblemished angel. As in Cagliostro's brief,
Nicole detailed her distress at being held in the hated Bastille. She became
the poster-girl for the injustices associated with the Crown. Bets abounded
over who would be the lucky young buck to win her hand upon her release
from prison:

Walled off as I am from all humanity, shut up in these high towers
away from the world, I await with trust and confidence the decision
on my fate. Even here in this dark prison, this dread fortress cut off
from sight and sound of mankind, like a desert wasteland of silence
and solitude entombed within the heart of the teeming capital—
even here I cling to my faith that I will hear the words of cheer
and solace ring out: She is a citizen of France and is entitled to the
protection of the law. She is an innocent and shall so be declared
by the due processes of law.

At last, in mid-April 1786, after languishing in a limbo of word wrangling
among his legal team. Rohan's attorneys distributed his brief to an impatient

public. The longest of all the briefs, it was purposely issued in a limited edition of a thousand copies. Target predicted that this would cause a riot by the public, and he was right—the scarce copies were snapped up and then scalped for exorbitant sums. Target presented the cast-off cardinal as a wounded man, sustained solely by his devotional prayers. Public opinion pitied the abused cardinal, probably fettered in chains. For the fashion-driven French, the season's hottest colors in 1786 were yellow (for the straw of the Bastille), and red (for the color of the cardinal's attire). Hats and accessories with these colors predominated as the season's must haves.

A major break in the case exploded when the fugitive, Rétaux Villette, was apprehended in Geneva in March 1786. He must have been out to lunch when he chose Geneva, that Swiss beacon of tight-laced Calvinism, to blend in unnoticed. Predictably, a rowdy Villette provoked a brawl and got tossed into the clinker, where his true identity was unveiled. Negotiations between Versailles and Geneva facilitated Villette's extradition to Paris and the waiting drawbridge of the Bastille. With Villette in custody, the trial could commence in earnest. Rétaux's reluctant testimony would prove to be the damnation of Jeanne and the salvation of Rohan.

The trial of Cardinal and Company officially opened on May 22, 1786, before the sixty-four judges of the Paris Parlement. The tension was unbearable as Count Mercy explained to Joseph II: "The trial of Cardinal Rohan, still the focal point of interest here, builds inevitably to its climax. As is easily comprehensible, the curiosity of the Parisian public is at a fever pitch in anticipation of the terms of the judgment to be handed down in this trial which is unprecedented in the annals of French history."

The transcripts of the interrogations were read aloud in the courtroom for eight days, during which time the accused were barred from attending. Behind the scenes, deals were being brokered to win over a judge's vote, by either the king's allies or those in the Rohan camp. The queen weighed in with her own sentiments, confiding to several judges that "the Cardinal Rohan is the enemy of my rest and my reputation." Some of the judges shared the king's belief that the cardinal saw the theft of the necklace as a way out of his immense debt. Even the king's minister, Vergennes, who planted his flag in Rohan's camp, also succumbed to doubts, confessing to one of his ambassadors, "It is rare that someone with so much wit could have been so stupidly duped."

On May 30, 1786, at eight in the morning, the moment arrived for the magistrates to interrogate the suspects. The packed courtroom included international reporters describing every nuance and word exchanged that day. When each suspect appeared, he or she was required to kneel before the magistrates on a very low bench. Like most judges, their middle name was God.

Rétaux Villette, dressed in black like a Lenten penitent, was the first to be summoned. The imposing scene convulsed him into delivering a lifesaving performance. He admitted to all of his crimes, expressing his remorse, with tears glistening in his eyes. Many expected that his offending hand, guilty of the forgeries, would be chopped off. Yet, his earnest contrition before the magistrates would sway the outcome of his sentence. As he exited the courtroom with his head bowed, the judges commanded Countess La Motte to enter.

Jeanne waltzed into the chamber like a thoroughbred anticipating a triumph. She entered, dressed for success—tailored, stylish, but not flashy. She did a double take when she comprehended that she was expected to kneel during the proceedings. Valois descendants did not submit to such a humiliation. Instead of kneeling, she managed the lounging position of a courtesan—how appropriate. This lack of submission before the magistrates did not pass unnoticed—already a red flag against her.

Jeanne should have copied Rétaux's submissive style. Instead, she behaved as though she were a chum of the judges. She spouted one lie after another even when the evidence suggested otherwise. She admitted to dressing up Nicole and staging the rendezvous with the cardinal in the gardens of Versailles, but it was all a lark she claimed. Unfortunately for her, the judges weren't laughing. As usual for Jeanne, the blame rested with the others. To deflect attention from the overwhelming evidence against her, she hinted that certain secrets would prove her innocence. But they could not be disclosed in deference to the honor of the queen. This tease backfired on La Motte while exposing the queen to even more ridicule. The countess raised every shackle in the courtroom with the false allegation that Antoinette and Rohan addressed one another with the familiar pronoun "*tu*"—a liberty reserved only for the truly intimate. The courtroom erupted into a hail of discord, just what the countess intended. Jeanne had no idea how much damage she had done to her defense as she breezed out of the courtroom.

Next, came the main attraction, Cardinal Rohan. A lingering murmur greeted the appearance of the prelate. Rohan made a reverential splash as he entered the courtroom, decked out in every distinction of his religious office. The cardinal looked frail, a bit like Jesus on the way to Calvary, thanks to Target's coaching. The cardinal was invited to sit rather than kneel, a huge concession on the part of the magistrates.

Rohan convincingly answered all questions that were put to him. He rejected the charge that he knowingly recognized the queen's signature as a forgery. He acknowledged his blunder of failing to seek confirmation of the purchase from the king, believing that the queen had wanted to keep the deal under wraps. As for the serious charge of disrespecting the honor of the queen, Rohan protested that he was merely responding with sincerity to serve the queen. He admitted to only two errors in the affair: he chastised himself for being a tool of Madame La Motte's trickery, and his misplaced zeal to regain the queen's favor, nothing more. When he rose to leave the courtroom, he bowed to the magistrates. Rohan knew his manners, a talent that merited extra points in eighteenth-century France.

Following the cardinal's testimony, Nicole Leguay took her turn on the kneeler. At the moment Nicole appeared before the court, she had to breast feed her newborn baby boy—a very tender, staged distraction. Sobbing, she blurted out her responses to the few gentle questions that were posed to her. The judges contemptuously dismissed the prosecutor's charges that Nicole was a scheming whore; they paternally excused her, as some of the observers dabbed at the tears in their eyes. The poor lamb.

As a finale, the burly Count Cagliostro appeared like a streaking comet in the night sky, clad in a neon green and gold ensemble (and it wasn't even Halloween!). He immediately entranced the courtroom. When asked to identify himself, Cagliostro solemnly intoned, "I am a Noble Voyager, Nature's Unfortunate Child." The judges exhaled in relief; now the entertainment portion of the trial would begin.

The prosecutor asked if he was guilty of any crime. Cagliostro paused, sighed a regretful yes: "One alas, I murdered Pompey." But he protested that the deed was unwillingly performed, since it was forced on him by the Pharaoh Ptolemy.

The prosecutor brilliantly participated in the fantasy, replying in a deadpan voice, "I have never heard of that murder. It must have been during my predecessor's term of office."

Cagliostro radiated solid Teflon; no misdeed would stick to him. Cagliostro's unintelligible answers mesmerized even the seasoned magistrates. No one would dare find the count guilty of anything; he was an accomplished showman, but not a criminal. As the costumed Cagliostro exited stage left, all eyes shifted to the judges. It was up to them to decide the fate of this oddly mixed group of roomies confined in the Big House.

> Peter Marshall: According to that old song,
> what's breaking up that old gang of mine?
> Paul Lynde: Anita Bryant.
> *Hollywood Squares TV Show*

Chapter 39

The Joint Is Jumping

On May 31, 1786, the long-awaited decision of the Parlement was to be announced. The streets around the courthouse overflowed with spectators by five in the morning. Before the court was called to order, nineteen stone-faced top guns of the Rohan clan, dressed in black entered the courtroom, bowing to the judges. Never did humility package itself in such ostentatious pride; the judges were impressed.

As dawn broke, the Prosecutor General, Joly Fleury, unsealed the seven recommendations to the court that comprised a summary of the Crown's wishes in the resolution of the case. He read each one aloud for the magistrates' consideration, beginning an exhausting day of deliberations that would end with the weary judges rendering their verdicts. Once again, the defendants were banned from attending the session. The first six decisions would all be unanimous and more or less in accord with the recommendations of the Crown; the seventh verdict would be the tricky one.

First, the sales contract and the queen's signature were declared forgeries. This was the easiest of all the decisions based on the evidence at hand.

Second, the Parlement determined Rétaux Villette to be an amoral drifter and an indulgent accessory in the case. His contrite appearance before the judges the previous day saved his pretty butt; he was banished for life from France, and his goods were forfeited to the king. He was lucky to get off with such a lenient sentence.

The third verdict dealt with Nicole Leguay. The queen's impersonator starred as the darling of the courtroom. Any punishment against her would have incited a vehement backlash. A ditty, reflecting popular sentiment, circulated all over Paris, equating Antoinette's majesty as synonymous for the Reigning Strumpet:

> Says the Queen—Ah, you foxy little flirt,
> it suits you well to play my role as Queen;
> Replies Mademoiselle Leguay—
> And why not, my Sovereign?
> You so often play mine!"

The Parlement acquitted Nicole Leguay on the grounds of insufficient evidence.

Number four revealed Count Cagliostro's destiny. He was acquitted without reprimand from the court, totally exonerated. This was the reward for making yourself completely credible while expressing yourself unintelligibly. Now that's real magic.

The fifth verdict was a stiff one. The absent Nicolas La Motte was condemned in absentia to be flogged and beaten naked, with rods; to be branded with a hot iron on the right shoulder with the letters G.A.L., signifying a life sentence in the king's galleys. He also had to fork over all of his earthly goods to the king. You could hear an audible hiss of delight with this sentence—no public sympathy for him. The count literally got away with grand theft as he remained a fugitive, unscathed, in England.

Verdict number six stood out as the harshest of the lot. Madame La Motte was condemned to be stripped naked, flogged with rods and to be branded on both shoulders with a hot iron with the letter V—*voleuse* being the French word for a female thief. She would spend the rest of her life in prison. All of her ill-gotten goodies would be forfeited to the king. This verdict was not easily achieved because some magistrates recommended a more extreme sentence for Jeanne—death on the gallows.

But it was bye-bye harmonious voting when it came to the last verdict concerning the fate of Cardinal Rohan. The courtroom burst into a volley of verbal assaults the moment the prosecutor uttered the last syllable of his recommendation. The sticking point centered on the prosecutor's demand that Rohan "was guilty of criminal temerity, of disrespect to the sacred persons of the Sovereigns; in betaking himself to the Grove of Venus in the belief that he was there to meet Her Majesty, The Queen of France; and to the effect that he has contributed to the deception of the jewel merchants by allowing them to believe that the Queen had knowledge of the necklace transaction."

After hours of rancorous debate, the judges concluded that Rohan did not act with malicious intent in the purchase of the necklace. Rather, he was the victim of a monumental scam. They believed the cardinal when he quipped, "I employed all the resources of my intelligence to prove that I am an ass." Where the judges differed sharply was on the question of *lèse-majesté*—whether the cardinal disgraced the honor of the queen. For hours, the magistrates exchanged insults with one another over this issue. To spike the tension in the courtroom, the wary judges were sensitive to the thousands of Parisians outside the building, impatiently clamoring for the cardinal's acquittal.

The Parlement announced the verdict at ten in the evening. By a slim margin of three votes, the court cleared Rohan of all charges, proclaiming him innocent. With this decision, the judges implied that, given Antoinette's questionable reputation, it was reasonable to believe that she would arrange a tryst in the dark of night. The judges simply echoed the feelings of most Frenchmen, delivering an unprecedented slap in the queen's face that propelled every pulse to soar.

The verdicts sped from the courtroom faster than an assassin's bullet, stoking jubilation throughout Paris. The judges departed the court to the cheers of the populace. Cardinal Rohan was summoned to the court to learn the verdict. Overwhelmed with joy, the frenzied crowd escorted him to his mansion where he delighted in the acclaim of thousands; his freedom was all too brief when he was ordered to spend one more night in the Bastille to await the king's orders.

Louis XVI reacted swiftly, but unevenly, to the rulings of the court. The king stripped Rohan of his offices at Versailles and exiled Rohan to his abbey at Chaise Dieu. Noting his distaste for Masons and ESP quacks, Louis also expelled Cagliostro from his kingdom. Besides these actions, the king did nothing more. Louis lamely lamented, "The affair has been decided outrageously. The Parlement perceived in the Cardinal only a prince of the Church. While what they ought to have seen was a man unworthy of his ecclesiastical character, a great nobleman degraded by his shameful connections." By not punishing the Parlement for the offensive verdict, Louis signaled a green light to disrespect the monarch without adverse consequences. The royal couple would suffer the most among the participants in the diabolical scheme.

Antoinette felt betrayed when she heard of the verdicts. She recoiled at the implicit message signaling her as a foul foreigner polluting the throne of France. She barricaded herself in her apartments for several days, bemoaning the malevolent star, the Lisbon Curse, that despoiled her life. She jotted a note to Gabrielle Polignac: "Come and weep with me, come and console my soul, my dear Polignac. The verdict which has been given is a terrible insult. I am bathed in tears of grief and despair. I can be satisfied with nothing when perversity seems to search for every means to torture my soul." Antoinette was an emotional mess.

"In scandal as in robbery,
the receiver is always as bad as the thief."
Lord Stanhope, the Fourth Earl of Chesterfield

Chapter 40

A Messy Aftermath

$\mathcal{F}$ollowing the verdicts, the lives of the key players in The Affair of the Diamond Necklace took different paths.

Once Rohan disappeared in disgrace, public opinion viewed him as a twice victimized example of the tyranny of the Crown. Although declared innocent, he was still punished after spending nine months in the Bastille. In keeping with the bizarre nature of the entire scandal, Rohan executed an about-face in behavior after he left the allure of Paris. He became a model priest, earning respect from his fellow clerics. In December 1788 the king relaxed some of the restrictions of the cardinal's exile, allowing Rohan to make a triumphant return to his diocese of Strasbourg. In a more curious twist of fate, he would be elected to the First Estate of the Clergy when the Estates General met in 1789 at Versailles. When turmoil erupted about the clerical oath to the constitution in 1790, he resigned his seat in the National Assembly and emigrated from France to his estate in Baden across the Rhine. There, he lived an exemplary life and died tranquilly in his bed in 1803.

The punishment of Madame La Motte took place on June 21, 1786. The gutsy adventuress knew that she had been found guilty but remained unaware of her sentence. Charles-Henri Sanson, the king's executioner, attempted to keep the time and place of the punishment under wraps. But word leaked out, attracting scores of the curious. At five in the morning, Sanson led the delusional Jeanne, dressed for a tea party in a silk gown of brown and white, into the courtyard of the Palace of Justice where the scaffold awaited. Her Valois superiority disintegrated as she heard the executioner read her sentence. Morphing into a feral animal, Jeanne had to be restrained. She was stripped naked, with her voluptuous figure catching the excited eyes of many male spectators, and then she was laid on her stomach and whipped. Next came the horrifying branding of the letter "V" on both shoulders. The writhing La Motte screamed that it was the queen who should be branded, not her. Most in the crowd couldn't agree more. The smell of the burnt flesh got stuck in everyone's nostrils, elevating Jeanne to the status of royal victim.

La Motte's sentence marked a missed opportunity for Louis to intervene. The king's clemency would have enhanced the monarchy's reputation rather than this medieval torture. Anger against Parlement's beastly sentence reverberated through the city along with blame directed at the heartless queen.

After her harrowing ordeal, La Motte was transferred to the women's prison, Salpêtrière. Dressed in a coarse gray dress, she occupied the section of the prison reserved for hardened female prisoners. A devoted camp of admirers cropped up during her incarceration. It became fashionable for the elite to visit the countess and offer solace. The Duchess of Orléans organized a charity to raise funds to ease the countess' dreadful prison conditions. And the biggest surprise of all was when Madame Lamballe, the queen's bosom buddy, stopped by one day to express her sympathies.

The scandal's notoriety did not fade with Jeanne's imprisonment. A year into her sentence, Jeanne escaped from Salpêtrière on June 8, 1787. Such a feat could not have succeeded without the aid of highly-placed supporters. Rumors hinted that the Duke of Orléans was involved; whether true or not, he applauded the outcome. Jeanne fled to England where she caught up with her husband. While their reunion was cordial, their marriage was over.

Safe in London, Madame La Motte set to work writing her story, "The Justified Memoirs of the Countess of Valois of La Motte." In these pages, she flipped on her nuclear bitch switch, targeting Antoinette with the toxic fallout. Jeanne sensationally exposed her victimization by all the players in the scandal, but she focused on the evil, greedy, and sex-crazed queen. Published in 1789 as the Revolution was gaining momentum, this revenge tell-all confirmed Antoinette's belief that a curse trailed her every move. Madame La Motte died in London on August 23, 1791, succumbing to injuries she suffered after falling from a third story window while trying to evade creditors pounding at her door. She died as she lived—a loose cannon chasing the elusive aura of nobility while ruining the lives of all she met along her way.

Aware of the harsh sentence awaiting him in France, Monsieur La Motte slipped out of London and hid in Scotland. He thwarted the efforts of detectives to have him hauled off to France to face judgment. In August

1789 Nicolas boldly returned to France with encouragement from Parisian radicals where the Revolution was turning the known world upside down. Nicolas gambled that a more favorable court would expunge his verdict. It took several years, but in 1792 the sentence against him was reversed. Of all the swindlers involved in the robbery, he literally got away with his crime. Citizen La Motte eventually returned to his hometown, Bar-sur-Aube; he remarried and supported himself with a succession of petty jobs. He outlived all the parties to the melodrama, dying in Paris in 1831 at age seventy-six.

Nicole Leguay's future seemed radiant following her release from prison. Her gallant attorney, Maître Blondel, offered his residence as a safe haven. She delighted in a micro-burst of celebrity, only to be dumped into obscurity. In April 1787 she married her deadbeat lover, Toussaint Beausire. The marriage quickly disintegrated after Toussaint physically abused his wife and then abandoned her. Nicole died in 1789 at age twenty-eight, destitute, and a charity case in a convent.

After his banishment from France, Rétaux Villette, the forger of the scented letters, made his way to Venice. He wrote his memoirs in 1790, claiming he was "used by all and abandoned by all." Not surprisingly, his life spiraled into a pit of destructive living. In 1797 he died when he was thirty-nine, penniless and friendless.

Count Cagliostro and Serafina first sought refuge in England. There, he published an open letter to the French, exhorting them to awake from their slumber. This letter trumpeted a call for revolt to revamp the corrupt system of government. For once, his skills as a seer proved true. He foresaw the demolition of the hated Bastille to be replaced by a public promenade. He further predicted the convocation of the Estates General that would usher in great changes in France. His letter caused a sensation when it was released in Paris, inciting calls for reform. After leaving England, Cagliostro led a nomadic existence until he unwisely entered the Papal Estates. He was hauled off to Rome to face the Court of the Inquisition. His Masonic affiliation, practice of sorcery, and incendiary letter inciting rebellion were used against him during his trial. He was found guilty and sentenced to life in prison where he died in 1795—a sad end for a man who was once the idol of thousands. Serafina fared no better, shut up in a convent for her remaining days.

And last of all, the story that began with two jewelers, Boehmer and Bassenge, came full circle with them. The agreement forged in 1785 to amortize the debt from the income of the Cardinal Rohan's abbey fell apart when church property was nationalized during the Revolution. Once they received their last payment in February 1790, both businessmen lost the cash needed to repay their creditors, forcing the jewelers into bankruptcy. Their heirs would wage a legal battle against the Rohan family for decades. In the last half of the nineteenth century, the Rohans repaid the outstanding balance to the descendants of the unlucky jewelers, putting a final close to the saga.

Perhaps Napoleon Buonaparte scored the best interpretation about the necklace debacle. While confined to the desolate island of St. Helena, the deposed emperor reflected on the scandal, declaring, "The Queen was innocent, and to ensure the greatest possible publicizing of the fact, wanted the Parlement of Paris to proclaim her innocence in its judgment. But instead, as it developed, she was deemed guilty and the monarchy discredited."

The Affair of the Diamond Necklace destroyed the queen's image forever, enshrining her as the most hated woman in France—the real Queen of Mean. To confirm this new reality, the police commissioner of Paris sent an opaquely worded note to Versailles suggesting Her Majesty postpone any planned visits to avoid unpleasantness.

> "If my critics saw me walk across the Thames,
> they would say it was because I couldn't swim."
> *Margaret Thatcher*

Chapter 41

Rough Seas from Now On

Grateful that Louis never doubted her innocence, Antoinette grew closer to her husband. Their renewed closeness resulted in another pregnancy. She wrote to her brother Joseph about her pique of having to bear another child. He rebuked her in his reply, reminding her it was her duty to provide as many heirs as possible. Antoinette had no desire to emulate her late mother's many pregnancies. Most of her close female friends shared the same sentiments, preferring not to be assembly-line baby mills. Such a fate would ruin their health and disrupt their complacent lives. The queen was determined that this would be her last child.

Once Antoinette pulled herself together after the trial, she took to heart her unfavorable polling numbers. She tried to repackage herself as a reformed material girl, making changes in her dress and behavior. She wrapped herself in the mantle of motherhood, devoted to the care of her children. She rededicated herself to her charities. Nothing seemed to make a dent in her quest for rehabilitation. Once Antoinette realized her sincere efforts went unappreciated, she dropped out of sight when seven months pregnant, sheltering herself in the privacy offered by the Petit Trianon. On July 9, 1786, the last of Antoinette's children was born, a girl, Sophie Hélène Béatrice. This baby provided the boost that the family needed.

After the ruinous necklace trial, Louis took his first trip beyond the vicinity of Versailles since his journey to Rheims eleven years earlier for his coronation. Louis, keenly interested in naval affairs, decided to inspect the port of Cherbourg in Normandy. The king would always treasure these nine days of travel as the happiest of his reign. His spirits lifted with the warmth showered on him by the local people. The king questioned his handlers: "Why do I receive here such testimonies of love to which I am not accustomed elsewhere?" Louis answered the unresponsive bowed heads himself: "I understand; they must have given me a bad reputation around Versailles."

Louis was unaware that his aides had plotted the path of the trip to deliberately avoid "the unhappy state of the interior provinces where misery reigns and where the tax devours the bread of the people." Louis erroneously concluded that discontent in France did not exist beyond the pernicious confines of Paris and Versailles. Louis animatedly wrote to the queen: "The love of my people has resounded to the bottom of my heart; judge if I am not the happiest man in the world." Upon returning to Versailles, the king sought out his toddler son, Duke of Normandy, shouting, "Come here my strong little Norman; your name is a good luck charm."

All of France speculated about Antoinette's future after the infamous necklace trial ended. Voices from all segments of French society urged that the queen be confined to a convent, or better yet, sent back to Vienna. The queen was devastated by these appeals for her removal from her family; the outraged Louis dismissed these demands as wild talk.

Thomas Jefferson was the American ambassador to France at the height of this national obsession concerning the queen's fate. He traveled throughout France for several months in 1787 and witnessed firsthand the increasing discontent. When Jefferson returned to a seething Paris, he noted the hostility directed against the privileged lot cocooned in Versailles, and particularly toward the queen. Jefferson echoed the feelings of agitated Frenchmen who believed that needed changes could take root provided one obstacle were removed. Quite simply, the queen had to go. In 1821 when he was seventy-seven, Jefferson reflected on his years in France. He bluntly declared when speaking about Marie Antoinette, "I should have shut up the Queen in a convent, putting harm out of her power." He echoed the widespread opinion that was widely held in pre-revolutionary France, "I have ever believed that had there been no Queen, there would have been no Revolution."

Indeed, the Crown teetered on bankruptcy during Jefferson's ambassadorship. But the primary cause for the brewing unraveling of France lay in the unresolved economic crisis sparked by the enormous sums France had borrowed to clinch the independence of Jefferson's homeland. However, Antoinette would be blamed for the country's economic woes. The Austrian Woman would garner a second title, "Madame Deficit."

"When someone is going downhill,
everyone likes to give him a kick."
Proverb

Spotlight Four

The Days of Diminishing Majesty

Chapter 42

It's the Deficit, Stupid

The French Revolution was a process percolating long before the fall of the Bastille. Evidence of cracks in the autocratic edifice became apparent by the summer of 1786. The financial mess of the State's revenues, ruined by the cost of the securing victory for the American colonies, required urgent attention. An edgy discontent surfaced throughout the country with calls for reform spouting from every tongue. And the public mostly targeted the Austrian Woman as the source of economic woe.

The bumpy road to fiscal disaster began when Finance Minister Turgot and his reforms met defeat in 1776. Several ministers followed him, each hopelessly inept at resolving the budget mess. Meanwhile, Parisians were abuzz about a Protestant money wizard from Switzerland—Jacques Necker. Through his own self-promotion, Necker's abilities reached the king's ears. With so many businessmen clamoring for his appointment, Louis XVI felt pressured to offer him the post of taming the Treasury. In June 1777 Monsieur Necker arrived on the job ready to impress, accompanied by his glamorous wife, Suzanne, who served as his political handler, and his precocious only child, Germaine.

Almost everyone extolled the banker from Geneva, including the banker himself: "To my great surprise, I seek in vain something to reproach myself for." Necker would discover that the natural snobbery of the courtiers at Versailles would eventually reduce him to his bourgeois foreign roots.

Necker impressed Louis with his personal thriftiness, refusing to accept a salary. He instituted economies in Louis' and Antoinette's households that both royals supported. He streamlined government services, and encouraged commercial enterprise. And his golden boy reputation encouraged investors to loan the Crown needed funds. However, some of the immediate savings were offset by the salaries and gifts heaped on rapacious courtiers like the Polignacs.

In the long term, Necker's retrenchments might have made a difference but for the steep price tag to fund the conflict across the Atlantic. Despite his firm disapproval, Necker bent to the vociferous popular will pressuring him to bankroll the American revolt. He raised the staggering funds necessary to fund the war against Britain, securing loan after loan. And the former Finance Minister Turgot predicted a nightmare would ensue from such unbridled borrowing. He wittily couched his warning, "Only a saint can perform miracles, and for that Necker would have to become a Catholic."

In February 1781 Necker brashly published a ponderous report of the nation's finances. Even though it was not a lusty page turner, thirty thousand copies flew off the shelves. Necker presented a robust portrait of France's financial condition, solidifying his reputation as the oracle of finance. However, he glossed over the looming debt for the American war. And it was hard to fault him entirely on that score, given that he had warned of the folly to underwrite the conflict. However, not everyone applauded Necker's best seller. Old Maurepas sniped, "It's about as true as it is modest."

With the success of his fiscal summary, Necker seized the moment to propel his career forward.

Necker's dreams for long-range financial reforms rested on becoming a member of the king's council. Unfortunately, being a Protestant barred him from a seat on the council. Louis chose not to bend the rules to accommodate Necker's religious affiliation. By May 1781 Necker hounded Louis not only for council inclusion, but also for control of the war and naval budgets. A shocked Louis hesitated as he canvassed his ministers. Both Maurepas and Vergennes threatened immediate resignation if the king sided with the pompous Protestant. Since Louis had grown weary of Mr. know-it-all Necker, he agreed with his ministers to sack the man from Geneva. But on the way out of the palace, Necker confidently muttered under his breath, à la Schwarzenegger, *"I'll Be Back."*

Despite Necker's ouster, the impact of his fiscal summary continued to boost investors' spirits. This euphoria fed off the defeat of the hated England and the birth of an heir to the throne. Times were good.

As for Necker's replacement, two mediocre men failed magnificently in quick succession. The third challenger, Charles Alexander Calonne, a forty-seven-year-old redhead from Flanders, touted impressive credentials. Although the king wasn't jazzed about the slick, sophisticated Calonne,

Louis appointed him as finance minister in November 1783 with Vergennes' prodding.

Calonne personified the consummate courtier of the era, down to his trendy shoe buckles. He was witty and urbane, possessed an enviable art collection, and stocked an impressive wine cellar of more than one thousand bottles. When he arrived at Versailles, he reveled in the social swirl of entertainments, ranking Madame Polignac's soirées as his personal favorite. Like Necker, Minister Calonne dared not levy any new taxes, fearing the evil disposition of the Paris Parlement. He borrowed extensively to keep the Crown afloat during his first two years in office, praying that the royal edifice didn't implode.

In early 1786 Calonne confronted an accounting nightmare—looming State bankruptcy. Alarmed, Calonne feverishly devised a bailout program. In August 1786 Calonne presented a dumbfounded Louis with a report that spelled out the crisis and provided an audacious solution. The crux of this plan advocated significant tax, bureaucratic, and social reforms. Calonne's proposals were an impressive reordering of the kingdom, but required the salesmanship of a P.T. Barnum.

Aware that the venomous magistrates of the Paris Parlement would never register these decrees, Calonne proposed a clever alternative: to convene an Assembly of Notables, a group consisting of noblemen, prelates, provincial luminaries, and sympathetic supporters from the various Parlements. Last used in 1626, this strategy provided a method for a king to achieve political goals. Desperate for a solution to erase the red ink, Louis accepted the plan. An anxious Louis rubberstamped the one hundred forty-four nominees that Calonne proposed—each supposedly on board with the plan. But the handpicked delegates would not translate into the expected "yes" men.

On January 24, 1787, the delegates gathered at Versailles but the proceedings immediately hit a snag. The architect of change, Calonne, fell ill. Then the sudden death of Foreign Minister Vergennes cast a dark gloom on the king's mood and, worse still, removed Calonne's chief supporter of his proposed reforms. During a month of imposed idleness, the assembled delegates bickered about the issues. A recovered Calonne addressed the notables, pinning the blame for the financial woes on the mismanagement of his predecessor, Necker. This strategy backfired, as most of his listeners were Necker fans. Calonne's courtly manners deserted him when he offered the delegates an either/or choice: either they back his proposals, or accept responsibility for fiscal ruin—not exactly a talented master of ceremonies.

The turned-off notables rejected most of Calonne's proposals. Part of the sticking point was a trust issue. Rumors circulated that Calonne had enriched himself through a real estate transaction at the expense of the king. Furthermore, the uncooperative notables declared themselves ineligible to raise taxes; only the Estates General could resolve that issue.

Calonne was now a wreck, as nothing panned out as he had planned. Behind the scenes in the king's council, puerile finger pointing reigned, unsettling the king even more. As Louis started to lose it, he lamented loudly that if Vergennes were still alive, "He would have rescued me from this mess."

The boxed-in king thought the world was collapsing on top of him. He felt misused by Calonne—Louis had expected him to extract him from this financial disaster. Louis banished Calonne to his estates in Lorraine, with no thank you note.

To make matters worse, the Parlement of Paris delighted in accusing Calonne of "financial irregularities" and launched a criminal investigation on charges of corruption. Calonne, disgraced and fearing arrest, fled to England, escaping the tempest brewing in France. The Parisians giddily burned effigies of Calonne along with his hostess at court, Madame Polignac. With great bitterness, Calonne sold his prized art collection to make ends meet. Convinced that Antoinette had manipulated his downfall, Calonne devoted himself to a campaign of slander against the queen.

"It's better to die than to preserve this life
by incurring disgrace.
The loss of life causes but a moment's grief,
but disgrace brings grief every day of one's life."
Chanakya

Chapter 43

Louis Leans on Antoinette

L ouis felt gobsmacked by the vast debt that had accrued during his watch. He felt betrayed by his handpicked notables who had been summoned to approve the required reforms. These men should have been his pillars of support. Instead, they gave Louis the shaft, shattering his tenuous self-confidence. He withdrew to his apartments, crumbled into a heap. He bemoaned his predicament to Antoinette, seeking her advice. Terrified to see her husband fall apart, the queen sought to rally him from collapse. She recommended two candidates as Calonne's replacement: either the popular Jacques Necker or the urbane archbishop of Toulouse, Loménie Brienne. Both options redoubled Louis' moans. The king disliked the egotistical Necker, and the idea of an agnostic churchman serving as his minister seemed immoral to Louis.

On April 30, 1787 Louis emerged from his funk and sourly appointed Loménie Brienne as finance minister. Louis needed a trusted ally on his team, so he lured Lamoignon Malesherbes out of retirement to become minister of the king's household, the same post he had held for nine months in 1775. Malesherbes enacted massive retrenchments in the expenses of the royal households, ticking off nearly everybody. While the savings were impressive, they barely made a dent in the colossal debt. The taxation system required emergency surgery.

Loménie Brienne, a well-liked insider of the Assembly of Notables, expected better odds at pulling off an agreement. But the ambitious archbishop got off on a bad foot, alarming the notables with spreadsheets predicting bankruptcy. Then, Brienne presented a reform package to the Assembly that resembled Calonne's with some added tweaks. Despite his sweet talking, the archbishop met with the same resistance as Calonne.

Beyond exasperation, Louis ordered Brienne to shut down the untrustworthy Assembly of Notables. The king resigned himself to the dreaded alternative of taking his case to the Parlement of Paris in the summer of 1787. The Parlement squealed with delight, betting it would gain ascendency over the Crown with this hot potato.

Count Mercy reported to Vienna: "It is unbelievable with what freedom the nation allows itself to criticize, complain of, and condemn the slightest operation of the ministers."

Another ambassador smugly declared, "Frenchmen are incapable of cool deliberation."

However, the French gladly blamed the Austrian Woman for the flood of red ink.

As the political landscape darkened in the summer of 1787, so did the hearts of the royal family. First, wishing to gauge the feelings of the public since the necklace fiasco, Antoinette decided to attend the opera in Paris. Hisses greeted her arrival in the royal box along with scattered shouts of "Madame Deficit." The humiliated queen scratched the capital from her travel options. Next, personal tragedy struck when the last of Antoinette's four children, eleven-month-old Sophie Béatrice fell ill. The baby, suffering a painful teething process coupled with periodic convulsions, died on June 19, 1787. The queen and king were heartbroken. The royal governess, Gabrielle Polignac, was abroad at the time of Sophie's death, prompting the queen to reach out to her sister-in-law Elisabeth to share her profound sadness. Elisabeth would become the queen's constant companion in times of sorrow.

At the time of Sophie's death, the society artist, Madame Vigée Le Brun, was putting the final touches to a painting of the queen and her four children. Forced to paint the baby out of the portrait, the viewer saw the eldest son pointing to his sister's empty bassinet—perhaps the most doleful depiction of royals ever painted. At the viewing of the mournful portrait in Paris, the indifferent reaction of the public compounded Antoinette's distress. The dispirited queen spent more time with her children and select companions at the Petit Trianon. Among her few pleasures were the afternoon horseback rides she and Fersen took together within her private grounds.

No need to consult an astrologer to predict that Brienne and the Parlement of Paris would lock horns. The Parlement defiantly refused to register the tax changes. In August 1787 Louis forced the misbehaving magistrates to register the tax. Within days, the Parlement retaliated by declaring that the king's actions were "contrary to the nation's rights." A behind-the-scenes deal was hammered out but the agreement unraveled at the last moment. A rattled Brienne proposed a desperate alternative with the promise to convene the Estates General in five years.

What was the Estates General? Established in 1302, this body advised the Crown and approved new taxes. It represented the three segments of French society: the clergy, the nobility, and the substantial rest, known as the Commons. After last being convened in 1614, French kings had bypassed this body and used the Parlement of Paris to register any new taxes the king imposed. But the Parlement of Paris signaled that it would no longer be a doormat to the king's demands.

Emboldened by its recent recall, the Paris Parlement rejected Brienne's arrangement, despite the appealing bait of an expedited convening of the Estates General. But the public's ears pricked up, insisting that the representative body meet soon. Determined to squelch the idea of an accelerated meeting, Louis summoned the Parlement of Paris for a royal session in November 1787 to approve an income tax with no class exemptions, as well as long delayed civil rights for France's seventy thousand Protestants.

Prior to a vote, a royal session allowed debate, carrying the downside of acrimonious arguments. During this particular session, the knives were not left on the breakfast table. Louis sat through seven hours of verbal combat, and his occasional dozing off did not improve his temper. Louis' patience frayed after endless calls for a prompt meeting of the Estates General. In a flash of frustration, the king considered there to be a majority vote and ordered the justice minister to register the two edicts. Louis barked out, "I ordain it." After an awkward pause, the Duke of Orléans rose from his seat and questioned the king's mishandling of the royal session. A shocked silence greeted this public rebuke of the monarch. Louis threw a royal fit, snapping back to his devious cousin, "It is legal, because I wish it." But Louis did not hold his ground and eject his cousin. Instead, less than majestically, Louis bolted for the door and stormed out of the building.

Momentarily muted by Louis' shocking behavior, the members of the Paris Parlement resumed their deliberations. Technically, they could continue their discussions for, in his haste to flee, the king had failed to dissolve the meeting. The Duke of Orléans encouraged the Parlement to reject the registration of the new tax forced on them by the king. It was not just their cherished privileges that the magistrates were protecting—they asked themselves why they should throw money at a government riddled with incompetence?

Although Louis convinced himself that he had resolved the issue of the money fiasco, the political crisis worsened. Following the royal session, the Parlement repudiated the king's edicts and declared them illegal. The year 1787 ended the way it began, with no resolution to resurrect the Treasury. The key power players at Versailles were in bad shape. The king and queen took to their beds with various ailments, as did the exhausted Brienne who was suffering from severe eczema. Mallet du Pan, an ardent royalist and journalist, identified the troubles at Versailles at the end of December: "They change political systems daily; there exists weakness and total incapacity."

Finally, the Paris Parlement crossed the line in April 1788 by informing Louis that "The will of the King alone is not enough to make law." These incendiary words goaded Louis to boldly abolish the Parlements in May and replace them with a revamped court system. Serious riots broke out all over France in support of the outlawed Parlements.

But it was not rioting that resolved the issue, but Mother Nature. In July a once-in-a-lifetime hail storm destroyed the grain harvest in the bread basket of France. Even the weather gods were insensitive to the king's plight. Investors kept their hands in their pockets, unwilling to lend a penny to the Crown. Louis confronted a ruined grain harvest, the evaporation of the tax revenue from the grain harvest, and the specter of starvation. Food riots quickly supplanted those protesting the ouster of the Parlements. As chaos sprouted everywhere, something had to be done to calm the national jitters.

In a bid to spark confidence in the Crown, Brienne convinced Louis to issue a decree convoking an expedited meeting of the Estates General for the first of May 1789. The news electrified the populace.

Lamoignon Malesherbes excitedly urged the king to modernize the medieval institution into a contemporary reflection of a new France:

> Sire, let a King at the end of the eighteenth century not convoke the three orders of the fourteenth century; let him instead call together the proprietors of a great nation renewed by its civilization. A King who submits to a constitution feels degraded; a King who proposes a constitution obtains instead the highest glory among men and their liveliest and most enduring gratitude.

Louis admired Malesherbes, but recoiled at the notion of a constitution. Louis just wanted to resolve the financial mess and put an end to the disorder afflicting his realm like a plague of locusts. Malesherbes resigned his post, despairing over Louis' ingrained limitations.

Sadly, Louis' decree to convene the Estates General did nothing to lessen the wave of lawlessness that swept through France due to fear of famine. With no confidence in the government, the Paris stock market tanked. Lenders kept their hands in their pockets, unwilling to lend a sou to the Crown. The Treasury ceased all payments.

Having failed to solve the financial impasse, Brienne resigned after eighteen months in office. Although defeated, Brienne received a cardinal's hat for his valiant efforts. The king and queen would miss him, but the Parisians felt differently: they constructed a magnificent effigy of Brienne decked out in his priestly finery, and after being subjected to a mock trial, he was condemned and burned in a massive bonfire.

"The world turns on a dime,
the same now as it always has—
which is to say, money makes
the world go 'round. It's also what
makes the world go spinning out of control."
Joe Murray

Chapter 44

A Gloating Comeback

With Brienne limping out of the palace, his warm council seat was filled by a familiar face, Jacques Necker. The queen shepherded the appointment on the listless king. Although Louis leaned heavily on the queen, especially when he was neck deep in the blues, he tartly reminded her that he always had the final word. Nonetheless, Louis held his nose and reinstated Necker in August 1788 complaining, "They have made me recall Necker. I do not want him, and they will not be long in regretting what they have done."

Antoinette recognized that Necker enjoyed the acclaim of the public and the Paris Parlement, the two inducements nudging her to have him on her side. More urgently, the queen hoped he would exercise a calming influence over the deputies of the forthcoming Estates General. But the queen expressed her ill-ease to Count Mercy, "I have just written three lines to Monsieur Necker asking him to come here tomorrow at ten o'clock. I tremble—forgive me for this weakness—at the thought that it is I who am recalling him. My fate is to bring bad luck, and if his infernal machinations make him fall again or if he weakens the King's authority, I shall be even more detested." All of the above would happen, reflecting the queen's dread of the Lisbon Curse.

When Necker resumed office, he was automatically included in the king's council. His Protestant affiliation no longer carried the opprobrium that it did back in 1781. As he gathered the national purse strings, Necker dispelled the bearishness of investors, assuring them that happy days were here again.

In addition to Necker's triumphant return to office, the king swallowed another bitter reversal. He was forced by popular demand to resurrect the Parlement of Paris and its satellite courts. The Parisians were delirious when the magistrates returned to their seats in the Palace of Justice in September 1788. But this victory would be amazingly short-lived. The first order of business of the Paris Parlement required registration of the royal edict convening the Estates General. Feeling invincible, the Parlement's magistrates overreached themselves by asserting that the outdated parliamentary procedures of 1614 would remain unchanged. They also limited the scope of issues that the Estates General could debate. Overnight these justices unmasked their villainous designs to preserve the status quo.

In a flash, the populace turned on the Paris Parlement. Public demonstrations flared up all over France where the courts were located. Most magistrates kept a low profile or slipped out of town, hoping the furor would die down. The rising political star, Count Mirabeau, had predicted months earlier in April 1788, "Suddenly the Parlements by force of circumstances will be reduced to their true stature. Their entire strength lies in the distress of the government and the discontent of the people." His prophetic words were spot-on.

Almost overnight, scores of pamphlets and publications inundated the cafes, salons, and street corners, condemning the Crown and the Paris Parlement. Count Fersen described to his father in Sweden the topsy-turvy social climate, "The fermentation of spirits is general; one only speaks of constitutions, the women in particular join in and you know the influence they have in this country. In the antechambers, the servants are busy reading pamphlets, of which ten or twelve are published daily; at the moment it is a matter of fashion, and you know as well as I do the power that has."

Louis XVI and his council were left to resolve the thorny issues regarding procedures for the Estates General. First, there was the matter of the venue for the convocation. Necker advocated Paris as the ideal spot, actually a stab at maximizing his public appeal. Antoinette lobbied for a location at least thirty miles from Versailles. She was uncomfortable with the meeting being held near to Paris and its troublemakers. Louis should have heeded her practical advice, but instead, Louis mandated that the momentous gathering would be held at Versailles.

Two major issues remained unsettled: one was the size of each estate, and the other was the voting procedures. When the Estates General last met in 1614, each of the three bodies was composed of three hundred members, and voting was done by each estate with each bloc having one vote. This method guaranteed that the clergy and nobility would outvote the commoners in the Third Estate whenever their joint interests were threatened. Necker pressured Louis to double the representation of the Third Estate to six hundred members. To placate the populace, Louis, with Antoinette's support, agreed to increase the number of deputies in the Third Estate.

Incomprehensibly, Necker and the king waffled on the manner of voting, allowing the established tradition of voting to remain unchanged, unless all three estates agreed to a head count vote. This decision set the stage for dissension even before the first session banged its gavel to order. A nasty showdown was in the works.

As for the king's brothers, Provence supported Necker's pitch, while Artois made a strident appeal for maintaining tradition. Most of the princes of the Blood echoed Artois' sentiments; they pointedly asked the king, "Who can say where the recklessness of opinions will end?" Around this time the queen began attending the king's council meetings at Louis' insistence, an unprecedented move heaping more hostility on the foreign Antoinette.

"History isn't just the story of bad people doing bad things.
It's quite as much a story of people trying to do good things.
But somehow, something goes wrong."
C. S. Lewis

Chapter 45

The Merde Hits the Fan

*I*n 1992 Queen Elizabeth II made a speech referring to the year about to close as the *annus horribilis* of her reign. For Antoinette and her family, 1789 was the most unimaginable *annus horribilis* in the history books for any royal family, kicking off four years of non-stop hell. Count Mercy underlined the despair of the established order: "We are in an abyss which makes us face with terror the moment of the Estates General; they portend disastrous reverses for royalty. My dispatches provide but an incomplete idea of the revolution which is brewing in this monarchy."

Misery flourished during the winter of 1788–1789, one of the coldest in memory. The dismal grain harvest of the previous summer foreshadowed ever intense food riots. Louis and Necker tried to alleviate the pitiful conditions by purchasing grain abroad. The Duke of Orléans made the Crown look cheap with the touted sale of some of his art treasures to relieve the desperation of many Parisians. As his popularity soared, the duke congratulated himself, pleased to upstage the king. Louis nursed his ill humor toward the duke, while Antoinette fretted that Orléans was plotting to seize the throne.

As the king sulked, Necker preened. He fantasized that the public stage would belong to him, and not the king, when the Estates General opened.

⚜   ⚜   ⚜

Trying to gauge his kingdom's mood, Louis requested his subjects send him their most pressing concerns. Each of the three Estates submitted a combined fifty-five thousand "notebooks of grievances," each of which began and ended with reverence for the king. Three common themes emerged: topping the list was a more equitable system of taxation; next, the wish to maintain a Catholic monarchy with the king owning the initiative of making laws; and finally, the request for a constitution. The final expectation was a wish that gave Louis an instant migraine.

Tucked away in the tsunami of desires for the king's consideration were scattered appeals for the equitable treatment of women. One group of hard-working ladies from Caux, north of Paris, raised a simmering question: "Whether from reason or necessity men permit women to share their work, to till the soil, to plow, to run the postal service; others undertake long and difficult travel for commercial reasons. Will men persist in wanting to make us victims of their pride or injustice?" Women were serving notice that they were determined to get their fair share of the pie of freedom—a concept more revolutionary than the budding Revolution.

Voting began to elect the members of the Three Estates in March 1789. Excitement tingled all over France as delegates were selected. The majority of the 300 representatives of the elected First Estate were local parish priests. Most of the 291 nobles chosen to represent the Second Estate were conservative monarchists. Finally, the common people elected 610 deputies to the Third Estate; half of these gentlemen were aligned with the legal profession and the remaining half were not unsophisticated rubes.

Mirroring the expectations of the first day on a new job, most delegates journeyed to Versailles with rose-colored expectations. Louis hosted a reception welcoming each order individually. The king accorded the First and Second Estates the same gracious protocol. The Third Estate, though, got the red carpet yanked from under their feet. They filed past Louis, bowing in respect, as the squinting king barely uttered a word in greeting. Most of these provincial delegates were underwhelmed by their first impression of the king. Expecting a deity of sorts, instead they beheld a pockmarked, stout man with a plodding walk and a whining voice. One delegate, Barère, noted his disappointment: "His appearance was very awkward and gave everyone the impression of a very badly brought up, big fat boy."

What Barère did not know was that Louis always felt inept in official settings where all glances were focused on him. The king's gut instinct was to keep one eye riveted on the nearest exit. The outcome of this first meeting with the Third Estate could have been different if Louis had reached out to the brightest minds of the Third Estate with his signature down-home warmth. However, neither etiquette nor the king could have countenanced such a radical step.

On May 4, 1789, the sun beamed on the assembled grandeur of the French monarchy for its ultimate curtain call with the convening of the Estates General. It was inconceivable to embark on the convocation of these deputies without heaven's sanction. A splendid mass was to be celebrated in the local parish church of St. Louis. The half mile procession to the church teemed with people vying to witness this historic moment. It seemed that most of Paris showed up at Versailles to attend the spectacle. Flowers lined the route and the facades of buildings were festooned with tapestries. The day held the promise of a leap forward for the nation.

The parade of luminaries began with the deputies of the Third Estate. On a day that should have promoted national unity, centuries-old prejudices held sway. The members of the Third Estate were required to wear a uniform of black cloth suits with a white cravat; they resembled sullen school children being led into class after recess. Their appearance drew the loudest cheers from the crowd who depended on them for needed reforms.

The real headliner among the Third Estate deputies was the forty-year-old deputy from Aix-en-Provence, Count Honoré Mirabeau. He had an imposing body with a large, ghastly face that was disfigured from childhood smallpox. Watching from an excellent vantage point, Madame de Staël, Minister Necker's famous daughter, described Mirabeau: "It was difficult not to look at him once one noticed him. His huge head of hair distinguished him from all others. It was as if his strength derived from it, like the biblical Samson. His face mesmerized all eyes caught by its unique ugliness, and his whole person suggested a strange power." Mirabeau was the kind of guy who sent shivers up and down everyone's spine, no matter their gender.

Next in the foot parade came the Second Estate—the nobility. They were smartly turned out in their black silk suits with gold and silver embroidery. Their flashy plumed hats danced commandingly above the crowd.

Following the nobility, processed the First Estate—the clergy. They looked celestial in their religious garb, especially the bishops in their runway-worthy ecclesiastical drag.

Last of all, Louis XVI and the royal family progressed in the twilight of regal magnificence. Even the ungainly king looked impressive in his suit of gold. Louis was enthusiastically cheered by the crowd along the entire route. Most Frenchmen in 1789 felt their king was a good man who had been misguided by ministers, courtiers, and especially his foreign queen.

Marie Antoinette followed the king, wearing a dazzling violet and white gown glittering with diamonds. Yet, she felt out of sorts. She unsmilingly kept pace with the procession, fretting about the outcome of this national gathering on her doorstep. She was greeted with punishing silence that at one point was breached with taunting shouts of "Long Live the Duke of Orléans." At one poignant moment during the half-mile route, Antoinette looked up to a frail seven-year-old boy buoyed on a heap of cushions, watching the parade from a veranda of the royal stables. Antoinette flashed her brightest smile on her eldest son and heir. The amiable child weakly waved at his mother. Given the crowd's frosty reception and her son's ailing health, how could anyone have expected Antoinette to be in a chipper mood?

Louis was greeted with enthusiastic cheers as he entered the church. The queen followed him. The quiet was too embarrassing to ignore. The king took a snooze during the bishop's sermon. Suddenly, ears perked up when the bishop condemned the court for its obsession with pleasure while the peasantry struggled. The bishop reprimanded Antoinette for her extravagances at the Petit Trianon and her Hamlet, which he termed "a puerile imitation of nature." Enthusiastic applause broke out in response to the bishop's message, rousing the king from his nap. The queen put on a stoic facade as she smarted under this public shaming.

The Estates General convened the following morning in the Salle des Menus-Plaisirs, a royal warehouse repurposed as a meeting hall. After two frustrating hours to get everyone seated, Louis arrived at noon, attired in the pomp of royalty. He basked in the deafening cries of "Long Live the King," taking his seat on a throne of crimson and gold. Next, the queen appeared— not one peep greeted her. Tears trickling down her face, Antoinette sat in an armchair two steps below the king on his left. Mirabeau leaned over to a neighbor and whispered, "Behold their victim." Some observers noted that the queen seemed agitated, fidgeting with her fan. She felt uneasy with so many deputies disapprovingly staring at her. Antoinette would have preferred to be at the Petit Trianon than in the company of these hardened Hottentots. Meanwhile, Louis welcomed the deputies:

> This day which my heart has anticipated for a long time has finally come, and I see myself surrounded by the representatives of the nation which it is my glory to command. The debts of the State, already immense at my accession to the throne, have increased even more during my reign: a costly but honorable war has been the necessary consequence. A general uneasiness, an exaggerated desire for innovation have seized upon the public mind, and

we hurried to allay matters by assembling wise and moderate counsel. It is in such confidence, Messieurs, that I have brought you together. I am assured that you will propose to me the most effective means of reestablishing the finances of the kingdom and to strengthen the public credit. May a happy understanding reign in this assembly.

Louis' speech drew a tepid response from most of the Third Estate delegates. They were disappointed by the narrow focus on the financial crisis at the expense of adjustments to the social order.

Then, Minister Necker, the main attraction, bombed with his presentation. Like a vampire, Necker sucked the life out of his listeners, delivering a three-hour harangue filled with torturous accounting figures. Except for an equitable tax system, Necker offered no specifics for reform. He concluded his rambling speech by reminding the deputies to follow the voting procedures of 1614. Suddenly, Necker's stock nosedived in the eyes of the Third Estate.

As the members of the Third Estate shuffled out of the hall, no doubt hungry after hours of empty rhetoric, they had to ask themselves, "But where's the bouillabaisse?" Already, on day one, the members of the Third Estate braced themselves for the fight to come.

Inexplicably, the upset of the ceremony was the lukewarm greeting that Antoinette received as she exited the hall. Surprised, she dropped one of her signature curtsies in recognition. The applause redoubled, and her second curtsy was prolonged and very low indeed. She still had the knack to wow a crowd, even an unfriendly one. But the queen was not fooled by this delayed acclaim. She understood that these representatives of the people were sending her a clear message: behave yourself, and you will be tolerated; misbehave, and you will be shipped back to Vienna.

As Louis returned to the palace, he lamely expected the Estates General to resolve the financial crisis and obediently disband. The queen did not share his optimistic outlook. She sensed that this gathering would spark further unrest throughout the realm. But neither Louis nor Antoinette could ever have imagined how their lives would be forever altered within the next five months. Dizzying changes arose that left them vulnerable, bewildered, and afraid. Neither of them possessed the political skills to keep their world from spinning out of control.

"The truth is you don't know what is going to happen tomorrow.
Life is a crazy ride, and nothing is guaranteed."
Eminem

Chapter 46

The Estates General Mutates

The king's master of ceremonies, twenty-seven-year-old Marquis Dreux-Brézé, oversaw the antiquated protocols that the Third Estate deemed unacceptable. From the outset, he clashed daily with the Third Estate. Strictly adhering to the rules of 1614, Dreux-Brézé treated the Third Estate with a lesser level of respect than the protocol he offered the First and Second Estate; yet, the deputies of the people were not about to accept a less-than-equal status.

With no compromise on how to proceed, the frustrated deputies of the Third pledged to defer the nation's business until all representatives from the three estates were united in one national body. The Third Estate viewed the clergy as the most likely to join them. The Third daily sent one of their deputies—the golden-tongued Guy-Jean-Baptiste Target, the skilled lawyer who had defended Cardinal Rohan in the diamond necklace trial—to sway the clergy to jump ship from the First Estate. Target's oratory skills could seduce the Holy Savior. To foil a rebellion within their ranks, the bishops suggested that representatives of all three estates meet in an effort to reach a compromise.

Meanwhile, the king and queen were borderline delusional, hoping that the impasse among the three estates might trigger their dissolution. In the real world, the Third Estate was busy plotting, not packing.

⚜   ⚜   ⚜

That old saying "Timing is everything" never seemed more timely. The king's first-born son and heir, Louis Joseph, suffered poor health for years. A year earlier Antoinette spoke of her distress regarding her senior son to her brother Joseph: "My elder son has given me a great deal of anxiety. His body is twisted with one shoulder higher than the other and a back whose vertebrae are slightly out of line and protruding. For some time he has had constant fevers, and as a result is very thin and weak."

The sweet tempered, intelligent little fellow had entered the final stages of spinal tuberculosis. An urgent summons beckoned the royal couple to hurry to the nearby chateau of Meudon where the young prince had lived since March 1788, hoping that the healthier air would rally the child. The doctors gently prepared the parents that their precious son was near death. The helpless royals, overwrought at losing their heir, sobbed in each other's arms. At dusk, a disconsolate Louis returned to Versailles, but Antoinette refused to budge. She remained with her child until he drew one last little breath at one in the morning on June 4, 1789.

The emaciated body of the little prince was placed in a small white coffin draped with a silver cloth, and the crown and sword of the Dauphin of France. Unfeeling etiquette forbade the king and queen's presence at his funeral. It fell to Madame Lamballe, as head of the queen's household, to oversee the religious rites and subsequent burial. This long-suffering boy, whose birth was greeted with wild delirium almost eight years previously, would now be barely remembered.

Following the death of their son, Louis and Antoinette locked themselves away, refusing to see anyone. The entire court lined up on June 7 to pay their respects to the grieving sovereigns. The Third Estate sent a delegation, ostensibly to offer their condolences, but, they insisted that the king meet with them. They insensitively pressed the king to determine if he was on their side. Offended by their politicking, Louis bitterly inquired, "Are there no fathers among the Third Estate?" Louis admonished them to demonstrate their attachment to him by cooperating with the other two estates.

Marie Antoinette also felt violated by the lack of respect for her dead child. Her son's significance was brushed aside by brash politics. The queen was distressed by an unfeeling populace obsessed with reform and impatient with any delay; it opened a wound between her and the French that would never heal. More than two years later in December 1791, she would write in a letter that she still mourned the loss of her bright boy: "At the death of my poor little son, the Dauphin, the nation hardly seemed to notice."

On June 14 the royal family arrived at Marly for a week of mandated mourning. At Marly, the royal couple divorced themselves from public view, to give vent to their grief. The drama in the Estates General would have to wait. Secluded at Marly, Louis and Antoinette were bombarded with calls from their closest kin to rein in the out of control deputies. Instead of the family coming together, arguments and slamming doors sabotaged most conversations. The king's brother Artois was the loudest, demanding that the Third be dealt with severely. Distracted by their loss, the royal couple was vulnerable to the bellicose advice of family members. Worn down, Louis summoned his council and family to help him craft a strategy to deal with the Third Estate.

While Louis was fretting about what to do next, the Third raced forward with a provocative symbolic change. They ditched the medieval title of the Estates General and began referring to themselves as The Commons. Next, they selected Sylvain Bailly, the famed astronomer, to be their president. A big break came on June 13 when three priests from the First Estate joined The Commons, followed by sixteen more priests over the ensuing days; expectations soared that mass defections would follow. The Commons re-branded themselves again with a more satisfying name, the National Assembly. They boldly declared that their first order of business would be to give France a constitution. Not one deputy proposed to first seek Louis' approval.

Soon, the political situation became quite fluid. More than a hundred clergymen switched sides to sit with the National Assembly. The Duke of Orléans demanded that deputies from the three estates sit with the National Assembly. But not everyone was swept up in jumping ship. The archbishops of Paris and Rouen went to Marly and begged Louis to snuff out the impertinence of the Third Estate. Fifty nobles also petitioned the king to dissolve the Estates General entirely. It appeared that the institution of the Estates General was in peril. The king knew he had to respond once the week of prescribed mourning ended on June 20.

Louis' council was evenly divided on a response. Half supported the idea of the Estates General meeting as a single body, while the other half urged maintaining tradition. Necker lectured the king: "Resign yourself, Sire, to an English style constitution. Anticipating the wishes of your nation, you will accord it today what it may force from you tomorrow." Louis' brother Artois nearly assaulted Necker, calling him a string of epithets. With pressure from his wife and brothers, Louis was convinced to announce an address to the Estates General on June 23.

The king ordered the Salle des Menus Plaisirs, where the Third Estate met, to be closed in preparation for the forthcoming showdown. Early on June 20, the beleaguered Dreux-Brézé informed the presidents of the three estates of the king's orders. This news did not reach most deputies of the Third who were surprised to find the hall locked when they arrived. Milling about in the rain, one deputy suggested they gather at the empty tennis court. Once the deputies assembled, simultaneous suggestions flooded the arena. Above the din of voices, Jean-Joseph Mounier, a legal genius from Grenoble, proposed they focus on providing the nation with a constitution. With no furnishings in the building, President Bailly stood on a door resting on wine barrels, and exhorted the deputies, "To swear never to separate, and to meet whenever circumstances demand it until the kingdom's constitution is firmly established on solid foundation." The response was a unanimous chorus of "I swear." Hats were thrown in the air and deputies tearfully embraced as they rapturously signed the oath. The moment would be forever known as The Oath of the Tennis Court. There was no turning back; France would get its constitution.

A host of talented wannabes would compete in the struggle for leadership of the National Assembly. But the man of the hour in the summer of 1789 was the fearsome Count Honoré Mirabeau.

Mirabeau was a comic-book hero made flesh. Just imagine Quasimodo on serious steroids, with a law degree from Harvard. He was the undisputed peacock parading among mere roosters. His name was linked with scandalous love affairs, several imprisonments initiated by his own father, and inflammatory writings penned while he was in jail. And his bad-boy image was further enhanced by the racy gossip that he slept in what was then termed "the Italian style," meaning buck naked. His life was about as steady as an EF-5 tornado. But no one better understood the high stakes that were at play at the onset of the Revolution. He was an unerring observer, and the best judge of character in the playbill of political stars. The quintessential politician, he steadily mastered the tightrope he had to walk to make radical change an acceptable success. He pinpointed his task: "When you undertake to run a Revolution, the difficulty is not to make it go, but rather to hold it in check."

"It's not enough to succeed. Others must fail."
Gore Vidal

Chapter 47

The Monarchy Unravels

*A*stonishingly, the events at the Tennis Court did not spook Louis as they should have. He fluffed it off "as just a phase," but his family decried the audacity of the Third. The king convened his ministers while still at Marly to finalize his counter offensive. Assisted by a disgruntled Necker, the king drew up a blueprint for the changes he would allow, based on the most requested reforms found in the notebooks of grievances. Louis parted ways with Necker on several key issues: the king insisted on the 1614 voting ritual; he refused to allow French soldiers to be promoted on merit; and he trashed the idea of a written constitution. Necker, fuming at having his advice dismissed, silently planned a course of retribution.

On June 23 Louis entered the Salle des Menus-Plaisirs amid scattered applause from the First and Second Estates while the Third sat on their hands; they were furious that they had been forced to wait in the rain for an hour before being granted admission to the hall. As everyone took their place, even the dullest deputies noticed that Necker was AWOL.

Louis chastised the deputies: "The Estates General have been open for almost two months, and they have not been able to come to an agreement on the preliminaries of their operations. A perfect understanding should have been born from love of the fatherland alone, and now a fatal discord throws alarm into everybody. I owe it to myself to put an end to these fatal divisions."

Louis then instructed the minister of justice to read fifteen articles requiring the deputies' obedience. Among the orders were the adherence to the centuries-old meeting and voting procedures and the inadmissibility of a National Assembly. After the announcement of these articles, the king chided the representatives: "Never has a king done so much for any nation, but then what other nation could have merited it more than the French?"

Louis next offered his plan of reforms. Among the king's thirty-five proposals were: the liberty of the press; the elimination of the detestable *lettre de cachet*; the abolition of social privileges in the collection of taxes; the publication of an annual budget; and fixed expenditures for the royal households. This package of reforms was the most he was willing to grant in terms of a compromise. In the future, he would always fall back on this offer as the best deal for his kingdom.

Finally, the royal lecture concluded with this admonition, "Reflect, gentlemen, that none of your projects, none of your proposals, can have the force of law without my express approval. I am the natural guarantor of your rights. Therefore, I command you to separate immediately and to come tomorrow morning, each to the chamber allotted to your order, to resume your sessions." Tough words for sure, worthy of a descendant of Louis XIV. But the king's family jewels didn't measure up to those of the Sun King.

The course of French history might have been different if Louis' reforms had been presented at the opening of the Estates General on May 5. No matter what the king offered now, it would not compensate for rejecting a National Assembly and a constitution for France.

As Louis and his retinue exited the hall, the clergy and nobility extended polite applause. After the clerics and nobles filed out of the hall, carpenters rushed in to remove the royal props. The Third Estate deputies would not budge. Mirabeau, known by the code name, Thunder, broke the silence with a reverberating tirade. He challenged the deputies to rededicate themselves, "I demand that you put on your legislative powers and withdraw into the religion of your oath which allows us to disband only after having made a constitution."

Listening in the rear stood the master of ceremonies who reminded the deputies of the king's orders to vacate the hall. Mirabeau bolted out of his seat and with a withering look, dismissed Dreux-Brézé: "Go back and tell your master that we are here by the will of the people, and we shall relinquish our seats only at the point of bayonets."

Dreux-Brézé scurried off to inform Louis of the defiance of the Third. The king, already in a foul mood, had found on his desk an impertinent letter of resignation from Necker. With Dreux-Brézé's disturbing news flash, the king unleashed a flurry of profanities that rattled the palace shutters. Predictably, Louis established a pattern of delivering muscular rhetoric, followed by barricading himself in his library, reciting a litany of misgivings.

The king's sister, Madame Elisabeth, kindly excused her brother's indecisive nature: "He is always afraid of being mistaken; when his first impulse is passed, then he is tormented by fear of doing injustice."

Soon after, the deputies of the Third dispersed, but not before vowing to encourage members from the other two estates to join them. They declared in a unanimous vote "that the person of each deputy is inviolable" and that no one, not even a king, could harm a member of the National Assembly. Such a person would be deemed as "infamous and a traitor to the nation, and guilty of a capital crime."

"Extremism in the defense of liberty is no vice.
And moderation in the pursuit of justice is no virtue."
Barry Goldwater

Chapter 48

Paving the Way for Rebellion

$\mathcal{T}$he provocative parliamentary exercise on June 23 became the pivotal moment in the birth of the Revolution. A group of six hundred subjects rewrote the rules of the game, ending autocratic rule in France. Louis could choose to either hop on board or be jettisoned along the roadway.

When the king's changes were released, along with the news of Necker's resignation, hostile mobs flooded the courtyard of the palace. Antoinette was frightened by the ugly mood of the crowd and knew it was time to mend fences with the popular Necker. The queen felt he had to be kept on, no matter the consequences. Necker received an urgent summons to make tracks to Her Majesty's apartments. A huge crowd engulfed Necker as he sauntered from his residence to the palace. The agitated mob roughly pushed aside the confused guards and started to rush the palace. The petrified courtiers were relieved when Necker, basking in the public's attention, exhorted the protesters to wait for him outside the palace. This man they obeyed.

After enumerating the need for his services, Antoinette escorted Necker to the king's apartments. The meeting was a stormy affair. Louis ranted about the magnanimous offers that he had presented earlier that day. And Necker's response—abandonment of his sovereign. The tense interview ended with Louis refusing to accept Necker's resignation, resulting in a hostile truce. Meanwhile, a confident Necker reappeared before the cheering crowd assuring them he had retained the king's confidence. An illusory order reestablished itself.

Over the following days, sizable defections from the First and Second Estates swelled the ranks of the newly-minted National Assembly. Louis could not compute how his orders of June 23 could be ignored. Four days later on June 27 a sullen king accepted defeat. The tipping point came when Louis got word that a Parisian mob was set to march on Versailles to coerce him to recognize the legislative body of the people. Louis ordered the loyal holdouts of the nobility and clergy to join the National Assembly "to achieve my paternal goals which are necessary for the safety of the State." Once all the deputies were gathered under the same roof, Bailly magnanimously welcomed them: "Now the family is complete."

Louis XVI's public acknowledgment of a national body whose goal was to give France a constitution marked the dawn of the new order. The news of the king's capitulation swept through the nation like a tidal wave. An effervescent crowd milled outside Versailles, shouting for the king to appear. Louis and Antoinette dutifully complied. But their smiling faces barely masked the anxiety that flooded their hearts. Louis' public acceptance of a new political paradigm was purely a move to play for time. He was still determined to enforce his reforms of June 23.

While the political drama stewed at Versailles, the emboldened have-nots seized this moment to vent their frustrations. With the populace of Paris approaching a seething volatility, Louis worried that a revolt would soon rock the city. A police force of fifteen hundred officers and five thousand unmotivated troops protected the city. A nervous Louis hurriedly ordered increased forces to be deployed to Paris.

The cost of bread rose daily in the early summer. Although the harvest of 1789 was far better than the previous year, it would be weeks before that grain would show up on the market. With speculators hoarding flour, empty bellies had no respect for law and order, triggering spontaneous riots throughout France. The government purchased grain abroad, but not enough to lower the price or calm the fears. The national chaos increased.

Surrounded by soldiers, most of whom were Swiss and German mercenaries, the Parisians feared a major crackdown was in the works. Two companies of the Gardes Françaises, the native-born infantrymen of the king's household, who numbered about thirty-six hundred soldiers, defied orders to confront the rioters. Their commander confined these men to their barracks for insubordination.

Disorder reigned in the streets as unwitting pedestrians and visitors were accosted and forced to declare their support for the National Assembly. Those who hesitated got roughed up until they professed allegiance. This sort of intimidation would escalate to summarily hanging unpatriotic suspects from the nearest lamppost.

By July 6 troops reached Paris with orders to protect bridges and vital buildings. As troops patrolled the city, the edgy urban dwellers sought to arm themselves against the Crown's rumored repression. It would take just one spark to light the fuse of the populace's pent-up fury. That event exploded on July 12, and the repercussions would continue for several unforgettable days.

In the meantime, the National Assembly deputies often resembled caretakers of a madhouse, coping with the onslaught of reform initiatives while deflecting cheers and jeers from the public galleries. A parade of pushy petitioners, starry-eyed well-wishers, and tiresome whiners occasionally occupied the podium. British visitors, accustomed to the more orderly Parliament in England, were surprised by the carnival atmosphere that prevailed in the chamber. And a French gentleman marveled at the many females who crowded the visitors' gallery: "There are women who never miss a session, who stay there five and six hours at a time. Don't they have husbands and children waiting?"

But work did get accomplished. Threatened by the foreign mercenaries descending on Paris, the prophet Mirabeau predicted that the increase of troops "might provoke the most prudent minds beyond the bounds of moderation, and that the people might commit excesses, the original idea of which would have horrified them."

Louis responded, "The troops were only intended to prevent fresh disturbances, to maintain law and order, and to ensure and even to protect the freedom which must reign in the deliberations of the assembled deputies. Only men of evil intent would mislead my people over the precautionary measures I am taking."

Almost as a postscript to his message, the king heightened apprehensions among the deputies suggesting, "If the necessary presence of these troops in the neighborhood of Paris should still cause umbrage, I should proceed on the request of the Estates General to transfer the Assembly to Noyon or to Soissons, and then go myself to Compiègne in order to maintain the necessary contact with it." The deputies smelled something rotten coming their way. And just imagine their indignation at still being referred to as the Estates General! The National Assembly felt that the laconic king needed a jolt in his ample derriere, while Louis reckoned that deputies, such as

Mirabeau, required a timeout in the Bastille. A high-noon rendezvous was ticking closer.

Meanwhile, Louis could not stomach another twenty-four hours with Necker. The final straw was as an explosive argument between them about the troops taking up positions in Paris. On July 11 during lunchtime, Necker received a terse note from Louis informing him that he was fired. Necker didn't even finish his meal; he and his wife packed a few necessities and picked the quickest road to safety from the royal wrath.

Louis urgently formed a new cabinet appointing as minister of war the septuagenarian Marshall Victor Broglie who would also command the troops in Paris. Louis appealed to him: "I need someone near me on whose loyalty I can count and who knows how to command troops. I will not try to conceal the fact that the situation is rather critical, but I count on your zeal and attachment to me. Please come to Versailles as soon as you can."

Marshall Broglie predicted that unrest would break out in the capital as soon as news of Necker's departure hit the streets. He sent an anxious note to Baron Besenval, his man in the trenches in Paris: "As I am apprised from many quarters, there is reason to fear a violent insurrection tomorrow. If there is violence we cannot defend the whole of Paris and you must confine yourself to the plan for the defense of the Bourse, the Royal Treasury, the Bastille, and the Invalides." Broglie, aware of the limitations of his forces, chose to protect the citadels of primary concern.

To replace the ousted Necker, Louis chose Baron Breteuil. Louis' brother Provence assured the king that "Breteuil was the only man capable of saving France." Breteuil, a firm subscriber of autocratic rule, would enter office with like-minded men. He was bent on preserving the stale status quo.

To bolster his image as a tough guy, Breteuil swore: "If it is necessary to burn Paris, then we will burn it."

"I prefer liberty with danger, than peace with slavery."
Jean-Jacques Rousseau

Chapter 49

This Can't Be Happening

*B*y late Sunday morning, July 12, news inundated Paris that Necker and his allied ministers were toast. The replacements under the leadership of Baron Breteuil stirred ardent resentment. Most Parisians suspected that the queen and the king's brother Count Artois had orchestrated Necker's downfall. Artois had recently branded Necker as "nothing but a fornicating foreign bastard."

The average person equated the loss of Necker with imminent repression and steeper bread prices. Worried Parisians rushed to the sanctuary of the Palais Royal to voice their apprehensions. By Sunday afternoon the grounds of the Palais Royal teemed with hyperventilating citizens listening to impromptu harangues.

One of the fellows on a soapbox was the lackluster lawyer Camille Desmoulins, a laughingstock in the courtroom due to a stammer. Miraculously on this day, his speech flowed like a Pentecostal preacher: "Citizens, you know that the nation asked for Necker to stay, and now he's driven out. Can they defy you more insolently? After this, they will stop at nothing. Tonight they are plotting, perhaps already preparing a St. Bartholomew's massacre of patriots." Everyone was spellbound with his numbing prophecies. He finished with a vow that all rapt listeners took to heart: "I who have been timid now feel myself to be a new man. Now I can die with joy for so glorious a cause, and pierced with blows I, too, would write in my own blood, 'France is free.'"

Before his believers dispersed, Desmoulins entreated them to arm themselves against the troops. Desmoulins suggested that they identify themselves to one another by wearing a badge of solidarity; the crowd chose the colors of Paris—red and blue. Pumped with hate, the people scattered into the streets with two purposes: get as many arms as possible, and hunt down any hoarders of grain.

The rioters imposed impromptu martial law on Paris; theaters and commercial businesses wisely boarded up shop. The rioters divided into groups as they roamed the streets looking for arms. One group got sidetracked at the Wax Museum owned by Monsieur Pierre Curtius. They "borrowed," with Curtius' quick assent, the busts of Necker and the Duke of Orléans as inspirational motivators for their rampage through Paris. Marauders rushed through the streets breaking into any site that might store arms and ammunition. At the monastery of Saint Lazare, the rioters scored a bonanza when they uncovered fifty wagons of grain and countless casks of wine. They hauled the grain off to the public markets, but they consumed the wine on the spot as the trembling monks either hid themselves or took flight.

Unimaginably, The Duke of Orléans capped off the drama of the day with an appearance at the king's ceremonial bedtime service. Orléans was the last person Louis wished to see on that tense day. Worst of all, the king considered the duke's radical enclave of the Palais Royal to be one of the primary incubators of his troubles. Since the duke was the man with the highest rank present that evening, the honor fell to him to present the king's nightshirt. Orléans bowed and offered the garment. The king snatched his nightshirt and barked out to his cousin, "What do you want here?" Orléans replied he wished to know the king's orders. The king shouted for him to get out and return to his nest of iniquity. The king's harshness humiliated the duke and he withdrew to cast his fate irrevocably with the dissenters.

Although the Duke of Orléans contributed to the fall of the monarchy, he was more of a collective participant than a leader of the events. Mirabeau tried for a year to persuade Orléans to parlay his popularity with the people into a significant role, perhaps even to ascend the throne. To Mirabeau's disappointment, the duke did not take the plunge. Later, Mirabeau would dismiss him as "a eunuch who has the desire but not the potency." Thereafter, Mirabeau resigned himself to pursue the king and queen in his quest to establish constitutional monarchy in France.

A new municipal government was hastily installed on July 13 along with the formation of a local militia. Rioters besieged city hall and demanded that Jacques Flesselles, the provost of Paris (a sort of mayor) hand over any arms in his possession. Flesselles mollified the mob by distributing several hundred guns. The crowd roared for more, prompting Flesselles to send them to the Carthusian Monastery where he guaranteed they would find more weapons. Finding no arms there, the infuriated mob scurried back to the deceitful provost, prepared to hang him on the spot. Somehow Flesselles convinced them that the Invalides had a huge arsenal of weapons, including thousands of muskets and some cannon stored in its cellars. He also blurted out that the Bastille had a sizable arsenal, too. The shaken, but still breathing, provost was abandoned like a rag doll as the militia hastened away.

The Invalides, a landmark building from the reign of Louis XIV, was a hospital and retirement home for the military. The crowd demanded weapons from the governor of the Invalides, Count Sombreuil. The gentleman pleaded that he needed instructions from his superiors. The militia bought his story, but swore to return. When the mob dispersed, Sombreuil sprang into action, covertly transferring barrels of gun powder to the Bastille for safe keeping. The same impatient crowd showed up early the next morning on July 14, expecting an affirmative answer from Sombreuil. He apologized that he had not yet received a reply to his request. Stampeding men swept Sombreuil aside, swarming the Invalides. The veterans in residence fraternized with the rioters, guiding them to stored weapons. In the confusion, Sombreuil miraculously escaped the mob and fled the scene.

Baron Besenval's troops, stationed near the Invalides, defiantly stayed put in their barracks, ignoring Besenval's orders. Any further hopes for the king's army to save the day evaporated on the spot. Thomas Jefferson noted this inglorious moment: "It was remarkable that not only the Invalides themselves made no opposition, but that a body of five thousand foreign troops, encamped within four hundred yards, never stirred." It was during the invasion of the Invalides that the Baron Besenval sheepishly withdrew his forces from the center of the city.

Finally, the emboldened rebels had plenty of weapons. But without gun powder and cartridges their arms were emasculated appendages. They knew the fortress of the Bastille possessed a vast supply of both requirements—their obvious next stop.

As a prison, the Bastille stood nearly empty. No one knew the prison better than the forty-nine-year-old Governor Launay. He was born there and inherited the post of governor from his father. Not a harsh jailer, he housed seven prisoners, and none of them were languishing in irons. Their cells ranked just below flophouse standards. Four prisoners were convicted forgers, two were insane, and the seventh was a nobleman detained at the request of his family for being a serial sex offender.

On July 14 rioters massed outside the Bastille, demanding that Launay release all of his powder and cartridges. The governor flatly refused until he received orders from Versailles. Two delegates from city hall entered the Bastille to negotiate with Launay. With a force of one hundred men, Launay faced a nasty crowd of thousands surrounding him. He promised the municipal officials that he would hold his fire unless attacked. In the meantime, he sent a desperate message to Baron Besenval pleading for immediate reinforcements. The baron responded with a useless note: "Monsieur de Launay is to hold firm to the end; I have sent him sufficient forces."

The situation grew uglier as the standoff wore on. Gunfire erupted from both sides with the besiegers claiming that Launay had fired first. With no help from outside, Launay proposed to allow the crowd access, provided he and his soldiers could safely depart. If not, he would blow up the entire neighborhood with the stored gunpowder—not the most diplomatic gesture of surrender.

This ultimatum infuriated the crowd even more. They screamed, "Down with the bridges, no capitulation." At this point the wildly desperate Launay ordered a corporal to unbolt the heavy wooden doors. The crowd became an unleashed weapon and within minutes they filled the Bastille's inner sanctum.

Once inside, they seized Launay. Everybody demanded his head on the spot. Terrified, the hapless governor was marched off to city hall being severely beaten along the route. He arrived at city hall a battered mess, hoping his safety was now more secure. But the mindless mob spontaneously slaughtered Launay on the steps of city hall and shoved his head on a pike to wild cheers. Atop the pike, a sign proclaimed, "Launay, governor of the Bastille, disloyal and treacherous enemy of the people."

But this vengeful crowd was not done; they remembered Provost Flesselles' deceit as well. They dragged Flesselles out of city hall to face a summary trial at the Palais Royal enclave. But the venom of the crowd was so overpowering that they murdered Flesselles along the way. His head joined Governor Launay's on an accompanying pike. Now, with two heads swaying atop pikes, the delirious crowd marched off proudly displaying their prizes.

This macabre conga dance would become a frequent sight through the streets of Paris for months to come.

As the disturbances in Paris reached their climax on July 14, Louis XVI's belligerent brother Count Artois insisted that the king use brutal force to split open some rebel heads. This would forever be Louis' dilemma: How do you justify the slaughter of your people to maintain your crown? To Artois' draconian demand, the king replied:

> I have thought this over. To resist at this moment would be to expose the monarchy to peril; it would lose us all. I have retracted my orders; our troops shall quit Paris. I shall employ gentler means. Do not speak to me of a show of force. I believe it more prudent to temporize, to yield to the storm and above all to bide my time for the awakening of the men of good will and the love of the French for their King.

These sentiments summarized what would become the king's mantra in times of crisis. As indecisive as he was as a leader, the king remained constant in his determination to refrain from spilling the blood of his subjects. Receiving Louis' reply, Artois' passions bordered on contempt for his brother.

All through the day of July 14 Louis received bulletins of the mayhem prevailing in Paris. In the afternoon, Louis learned of the plundering of arms at the Invalides. Later in the evening, Duke Liancourt, the first gentleman of the bedchamber, filled in Louis on the fall of the Bastille, the murders of Governor Launay and Provost Flesselles, and the collapse of his military forces under Baron Besenval's command. The demoralized king felt battered by the endless stream of bad news.

And the news suddenly got worse. Salacious pamphlets about the queen were unearthed in the bowels of the Bastille. These writings about the queen were hidden from the public by the efforts of the crown censors. These smutty pamphlets, coupled with Jeanne La Motte's recently published X-rated memoirs, suddenly flooded the market, cementing the general perception that the Austrian Woman was an out-of-control, sex-crazed, power-hungry bitch. Overnight, Antoinette was popularly referred to as the reincarnation of Messalina, the sex-addicted, politically ambitious wife of Emperor Caligula from the Roman empire—nobody's role model.

The following morning Louis entered the National Assembly announcing that the troops protecting Paris would be withdrawn to ease the fears of the people. Once the king departed, the Assembly selected a group of eighty-eight deputies to go to Paris to deliver the olive branch from the king, with Lafayette serving as spokesperson.

Once in Paris, Lafayette encountered the newly-formed militia, suddenly baptized as the National Guard. Their members insisted that Lafayette assume command. Dreaming of being France's version of General Washington, Lafayette accepted the challenge.

Next, Parisians fingered the astronomer Sylvain Bailly to be their first mayor of Paris, replacing the murdered Flesselles. Bailly—aware that his predecessor's head perched above him on a pike—reluctantly accepted the sensitive job of restoring calm and order. Within weeks, Bailly discovered what a thankless job he had assumed. He lamented the lack of order in Paris sighing, "Everybody knows how to command, and nobody knows how to obey." Bailly would never know another day's peace.

All of the visiting deputies received the new cockade of red, blue, and white to wear in their hats. After the fall of the Bastille, this badge became the de rigueur article of dress symbolizing the new French nation. Red and blue represented the colors of Paris, and white, the Bourbon dynasty.

The tricolor cockade, the national emblem of unity, appeared everywhere overnight, becoming a passport to personal safety. It immediately became a staple of the uniforms of the National Guard who were replacing the royal armed forces. The fashion houses were in a tizzy to weave this patriotic advertisement into every fashion adornment. Cockades, made out of fabric in the shape of a rosette, normally about three to four inches in diameter, were usually pinned to the hats of men and women. Ladies incorporated them in their coiffures, shoes, and fans. No matter who you were, you were wise to wear one.

Expecting to be hailed as heroes, the deputies of the National Assembly were instead pelted with angry shouts as they proceeded from city hall to Notre Dame Cathedral for a thanksgiving service. The Parisians were not content with the king's half a loaf of withdrawing forces. The crowd clamored for the return of Necker and the ouster of the beastly Baron Breteuil and his clique of ministers. Suddenly, the deputies became desirous of returning to a calmer Versailles.

As the people of Paris loudly voiced their demands, the National Assembly at Versailles became a furnace of fiery debates. The most disturbing speeches in the Assembly that day concerned the spread of violence in Paris. The Assembly whitewashed the murder of Crown officials as unavoidable atrocities, insisting that the anger of the people had been tested beyond human limits. Some deputies justified the violence by invoking Thomas Jefferson's admonishment: "The tree of Liberty must be refreshed from time to time with the blood of patriots and tyrants."

As the visiting deputies from the Assembly worked to diffuse the public anger in Paris, a building contractor named Palloy was also busy. On July 15 he appeared at city hall offering his services to dismantle the Bastille. Municipal officials consented "that the Bastille should be demolished without delay." Palloy won the contract, turning it into an entrepreneur's dream. Within weeks, the tumbling remains of the Bastille topped the list of sights to see in Paris. The imaginative Chateaubriand hailed the emergence of the latest in-spot, noting the predictable behavior of tourists, no matter the century: Makeshift cafes were set up under tents, people squeezed into them; numerous carriages paraded or stopped at the foot of the towers. Elegantly-dressed women, fashionable young men, placed on different levels of the Gothic rubble, mixed with the half-dressed workers, who were demolishing the walls to the cheers of the crowd.

On July 16 Louis met with his cabinet and family. The queen and Count Artois voted for fleeing to the fortified town of Metz. Broglie warned that he could not assure them a safe passage due to the unreliability of the troops and the hostility of the populace. The king's brother Provence urged Louis to hold his ground at Versailles. Antoinette persisted in her pleas to leave Versailles, but the king would not commit himself. As the king pondered the situation, he felt the only solution was to capitulate to the demands of the Parisians. The National Assembly was notified of the king's decision: Breteuil would be dismissed; and Necker recalled. The king promised to go to Paris and personally acknowledge these changes. Mirabeau, the seer of the Revolution, gloomily remarked, "This is how Kings are led to the scaffold."

"The measure of a man is what he does with power."
Plato

Chapter 50

The Parisians Rewrite the Rules

*A*ntoinette begged Louis to abort such a dangerous visit to Paris. He comforted her but proceeded with his plans. Anticipating that he might be assassinated, Louis wrote his will and received the sacraments. He appointed his brother Provence, Lieutenant-General of the kingdom, with authority to act for him in his absence. The phlegmatic king left Versailles at nine in the morning with his family forlornly watching from the palace windows. Twelve bodyguards and thirty-two deputies selected by a random drawing from the National Assembly accompanied Louis to Paris.

Antoinette was an emotional wreck during the king's absence. She prepared a brief speech to deliver to the National Assembly just in case the king failed to return: "Messieurs, I remit to your hands the wife and the family of your Sovereign; do not allow that which has been joined in Heaven to be separated on earth." During the unsettling hours of waiting, she fretted, wept, prayed, and scanned the road for any sign of her husband's carriage. During the vigil at her window, the queen uttered with bitterness, "Today we pay dearly for our infatuation and enthusiasm for the American War." You know what they say about hindsight.

While Louis' carriage headed for Paris, other coaches carrying VIPs were speeding for the French border. The night before, the king ordered his brother Count Artois, the Polignacs, Baron Breteuil, Prince Condé, and Reverend Vermond to leave France until the public turmoil abated. It did not take much to convince them to flee because a bounty had been placed on all of their heads by the radicals in Paris. Antoinette suffered a significant loss with their departure, especially losing Gabrielle Polignac and Vermond. Her social world was shrinking, as were her hopes for a stable life.

When Louis arrived in Paris, the city was almost unrecognizable. The streets overflowed with the newly-formed National Guard under the command of Lafayette. From Louis' carriage window, it appeared that everyone brandished a weapon. The king heard the repeated refrain of a popular song of the time: "Where is one better than in the arms of one's family?" This should have been a huge hint to Louis that the Parisians were determined to uproot him from that sinkhole of Versailles.

To hammer home this point, Sylvain Bailly, the neophyte mayor of Paris, presented the keys of the city to Louis, coupled with a trace of sarcasm: "I bring to your Majesty the keys of your good city of Paris, they are the same ones which were presented to Henry IV. He had reconquered his people; now it is the people who have reconquered their king." This dig contrasting the first Bourbon king with the current one drew a cool reaction from Louis. The king slowly proceeded to city hall where he was handed the newly designed tricolor cockade. With resigned good grace, Louis attached it to his hat, earning approval from the surly crowd that demanded royal contrition. Meanwhile, rumbling groans shook the tomb of Louis XIV.

Ambassadors, including Thomas Jefferson, commented on the day's events. They wrote home describing the humbling of the French king and the upheaval of the governing system, all of them labeling it a revolution. Jefferson reported to his boss in America, Secretary of State John Jay: "The King made apologies such as no Sovereign ever made and no people ever received." Perhaps the most poignant report home came from the queen's avatar, Count Mercy. He detailed the dreadful events befalling the Crown: "However unbelievable the Revolution that has just been accomplished may appear, it is nonetheless absolutely certain that from now on the city of Paris has assumed the role of King in France, and that it can, if it pleases, send an army of forty to fifty thousand citizens to surround the Assembly and dictate the laws to it."

Content for the moment with their victory over Louis, the jubilant people of Paris allowed the bewildered man to return to Versailles. At half-past ten in the evening, a weary king arrived at the chateau. Immediately surrounded by his overwrought wife, concerned family, and jumpy members of his court, the king, amid tears, proudly told his queen, "Happily there was no bloodshed, and I swear French blood will never be shed by my order."

After Louis' acceptance of the new political pyramid, most observers considered the Revolution to be over. In reality, the Revolution was just gaining steam. The bloodthirsty Parisians continued their killing streak after the fall of the Bastille. On July 23 they murdered two more perceived enemies of liberty, Joseph Foulon, a member of Breteuil's council, along with his son-in-law, Bertier Sauvigny.

Gouverneur Morris, an American citizen and patriot of the American War, was in Paris at this time of civic disintegration, promoting the interests of American tobacco growers. By chance, he witnessed a sickening parade of body parts:

> After dinner, I was walking a little under the Arcade of the Palais
> Royal, waiting for my carriage. At this very moment, the head
> and body of Monsieur de Foulon are introduced in triumph. His
> crime is to have accepted a place in the Ministry. This mutilated
> form of an old man of seventy-five years is shown to Bertier, his
> son-in-law, the Intendant of Paris, and afterwards he also is put to
> death and cut to pieces, the populace carrying about the mangled
> fragments with savage joy. Gracious God, what a people!

Meanwhile, Antoinette had to find a replacement for the governess to the Children of France following Gabrielle Polignac's unexpected departure. Antoinette wisely selected the solidly virtuous forty-year-old widow, Madame Tourzel. In a letter to Tourzel, Antoinette described her children, reflecting her keen maternal involvement. The letter offered a peek into the queen's matured character:

> My son is four years old, and four months, minus two days. His
> health has always been good, but even in the cradle we noticed
> that his nerves were delicate and that the slightest unusual noise
> affected him. For instance, he is afraid of dogs because he heard
> them bark next to him. I never forced him to see them, because
> as his reasoning faculty develops, his fears will disappear. Like
> all strong, healthy children, he is thoughtless, light-headed, and
> violent in fits of anger; but he is good-natured, gentle, and even
> affectionate when his thoughtlessness does not get the better of
> him. He has an enormous sense of pride, which properly directed,
> he might one day turn to his advantage. Until he feels at ease
> with someone, he knows how to control himself and master his

impatience and anger, so as to seem gentle and friendly. He is extremely reliable when he has promised something, but he is very indiscreet; he easily repeats what he has heard; and often without intending to lie, he adds things according to his imagination. This is his greatest fault and must be corrected. I repeat—he is good-natured; and by being sensitive and firm, but not too strict, one can always get him to do what one wants. But strictness would make him rebel, for he has a strong character for his age. For example, from earliest childhood, the words "I'm sorry" always shocked him. He will do and say anything you want when he is wrong; but he will only pronounce the words "I'm sorry" with tears and great difficulty.

My children have always been accustomed to having complete trust in me, and when they do something wrong, to tell me so themselves. When I scold them, I look more hurt and sad about what they did than angry. I have accustomed them that a yes or no from me is irrevocable, but I always give them a reason befitting their age, so that they do not think that it is moodiness on my part. My son does not know how to read and has difficulty learning; but he is too distracted to concentrate. He has no idea of rank in his head and I would like that to continue; our children always find out soon enough who they are. He is very fond of his sister and has a good heart. He was born cheerful; for his health, he needs to be outside a great deal, and I think it is best to let him play and work on the terraces, rather than have him go any farther.

Antoinette was a mother hen who kept a close eye on her precious chicks. Even though her son was the heir, Antoinette emphasized that Madame Tourzel treat her charges equally, noting that both children were equally cherished by their parents. The queen's mention of her son's pride revealed her expectations that he would become a great king of France since he carried the blood of Empress Maria Theresa. The queen's advice was no doubt colored by the uneven upbringing she had experienced in Vienna. Antoinette promised herself that her children would be better prepared for the destiny awaiting them.

When the wildly popular Necker returned to office, Antoinette granted him an audience. Expecting Necker to be grateful for his reappointment, Her

Majesty emphasized in their brief tête-à-tête that Necker was a fortunate man to regain the king's favor. Aware that the political table settings were reset, Necker dealt the queen a serving of reality, "My zeal to serve the king is a duty but I have no obligation to be grateful." Necker's words stunned Antoinette into momentary silence, prompting him to take advantage of the queen's shock by grabbing her hand, kissing it, and bowing out of her presence. He might as well have puked all over her gown. How dare this commoner seize her hand without its being offered! You never touched the person of the monarch without their permission. Apparently, the beatific aura of the royals was beginning to disintegrate.

After the delirium of toppling the Bastille had ebbed, an unease rippled through France, known as the summer of the Great Fear. Rumors proliferated of a royalist plot to suppress the budding Revolution with wild tales of the queen luring foreign troops to overrun France. The scarcity of grain and its suspected hoarding by wealthy producers did not improve the people's temper either. Throughout the kingdom the king's agents and army soldiers fled their posts in large numbers. Many municipalities stepped into the vacuum to establish their own form of local government and defense. Peasants forced nobles to destroy legal documents spelling out their feudal obligations. For those lords who proved to be stubborn, burning their chateau solved the impasse nicely. France was becoming a nation of chaotic crazies. The Venetian Ambassador wrote home, "There no longer exists executive power, laws, magistrates or police. A horrible anarchy prevails."

"You know the world is going crazy when
the best rapper is a white guy, the best golfer
is a black guy, the tallest guy in the NBA is Chinese,
the Swiss hold the America's Cup,
France is accusing the U.S. of arrogance,
Germany doesn't want to go to war,
and the most powerful men in America are named
'Bush,' 'Dick,' and 'Colin.'"
Chris Rock

Chapter 51

The Deputies Go Rogue

*M*ost deputies in the National Assembly fretted about the lawless behavior popping up everywhere. The environs of Versailles seemed especially unstable, prompting Necker to urge the government to move to Compiègne, about sixty-five miles away. Even though the queen was pushing for the same objective, Louis refused to budge from his ancestral home. Beneath the fear that stoked the violence festered a suspicion that the queen was plotting to squash the Revolution.

An innocent target of the imagined royal crackdown snared a visiting Englishman, Arthur Young, a respected agronomist and advocate for small farmers. In the summer of 1789 he traveled through France interviewing farmers, observing planting practices, and collecting soil samples. Passing through Clermont, he was nearly torn to pieces. The half-crazed villagers were ready to dispatch him on the spot for being a foreign emissary of Antoinette. He related his harrowing experience: "They declared that I was an agent of the Queen intending to blow up the town with a mine and send all who escaped to the galleys. The care that must have been taken to render the character of that princess detested among the people is incredible; and there seems everywhere to be no absurdities too gross, nor circumstances too impossible for their faith." Fortunately, Arthur Young defused the crowd's irrational anger and got out of town fast, but not before scooping up some soil samples.

The National Assembly barely took a collective breath in August 1789. They usurped the legislative powers of the king, allowing him the right of only casting a veto of legislation. The Assembly passed the first of two significant decrees. First, while debating how to restore law and order in France, the deputies suggested dismantling many seigniorial rights that aristocrats and clergy had enjoyed for centuries. Several big names in the pantheon of French aristocracy concluded that "this insurrection, however damnable, can find its excuse in vexations," meaning the abuses of feudalism. Like the lyrics from the song, "Don't the Girls All Get Prettier at Closing Time," the deputies got carried away with the renunciation of their privileges. By two in the morning on August 4, the deputies basically handed over the keys to the castle, erasing centuries of oppression. Count Ségur would recall the giveaway years later:

> Whatever the language of freedom, its valor pleased us; equality seemed convenient. It is pleasant to climb down when you can climb back up as soon as you like; we unthinkingly appreciated both our patrician advantages and the attraction of a plebeian philosophy. Even though our privileges and the vestiges of our former powers were crumbling beneath our steps, the little game pleased us. We saw the spectacle, not the danger.

With the sobering approach of dawn, remorse set in. The National Assembly amended the original wording of the legislation over the following week allowing plenty of escape clauses for the entitled. Even the champion of the people, Count Mirabeau, warned his valet not to forget his station in life. When the boss is accustomed to traveling first class, you can't expect him to join his gofer in cheesy economy.

The second accomplishment adopted was The Declaration of the Rights of Man and of The Citizen, "affirming that men are born free, and remain free and equal in rights." The text, primarily written by Lafayette, with Thomas Jefferson whispering in his ear, was very similar in spirit to the founding documents of the American revolutionaries. This declaration became a cornerstone of French political thinking. A reading of its fine print, though, exposed the limited extent of these freedoms; white Catholic French males over twenty-five were awarded the rights enshrined in the text, but it excluded thirteen million females. Even before the ink dried, its implementation would be rocky.

Both pieces of legislation made Louis huff and puff that he alone made laws. Louis put the Assembly on notice that he would not accept the Declaration of Rights unless they drew up a companion Declaration of Duties. Louis was particularly incensed by the proposal to dismantle seigniorial rights: "I will never consent to the spoliation of my clergy or my nobility." There goes the king again using words such as 'never'—not a credible negative in his oratorical arsenal.

Luckily, for Louis, a growing backlash sprouted from both nobles and clergy in the Assembly who feared a total collapse of the social order spelling their personal ruin. Suddenly they wanted to bolster the king's authority, not diminish it. The king counted on their support to shift the power throttle back into his grasp and impose the reforms he offered two months earlier on June 23.

But the more radical deputies believed the national mood would not permit any turning back. And by now Louis' threats of royal resistance were not taken seriously. The local odd-makers were bullish that the king would back down and approve what he now resisted. He just needed a forceful nudge in that direction. That unpleasant shove was already on the horizon.

"We're mad because we've been had."
Sarah Palin

Chapter 52

Kiss Versailles Goodbye

*D*uring the late summer of 1789 some outspoken delegates in the National Assembly urged the government to move from Versailles, by force if necessary. Barnave, the firebrand visionary from Grenoble advocated that the king take up residence in the Tuileries Palace in Paris. This move would benefit the advances of the Revolution and secure the king's compliance to the will of the people. Barnave's colleagues listened lukewarmly, but nothing came of his suggestions.

However, in Paris this message was at the forefront of the vitriolic rhetoric of two radicals, Jean-Paul Marat and Camille Desmoulins. With the king in Paris, royal authority would stem from the people and no longer from God's Anointed One.

Louis, prodded by his advisers, decided to bolster security at Versailles by ordering the Flanders Regiment, a force of eleven hundred infantrymen, to redeploy to the chateau. Upon their arrival, they were offered the customary welcome of a fraternization meal with the soldiers already assigned to Versailles. But their reception on the first of October was different from the normal meet and greet. A sumptuous repast was served on the stage of the palace Opera House, where the king and queen had dined on their wedding night nineteen years earlier. In appreciation of their arrival, the royal couple made a cameo appearance, exciting the troops. Fueled by the flowing wine, the men loudly belted out a popular song:

Oh, Richard, oh my king,
The universe abandons you.
On the earth there is only myself
Who cares about you!

The display of loyalty boosted the spirits of the royal couple. Their four-year-old heir, Louis Charles, a captivating charmer, was engulfed by these burly army guys. The royals departed the Opera House with revived spirits, feeling their personal security was now tighter.

The next morning the Parisian newspapers decried the evening's reception as a reactionary bacchanal with the Austrian Woman serving as the mistress of ceremonies. Yellow journalism at its worst blared that the sacred tricolor cockade had been trampled underfoot. The news of this desecration sent agitators into a rage, vowing no more violations of the national symbol. Camille Desmoulins fed the anger of the crowd, demanding that the king be brought to Paris to purge him of traitors hostile to the cause of the Revolution.

The morning of October 5, 1789, began at Versailles with its predictable rhythm of activities. After the usual morning rituals, the king decided to hunt, and the queen stole away to the Petit Trianon. In Paris, the same day began in a ferment. Alarm bells sounded as women converged on city hall, seeking revenge over the abuse of the national cockade. They also wanted bread which was scarce. A shout went up that it was the queen who was scheming to have them starve. In no time at all, another cry "to Versailles for bread" arose. By ten in the morning, women set out on foot for the palace and Antoinette's breadbox.

It rained intermittently during the muddy trek from Paris further dampening the mood of the protesters. By midafternoon, routine at Versailles receded into ancient history. The vanguard of ragtag women began trickling into Versailles after the twelve-mile trudge from Paris. Eventually, six thousand women and a smattering of paid male informers were pressed against the shuttered gates of the palace, armed with pikes, pitchforks, brooms, some muskets, and even a cannon. Most were market workers, known as *poissonardes* for the knives they carried to cut fish and other edible commodities that they sold on the streets.

The palace staff was terrified. A page, frantically dispatched from the palace, found the queen at the Petit Trianon, exhorting her to return to the chateau immediately. Without looking back, the queen hurried to Versailles, not imagining that she would never again enjoy her private hideaway. The king was also tracked down during his hunt, and sped back to the palace.

Once Louis rounded up his advisers, the sniping began. Heated opinions were hurled in a barroom fashion before the king. Some urged getting out of harm's way in a hurry, while others advocated standing firm. When Louis asked Antoinette for her preference, she told him she could be packed in a jiffy as soon as he gave the signal. The minister of the royal household, Saint-Priest, seconded the queen's views, urgently advising the royals to flee for the more fortified chateau of Rambouillet, twenty miles from Versailles. Saint-Priest bluntly warned Louis, "Sire, if you let them take you to Paris tomorrow, you will lose your crown."

The king's brother Count Provence and Minister Necker pressured Louis to stay put at Versailles. The befuddled king kept muttering, "Imagine, a fugitive king, a fugitive king!" There was a suggestion at one point for the queen and her children to leave without the king. But Her Majesty dismissed that option as unacceptable, saying she would rather die at the feet of her sovereign. Years later, François Hue, the dauphin's valet, bemoaned the mistake of not hurrying to Rambouillet: "If only it had been God's will that it should be followed." But God had nothing to do with this man-made mess.

Wave after wave of sodden women surrounded the palace, chanting for bread and screaming that the Flanders Regiments be punished for desecrating the cockade. They were determined to force events in their favor and to haul Louis and the National Assembly back to Paris for better supervision.

A portion of these women detoured to the National Assembly, swarming the male bastion of legislation. The intruders peppered the deputies with belligerent questions about the scarcity of bread. It was an uncomfortable moment for the deputies who normally received acclaim from the visitor's gallery. The President of the Assembly, Jean-Joseph Mounier, promised a prompt investigation. A few gals advised Mounier to "Shut the f**k up" as they commandeered the podium to berate the deputies. Some of these ladies began shedding their outer clothing to dry it out. Many deputies blushed at such unbecoming behavior as they scrambled for any ruse to get these harpies to go elsewhere.

Meanwhile, back in the palace, Louis finally consented to leave for Rambouillet. The queen swiftly alerted her children's nannies to be ready to leave within fifteen minutes. But it was too late. A restive, drenched crowd intentionally blocked any carriage exits, determined to keep their prizes captive. At one point, some vigilant rioters espied the gates of the king's stables opening as carriages were being led out. Alarmed that the king might flee, a crowd rushed the carriages to cut the harnesses, leading the horses away with them. The royals were trapped.

With tip-toeing out of the palace no longer an option, the ministers pressed the king on another possible way to appease the mob. They suggested that Louis sign the two decrees that he had been stalling on since August—the Declaration of Rights and the abolition of feudal privileges. The beleaguered king agreed, hoping his signature of approval would calm the explosive situation. This delayed acceptance did nothing to diffuse the wrath of the mob. What would it take to satisfy these people?

In the meantime, the Assembly deputies found a solution to their home invasion. They suggested that the women choose from their cohorts a delegation to appeal directly to the king. President Mounier and several deputies accompanied twelve handpicked women to petition the king. The convoy of deputies and spokeswomen had to fight their way to the palace gates. One of the guards recognized the pleading Mounier and, through a split-second opening of the gates, ushered this group into the palace. The king's daughter, Marie Thérèse, recalled years later her shock at the appearance of these women, who looked like scantily clad savages. The ten-year-old sheltered princess had never come face-to-face with such desperate people, the real face of France.

Louis always performed at his best when mixing with the common people. The female delegates were overcome by the king's warmth, as he promised them bread. One damsel fainted in Louis' presence, spurring the king to tend to her. The grateful delegation, still dazed from the royal interview, exited the king's apartments with a written order in the king's hand for flour from the royal warehouses. The court hoped that it had dodged a bullet, praying the marchers would troop back to Paris with their flour.

Since the fall of the Bastille, the have-nots of Paris had grown more defiant, aware of their mushrooming clout. The delegation that saw the king recounted the king's goodness. Incredulously, they were booed by the crowd and even called traitors. The agitated rioters were not in any mood to make nice. And they wanted more than bread for their trouble. Refusing to budge, the demonstrators sniffed the soured scent of royal weakness in the damp evening air.

> "And especially don't f**k with the vegans!
> Say 'I'm sorry' and run away as fast as you can.
> Don't f**k with the vegans because they will
> f**k you up ... BECAUSE THEY'RE HUNGRY."
> *Margaret Cho*

Chapter 53

A Fright to Remember

*H*ours later Lafayette arrived with a force of fifteen thousand men of the National Guard from Paris. Earlier, these troops had angrily defied Lafayette's orders to remain in Paris, threatening to lynch him. Hoping to avert an unparalleled bloodbath at Versailles, Lafayette led the National Guard rowdies, all the while fearing that the court and the National Assembly would perceive his move as a coup attempt. Arriving at Versailles, the troops from Paris fraternized with the local National Guardsmen. The troops loyal to the king on the opposite side of the palace gates felt like toy soldiers. How do you enforce "No Audiences Today" to such a throng—six thousand defiant warrior-women and thousands of armed men?

The mud-splattered Lafayette entered the National Assembly, hoping to calm the nervous deputies. Lafayette predicted that national law and order would return once the king sent away the Flanders Regiment and replaced the royal bodyguards with National Guardsmen. Furthermore, the king needed to make a conciliatory gesture with the national cockade to regain the confidence of his people. Lafayette knew he was walking a tightrope of delicate diplomacy among the opposing factions in the Assembly.

At midnight Lafayette was permitted to see the king. Accompanied by several aides, Lafayette ascended the staircase to the king's chambers, passing glowering courtiers who condemned him as a villain. Lafayette bowed before Louis, confidently telling the king that the palace was secure and Louis could count on the loyalty of the National Guard; both assertions were exaggerations. But Lafayette had to save face before this suspicious audience. He proposed to the king the same suggestions he had presented to the National Assembly, slipping in just one more detail—moving the royal family to Paris. Gasps echoed through the room. Louis agreed to the requests, except for the last one, saying he would reflect on it before giving an answer. Lafayette wished all a good night's sleep, and exited the palace. Just before two in the morning, the exhausted royal family and courtiers drifted off to their beds.

Lafayette made his rounds of the opposing armed forces to ensure that the National Guardsmen and the royal guards did not come to blows. It seemed tempers were subsiding, and fatigue was setting in with the help of lots of wine. After several hours of supervising, Lafayette plopped down fully dressed on a sofa in his family's nearby townhouse at five in the morning. He was jolted awake less than an hour later with news of an invasion of the palace.

A group of about two hundred screaming women had barged into the palace through a vulnerable gate. The horde of rioters dashed up the stairway rushing for the queen's apartments, shouting "Death to the Austrian." A bleeding Swiss guard burst into the antechamber of the queen's bedroom alerting the two female attendants to save the queen. Moments later the guard was murdered and decapitated. The shrieking ladies roused the half-asleep queen, urging her to make haste. In her nightgown and a cape, clutching her slippers, Antoinette and her ladies hurried to the paneled door concealed behind a large Gobelin tapestry and accessed a secret staircase connected to the king's suite of rooms above.

The fleeing fugitives could hear the cackles of the invaders spilling into the queen's bedroom below them. The furies pierced with their pikes the elegant walls and regal bed. Finding the king's door locked, the frantic queen and her ladies pounded on the door for admittance before the mob below discovered the secret stairway. After what seemed a lifetime, an alert attendant heard their cries and swung open the door as the shaken group spilled into the safety of the king's apartments. When the noise of the invasion awakened Louis XVI, he darted off to gather up his sleeping son. The entire family tearfully reunited in the ornate antechamber to the king's bedroom, shaken by the deafening threats from the crowd massed outside.

Startled awake by the news of the palace break-in, Lafayette swiftly secured the inner palace with his troops. He burst into the king's apartments, relieved to see the royal family safe. He prompted the king to address the agitated crowd. Louis strode onto the balcony reminding the rioters that he was "assured of the love of my good and faithful subjects." Roars of approval and "Long Live the King" rang out. They were satisfied to see that Louis had not escaped during the wee hours. The king also announced that the rumored disrespect to the nation by the Flanders regiment was a serious falsehood. With disbelief etched on the crowd's faces, Lafayette took a tricolor cockade and pinned it to one of the king's royal guardsmen. Suddenly, the public expressed their acceptance with lusty cries of "Long Live the Nation."

No sooner had the king vacated the balcony, when demands exploded from the crowd, "Where's the Austrian Woman?" Some feared that the queen had fled with her children during the night. They wanted to make sure that they were not being deceived. Lafayette invited the queen to appear on the balcony. The ashen Antoinette hesitated, not exactly feeling bulletproof. She grabbed each of her children by the hand and walked resolutely onto the balcony. Antoinette showed herself, still wearing her nightgown and her hair undone. Boos immediately erupted as the crowd snarled, "No children, no children." She shooed her children back into the palace, and faced the glaring mob—definitely not an Evita Perón moment. The queen expected to be shot to death within seconds. With all eyes and weapons fixed firmly on her, the queen could hear muffled sobs coming from within the balcony doors.

To break the unbearable tension and prevent a tragedy, Lafayette appeared next to the queen, bowed before her and kissed her hand, probably saving her life. Some scattered shouts of "Long Live the Queen" could be heard at last. Marie Antoinette, with her arms crossed over her chest, curtsied to the throng and reentered the palace, engulfed by her relieved family.

The queen and the king retired to an adjoining room with several ministers from where they could hear the deafening cries, "To Paris, to Paris." Seeing no way to evade the trap that ensnared him, the king resigned himself to leave for Paris. But in private, Antoinette made Louis promise her that when the opportunity to flee presented itself, he would act decisively. Louis pledged his agreement. Once more Lafayette appeared on the balcony followed by the royal couple. The king proclaimed, "My friends, I will go to Paris with my wife and children." Cheers of delight sprang from the crowd.

The dazed king and queen began the doleful task of vacating Versailles. At half-past noon, the king and his entourage descended the palace staircase for the last time. The caravan of cushy carriages lurched away from Versailles for a grueling crawl to Paris. As a forlorn Louis entered the carriage, he implored the count in charge, "You are now the master here; try to save my poor Versailles."

The count's wife eerily noted, "The only noise heard in the chateau was that of the doors, the blinds, and the window shutters which were being closed for the first time since the reign of Louis XIV. My husband made all of the arrangements for the defense of the chateau to prevent pillage."

This unprecedented procession from Versailles resembled a Fellini film. An endless stream of carriages transported the disbelieving residents from the cocoon of Versailles. Leading the pack was the ornate carriage transporting in numbed shock: the king; his queen; their two children; Louis' sister Madame Elisabeth; his brother Count Provence; and the royal governess, Madame Tourzel. Louis barely uttered a word during the dreadful journey. The queen focused on soothing her son, who was terrified by the continual burst of celebratory gunfire along the route. General Lafayette rode next to the monarch's carriage, serving as their escort. The very sight of him made Antoinette ill; she was convinced that he had failed to protect the royal family the previous night. From that day forward, his name was mud.

In contrast to the mummy-like occupants of the carriages, the marchers behaved like drunken revelers at Mardi Gras. They were deliriously conveying to Paris the pliable monarch; his stone-faced wife; their once glittering courtiers; and, the subdued deputies of the National Assembly. Amid squeals of delight, the rabble reveled in the outcome of their exploits. Spectators along the route grasped the significance of this ballsy venture, cringing at the site of the two clownish heads of the queen's bodyguards, waving on pikes with mouths open in silent protest. The triumphant marchers chanted that now they had in their clutches "the baker, the baker's wife, and the little apprentice, assuring plentiful bread for all."

Count Fersen lamented the cavalcade to his father in Sweden: "I returned to Paris in one of the carriages that followed the King. We were six and a half hours on the road. May God preserve me from ever again seeing so heartbreaking a spectacle as that of the last two days."

After being humiliated with a "Welcome Home" at city hall, the exhausted royal family entered the shabby palace of the Tuileries. The little heir jolted everyone out of their stupor as he blurted out, "Mama, it is very ugly here."

Trying to console the child, Antoinette reminded him, "My dear son, if this chateau was good enough for Louis XIV, then we must not be more demanding than him." But in her heart, she knew the kid was right. The place was a dump.

"The man forgot not, though in rags he lies,
And know the mortal through a crown's disguise."
Mark Akenside

Spotlight Five

The Days of Dread and Dodging

Chapter 54

They're Not in Kansas Anymore

On October 7 the royal family awoke to their new surroundings in the neglected Tuileries palace. When the queen beheld her image that morning in a mirror, she noticed that hair at her temples had turned a grayish white. Thank God for good cosmetics! Large crowds outside the palace walls demanded that the royals show themselves often. With the proximity of a compliant king, all would proceed smoothly with the Revolution. At least that was the word on the street.

Most governments abroad shared the same outlook as the people of France, delighted to see the proud Bourbons minimized on their throne. There were three notable exceptions: Sweden's Gustavus III, an unabashed Francophone, condemned the removal of king and queen from Versailles; France's Bourbon cousins in Spain urged a crackdown before the revolt trickled over its borders; and Catherine II of Russia deemed it odd that Louis XVI could be reduced to his state of pitiful weakness, remarking, "It must be sad to find that your last hope is your rosary beads."

The traumatized French royals cautiously adjusted to their uncertain circumstances. From day one in the Tuileries, no matter the consequences, Louis and Antoinette swore to never again be separated from each other nor from their children. After the horrors of their last night at Versailles, the royal couple insisted that their bedrooms be in close proximity to their children. The king had a suite of three rooms, excluding his bedchamber, on the first floor that adjoined the queen's suite of rooms. The king's bedroom was directly above the queen's, and his son's bedroom abutted his, and that of his daughter nearby. This arrangement eased some of their fears in the event there would be a sequel to the nightmare of October 6.

To render the Tuileries Palace more hospitable, renovations began immediately. Louis ordered some furnishings be brought from Versailles. Antoinette, who had been driven out of her familiar surroundings at Versailles, oversaw the makeover of her new domain. She accepted nothing less than her customary exacting standards, and she got what she wanted. With a much smaller palace to maintain, two thirds of the staff from Versailles awoke to pink slips on October 7.

Antoinette found a moment on that first day in the Tuileries to pen a hurried note to Count Mercy, who had skipped town temporarily after the frightening events of July. The queen described her situation, proving herself to be made of the same tough fiber as her mother:

> What has happened during the last twenty-four hours seems incredible. No description of it could be exaggerated; and indeed, whatever could be said would fall short of what we have seen and suffered. Rest assured I am well. Forgetting where we are and how we got here, we should be content with the mood of the people. I talk to the people, the militiamen, and the market women. I have been very well received, and the people asked us to stay. I told them that as far as the King and I are concerned, it depended upon them whether we stayed, for we asked nothing more than that all the hatred should stop and that the slightest bloodshed should make us flee in horror. Prudence and patience are my lot; and above all, courage.

No matter where the royal family lodged, court etiquette remained a fixture of daily life. The queen sorely missed her members-only enclave of the Petit Trianon and her idyllic village of The Hamlet. She had to adapt to the omnipresent prying eyes of servants, some of whom spied for the leading revolutionaries. In her more confined world, there would never be enough keys for all the locks she wished to secure. She resigned herself to embrace court etiquette, seeing through a different lens that these ceremonial rituals were a stabilizing force to remind everyone of her family's God-given station. Custom dictated that the royal family dine in public on Sunday and Tuesday afternoons. As hostess to the court, the queen provided entertainment in her suite of rooms three times per week. Beyond that, both the king and queen refused to resurrect balls, concerts, plays, etc. It was as though they were in mourning after losing their freedom.

The routines of Versailles resumed at the Tuileries, but with fewer courtiers in attendance. Almost every day, a duke, marquis, or count was noted to be absent, as emigration abroad became fashionably expedient.

Louis' passion for hunting took a big hit with the relocation to Paris. Louis was informed he could hunt in the nearby Bois de Boulogne, but he bristled when he learned that a detachment of National Guardsmen would accompany him. He balked at this affront and in protest, he at first refused to hunt. However, within months, restrictions eased, and the king would often ride out to visit his aunts at Bellevue or else do occasional stag hunting. This outlet of physical exercise and enjoyment of his horses kept the king from cascading into a permanent depression.

Antoinette consoled herself by taking frequent walks with her children in the palace gardens. An occasional ride in her carriage to visit a charity organization or a hospital were scheduled in hope that the public might soften their hardened image of her. On rare nights, she attended the theater, but most times she refused to venture beyond the palace gates.

The most difficult adjustment for the royal family was the omnipresent and unfamiliar National Guardsmen who hovered in watchful attendance. Six of them were assigned to the king whenever he walked out the front door with orders to protect the sovereign. Their true task was to serve as spies and to report any unpatriotic behavior.

Antoinette was forever scarred by the nightmares that plagued her, especially the heads of her brave bodyguards bobbing outside her carriage window during the forced march from Versailles. Receiving a deputation from city hall, the queen revealed, "I have witnessed everything, known everything, and forgotten everything." This sound bite was aimed at placating her captors, while Antoinette's true sentiments were more complicated. But she recognized the urgency of winning back the people, saying, "We must inspire confidence in this unhappy people. It is only an immense patience that can bring it back to us."

A committee established by the National Assembly conducted an official inquiry regarding the events of October 6. The National Assembly was caught off guard at how a volatile crowd so easily cowed both the royals and the elected representatives of the people. The mostly middle-class deputies resolved to prevent any repetitive surge of mob rule that was becoming an unacceptable pattern.

Everyone near the royals recognized the perilous implications of being carted off to Paris like bedecked circus animals. The king's sister, Madame Elisabeth, was not fooled by the hollow cheers from the crowds at the palace windows. She adored her brother and bombarded him with bracing advice, including a call for civil war. Yet, she always respectfully acceded to Louis' ineffectual responses. She does not paint a Greuze-like rendering of a tender departure from Versailles, writing to a friend, "We have left the cradle of our childhood. Why do I say left? They abducted us! What a journey! What frightful scenes! Never, never will they be effaced from my memory. What is certain is that we are prisoners here. My brother does not believe it yet, but time will show him. Our friends are here; they agree that we are lost."

> "Do you ever have the feeling of impending doom?"
> *Linus van Pelt*

Chapter 55

Changes by the Hour

*W*ithin days of his forced change of residences, Louis XVI finally got to vent in a letter to Charles IV, King of Spain. In this surreptitious correspondence, Louis revealed his strategy in this chess game of survival. He juggled placating the rebels on his doorstep with inspiring loyal subjects to reverse the descent into anarchy:

> I have chosen Your Majesty, as head of the second branch of the Bourbon family, to place into your hands this solemn protestation against my enforced sanction of all that has been done contrary to the royal authority since 15 July of this year and at the same time declare it my purpose to carry out the promises which I made by my declaration of the previous 23 June. I beg Your Majesty to keep this protest secret until the occasion when its publication could become necessary.

While Louis confided in the king of Spain, Antoinette also was churning out her own missives. Like the king, the queen pursued a dual-track policy. On the home-front she tried to appease "the monsters" that surrounded her; yet in her increasingly desperate letters abroad, she advocated foreign pressure to restore autocratic rule. Antoinette's primary goal after the events of the October days was to reassert the royal authority by escaping from Paris. Unlike his wife, Louis felt that there might be a way to slowly restore his authority by staying put in Paris; the laws of inertia came easily to him.

With the chastened royal family in Paris, Count Mirabeau calculated that the perfect moment had arrived to offer his services to the Crown. Alarmed like Antoinette by the disturbing events of October 6, Mirabeau feared the Revolution might descend into madness. He and the queen shared a mutual acquaintance, Count La Marck, whom Mirabeau approached to sound out the queen on a possible détente. He conveyed to La Marck, "The king and queen are lost if they do not leave Paris. I am working on a plan. Would you be in a position to go and assure them that they can count on me?"

This overture should have been met with Hosannas, but it didn't fly at all. Rarely disposed to ponder political options, Marie Antoinette promptly replied, "I trust we will never be so unfortunate as to be reduced to the painful extreme of seeking help from Mirabeau."

Given Mirabeau's tirades against the Crown during the previous five months, one can sympathize with the queen's abhorrence of dealing with "the monster." But within nine months, Antoinette would be forced to reconcile to the starker realities of the Revolution.

The deputies of the National Assembly resumed their legislative duties in the former riding school of Louis XIV, adjacent to the Tuileries palace. Having the government in Paris was a boon to the various political clubs whose headquarters were rooted in the capital. Much like social media today, the clubs served as the power brokers, influencing the legislative agenda in the Assembly. Such an arrangement paved the way to grandstanding, jealousies, and power grabs.

Once in Paris, one of the first decrees enacted by the Assembly dealt with a liberation of dress codes. The deputies abolished the distinctive dress formerly required for each of the three estates. With this fashion manifesto, it could be a challenge to identify a wealthy grocer from a provincial lord in the Assembly Hall.

The deputies also tackled more sensitive issues, such as the title of the king. Louis XVI would no longer be called the King of France and Navarre; instead more constitutionally the King of the French. Louis' head was spinning with the onslaught of changes to the former order. He uneasily signed decrees, aware that the monarchy was being eviscerated with his compliance.

The month of November produced some of the most radical laws passed by the Assembly. The lawmakers abolished the once powerful Parlements. Future judges would be elected by the people and paid a salary by the State. In arguing for the dissolution of the Parlements, one deputy voiced aloud the thoughts of most of the members of the National Assembly, especially after the bloody events of the preceding summer and October 6. He thundered, "Who had accustomed the people to unlawful assemblies and to resistance?" Not waiting for a reply, he shouted, "The Parlements." What used to be the bane of the monarchy for centuries was swept away without a murmur.

Also in November, another explosive issue, the demand for women's equality, unsettled deputies in the Assembly. Women played a role in the politics of France. Their influence proliferated through the sophisticated ladies who hosted weekly salons, various female organizations, the Parisian market women with their unfiltered mouths, and the thousands of women who guaranteed the success of spontaneous street riots. Women felt they rightly earned a piece of the power pie after their brilliant coup to force the royal family, court, and government to decamp to Paris.

A group of feminists submitted the Women's Petition to the National Assembly, demanding equality with men on all levels. They expected serious consideration and debate. They got neither. The Assembly refused to even look at the petition. Most deputies were still irate that women orchestrated their eviction from their former digs at Versailles. If the male deputies had read the ten articles that composed the petition, they would have imprisoned all of these unladylike ladies. Within a few years, all of the female leaders would be punished by the men running the show.

The most contentious headache for the Assembly dealt with the urgent need to generate revenue. Before they could tackle this matter, a reorganization of the national map was mandatory. Traditionally, France was divided into thirty-four provinces, each with different customs for conducting business, resulting in a non-cohesive political system. The Assembly radicalized the map of France by devising a grid system to divide the country into eighty-three departments of equal size. Previous ministers of the king had vainly attempted such a reorganization only to end up with bleeding ulcers. This plan envisioned a threefold advantage: to facilitate an equitable tax collection throughout the land; to empower local citizenry to overtake the clout of the nobility; and to advance national unity by erasing provincial jealousies. Nice on paper, but messy in practice.

Back to the money trail. With Jacques Necker leading the king's cabinet, the once financial idol exposed himself as a Midas has-been. He impressively failed to resolve the financial crisis, thereby allowing an unconventional bishop to save the Treasury. The bishop of Autun, Charles Maurice Talleyrand—who irreverently lived a life more aligned with that of a swinging single—preached that "great dangers demanded equally drastic remedies." The bishop proposed a confiscation of Church lands to be offered for public sale with the State picking up the tab for each clerics salary. Count Mirabeau, a close confidant to Talleyrand, endorsed this remedy as a providential solution.

The debate in the Assembly Hall exposed the raw anticlerical sentiments that permeated segments of society. The radical Protestant deputy, Barnave, reminded his fellow deputies that "the clergy only exists by virtue of the nation; thus, the nation can destroy it." Not surprisingly, most of the clergy railed against this land grab, citing the sacred nature of their place in the nation.

In November 1789 by a vote of 510 to 346, the Assembly approved the nationalization of Church property and the estates of wishy-washy noblemen who had fled France. The proceeds of the real estate auction sale of the century would provide the backing of a paper currency, called the *assignat*. In the meantime, the Assembly intended to hammer together a more permanent tax solution.

Another thorny social issue demanding attention centered on the miniscule non-Catholic population. At last, the persecuted communities of Protestants and Jews were invited into the nation's wary embrace. Protestants acquired full citizenship by the end of 1789. Jews also gained equal rights along with the opportunity to hold public office.

In hindsight, 1789 was a memorable year for the people of France. Except for women and people of color, whose struggle for equality seemed an eternity away, the future seemed brighter, if less certain. Now if only the Revolution would allow itself to catch its breath for a spell.

"Those who make peaceful revolution impossible,
make violent revolution inevitable."
John F. Kennedy

Chapter 56

Oh, Happy Day!

*B*efore the details of the happy day, a most dreadful one surfaced for Antoinette. A courier from Vienna arrived with the news that Emperor Joseph II had died of tuberculosis on February 20, 1790. Antoinette was aware that the emperor's health had been failing, but she did not know his situation was terminal. Even though tensions had surfaced between brother and sister on how best to respond to events in France, they still adored each other. With her dearest relative now gone, the queen felt that links with her native Austria were shaky. Joseph left no direct heirs, causing the imperial crown to pass to Antoinette's brother Leopold, who was practically a stranger to her. The queen verged on despair with the bad timing of events—how much longer would The Lisbon Curse trail her?

Another significant moment of early 1790 heralded Louis' revival from inaction. With Necker's prodding, Louis roused himself to remind the nation that he was indeed the head of State. Uninvited, the king strode into the Assembly Hall on February 4, 1790, announcing that he was the true leader of the Revolution:

> It is time gentlemen that I should associate myself more closely
> and in a still more direct and open fashion with the successful
> carrying out of all that you have planned for the benefit of
> France. I will do more in agreement with the Queen who shares
> all my sentiments. I will educate my son in the new principles of
> constitutional monarchy and freedom with justice.

Louis rocked the assembled deputies with this unexpected message. With few exceptions, they sang the king's praises, proclaiming him "The Restorer of Liberty." They jubilantly escorted him back to the Tuileries. The honeymoon between Louis and the Assembly would glow for a few months, before the Assembly resumed dismantling more of the king's authority and way of life.

After nine months of waiting, Mirabeau finally got his face time with Antoinette. The royal family had received permission to spend the summer at the queen's private residence of Saint Cloud. On Sunday morning July 3, while most of the chateau was stirring from their beds, Antoinette and Mirabeau secretly met. Months earlier the queen had rebuffed such a meeting, but the mercurial political climate caused Antoinette to stow her prejudices. Mirabeau was convinced that the queen would fall under his commanding, but unglamorous spell. The exact reverse occurred when Antoinette charmed him. The queen, who could transform adversaries into ardent admirers, ensnared Count Mirabeau with her regal mystique.

The upshot of the clandestine interview was Mirabeau's pledge to wield his significant influence for the royals' benefit—in exchange for generous remuneration. For this big fellow who lived big, his huge debts would now go poof. To be fair to Mirabeau, he risked plenty by embarking on this dicey path of rescuing the Crown from the radical forces besieging it. But his large ego propelled him to live life on the edge. As he left the queen, Antoinette offered her hand to him to kiss. With that regal token of trust, Mirabeau blazed with expectations of honors for himself. Upon entering his carriage, Mirabeau gripped the coachman's arm and excitedly whispered, "She is great, noble, and unfortunate; but I shall save her." He was no handsome knight on a white steed, but if anyone could remedy the ugly situation, Mirabeau was the guy for the job. After the meeting, he confided to a friend, "The King has only one man on whom he can depend—his wife!"

Flight from Paris was Mirabeau's first major recommendation to the royals. Antoinette loved the concept but not the details. Mirabeau advocated that the king escape to Normandy, rally loyal armed forces and subdue the firebrands in Paris. This policy would likely inflame a civil war that in Louis' mind was more frightening than his loss of power. The royal couple shuddered at such a prospect as the queen explained to Mercy, "How could Mirabeau believe that the moment would ever come for us to provoke a civil war." It seemed any ideas from Mirabeau were going to be a hard sell.

Now back to the happy day mentioned earlier. As the first anniversary of the storming of the Bastille approached, Bishop Talleyrand made a pitch in the National Assembly for a holiday:

> A festival of Federation should be celebrated with utmost dignity; that such a festival by inspiring thoughts of the glorious past, by strengthening fraternal ties among citizens, and by making public the patriotism of all Frenchmen, will prove to any existing enemies of the Revolution, the vanity of their attempts to destroy it.

Talleyrand's vision for a national holiday lifted everyone's spirits, making him the darling of the moment. The National Assembly embraced the bishop's proposal on June 21.

A burst of patriotic zeal seemed to dispel a centuries-old class system. Volunteers from all ranks of society massed together and in three weeks constructed a stadium in the Champs de Mars, a vast space normally used for military drills. Delegations from all parts of France gathered to mark the unifying occasion. Given that Talleyrand sparked the impetus for the celebration, Louis felt obligated to tap him as the master of ceremonies. Antoinette wished to skip this sham of a holiday, confiding to Count Mercy, "One has to participate, but oh, how I dread it."

The fourteenth of July was a rainy day, but that did not dampen the jovial spirits of an estimated 400,000 participants, huddled beneath a sea of tricolor umbrellas. All in attendance were overcome with the emotional significance of the day.

Earlier in the morning, 50,000 National Guardsmen marched eight abreast toward the Champs de Mars with members of the National Assembly joining them along the route. These soggy, but high-spirited patriots arrived at the venue at one in the afternoon where, at the center of the stadium, stood the Altar of the Fatherland. The royal family, who had traveled from Saint Cloud, was purposely visible from the sidelines. The king no longer merited center stage, reflecting the paradigm of the new political order.

Antoinette had learned that ladies attending the festivities were wearing white dresses. Hoping to woo the crowd, the queen wore an unadorned white dress with a huge tricolor sash. Her hair was simply done and finished off with tricolor feathers and matching ribbons. She looked the part on the outside, but inwardly, she disdained this ominous celebration. Antoinette garnered some kudos when the public saw the five-year-old heir wearing a spiffy uniform of the National Guard. With fraternal feelings flying high that day, the queen was surprised by the warm public reception she received. Apparently, the huge crowd cut the Austrian Woman a bit of slack in the spirit of national unity.

The highlight of the day's festivities included a solemn rite requiring all in attendance to take an oath to the unfinished constitution. Appearing like Sir Lancelot, Lafayette rode his white charger to the altar and administered the oath. It was perhaps the only day in the history of the Revolution when harmony prevailed in all hearts throughout the nation. It appeared that the Revolution had run its bumpy course, and sweet France could now resume a more tranquil existence.

Bishop Talleyrand pulled off a showstopper of a mass theatrically embracing everyone present with a pontifical benediction. The ceremony ended with a magnificent *Te Deum*, accompanied by a twelve-hundred-piece orchestra. There wasn't a dry eye in sight. Once Talleyrand divested himself of his soaking priestly garments, he made a beeline for the gambling tables of the Viscountess Laval where he racked up a winning evening.

After the day's official festivities, Paris became party central. The former site of the Bastille reigned as the chic place to be. Still working every angle to enrich his pockets, Pierre Palloy, the demolition contractor of the fortress, staged the entertainment. He packaged every remnant from the Bastille into a sought-after souvenir. For an entire week, festive events blanketed Paris. Many out-of-towners from the provinces, along with loads of foreign visitors, made the most of their stay in the capital. Most merchants were thrilled with the holiday, confident it would grow in the years to come.

Following the brouhaha of the national festivities, few noticed the departure of a once-revered figure, Jacques Necker. Pestered by the National Assembly for a reckoning of revenue, Necker issued a report describing a Treasury flush with cash. The ridicule that followed such folly sealed Necker's disgrace. He knew he was washed up and an embarrassment. On September 4, 1790, Necker submitted his resignation and slinked out of Paris. For the third and final time, the banker and his wife headed for the Swiss border. He endured an unpleasant road trip as stones and insults were hurled at his carriage. Jacques Necker settled into an obscure life of endless writings that no one bothered to read. He died a forgotten man in 1804 after suffering a stroke. His daughter, the famed Madame de Staël, vigilantly kept his memory alive during her lifetime. She frequently visited her adored father's body, preserved in alcohol in a black marble pool in the family mausoleum. Rich and famous folks can be weird.

Never far from Antoinette's thoughts during this time was her absent friend, Gabrielle de Polignac. In August 1790 the queen smuggled out a note to Gabrielle in Switzerland: "I don't know if this letter will reach you. I won't tell you about my children; their governess will send you news about them. My God, only death could make me stop loving you. Remember me often to your daughter, your husband, and Armand [Gabrielle's son], all three of whom I love with all my heart." Such furtive communications sustained Antoinette's spirits.

Another personal setback befell Marie Antoinette in October 1790 when she lost one of her mainstays of support in France. The wily Count Mercy cleverly convinced Emperor Leopold II that his services would be better utilized elsewhere, beyond the French borders. Accordingly, Mercy was reassigned by Leopold to serve as his emissary in the Austrian Netherlands. Mercy, relieved to quit Paris and its cauldron of unpredictable violence, would never return to France. Antoinette continued to rely on Mercy's guidance despite the geographical separation, exchanging a steady stream of messages that suited Mercy's desire to advise the queen from a more secure venue. As 1790 came to a close, it was hardly a better year than 1789. And 1791 would be even worse.

"Red skies and bluest twilight,
Sweet sun without end
I can pen for all but me."
Victoria Anderson-Throop

Chapter 57

To Flee, or Not to Flee?

*B*eginning in July 1789 Antoinette pressured Louis to escape to a more secure base of operation. Given his chronic indecision, the king would not commit himself to a definitive plan, hoping that the political pendulum would swing back in his direction. But the hemming and hawing melted away after the legislative events of December 1790. The matter that finally goosed the king into action regarded the nationalization of the French Catholic Church.

During the first half of 1790, the National Assembly waded into the quicksand of the operation of the Church. During the kissy-face celebrations of July, the National Assembly put the finishing touches to legislative measures that would shatter forever the fragile foundation of the Revolution. Perhaps on this occasion the National Assembly should have kept its reformist mouth shut for the ultimate good of the nation. But anti-clerical deputies wanted to dismantle the Church's powerful hierarchy, whom they considered far too wedded to the status quo.

The deputies passed a series of laws known as The Civil Constitution of the Clergy. The law authorized major changes: the one hundred seventy-six French bishops in 1789 would be reduced to eighty-three bishops, one for each of the governmental departments; bishops were to be elected by the people; bishops' salaries would be slashed and bishops would reside year-round in their diocese; parish priests would also be chosen by local residents with non-Catholics having a vote; and salaries of lowly clerics would be enhanced and paid for by the State. Most controversial of all, Rome would have to butt out of the business of the French Church. This hot-button issue paved the way for what would eventually make France a secular State.

Louis agonized over this pending legislation and urged deputies to temper their proposals, while he stalled for time. The king dispatched missives to Rome seeking guidance with such radical changes. Irritated, the Assembly staged a showdown in November, requiring all clergy to swear an "oath of loyalty to the nation, the law, and the King" by the first of January 1791. Louis had to accept or veto the package by New Year's Eve. Louis' sister, the convent wannabe Madame Elisabeth, fell to her knees, begging her brother to reject the abominable legislation. Even the queen urged her husband to stand tough against this outrage.

Someone placed an anonymous note in Louis' prayer book: "You are a slave, Sire. You cannot dissemble it from yourself. You have without any difficulty sanctioned all the blows directed at your royal authority. Step by step you have sacrificed to your masters: your God, your crown, your nobility, your Parlements, your ministers, your defenders." Such a discovery at mass must have caused the king to shrink in his pew. After assaults from all quarters for failing to exercise leadership, Louis sank into a dark space. He barely spoke, and for a month he ignored the decree sitting on his desk. With dread and moral disquiet, His Majesty the Milquetoast caved once again to the relentless pressure from ministers and deputies of the National Assembly; on December 26, 1790, the king signed the law. Louis now wished he were dead.

In early 1791 a handful of bishops and half of the parish priests took the oath of allegiance to the constitution. Conditions were ripe for a ruinous schism in the most Catholic of countries. The clergy who did not swear to the oath were branded as "non-jurors" and subject to harassment, or even imprisonment. One sensible bishop suggested a compromise requiring all the clergy to take the oath, while providing an out for those truly opposed by allowing them to withhold "mental assent." A clever resolution that screamed political practicality. Naturally, Rome shot down such a solution.

Louis tried to sweet-talk Pope Pius VI, begging for a bit of slack in this crisis capable of tearing France asunder. The king got his answer in mid-March 1791. While sympathizing with Louis' political firestorm, the pope scathingly condemned the Revolution and the sacrilegious oath. He declared that any clergy who took the oath would face immediate excommunication, and any election of bishops by the people would be considered unsanctioned by Rome. The pope's response was clear to the king: Louis had to submit to the orders of Jesus' successor on earth.

The Church in France was now splitting apart, and so were Louis' nerves. For many Parisian militants, the pope's orders were not only an insult but a direct threat to the autonomy of the nation. Effigies of Pius VI were burned, and the pope was condemned as an enemy of the Revolution. With Easter Sunday falling on April 24, Louis believed he could engineer a way to satisfy his opponents and preserve his soul.

Complicating Louis's tenuous position, two months earlier in February, the king's surviving aunts, Adélaïde and Victoire, kicked up a lot of dust in the national dialogue about the meaning of liberty. The king's aunts, living in comfortable obscurity just outside of Paris, felt "inspired" to make a pilgrimage to Rome to commemorate Holy Week in the pope's company. In reality, these old dames decided it was time to bolt for the border, escaping the madness that surrounded them. The final straw for them was the overturn of the established religious order. They had endured enough of the lunacy.

Louis doted on his two surviving aunts and secretly supported their plans. He believed their departure beyond the chaos of a seething France would make his own potential escape less complicated with them safely out of the country. The king wanted his sister Elisabeth to leave with them as well, but she refused to budge from her brother's side. To travel abroad, the aunts needed passports from their nephew, which he issued on February 19. The aunts took to the road the same day with an entourage of twenty—no skimping for these royal daughters of King Louis XV.

A national howl erupted over the aunts' travel plans. They were detained for eleven days in Burgundy. Louis vehemently defended his aunts declaring, "My aunts being mistresses of their own persons may travel wherever they wish like all other citizens." Louis was right. But royals were not considered ordinary citizens, a fact Louis XVI experienced on a daily basis. Permission for the aunts' journey became the heated topic in the Assembly. The outspoken Barnave made impassioned pleas that the aunts be compelled to return to their residence.

But it was the oratorical genius of Mirabeau that won the day for the old gals. He humorously predicted international jeers while the Assembly squandered the people's expectations for reform by becoming sidetracked with two old biddies. Conscious about its public perception on the world stage, the Assembly begrudgingly granted the feisty old broads the freedom to continue their travels. It was useful to have Count Mirabeau on the king's payroll.

After the aunts bailed, rumors of a clandestine flight of the royal family ignited tempers in Paris, convincing many that the king was anxious to emulate his aunts. Many Parisians and leftist politicians were convinced that the queen spearheaded an effort to bring in foreign troops once she reached the French border. These passions set the stage for the hotheads in Paris to keep a closer eye on the king's movements.

But first another unfortunate twist of fate complicated matters for the royal family. On April 2, 1791, the magnificent Mirabeau suddenly left this earthly realm. A week of mourning for Mirabeau was mandated by the Assembly, according him a funeral reserved exclusively for heroes.

Mirabeau's last words were not exactly comforting to the king and queen: "I take with me the death of the monarchy. The factions will prey upon its remains." Obviously, Mirabeau's sharp assessment of political events did not desert him at his end. Nor did one organ of his body. It was whispered confidently about town that the coroner found Mirabeau's penis to be defiantly erect after his peaceful death. Mirabeau would have enjoyed a hearty laugh with this prominent farewell.

Antoinette chalked up another defeat with Mirabeau's passing, moaning, "We have lost our last hope."

Count Fersen, already planning a flight for the royals, lamented, "It is a terrible blow because he was on our side, working for us and becoming useful. He would have been of the greatest help to us in the execution of our plan."

Even Count Mercy missed Mirabeau: "Why is everything going against us? There is no fighting such bad luck."

The excommunicated Bishop Talleyrand, who had pledged his oath to the Civil Constitution of the Clergy, decided to step into Mirabeau's vacant shoes as unofficial counselor to the Crown. He contacted Louis through an intermediary: "This message comes from the bishop of Autun, who makes known his desire to serve Your Majesty. He has bid me convey that Your Majesty may test his zeal and reliability by assigning him some task in either the district or the National Assembly. His ability to execute your wishes will prove his zeal." Louis would have sooner supped with Lucifer than place his trust in this disreputable bishop. The note received no response, but Louis did stash it away in his palace safe. Through Louis' prejudices and perhaps justified sentiments regarding Talleyrand's loyalty, the king forfeited one of the keenest political minds of the era.

Louis planned to celebrate the Easter holidays at Saint Cloud, allowing him to receive the services of a priest faithful to Rome. His family would depart the Tuileries on April 18, 1791. News of the royal schedule incited a mob to besiege the gates of the palace. The crowd would not allow the king's carriage to proceed. The king's conscience be damned; he had to obey the new law like everyone else and receive the sacraments from an oath-abiding cleric. Further, the agitated crowd suspected that the royal family was plotting to make a run for the border during their stay at Saint Cloud.

Lafayette, still leading the National Guard, used entreaties and threats to convince the crowd to let the king pass, but the protesters redoubled the booing. Even Lafayette's soldiers' sympathies rested with the will of the mob.

Mayor Bailly showed up and gingerly appealed to the crowd to grant the royal carriage access to the road. He was shouted down with a barrage of obscenities. Prudently, Bailly stepped out of the undesirable spotlight. Lafayette boldly advised the mayor to hoist the red flag, signaling imposition of martial law. Bailly refused; he feared this draconian move would lead to a bloody confrontation, and possibly the loss of his own head.

At one point in the standoff, Louis poked his head out of the carriage to remind the crowd of his goodness: "It would be surprising if I, who have given freedom to the nation, should not be free myself."

Few of the responses to the monarch would be acceptable in polite society, but one in particular stood out, "We pay you twenty-five million a year; do what we tell you, fat pig!"

For two hours near riot conditions prevailed as curses and insults were hurled against Louis, Antoinette, Lafayette, and Bailly. Having endured enough humiliation for one day, the distraught monarch stepped down from the carriage and reentered the palace. As Antoinette descended their carriage, she hissed at Lafayette that the world would now know that she and her family were inmates of a palatial prison. The standoff at the palace gates forced Lafayette to concede that the Revolution was now charting a perilous path.

Hailed just the year before as the Restorer of Liberty, Louis XVI was now denied his own liberty. For months, the king had wrestled with the prospect of flight from Paris; now his indecision dissolved—he was determined to get out of Dodge. Shut up in the Tuileries, Louis huddled with his wife, giving her the green light to proceed with plans for a change of scenery. Count Fersen noted in his diary, "It is now more evident to the King that it is time to act with all due haste."

On the day following the aborted trip to Saint Cloud, a smarting Louis addressed the National Assembly, decrying his circumstances. The king affirmed his acceptance of the Civil Constitution of the Clergy but insisted on his personal right to travel within twenty miles of Paris. Many of the delegates commiserated with him offering their tepid regrets. But these deputies felt uninspired to contradict the voice of the Parisians over the matter of non-juring priests.

But Lafayette refused to submit to mob rule. He demanded, and received, broader leverage in dealing with the National Guard. He strengthened discipline and dismissed those guardsmen who had defied his orders on April 18. This would have been the perfect opportunity for Louis to reschedule a visit to Saint Cloud, to test the reformed National Guard. But Louis would not tempt another humiliation, and Antoinette's feelings about Lafayette were beyond repair.

On Easter Sunday, April 24, 1791, the royal family obediently attended mass and received communion at a church near the palace officiated by a State approved priest. The crowd roared its approval for compliance with the new religious order. Like a pair of marionettes, the royals outwardly smiled, yet seethed within, wanting to be rid of these gross degradations. The king and queen could barely contain their impatience to put vile Paris in their rearview mirror.

> "Desperation is the raw material of drastic change.
> Only those who can leave everything behind can hope to escape."
> *William S. Burroughs*

Chapter 58

An Oldie, but Goodie, Gets Airtime

*A*t this juncture in the Revolution's trajectory, it was evident that something had to give way. Like two tectonic plates stressed to the max, a sudden jolt could irrevocably alter the political landscape. The flight of the royal family would be this earth-shattering event. But on the eve of this shift in the Revolution, a prophetic letter from Guillaume Raynal, the last surviving luminary from the Enlightenment, was read to the National Assembly.

Raynal had been exiled from France for his dangerous writings in the early 1770s. Few men had written more eloquently about the rights of man and the abolition of slavery than Raynal. He urged Frenchmen to adopt England's style of constitutional monarchy that he had long admired. He received permission to return to France in 1787, and to Paris in 1791. When he arrived in Paris, Raynal was horrified by the detour into chaos taken by the Revolution, prompting him to publish an unsolicited state-of-the-nation speech that ignited a firestorm when it was read to the members of the National Assembly on May 31, 1791. It served as an accurate commentary of the instability afflicting France:

> Returning to this capital after a long absence, my heart and
> thoughts are turned toward you. You would have seen me before
> the feet of this august Assembly, if age and my infirmities allowed
> me to speak to you of those other great things which now need
> be done in order to establish in this unhappy land, that peace,
> liberty, and happiness which is your intention to procure for us.

Not long ago I dared to speak to Kings of their duty. Suffer me
today to speak to the people of its mistakes and to the people's
representatives of the great dangers which menace us. I shall not
hesitate to say that I am profoundly grieved by the crimes which
are covering our nation in mourning. I am appalled to realize
that I am one of those who once battling against arbitrary power,
may have given arms to license rather than to liberty. You cannot
without falling into the greatest error, attribute to us the false
interpretations which have been made of our philosophy.

At this point, some deputies began booing and murmuring among themselves.
After a call to order, the reading continued:

About to die, what do I see about me? Religious dispute, civil
dissension, fear on the part of some, tyranny and ambition on
the part of others, a government which has become a slave to the
forces of the gutter and become a sanctuary for men who want to
dictate or to violate the law, soldiers without discipline, heads of
State without authority, ministers without means, power over the
State existing in certain clubs where gross and ignorant men pass
judgment on political matters.

Now all hell broke loose on the Assembly floor. The left-leaning deputies
demanded that the reading be suspended. The President of the Assembly
forced order, and again the reading to proceed:

Such, and I tell you the truth, is the state of affairs in France. I dare
to tell you not only because I must, but because I am eighty years
of age [he was actually seventy-eight at the time], because no one
here can accuse me of regretting the former despotic monarchy,
because in denouncing in your presence those citizens who have
irresponsibly set fire to our kingdom or who have perverted
public opinion by their writings, no one can accuse me of being
insensible to the value of the freedom of the press. I was full of
joy and hope when I saw you laying the foundations of public
felicity, abrogating feudal abuses, proclaiming The Rights of Man,
and bringing the divers regions of our nation under one common
law and a uniform government. My eyes fill with tears when I see
unscrupulous men using the lowest form of intrigue to stain this
Revolution, when I see the honorable name of patriot prostituted
and behold license triumphantly marching under the banner of
liberty.

Once again shrill voices pierced the chamber. Unbelievably, the reading was allowed to conclude:

> In this city, which is the city of light and of civilization, I see people welcome with ferocity the most culpable of propositions and smile at accounts of murder, boasting of its crimes as though they were conquests. Such people do not realize that the smallest crime can be the beginning of an infinity of calamities. The lightheaded behavior of people laughing and dancing on the brink of an abyss has disturbed me more than anything else.

Raynal's description of the precarious path of the Revolution unsettled most deputies. They loudly condemned the message, outraged at being exposed for behaving like two-bit opportunists. Raynal was the kind of man they needed—a convincing voice of reason, from The Age of Reason. But like the fate of most prophets, Raynal's words were dismissed as the out-of-touch drivel of a man who no longer mattered. To get even with this nasty critic, the National Assembly would eventually seize his property. What a noble race—the politician!

"It has been said that politics is the second
oldest profession. I have learned that it bears
a striking resemblance to the first."
Ronald Reagan

Chapter 59

No Turning Back Now

Most of the arrangements for escape were in place by the spring of 1791. Louis had been secretly corresponding with General Bouillé, stationed near the French border even before the showdown outside the palace gates. Besides the escape plan, the king and the general sketched out a course of action to pursue once Louis was freed from what the queen termed "the insolent monsters" in Paris. By March 1791 the king was ninety-five percent on board for flight. When the ignominious standoff unfolded at the palace gates, Louis became the loudest advocate for skipping town. However, each time a date was set, unforeseen snags forced a postponement. Aware that palace servants loyal to the Revolution spied on their every move, the royal couple strove to portray a monotonous normalcy. Meanwhile, Antoinette met secretly with Count Fersen to fine-tune the escape plans.

Financing the enterprise became the first order of business. Louis no longer had unbridled access to the Treasury. A request from him for a large sum of money would raise a red flag. Count Fersen offered to advance the king the bulk of the expenses from his own pocket and to borrow the rest from trusted friends. The royals were lucky to have the Swede's unwavering support. Odd how none of Antoinette's relatives offered to pitch in one dime to help out.

With the funds secured, attention focused on the escape route. Bouillé wanted the shortest itinerary along the best maintained roadways. Louis rejected the proposed routes and insisted on one of his own. Having already prepared detailed maps, the king targeted the fortified town of Montmédy.

The royal family would not reside in the actual fortress, but rather in the nearby Chateau of Thonnelle, which nestled a convenient two miles from the Austrian border—just in case.

While General Bouillé disagreed with Louis' plan, he dispatched François Goguelat, a survey engineer, to scout the one hundred and fifty-mile route from Paris to Dun, where Bouillé would be waiting for the royals. Goguelat did a meticulous reconnoitering job, evaluating each of the relay stations for possible revolutionary hotheads, noting that the village of Varennes would be the safest of all the stops. He signaled the thumbs up to the king's preferred pathway to freedom.

The pivotal item on the to-do list concerned the means of transport. Both Fersen and Bouillé stressed that the success of the operation hinged entirely on secrecy and speed, thereby requiring small, swift carriages. The king and queen would travel in one nondescript cab and their children in the second vehicle. Both Louis and Antoinette firmly overruled Fersen and Bouillé on this vital detail. After the frightening events of October 1789, the royal parents were terrified by any separation from their children.

The royal couple insisted that their party of six depart in one regally correct carriage. The dumbfounded Fersen asked why six passengers instead of four? The queen made it clear that the king's sister Madame Elisabeth and the royal governess Madame Tourzel would join the royal family.

A flabbergasted Fersen had to come up with a better arrangement. He desperately needed an extra seat for a competent military man to protect the royals. Fersen first suggested that Madame Elisabeth escape on the same night in the company of the king's brother Provence and wife. But Louis was not about to permit his devoted sister to be separated from his side. Undaunted, the Swede then tried to jettison Madame Tourzel from the travel manifest. Now it was the queen's turn to stomp her foot with an emphatic no. And Louis backed her up. Overruled again, a frustrated but equanimous Fersen had no choice but to accommodate the monarchs and scratch his point man from the lineup.

Fersen recognized that a party of this size required a carriage intended for long journeys, known as a *berline de voyager*, the stretch limo of its day. The carriage ordered was loaded with the latest bells and whistles, including a smart interior upholstered in a plush white velvet. The heavy vehicle would travel at a slow pace even with a team of six horses. And it was the type of conveyance that screamed, "VIPs inside!"

Next, the planners obtained the required identification documents. The necessary passports were obtained on June 5, 1791, at the request of the Russian ambassador to Foreign Minister Montmorin, who signed and issued them without any suspicions, followed by Louis' countersignature. The traveling party would consist of the Russian Baroness de Korff (Madame Tourzel) and her suite of five. Among them were her two young daughters, Amélie and Algaë (Madame Royale and her disguised brother); the trusted governess to her children, Madame Rochet (the queen); Monsieur Durand, valet to the baroness (the king); and finally, her maid, Rosalie (Madame Elisabeth). So reminiscent of the cast members from one of Marie Antoinette's frothy productions at the Petit Trianon!

Another five individuals completed the De Korff party: two nannies of the royal children; Monsieur Valory serving as scout leading the carriages; Monsieur Malden riding shotgun atop the box of the large berline; and lastly, Monsieur Moustier serving as the sweep following the small carriage carrying the two nannies. Moustier purchased three used yellow livery uniforms that he and his buddies would wear during the journey.

General Bouillé appointed the Duke of Choiseul to serve as an advance man. (The duke was the nephew of the powerful former foreign minister who had arranged Antoinette's marriage more than twenty years earlier.) Count Fersen had questioned General Bouillé's choice for this very key part of the mission that required a trained army veteran: "If it is possible, try not to send me the Duke of Choiseul. No one could be more devoted, but he is a bungler and too young." The Swede's advice was bypassed, and drawing room pedigree bested pragmatic judgment.

With the serious issues resolved, Antoinette prepared the list of items to be packed in the carriage and those that would be sent ahead to their destination. The queen had an entire wardrobe made and smuggled out of the palace to await her at Montmédy. She packed the king's crown and royal robes to remind the populace of his God anointed position. She ordered a magnificent traveling case for her favorite perfumes and cosmetics. She commissioned an exquisite *nécessaire*, a sort of carry-on bag, made of the finest walnut and fitted out with a silver tea set and other niceties—just imagine a pricey picnic basket fabricated by the most elegant designer in France. No matter where they were, they had to look every stitch the royal family.

Everything seemed in place for a departure at eleven in the evening on June 20.

"Quiet on the Set—Lights, Camera, Action!"
A Fabled Hollywood Studio Instruction

Chapter 60

Oy Vey, Varennes!

SPOILER ALERT: Brace for a major nail-biter.

Of all of the events in the life of Marie Antoinette, few can compare with the near impossible escape from Paris, followed by the unbelievable outcome of the journey.

Before the flight, Louis and Antoinette had received warnings about the frightful risks of such an undertaking. They were urged to reconsider their plans by supporters of the monarchy already safely abroad. Count Mercy warned Antoinette in early 1791 that, "Escape has become impossible at this time. Every village could be an insurmountable barrier. If you can only persist where you are, you can be sure that the mad creations of the revolutionaries will destruct by themselves. I tremble to think of the catastrophe that would arise if the enterprise fails." Louis and Antoinette fully realized that the stakes were high. But the royals were the ones undergoing the daily threats and provocations. The advice from well-intentioned individuals safely abroad in secure settings only increased the royal couple's determination to enjoy that same freedom. For Louis and Antoinette, the risks of fleeing outweighed the dangers of staying.

On Monday, June 20, 1791, Louis closeted himself the entire morning in his office. He composed a letter entitled, "A Declaration from the King Addressed to all Frenchmen About his Flight from Paris." Louis spelled out his reasons for abandoning the toxic atmosphere of Paris. Louis declared his intentions to reclaim some of his former royal privileges, to regain his personal liberty, and to assure the safety of his family. More importantly, he expressed his impetus to flee Paris was based on his loathing for the nearly completed constitution and the rape of the Catholic Church:

> Frenchmen, and above all, you Parisians, inhabitants of a city which the ancestors of His Majesty have pleased to call the good city of Paris, distrust the suggestions and lies of your false friends [he refers here primarily to the Jacobin members of the National Assembly], come back to your King; he will always be your father, your best friend. What a pleasure he will not take in forgetting all his personal injuries and beholding himself once again in your midst, when a constitution freely accepted by him shall cause our holy religion to be restored.

Louis made it clear that his autonomy in decision making had been intolerably compromised. And the religious fabric of France had been torn asunder. The king presented the people with a choice: either a benevolent monarch or a godless anarchy. The sore spot in the letter was the reprimand to the National Assembly and its odious constitution that Louis had sworn to uphold. Furthermore, he scolded the cheeky Parisians, lamenting that he had endured enough of their disrespect to remain even one more night in the same city as they.

In the afternoon Louis discretely disclosed to his sister Elisabeth the risky events that were beginning to unfold. Without a blink, Elisabeth was solidly on board.

At the same time, Antoinette summoned to her sitting room Léonard, her hairdresser. As a last-minute choice, Antoinette drafted Léonard into the scheme. The queen dreaded the spectacle of roughing it without an elegant coif in such a remote outpost as Montmédy. God only knows what Fersen must have thought about this addition.

Antoinette questioned Léonard if she could depend on his unswerving loyalty. After nearly twenty years on the job, Léonard effusively declared his devotion. Satisfied, the queen handed him a letter and instructed him to proceed immediately to a particular address. He was to follow without question the orders of the man who was to receive this letter, the Duke of Choiseul.

The hairdresser hopped into a taxi for the designated residence, allowing his imagination to soar. Upon arriving and handing over the letter, Choiseul read that it was full steam ahead for the plans. Choiseul instructed the stylist to follow him and, within moments, their taxi left Paris.

Léonard became agitated as the cabriolet passed the outskirts of Paris. With no overnight bag, not even a teasing comb, the stylist informed the impassive duke that he had an appointment with an important client requiring his immediate return—so much for his promise to follow instructions blindly. As they traveled further from Paris, the hairdresser's mini-meltdown escalated into a fit of hysteria. To calm his convulsive companion, Choiseul informed Léonard of the royals' impending escape. Dumbstruck, Léonard learned that he was to be entrusted with spiriting the queen's jewels out of Paris, as well as do her hair in Montmédy. Choiseul warned Léonard to strike a macho-man pose as they were about to enter the next relay stop and could not draw unnecessary attention to themselves. Fortunately for Choiseul, Léonard belonged to a theater company in Paris, so he tried to project believable virility.

Later in the afternoon Marie Antoinette gave the impression that June 20 was just another day at the Tuileries. Parisians observed her taking her children for a leisurely walk in the park. While her son was scampering about, Antoinette soothed her daughter that she was not to fear unusual events later that evening. On her return to the palace, the queen notified the officer on duty that she would be going out again the following day.

Every night after the monarchs ceremoniously went to bed, government officials, courtiers, servants, and other visitors would make a dash for the palace doors to hail a long line of waiting cabs. It offered the ideal moment for the royal family to blend in with the ritualized evening exodus. No one played his part better in the tightly orchestrated stab at freedom than Count Fersen. Since he was the most visible participant of the operation, impersonating a street cabbie, he had to be the most convincing. He had scrutinized the habits, manners, and street talk of the cab drivers. On the night of the escape, he fit in perfectly with all the other cabbies waiting for their fares, shooting the breeze with the rest of the guys.

Shortly after ten in the evening the plan sprang to life. Marie Antoinette played her first gutsy move to start the escape clock ticking. She and Madame Tourzel sneaked past the guard on duty in the halls outside the bedrooms of her children. The queen first awoke her daughter and instructed the girl's maid, Madame Brunier, to dress her. Then she went to her son's room and woke him, telling him he was about to embark on a great adventure. His maid, the devoted Madame Neuville, dressed him as well. The dauphin protested at being forced to don a girl's dress; he insisted on wearing his military uniform. His mother soothed him and told him this was only a disguise and at the end of the charade he would wield his sword in triumph. The prince's initial reservations melted away, convinced that he was playacting, just like at his mama's theater at the Petit Trianon.

When the children were gathered together, the queen revealed the escape plan to the nannies. She informed these women that their services were required to accompany the royals to a more secure location near the border. The disbelieving maids would immediately leave the palace to a waiting carriage that would whisk them to a location beyond Paris where the royal family would later join them. Fortunately, the queen's staff could never do enough for her which Marie Antoinette never took for granted. Both ladies pledged their unquestioning loyalty to the queen.

Antoinette, Madame Tourzel, and the children descended a back stairway to a vacated apartment on the ground floor of the palace that led to an outside street. These rooms had recently been abandoned by the king's first gentleman, Monsieur Villequier, who had emigrated to a more tranquil foreign residence. With a purloined key, Antoinette unlocked the door of the vacant apartment that opened to a courtyard that lead to the street. Slouching by his cab, Count Fersen spotted Madame Tourzel crossing the street, carrying the young prince and grasping Madame Royale by the hand. Fersen helped his fares into the cab and slowly drove around the streets to return for the rest of the fugitives.

With the royal children and Madame Tourzel safely out of the palace, the queen sped off to her bedroom via the same back staircase to prepare for bed according to the required etiquette. Meanwhile, the king was performing the same ceremony in his bedroom, with Mayor Bailly and General Lafayette in attendance.

For weeks, rumors abounded of a planned escape by the royal family. Consequently, Bailly and Lafayette wanted to be certain that nothing fishy was afoot. Lafayette made small talk with Louis, discussing details regarding the forthcoming festivities for the religious holiday of Corpus Christi. These unwelcomed visitors persisted in a chatty mood that translated into the loss of precious time. At last, Lafayette stopped to take a breath, which cued the king to approach the royal bed, say his prayers, have his boots removed, and allow himself to be undressed. At this point the usher on duty tapped the floor with his stick and announced, "It's the moment to withdraw, Gentlemen." Everyone bowed and backed out of the royal presence.

While the king and queen were being readied for bed, Madame Elisabeth slipped out of the palace, unrecognized in her disguise as a maid. Upon noticing Fersen, she bolted for his cab and hopped in. When entering the carriage, she accidentally stepped on her little nephew who was asleep under Madame Tourzel's dress. The little guy let out a muffled groan but didn't cry. So far, so good.

Once the king's valet snuffed out the candles and drew the bed curtains, he left the room to change into his night clothes. As the door shut behind the valet, Louis jumped out of bed and used a hidden staircase to escape to his wife's bedroom below. Moments later the valet reentered the room and settled into the folding cot next to the State bed. He attached the long cord to his wrist that stretched from the king's person, in case His Majesty required his assistance during the night. Certain the king was sound asleep, the valet drifted off to sleep.

Louis changed into his disguise in Antoinette's bedroom. With a cane in hand, he casually walked down the main staircase of the palace and nonchalantly bent down before one of the guards to adjust a buckle on his shoe. Unruffled, he straightened up and strolled out of the front entrance of the palace, unrecognized by the guards on duty. What *chutzpah*! An experienced actor could not have delivered a more convincing performance. This unbelievable feat came off without a hitch because every night for several weeks at the same hour the Chevalier Coigny, who bore a physical resemblance to the king and was privy to the scheme, would leave the palace dressed in similar clothing that Louis wore as a disguise. Not one of the National Guard soldiers on duty suspected any alteration to the routine, proving no security is ever fail-safe.

Lastly, came the queen's chance. She used the same exit that her children had taken two hours earlier. Very unexpectedly, as she entered the street, Lafayette's departing carriage passed within inches of her body. She and her escort, Monsieur Malden, became momentarily flustered with this close call that could have proven disastrous. They temporarily lost their way but regained their wits and headed for the waiting carriage. Meanwhile, the king became anxious about the queen's delay and suggested to Fersen that they should look for her. At fifteen minutes before midnight the queen appeared, and her delighted husband expressed his relief that they were all safely together, but forty-five minutes behind schedule.

Amazingly, the royals managed to evade the six hundred guards assigned by Lafayette to prevent just such a daring exploit. Seldom is credit given to these escapees for pulling off what seemed to be an impossible feat. Antoinette and Fersen had done their homework and should be applauded for succeeding in the most challenging segment of the daring flight. But a potential unraveling of the enterprise increased with each mile covered from its starting point.

Fersen drove the cab slowly to avoid suspicion, but it came at the price of another half hour gnawing away at the tight schedule. Once Fersen exited Paris at the tollgate of Saint-Martin, he poked around in the dark for the berline; more time was lost as Fersen searched for the well-hidden vehicle. Once discovered, the fugitives transferred from the cab into the more comfortable coach. Within thirty minutes the berline, pulled by six horses, entered the first relay post at Bondy. Here a fresh team of horses waited along with Valory, the lead rider. The relay posts appeared about every fifteen miles on the roads, and in the light of day many gawkers would gather to gossip about the conspicuous carriage.

At Bondy, Fersen reluctantly left the disguised voyagers. It had always been his plan to accompany the royal family the entire route, but the king decided otherwise. Louis may have felt that a foreign military man at the helm would not be a smart idea. Furthermore, if Fersen and the queen were romantically involved, this would not be the politically correct moment to share company. Louis warmly thanked Fersen for all that he had done, vowing never to forget the count's priceless assistance. In reality, Fersen was the superhero of this escapade, only minus the mask, cape, and tights. On the verge of tears, Antoinette admirably restrained herself. Fersen admonished the coachman not to hold back with the reins of his horses—it was full speed ahead. As Fersen gallantly removed his hat, he bowed toward the queen, and loudly exclaimed, "Godspeed, Madame de Korff." He then rode off at a gallop into the darkness.

After Bondy, the second relay stop was Claye, where the cabriolet carrying the nannies joined the exodus.

By mid-morning the tense fugitives began to relax, relieved that the most dangerous segment of the mission was behind them. Despite being behind schedule, the spectacular weather fostered a festive air in the berline. For the first time in two years, the royals did not feel like felons. Even the king lightened up, confessing his pleasure, "I have escaped from that town of Paris, where I have been forced to drink so much bitterness." He checked his watch, noting the time, eight o'clock in the morning. He chuckled aloud at the profound discomfort that General Lafayette was now suffering, confronting empty beds in the palace. The king pronounced, "Believe me, once my butt is back in the saddle, I'm going to be a far different person from what you have seen before." Even his wife could not doubt such hyperbole at this moment of relief. Their hopes for a reversal of fortune appeared within reach.

At one point, Louis emerged from the carriage to speak to the locals about the harvest and other small town matters—dangerous behavior lest he be recognized, but the king reveled at having no guards trailing his every footstep.

In the coach the king was in holiday mode as he recalled his cherished journey to Cherbourg in 1786. Oh, how the people truly loved him outside of the environs of Paris. Even the queen joined in the levity at one point by accepting the hospitality of the postmaster of Chaintrix, whose son-in-law recognized the king from a previous visit to the capital. The overwhelmed locals rolled out the welcome mat offering some freshly made clear broth to the travelers. In a gesture of thanks for their kindness, the queen gave the family two monogrammed small silver soup bowls from her travel service. While dallying with the provincials energized the royals' hopes of regaining the reins of power, this interaction wasted precious capital—speed and secrecy.

> "You might as well fall flat on your face
> than lean over too far backward."
> *James Thurber*

Chapter 61

Reclaiming an Unwanted King

The mood was far from cheery in Paris. By eight in the morning the city buzzed with the bombshell news that the king and his family were gone. A huge crowd surrounded the Tuileries, drifting into the palace to confirm that the monarchs were indeed absent. As the multitude sauntered through the royal apartments, they looked like customers window shopping in an upscale department store. One of the market women plopped down on the queen's bed, expressing her satisfaction with its plush appointment: "Now it's time for the Nation to be comfortable." Surprisingly, no vandalism occurred within the residence.

When Lafayette learned of the royal disappearance, he dashed off to the Tuileries where a hostile crowd berated him. He pledged to the crowd, "I will be responsible for the King with my own head!"

They shouted back, "You're damn right!"

Mayor Bailly arrived about the same time for a similar scolding from the restive crowd. Since the Assembly deputies were not scheduled to meet until nine that morning, there was not a minute to lose. Lafayette boldly drew up and signed a decree ordering the king's return to Paris:

The King, having been removed by the enemies of the Revolution, the bearer is instructed to impart the fact to all good citizens who are commanded in the name of their endangered country to take him out of their hands and to bring him back to the keeping of the National Assembly. The latter is about to assemble, but in the

meantime, I take upon myself all the responsibility of this order.
Paris 21 June 1791. Lafayette

P.S. This order extends to all persons of the royal family.

Several copies were hurriedly reproduced as couriers took off in various directions. For a brief time, Lafayette was the acting head of State. Lafayette's decisive action did little to lift the cloud of suspicion that tarnished his reputation. An accepted belief took root that both Lafayette and Bailly were accomplices in the escape of the royal family, forever blackening their careers. The crowd remained ignorant that Lafayette would have been the last man on earth that the queen would have allowed to aid in her escape from the Tuileries. Months earlier he had lectured her about the public's wish that she be divorced from the king and shut up in a convent. Antoinette would have opted to rot in the palace than seek his help.

As the day wore on, the ugly mood in the capital mushroomed. When the declaration Louis left on his desk was read to the National Assembly, the deputies unanimously cried foul. The king's disavowal of his oath to the constitution ranked as unpardonable in the eyes of many. One royalist-leaning deputy condemned the king: "Louis XVI, the King whose goodness had always seemed to excuse his weakness, has abjured in an instant all of his promises and all of his oaths. With this declaration, written and signed in his own hand, he has revealed to the universe that the honor and duty of Kings toward their people are utterly worthless."

All the deputies mimicked a famous Cuban, barking out, "Oh Louis, you gotta lotta splainin' to do!"

The royal family's escape from Paris was saddled with complexities, rating its chances of success as marginal. So why add to the high stakes of failure by leaving such a letter on your desk? That was the kind of vindication that you take pleasure to publish once you have safely reached your destination, certainly not before. Leaving this letter ranks as one of the major mistakes of Louis' reign. The damaging contents of the king's declaration would cause an unbridgeable rift in the trust between the king and his subjects.

The various political clubs zoomed into republican overdrive excoriating the escape. In particular, members of the rabid Jacobin Club screamed for an overthrow of the monarchy in favor of a republic. Someone placed a billboard on the gates of the Tuileries that read "House to Rent." Spontaneously, signs of ornamental royalty in Paris were removed, destroyed, or covered over. As one English traveler recounted, "All those who were so vain of announcing over their doors that they were tradesmen of the King or Queen have removed every word, emblem, or sign which would revive the remembrance of such a connection." Most of the newspapers took a hard line against the royal family. One particular publication captured the feeling of betrayal: "He has gone, this imbecile King, this perjured King. That scoundrel Queen who combines the lustfulness of Messalina with the bloodthirstiness of the Medici. Execrable woman, Furie of France, it is you who are the soul of this conspiracy!" No surprise that the public branded Antoinette as the culpable party in this national brouhaha.

While the focus of the hysteria remained on tracking down the royal family, less agitation surrounded the disappearance of Louis' brother and sister-in-law, the Provence couple. Their plan of flight called for the stealthy departure of the count and countess on the same night as the king. They resided in the Luxembourg palace, not far from the Tuileries, with a less stringent security force. On the evening of the anxious departure, Count Provence and his wife had dined according to their daily ritual with the royal family in the Tuileries palace, all pretending a casual parting after dinner.

Unlike Louis and Antoinette, Count Provence agreed with Count Fersen's advice of using small, fast carriages. The Provences, who loathed one another with equal ardor, split up into two small cabs following different routes. Both of their escapes came off without a hiccup. The moment the count's coach crossed into Belgium, the king's brother ripped the tricolor cockade from his hat, tore it to pieces, and threw it out of the window, exclaiming in his usual poetic style, "What a sham ornament of an unworthy spinelessness." Provence was in a jolly mood, not wasting much thought about the outcome of his brother's escape.

"Your dreams are ballbusters;
they're not The Yellow Brick Road."
Kelly Cutrone

Chapter 62

The Domino Effect

General Bouillé never anticipated the possible breakdown of the planned military escorts. He did not anticipate the blow-back that seven hundred and twenty cavalrymen stationed along the roadways might arouse among the local population. During the planning stages Count Fersen expressed his reservations to Bouillé about this show of force: "If you are not sure of your detachments, it would be better not to have any at all so as not to excite notice in the countryside." But General Bouillé was sold on an assertive cavalry presence and ignored Fersen's sterling advice.

Already several hours behind schedule, the royal party attracted more and more curious folks speculating on the identities of the berline's occupants at each relay stop. In the late afternoon at Somme-Vesle, the royals expected to meet up with the first detachment of military escorts under the command of the Duke of Choiseul. Then, the rest of the trip would be a breeze.

Choiseul and his forty cavalrymen, totally pumped to escort the king, formed ranks by one in the afternoon in Somme-Vesle. As the hours ticked by, there was no sign of the carriage. Word spread among the locals of suspicious soldiers loitering in the roadway. The officers informed the curious that the troops were waiting to escort a payroll for the army, a story these crafty country folk doubted. They suspected some highhanded operation against themselves, and they became menacingly restless. Choiseul felt that his position was deteriorating with the hostile crowd surrounding him. What would happen if the coach suddenly appeared? Would the escape plans be jeopardized? As the afternoon faded, Choiseul feared that the royals had either not yet left Paris, or even worse, were already unmasked. After all, Count Fersen had assured Choiseul that the berline would pull up no later than half past two in the afternoon. It was already after five.

With the crowd growing uglier and larger, Choiseul decided to bail. He scribbled a note and handed it to Léonard, ordering him to serve as a courier. The message alerted the military detachments further ahead that "there is no sign the treasure will pass today. I am leaving to join M. de Bouillé. You will receive new orders tomorrow." Along with the note, Choiseul forked over the queen's jewels to the hairdresser. Léonard took off in Choiseul's cabriolet to spread the word of a royal no show.

Choiseul finally rode away at half past five on that summer afternoon, a half hour before the huge berline eventually puffed its way to the agreed spot.

Upon arriving at Somme-Vesle, the entire royal party poked their heads out of the carriage in eager expectation of greeting Choiseul and his cavalrymen. Jeepers, there wasn't a soul waiting for them! Spirits sank fast among the travelers, wondering what could have possibly gone wrong. As Louis would dolefully recount, "I felt as though the entire earth had fallen from under me." Dismayed, the royal party knew they had no choice but to press forward a lot faster than the eleven miles an hour they were clocking. There was no turning back at this point.

Two more relay towns remained before the berline would arrive in Varennes. First came the large town of Sainte-Menehould where the royals were praying to find Choiseul and his troops. Instead of spotting Choiseul, they noticed cavalrymen relaxing outside the inn, while across the road, National Guardsmen were checking out the berline. It appeared that half the town had turned out to gawk at the coach. The agitated Antoinette managed to catch the eye of one of the officers, Captain Andoins, who had been tipped off earlier by Léonard that the royal party was not coming. The captain casually approached the carriage, but whispered like a ventriloquist, "Plans have not worked out; I gotta go so as not to arouse suspicions." The officer sauntered back to his buddies. All the adults in the coach could have used a triple martini at that point. They had to drive out of there pronto.

After the trembling berline pulled out of Sainte-Menehould, it groaned uphill to Clermont where at half past nine the jumpy travelers encountered a loyal officer, Count Damas, who warned the royals of danger all around them. Goodness, did anybody have some good news to tell them? Damas promised to catch up with them once suspicions calmed in the area. While they sped off to Varennes, the tension in the berline was worse than when they had sneaked out of Paris.

Meanwhile, at the previous relay town of Sainte-Menehould, the manager of the relay post, a twenty-eight-year-old man named Jean Baptiste Drouet, was fairly certain that the occupants of the berline were the king and his family. He kept looking at the king's image on the paper money he received from the "butler" of the Russian baroness. The likeness of the two was remarkable. And he thought the "governess" bore a resemblance to the queen whom he had seen several times during his seven-year stint in the army. After a lengthy huddle with the town fathers, the consensus emerged that Louis was headed for the border to return with an army of foreign soldiers who would overrun the countryside and crush the Revolution. Drouet, the best horseman in the district, was commissioned to ride like hell and intercept the berline. Like a greyhound in flight, Drouet and a buddy took off in hot pursuit of the royals. On the dash, Drouet met up with the driver returning with the horses changed at the relay stop in the town of Clermont. The driver told Drouet that the coach had taken the road to Varennes and not to Metz as Drouet had assumed. What a lucky break for Drouet!

The overwrought Léonard raced ahead with Choiseul's note alerting the cavalry at each relay station of the snag. It was already dark when he reached Varennes, barking out the same warning. The troops were dismissed for the night, except for François Bouillé, son of General Bouillé. He kept a vigil at the inn, with a team of fresh horses ready, just in case the berline did arrive. Léonard drove off in a frenzy for Stenay. Unfortunately, he took a wrong turn in the dark and headed instead toward Verdun, thus failing to meet up with General Bouillé along the route. The general remained clueless of the fiasco until it was almost dawn.

At eleven at night the travelers arrived in Varennes, a village of about one hundred souls, divided with an upper and lower town. The postilions searched in vain for the fresh team of horses in the upper town. Even the royals knocked on several doors, frantically inquiring about the horses, losing another half hour of precious time. No one knew about any horses. The rattled royals pleaded with the drivers to drive directly to Dun, offering them more compensation. The drivers from Clermont were adamant in their refusal. Their orders were to go as far as Varennes; they were needed for farm work the next morning in Clermont. The best the drivers offered was to take the carriage into the lower town of Varennes, opposite the inn.

About the same time, Drouet and his companion sped into town and spotted the unmistakable berline. Drouet darted off to the inn and urged the few drinkers at the bar to rouse the slumbering townsfolk. Drouet spit out his suspicions regarding the identity of the carriage occupants soon to pass before the inn. With alarms ringing urgently and shouts of "Fire" filling the night, most residents rushed from their beds to the center of town. All hearts trembled in the berline as the wound-up royals heard the frantic ringing of the bells; this could not be good news for them.

Four local National Guardsmen with drawn bayonets shouted "Halt" to the drivers. A group of five men, including Drouet, opened the carriage door and thrust in a lantern to take a good look at the occupants. The Russian baroness (aka Madame Tourzel) imperiously demanded to see the mayor. But the mayor was away on business in Paris. His substitute was a man named Sauce, the fellow holding the lantern. He requested their passports and took them into the inn for verification. Everything seemed in perfect order to Sauce. Drouet kept shouting it was the king and queen inside the coach, and they were bent on escaping from France to return with an avenging army.

Sauce just wanted to get rid of the unwanted travelers and let them drive on. But Drouet threatened Sauce that he would be guilty of treason if he allowed the coach to pass. If Sauce permitted the travelers to continue and later learned that it was indeed the king in his midst, he would be in very hot water. And likewise, if he detained the travelers only to discover that they were subjects of the Russian empress, the consequences for him could be equally disastrous. Citizen Sauce was in a pickle.

A practical guy, Sauce returned to the berline and politely invited the unwilling travelers to descend from the coach until "the emotions of the moment" died down. The "baroness" protested in her best uppity aristo talk, but Drouet and his pals shut her up with their drawn weapons. Already a crowd of villagers had surrounded the town center, carrying makeshift arms in response to the alarm bells. Ironically, the first item of interest the royals beheld on exiting the berline was the team of waiting horses for which they had been searching.

Sauce escorted the silent travelers into his flat located above his grocery and candle-making shop. The weary runaways climbed the narrow wooden steps to a two-room abode where Sauce instructed his surprised wife to provide hospitality for the strangers while he bought himself time. The queen requested clean sheets so her exhausted children could get some needed sleep. The stunned ladies of the party sat on humble straw chairs while the king paced back and forth. Drouet kept busy barricading the road that led out of Varennes to impede any attempt at liberty, but not before Bouillé junior sped off in search of Bouillé senior.

Sauce recalled that the local judge, Jacques Destez, had married a lady from the town of Versailles and spent a few years living there where he got to see the royal family up close. Sauce awakened Monsieur Destez and dragged the confused man to his store. Destez scanned the room full of people and recognized the king. Overcome with emotion, he sank to his knees and blurted out, "Oh, Sire." The charade was up—the royals were unmasked.

With calm resignation, Louis admitted to the stupefied spectators that he was their king. While the queen stood silently at a distance, the king began to embrace those present with a paternal familiarity. This was the social milieu where Louis' warmth glowed to perfection, not in gilded palaces. The king explained to the townsfolk the dire circumstances that provoked him to flee the poisoned capital, insisting that his destination was Montmédy and not Austria. He described the threats that he and his family had suffered: "I came to the provinces to find the peace and freedom that you enjoy. If I had stayed in Paris any longer, I should have been murdered." Gasps of horror filled the room as the spellbound listeners sympathized with his plight. Caught up in the emotions of the moment, the townspeople present pledged their unwavering support—definitely a selfie moment.

But that vow fell victim to the tricky realities at hand. These were uncertain times, and the punishment would be severe for thwarting the goals of the Revolution. Sauce had to allow circumstances beyond his control to settle the event that now threatened him and his family. He promised the royals to personally lead them at daybreak to Montmédy with a detachment of National Guardsmen. This offer galvanized the queen into action.

Fearing the collapse of the escape, Antoinette approached Madame Sauce, attempting to alter the outcome, woman to woman. Antoinette spread on her autocratic charm, appealing to Madame Sauce to convince her husband to let the royal party continue their journey without delay. She impressed on Madame Sauce how grateful the king would be if she accelerated their departure. With quivering hesitation, the grocer's wife expressed her deep respect for the king. But she pointedly reminded the queen that her role as a wife was to follow her husband's wishes. There exists no better image to capture the new social and political order of the Revolution than this intimate girl talk between the Queen of France begging for help from a grocer's wife in a humble provincial cottage—a commoner's defiant refusal to bow to the will of the monarch. Thwarted, the queen sank into near despair.

However, Louis didn't share Antoinette's bleak apprehensions. He felt confident that, before dawn, General Bouillé would arrive and remedy the situation. Sure enough around one in the morning the cavalry did arrive. It was not who the royals expected, but it was a sign of hope. Forty troops under the command of the Duke of Choiseul cleared the area of the peasants milling around Sauce's house. Choiseul flew up the steps to Sauce's rooms and breathlessly told the king he awaited his orders. Big Mistake! Louis answered on cue, "What should we do?" Choiseul suggested they escape together on horseback. But Louis hesitated, thinking it too dangerous for his family's safety. Louis remained convinced that Bouillé would soon arrive and escort the royals the remaining short distance. Louis declared, "Then we can leave here safely without violence of any kind."

In Choiseul's company was Monsieur Goguelat, the engineer who had originally surveyed the escape route. Coincidentally, having previously served as the queen's secretary, Goguelat implored the queen to urge her husband to comply at once with the bold offer. But Antoinette could not publicly challenge a decision by the king, no matter her sentiments.

Not long after, Count Damas rode up with his cavalry unit as he had promised the queen in Clermont. He drew the queen aside and spoke to her in German which angered the locals who shouted, "No German, speak French." Like Choiseul, Damas also encouraged the king to make a run for it. Louis, grateful for the offer, remained stationary. He reaffirmed that General Bouillé would arrive by five in the morning.

In the meantime, the young Bouillé, who had raced off to warn his father at Dun of the king's predicament, discovered that Bouillé senior had already left the town and returned to his headquarters at Stenay. Bouillé junior did not find his father until four in the morning. It took another hour to get his four hundred cavalrymen up and ready to ride out. With the country roads swarming with agitated peasants, it was slow going to reach Varennes.

As the tense night wore on, word sped throughout the neighboring hamlets of the incredible news from Varennes. The mood of the people opposed the king continuing his journey as rumors abounded that Austrian troops were rushing across the border to slit French throats. Before dawn broke, thousands of countryfolk carrying rudimentary weapons overran the small town of Varennes. The small group of loyal soldiers was no longer a match for this avalanche of keyed-up peasants. Resumption of the journey now seemed improbable without the intervention of a strong force on the king's behalf, causing certain bloodshed.

At six in the morning a wave of excited talk could be heard outside Sauce's shop along with the stomping of arriving horses. The relieved Louis knew it had to be the dependable General Bouillé. Instead of the general, two exhausted couriers, Citizens Bayon and Romeuf, arrived after riding non-stop from Paris. They sprinted up the steps where the king sat expectantly awaiting Bouillé. Barely breathing, Bayon panted to Louis, "Sire, Paris is in turmoil. Our families will be massacred. Nothing but your return can prevent bloodshed."

The queen was shocked to see Romeuf who had served in her household. Antoinette glared at him, demanding to know how he, of all people, accepted the task to come on this ignominious mission. Shifting his weight from one foot to the other, he uncomfortably averted the queen's offended gaze. The mortified Romeuf gave the king the order signed by Lafayette. Louis scanned the document and without saying a word, handed it to the queen. Outraged, the queen hurled it back to Romeuf who gently set the document on the bed where the royal children slept. After a sad silence, the broken Louis murmured, "There is no longer a King in France."

Marie Antoinette was not endorsing her husband's resignation. Exhausted and super stressed, she angrily lashed out at the two discomforted couriers as she hurled the despicable decree onto the floor, screaming, "What insolence!" She spouted that she would not permit such a filthy document to defile the bed where her precious children slept. And with searing scorn she demanded to know how it was that subjects dared to give orders to their king. As for Louis, he sat there quiet and dejected.

Some local folks, who had managed to squeeze into the room, watched this family drama unfold, their mouths agape. They began whispering animatedly among themselves. Perhaps all the pamphlets they had seen about the queen through the years were true. She was a controlling, haughty bitch. No doubt the king deferred to her, or so it seemed.

With this order from Paris, the town officials had two choices before them: accede to the wishes of the monarch to resume his trip; or obey the decree of the National Assembly. It took them less than thirty seconds to have the coaches turned around in the direction of Paris. When the peasant crowd, now numbering more than five thousand, saw this activity, they chanted in unison, "Long Live the King. Long Live the Nation. To Paris."

Louis requested a delay of several hours before setting forth, citing the exhaustion of his retinue, and still pinning his hopes for deliverance on General Bouillé's arrival. But the impatient crowd demanded an immediate departure. Before reentering the carriage, the king gave a key to Sauce, ordering him to retrieve a box in a hidden compartment in the carriage. Once Louis had the box, he, his wife, and sister destroyed documents that would have proved compromising if discovered on their return to Paris. They burned as many of them as possible and threw the remaining torn fragments out the window.

After the night of shifting fortunes, the bedraggled royal family and their entourage resumed their seats in the waiting carriages at half past seven in the morning. As the queen stepped into the berline she leaned into Choiseul, inquiring if Fersen had reached safety in Belgium. He reassured her that was the case, which provided a bit of solace for the queen.

Fersen did indeed arrive in Belgium after riding all night. There, he met up with the liberated Count Provence to whom he related the safe escape of the royal family from Paris. In a chipper mood, Fersen made his way toward Montmédy where he planned to congratulate the royal family.

With numbing weariness, the royal family began the nightmare return to Paris all the while desperately scanning the horizon for any sign of Bouillé. But no such luck. The general did arrive in time to espy in the distance the sad procession of the two forlorn vehicles hemmed in on all sides by thousands of locals and National Guardsmen, inching its way to a wretched destiny. The distraught general, peering through his spyglass, bitterly realized that any attempt at rescue would be folly with his inferior force. As tears streamed down Bouillé's face, he turned back and rode off to exile in Belgium.

Back in the berline, silence encased the stunned captives. But Antoinette was already forging future plans, if they survived this ordeal. The disastrous outcome of the flight convinced her to no longer trust incompetent French forces. From now on, she would seek deliverance of herself and her family by placing her confidence in foreign military powers.

"We must accept finite disappointment,
but never lose infinite hope."
Martin Luther King, Jr.

Chapter 63

Reentering the Gates of Hell

As the defeated escapees drifted from Varennes, a multitude of crudely armed peasants lined the miserable haul back to the capital. Jean Baptiste Drouet, the hero of the hour, proudly accompanied the berline to the gates of the Tuileries and lasting acclaim. It took almost four grueling days for the royals to reach the abandoned palace. The queen wanted to draw the window blinds of the coach but was reprimanded. The captives were forced to leave the windows open so all could gloat at the sight of the humbled sovereigns. The intense heat of June, along with the endless swirl of dust stirred up by the multitude pressed against the carriage, made conditions in the berline unbearable. The royals were drenched in sweat and caked with dust.

Fear flooded their hearts about the reception awaiting them in Paris. The captives suspected their prospects would be harsh once they reentered the Tuileries. At most stops along the reverse journey, huge crowds slammed the royals with insults. At Epernay, someone ripped the queen's dress as she was jostled by the crowd. As the royals glumly lunched there, one of the municipal officers snorted at the queen, "Do you see what happens when you decide to go traveling?"

After lunch, the captives once again faced the gauntlet of agitated citizens. One brassy woman gave the queen a forceful shove forward, jeering, "Step more lively, my little pretty! They're going to give you lots worse when you get back to Paris!" Even bottom-rung servants got better treatment.

Miles away, Count Fersen bumped into the disconsolate General Bouillé in Belgium who sputtered out the devastating news of capture. Fersen staggered in disbelief that the king had been seized. The Swede would always blame himself for the failed escape. He should have insisted on accompanying the royal family to their destination. He jotted down in his journal, "Learned from Bouillé that the King was taken. No one yet knows the details. The detachments didn't do what they were supposed to do, and the King wasn't firm." Fersen was obliged to inform his king, Gustavus III, of the disaster. The normally cool Axel rushed off a note to his father: "All is lost, my dear father, and I am in despair. The King was arrested at Varennes, just sixteen leagues from the border. Imagine my pain and pity me." The pain was far from over.

Late in the afternoon on June 23, the berline came to an abrupt halt, silencing the crowd of bystanders. Three deputies from the National Assembly chosen to represent the right, middle, and left factions approached the carriage. Respectively, they were Marquis Latour-Maubourg, Antoine Barnave, and Jérôme Pétion. Accompanying the deputies was a military officer, Mathieu Dumas, delegated to bring needed order to the various National Guardsmen escorting the fugitives. The distressed travelers were relieved to see at least one familiar face, Marquis Latour-Maubourg, holding out some hope for their safety. The other deputies were not on the queen's Christmas card list.

Madame Elisabeth appealed to Maubourg to safeguard the faithful three guards who were chained together atop the berline. Due to their prime visibility, they were taunted by the furious lookie-loos who wanted them lynched on the spot. The marquis did what he could under the circumstances and jumped into the cabriolet carrying the two nannies who also were being harassed by the mobs.

Both Barnave and Pétion entered the coach without the king's permission, neglecting to salute him. This impropriety shocked the royals. Barnave squeezed himself between the king and queen, forcing Antoinette's son to sit on her lap. Pétion nestled between Madame Elisabeth and Madame Tourzel, with Madame Royale sitting on her aunt's lap. It was going to be tight quarters for the remainder of the journey. Now all eight passengers were uncomfortable and uncomfortably quiet. Too bad someone didn't start humming a few bars of "Happy Talk."

Elisabeth took the lead in breaking the ice with the Assembly's representatives. She explained that the king had never intended to leave France. Realizing he needed to backpedal fast to minimize the retribution facing him and his family, Louis acknowledged that his sister spoke the truth. To convince the deputies of his sincerity, the king reported that while at Châlons, he attended a mass celebrated by a priest who had sworn the oath to the constitution. Pétion dismissed the peace offering. He sharply reminded the king that such a mass was the only kind the king should ever attend.

Then, Pétion disclosed a bit of news with smug pleasure. Locking eyes with the queen, he inquired if the royals were aware about the rumors sweeping through the capital that a foreigner, probably a Swede, had driven the royal family out of Paris. After a stony royal stare-down, the queen replied icily, "I am not in the habit of knowing the names of cabdrivers," whereupon she lowered the veil on her hat. An unmistakable signal to Pétion that any further conversation with him was to be conducted purely at Her Majesty's leisure and pleasure, meaning fahgettaboudit.

Pétion remained steadfastly disagreeable for the duration of the journey. Later, he would boast that the king's sister Madame Elisabeth tried to seduce him, no doubt at the queen's pernicious prodding. He proudly declared that he resisted her charms purely out of patriotic valor. Anyone familiar with Elisabeth would have known that that she was a formidable Attila the Nun; flirting was not part of this lady's DNA.

Barnave, seated next to the queen, possessed impeccable manners which fostered amiability between them. He and Antoinette explored some common areas of agreement when they chatted at overnight stops. Barnave was unprepared to be impressed with the queen's resolute character in the face of adversity. Like Mirabeau before him, Barnave embarked on a crusade to somehow salvage the Crown. As for the queen, she recognized that she was in a very tight spot. She had to cultivate this man's clout in the Assembly to assure her family's immediate survival.

The tension in the berline tightened as the captives and captors neared Paris on June 25 in the evening. Louis expressed his dismay to Barnave: "This is a very sad journey for my children. What a difference this and my trip to Cherbourg in 1786! At that time calumny had not yet misled public opinion. How prejudiced they are! They may disown me, but they will never change me; I shall always love the people." The king's impressionable little boy kissed his father's hand, promising, "Don't be sad, Papa, next time we'll go to Cherbourg."

Posters plastered throughout Paris alerted the public of the royal family's arrival. The placards warned, "Whoever shall applaud the king will be flogged, and whoever insults him shall be hanged." A tsunami of silence engulfed the dust encrusted carriage and its keyed-up occupants. As the berline crept toward the Tuileries, only church bells defied the total quiet, mournfully tolling as though a death had occurred. The berline passed through two rows of armed National Guardsmen with firearms shouldered in reverse as custom dictated in a funeral cortege. To compound his dismay, Louis' heart sank when he observed that not one man in the vast crowd removed his hat as a sign of deference to their king.

Endless crowds jammed the streets from every possible viewing spot, heeding the posted notices. At last, the berline crept through the palace gates at eight in the evening. Once the carriage halted, a pressure cooker of hate exploded. Shouts spontaneously erupted and the crowd surged forward as the royals shakily descended the carriage and wobbled into the palace. The most violent expressions of anger were reserved for the queen as she exited the berline. Everyone cursed her for manipulating every detail of the escape. As for the non-royals in the traveling party, they were taken to the Abbaye Prison for interrogation.

After entering the palace, Lafayette greeted the spent royals. He bowed to Louis and admonished him: "Sire, you know how attached I am to the person of Your Majesty; but I have never concealed from you that should you separate yourself from the cause of the people, I should be on the people's side." The rage within the queen to have to deal with this obnoxious man again was insupportable; she nearly slapped him for the way he addressed the king. Louis acknowledged the impeccability of Lafayette's integrity. Then, as though the previous five days had never occurred, Lafayette requested the king's orders. Considering the changed circumstances, the king suppressed a smile in response: "It seems to me that now I should receive orders and not give them."

The exhausted travelers retired to their respective suites in a palace that was now a maximum-security detention center. The consequences of the failure of this gutsy undertaking would reset once again the compass for the course of the Revolution.

Ultimately, the flight failed for several compelling reasons. First, there was the use of the large berline that slowed the travel and attracted undue attention at relay stations. Next, the route chosen was neither the most direct nor on the best kept roads. Third, with the royals several hours behind schedule, the military escorts grew uneasy and did not hold their assigned places. Lastly, there was the king's unwillingness to forcefully elbow his way out of Varennes when it became necessary. Even if all of the military escorts had appeared as promised, it is highly doubtful that Louis would have allowed armed resistance if he had met with hostile actions by the local populace.

The outcome supported Fersen's entreaties for having a capable military man in the party to make difficult decisions on the king's behalf.

Finally, two testimonies reflect on the role of destiny in the daring operation. The engineer Goguelat, who had a front row seat throughout the escapade, mused years later, "If one considers the chain of events that constitutes the destiny of men, a long chain whose entire combination can be altered by the removal of one link, one finds oneself forced to revert to Providence, whose powerful hand casts down thrones as it chooses." And Louis, the last to weigh in, wrote to the ashamed General Bouillé. The king generously accepted responsibility for the failed escape. No other words better describe the character of King Louis XVI as a commander-in-chief:

> You risked everything for me and did not succeed. Fate was against your plans and mine. Circumstances paralyzed my will and your courage, and all your preparations were nullified. I do not reproach Providence. I am aware that to succeed was in my hands; but it is needful to have a ruthless spirit if one is to shed the blood of one's subjects by putting up resistance or igniting civil war. The thought of such possibilities broke my heart, and all my resolutions melted away. Accept my thanks, Monsieur. I only wish it were in my power to give you some token of gratitude.

> "Power is not a pleasure.
> It makes you vulnerable."
> *Carla Bruni-Sarkozy*

Spotlight Six

The Days of Grasping at Straws

Chapter 64

Back in the Snake Pit

*I*n the mere four days that had elapsed since Louis' escape, a major shift took root in hearts of the people of France. Some wondered if it were necessary to have a king. Others felt the king should abdicate, and a regency set up for his son. Overall, a popular consensus emerged that Louis could not be trusted. His popularity plummeted, never to recover again. Most people remained sold on the conviction that Antoinette had engineered the diabolical escape to the border to inflict ruination on the Revolution. She had to be eliminated.

The morning following Louis' return, three members of the Assembly paid him an unannounced visit. They informed His Majesty that he was under provisional arrest, and his powers as chief executive had been suspended. Once a thorough investigation was conducted by the Assembly, the king would be informed if he were to be reinstated or dethroned. To Louis, this mortal world seemed madder by the moment. A resigned stoic, Louis did not challenge the Assembly's decision.

Louis' visitors required a detailed account of his motives to embark on such a flight from a city that loved him like a father. The king suppressed an urge to rebuke their insincerity, but instead repackaged what he had enumerated in his departure letter. Louis affirmed, "It was never my intention to leave my kingdom. I have never had any understanding on this subject either with foreign powers or my relatives. Lodgings for me and my family had been prepared at Montmédy. I chose that place because it was fortified, and my family would have been safe there. And being close to the frontier, I would have been in a position to oppose any kind of invasion in France." This last sentence was too much to swallow. When it was read to the Assembly, guffaws filled the chamber. Their king seemed hopeless even when lying.

After questioning the king, the representatives expected to interrogate the queen. They were informed she was currently indisposed, engaged in her bath; they would have to return. The queen was indeed in her bath. It was the only refuge where she was not supervised by guards. Antoinette avoided the grilling by the delegates since it was imperative that her narrative and that of the king coincided. The royal couple secretly exchanged notes that prepared the queen for the reappearance of the Assembly's interrogators.

From the moment they returned to the dismal palace, the royals were tightly guarded in the Tuileries, not even permitted to close the doors to their private suites. The queen always had two soldiers present in her company, even when she dressed. Anyone entering the Tuileries needed a pass from either Lafayette or Bailly. Both king and queen were barred from stepping foot outside the building; the palace grounds teemed with National Guardsmen, day and night.

In the seclusion of her bathtub, the queen wrote to those she cherished. She contacted Fersen first:

> I still exist. How I have worried about you, and how you must have
> suffered without news of us! Heaven grant that this may reach
> you, but do not answer it, for we would be compromised if our
> correspondence were discovered. Above all, do not come back here
> on any pretext. It is known that you assisted us in leaving Paris,
> and all would be lost if you were found here where we are watched
> day and night. But I do not care, for you may rest assured that
> nothing will happen to me, because the Assembly seems inclined
> to treat us kindly. I cannot write more now.

The queen's optimism reflected her networking with Barnave during the hellish return to Paris. Through a loyal intermediary, the Chevalier Jarjayes, the queen approached Barnave, whose influence mattered among his peers, asking, "I should very much like him to tell us what we are to do in our present situation. There is something to be done, I know. But what? During the course of our conversations, he must have realized that I am of good faith." Antoinette used all her charm and persuasion to get Barnave to salvage the Crown's desperate situation in the National Assembly.

How did the royals smuggle out of the heavily guarded Tuileries so much private correspondence? They still had a few trusted courtiers in their respective service who facilitated the dispatch and delivery of countless messages. One of Antoinette's ladies-in-waiting, Madame Jarjayes, served as post mistress with total circumspection. Also, writing in secret, Louis sneaked notes out of the palace. In one of his desperate messages to Emperor Leopold, the queen's brother, Louis pleaded, "if I am forced to be sacrificed on the scaffold like Charles I, then I am ready. But no war!"

"Study after study has shown that human behavior
changes when we know we're being watched."
Edward Snowden

Chapter 65

Monarchy or Republic?

The crisis of the botched flight preoccupied the Assembly around the clock. Seven committees were formed to provide recommendations for a course of action. Beyond their own investigations, the deputies canvassed opinions from all over France. A deluge of letters flooded the Assembly, most of which expressed outrage and feelings of betrayal regarding the king's behavior. Throughout France citizens swore oaths of allegiance to the National Assembly, yet the vast majority did not call for the king's removal. They trusted the Assembly to decide the choice that best suited the nation. Most of France needed a cooling off to be convinced that jettisoning the monarchy was in their interest.

But it was a different reaction in Paris where most political clubs demanded the National Assembly declare a republic or, at the very least, establish a regency. As the Assembly grappled with their options, they unenthusiastically leaned toward retaining the king. Here was the rub. The exhausted deputies of the National Assembly were just weeks away from finishing their task of providing France with a constitution that required the office of a king. Deposing Louis would mean starting the entire process anew. These deputies wanted to complete their job and officially bring the Revolution to a close. Furthermore, they worried that Louis' removal would trigger an invasion of France by the surrounding monarchs. Barnave pinpointed the ambivalence of most deputies:

Are we going to end the Revolution or start it all over again? If the Revolution takes one more step it could be a dangerous one.

> If it is in line with liberty, its first act could be the destruction of
> royalty. If it is in line with equality, its first act could be an attack
> on property. It is time to bring the Revolution to an end. Is there
> still to be destroyed an aristocracy other than property?

Barnave, the once incendiary voice in 1789, now seemed more restrained
and politically pragmatic in 1791. His reference to an attack on property
made the middle-class deputies nervous. The Assembly felt uneasy during
the summer of 1791 amid widespread strikes for higher wages, civil unrest
in rural areas, as well as ugly demonstrations by the unemployed in Paris.
Deputies feared that the Revolution was spiraling out of control.

Any reticence in the Assembly was overcome by an inflammatory letter
received from General Bouillé, the failed military leader behind the escape
plan. Bouillé publicly assumed blame for the attempt to save Louis and his
family. Bouillé boasted from the shelter of Luxembourg that he had shamed
the king into fleeing after the intolerable standoff at the Tuileries gates on
April 18. He taunted the Assembly, saying, "I arranged everything, decided
everything, and ordered everything. I alone gave the orders, not the King. It
is against me alone that you should direct your rabid fury." For extra sting,
Bouillé indelicately suggested where the deputies should ram "their infernal
constitution." While not exactly buying the confession, the letter supplied
the Assembly with the needed rationalization to maintain a constitution that
required a king.

The final report regarding the Varennes affair was submitted to the
Assembly on July 13 for its discussion and vote. The recommendations chose
to exonerate the king and maintain the monarchy. The Assembly's report
underscored: "It is for the nation, and not for the King, that a monarchy has
been established." The Jacobin faction blasted this solution, demanding that
Louis be branded as a traitor and immediately dethroned. After the shouting
match ended, the voting ruled in favor of Louis, declaring his innocence,
citing he had been "abducted." The National Assembly begrudgingly
absolved Louis while touting the nearly completed constitution.

General Bouillé became the primary fall guy for the Varennes mess-
up. He was condemned for plotting to use the king "as an instrument of his
personal ambitions." Fortunately, he was far away, beyond the vengeance
of the nation. But within a year, his name would become infamous as the
only designated traitor mentioned in "La Marsellaise," the patriotic song that
would become the French national anthem.

Choiseul, Goguelat, and Damas were all found guilty of the "abduction"
and imprisoned. Count Fersen was soundly demonized for his role but no
more than that. Madame Tourzel, the two nannies, and the three guards, who

had been jailed on their return from Varennes, were now released. But like the verdict in the Diamond Necklace Trial, the guilty party in this episode was none other than Marie Antoinette. The Lisbon Curse was on a roll.

Louis obtained conditional release from the national dog house. His office as chief executive would remain in limbo until the constitution was completed, whereupon the king would be required to swear his allegiance. Only at that juncture would he resume his responsibilities. The Assembly also ruled that any king who broke his oath to the constitution or led an army against the nation would immediately be forced to abdicate.

The decision of the National Assembly did not go down well in Paris. The more prosperous Parisians supported retaining the king to maintain stability, certainly not out of loyalty to the man. The common city dwellers and the radical patriots were irate. Seething crowds cornered the deputies of the Assembly, cataloguing all sorts of threats against them if they didn't depose the king. On July 16 Mayor Bailly was summoned to the Assembly and chastised for not maintaining order. The battered mayor was on the verge of screaming to all of Paris to take this job and shove it.

The most radical political group at the time was the Cordeliers Club. Founded in 1789, they were considered anarchists by the more conservative revolutionaries. They adopted as their motto: liberty, fraternity, and equality. The most notorious members of the club were the wild wolves: Georges Danton, Camille Desmoulins, and Jean-Paul Marat. They spearheaded the move to overrule the Assembly's decision on Louis, calling for a national referendum on the fate of the king. A petition execrating Louis and demanding his removal was placed on the Altar of the People in the Champs de Mars on July 17 where a large crowd had congregated to add their signatures. Early in the proceedings, two jinxed fellows were uncovered hiding under the altar. Their discovery sparked rumors that they planned to blow up the altar and kill as many patriots as possible. Both fellows were dragged off screaming, and lynched on the spot with the customary head on a pike.

When the Assembly learned of this atrocity, most members exploded. These spontaneous murders and rejection of the Assembly's role as legitimate legislators were unacceptable. Once again, Mayor Bailly was put on the hot seat. After conferring with his colleagues at city hall, Bailly reluctantly hoisted the red flag, signaling the imposition of martial law. When Bailly arrived at the tense Champs de Mars, the National Guard was already present. According to the rules of martial law, three warnings had to be issued by the mayor ordering the crowd to peacefully disperse. The organizers of the event knew the drill and agreed to vacate the stadium after the first of the three warnings.

A sizable group of people still waited in line to sign the petition that already bore about six thousand signatures. The organizers urged those assembled to remain calm as the National Guard entered and took up positions. Some in the crowd hurled insults and began pelting the guardsmen with rocks. A single gunshot rang out, just missing Bailly, but wounding a cavalryman and triggering a spray of gunfire by the guardsmen. Panic broke out as people fled in all directions to escape the shots. After the firing ceased, dead and wounded littered the field. Bailly counted twelve citizens and two soldiers among the dead. Some protesters insisted hundreds had been massacred; the truth appeared to be closer to sixty casualties. Regardless of one's political affiliations, most Parisians were horrified by this use of military force. They had become so accustomed to intimidating the authorities that they were rudely reminded of the flip side of dissent. Lafayette and Bailly became public enemies, vilified as being in the pay of the Austrian Woman. Within two months both men would be pounding the pavement for a new job.

At first glance, the suppression of the demonstration at the Champs de Mars was a blow for Robespierre and his radical allies in the Assembly. Barnave and his party of moderate-right Feuillants could claim a brief victory. Radical newspapers fell off the grid for self-preservation. Could it be that the rule of the mob was finally faced down? Antoinette congratulated Barnave on the Champs de Mars outcome, hoping that it meant that law and order would triumph.

Barnave responded by insisting that the queen write to her brother, Emperor Leopold, emphasizing two policies. First, Louis willingly accepted his role in a constitutional monarchy; and second, the king desired that the alliance between France and Austria be maintained in peaceful cooperation. The last headache that France needed was an international war on its borders.

Antoinette tried to wiggle her way out of this assignment. She appealed to Barnave: "My influence over him [Emperor Leopold] is non-existent. He has regard for the family name, and that is all." There was truth in the queen's remarks, acknowledging her relationship with Leopold was unlike her bond with her late brother, Joseph. In the end the queen had no choice but to follow Barnave's instructions.

But through a clandestine note to Count Mercy, the queen alerted him to inform the emperor that her words were not truly her own: "I had to give into the party leaders here. It is extremely important for them to believe that I am of their opinion, at least for some time to come. Although they are tenacious in their opinions, I have never seen anything but the greatest decency in them, and a genuine wish to restore order and the authority of the Crown." Blasphemy! Many émigrés, out of harm's way abroad, sneered at the queen's dealings with Barnave and his crew. They were convinced that Antoinette was sleeping with him.

Barnave hammered away that Louis and Antoinette zealously support the constitution. He urged the royal pair to dispel the widespread conviction that they spearheaded reactionary measures aimed at the Revolution's collapse. Barnave kept orchestrating public appearances of the royals to rally popular support, a wasted effort in the eyes of hardened Parisians. Barnave even coerced the queen to write to Count Mercy, urging his return to France as a sign of good faith in the achievements of the Revolution. Hands down, at age sixty-four, Mercy would have chosen a double dose of cyanide over a return to Paris.

Since Varennes, Emperor Leopold received notes of desperation from his sister, begging him to man up on behalf of her family. Louis also asked Leopold "to come to the aid of the King and kingdom of France."

Amid these appeals, Leopold of Austria and Frederick William of Prussia met in August 1791 at a spa in Pillnitz, Saxony. The two leaders stitched together a declaration that called on European monarchs to validate that the well-being of the French royals was a matter of common interest. It also encouraged a united armed intervention to prop up the French royals, if necessary. The pledge was worthless even before the ink dried, given that most powers were not on board with military action. The émigrés deemed the text toothless, causing the king's brother Provence to attach a cover letter full of threats against France. When Antoinette read Provence's document, she screamed out, "He has murdered us." When Provence's letter was read before the Assembly, the Austrian Woman was fingered as the mastermind behind the bellicose statement. Ultimately, the Pillnitz Declaration was like a stab of venom; everyone felt poisoned.

On September 3, 1791, a delegation of deputies from the National Assembly marched in solemn procession to deliver the constitution to the king in his council chamber. Louis congratulated the deputies and promised to carefully review the document. The king all but said, "I swear," to the national contract, commenting, "My journey to Varennes has convinced me that public opinion firmly favors the constitution."

One of the delegates expressed, "Now we will learn if the King will be the friend or the enemy of the nation. Everything hangs on his decision."

Louis was in a jam. He considered the constitution mostly an abomination because his royal powers were reduced to chopped liver. But the king knew his reputation was still in the sewer after the botched escape. If he rejected the constitution, chaos would surely erupt with nasty consequences for him and his family. If he accepted the constitution, he would be dishonest, but might survive to prove the constitution unworkable. Louis opted for the latter, and prayed for a miracle. After nine suspenseful days, the king announced that he would approve the constitution.

Louis trotted off to the Assembly on September 14 to take his oath to the loathsome document. The deputies responded to him in an undignified manner. Louis was mortified when he was forced to stand and remove his hat when he took the oath. The deputies remained seated and never removed their hats as a sign of respect. For Louis, this insulting reception was worse than the constitution itself. He barely held it together throughout the ceremony.

Louis' speech, drafted by Barnave and his cohorts, called for a general amnesty to reunite the nation and extinguish suspicion. To the delight of the crowd, the anguished king declared, "Frenchmen living under the same laws must recognize as enemies only those who infringe upon them. We have reached the end of the Revolution. May happiness return to our country." As the king exited the Assembly to stale cheers, many wondered if the king could be trusted. In their eyes, Louis was on strict probation.

Throughout the ceremony, the queen witnessed the proceedings from a private box. Later when the royals reached Louis' private apartments in the Tuileries, a tearful king sank into an armchair and blurted out, "Oh, Madame, that you should have witnessed this humiliation! All is lost! That you should have come to France to see this day." Antoinette did her best to console her husband and bolster his spirits.

Any chance of a rapprochement between the Crown and revolutionaries now seemed unlikely. How could the king ever trust deputies who insulted his office with spiteful delight? The queen unloaded her personal thoughts to Mercy: "It is impossible given the position here for the King to refuse the oath. You have enough experience of me to know that I would prefer a nobler and more courageous path, but there is no point in courting certain destruction. Our only hope lies in the foreign Powers." And those powers could not get their act together.

One bright spot did surface for the royals: the Assembly extended a longer leash to their captivity. Louis resumed his limited executive functions: appointing ministers and exercising the right of the veto. The king and his family obtained some respite from the stringent measures imposed since their return from Varennes, including more privacy and the freedom of closing their doors. Once again, they received and entertained ambassadors and courtiers. Modest movement of travel within the city limits of Paris was also granted. And last of all, they were accorded the reward to attend the theater. How lucky can you get?

On the last day of September 1791, the National Assembly formally disbanded to be replaced by a new representative body, the Legislative Assembly. Within two turbulent years the National Assembly had not only written a constitution, but enacted about five thousand laws. As the National Assembly disappeared from the main stage, so did Lafayette. He decided to run for mayor of Paris in October but was trounced in the election by Pétion. After his militaristic intervention during the Champs de Mars show of force in July, Lafayette's reputation was shot to hell. The chastened Lafayette retired to his estate, planning to emulate his hero at Mount Vernon in Virginia.

"Defeat is not bitter unless you swallow it."
Joe Clark

Chapter 66

Everybody's in a Bad Mood

Support for the constitution was hardly a universal endorsement. Basically, propertied males over twenty-five were considered fully protected by the constitution; all others were termed "passive citizens." Once again, women felt excluded and betrayed. Perhaps the most vocal of feminist activists in France was Olympe Gouges, a playwright and political essayist. Before the National Assembly closed shop permanently, she taunted the authors of the constitution by publishing a manifesto, "A Declaration of the Rights of Women and the Female Citizen." Olympe called on the National Assembly to give women the same rights as men. This call for equality was dismissed by the men in charge; they tagged Olympe as a dangerous troublemaker.

Meanwhile, Louis had secretly empowered his brothers with a limited authority to negotiate with foreign powers, with Louis retaining the final say. The brothers blithely ignored the latter stipulation, announcing that they acted on Louis XVI's behalf since he was now a puppet monarch. Louis' brother Provence exposed his serpentine prowess while protesting his devotion. He wrote to Louis lamenting his sadness that the unhappy king accepted a constitution that he privately detested. He ended his fraternal missive pledging, "Don't worry about your safety. We live only to be of help to you and we are working for you with ardor." In a scuzzy move, Provence circulated copies of the letter throughout France so everyone could share the brothers' unified stance against the constitution. Even in the Bible Abel got a better deal from Cain.

Louis lamely fired back to his brothers, "In adopting the principles of the constitution and executing them in good faith, I will make the people see the true cause of its misfortunes; public opinion will change, and since without this change, new convulsions will be inevitable. I will have more chance of achieving a better state of things by my acceptance, than by my refusal."

Although favoring the intervention of foreign forces, Antoinette reluctantly supported the king's stance in a letter to Mercy: "We must follow the constitution to the last letter of the law. I promise you that this is the best way to disgust them with it." But within a few months, the royal couple would be on the same page as they scanned the horizon for the first sight of their liberators.

Antoinette also described the strains on family relations to Fersen: "Our domestic life is hell, with the best will in the world, one can't discuss anything. My sister is so indiscreet, surrounded by intriguers, and above all dominated by her brothers abroad, that we cannot speak to each other; otherwise, we would be quarreling all day." The glittering social swirl of the court was now on a par with a rural nursing home. The royals obediently dined in public twice a week, and the queen hosted card games several times a week. The highlight of the social life at court might be the evening entertainment offered in the rooms of the Princess Lamballe, a hostess never credited with being a party animal.

On October 6, 1791, Louis XVI appeared at the inaugural meeting of the newly installed Legislative Assembly whose mandate empowered deputies to put meat on the bones of the constitution. Many of the new deputies were convinced that a conspiracy festered within the palace, led by the queen, to incite émigré forces abroad to invade France and restore the former order. With this mindset, the deputies went out of their way to belittle the king. Once again both Louis and Antoinette blanched at the blatant disrespect for the monarch. This was not the way to foster a fruitful relationship with the head of State.

The first two items of business the deputies tackled were sure to make Louis howl. First, the Legislative Assembly devised more stringent punishments for the disobedient non-juring priests; and, second, the deputies wished to make life miserable for the expanding émigré population headquartered in Coblenz. The moderate Feuillant party in the newly-elected Legislative Assembly was getting nowhere on these hot button issues with each successive compromise they proposed. The position of the Crown deteriorated daily, despite Barnave's backstage efforts to nudge it and the Legislative Assembly into the same bed. Neither side trusted him anymore.

Power was shifting from the Feuillants to the Girondin faction, the hip political club of the hour. As a group, they considered constitutional monarchy as heretical and were bent on discrediting Louis. A few months after taking the oath to the constitution, Antoinette convinced Louis to enlist foreign powers to restore their sovereignty. The queen churned out coded letters to sympathetic ears. What a huge departure from her carefree days at Trianon! Did she ever think of her delightful hideaway? Now, all of her energies centered on survival. She admitted to Fersen her weariness living under so much stress:

> I am in better shape than I would have expected given the
> prodigious exhaustion of spirit which comes from going out so
> little. I don't have a moment to myself between seeing all the
> people I have to see, as well as writing and the time I spend with
> my children. These two are my only solace. Try to understand my
> position and the part that I am forced to play every day; sometimes
> I barely recognize myself and find it difficult to believe that it is
> really me speaking! But what can one do? All of this is necessary,
> and believe me, we would be much worse off than we are now
> if I hadn't immediately adopted this policy. At least this way we
> gain time, and that is all we need. Oh, what joy if one day I could
> triumph enough to show all these rogues that I was never their
> dupe.

⚜   ⚜   ⚜

Before the brewing implosion of the established order, an unexpected fugitive arrived to offer his services to the royal couple. Count Axel von Fersen breezed into the palace on February 13, 1792, disguised as a diplomatic courier. He took his usual route to the queen's apartments. Antoinette had learned only that afternoon of his imminent arrival. Fersen passed the night hidden in the queen's apartments, running a huge risk of being discovered. This guy strolled through "hot zones" affecting a casual identity, while courting tremendous personal danger. If the guards on duty had ever learned that they had been fooled again by this cunning man, there would have been hell to pay among their ranks.

For Antoinette and Fersen this would be their last time together, an emotionally charged moment for both of them. They exchanged recollections about Varennes with the queen filling in the blanks of details that Fersen did not know. The following day Fersen saw Louis in the evening in Antoinette's rooms, presenting a plan of escape devised by King Gustavus III. The Swedish sovereign proposed an escape to Normandy where troops would land in the king's defense. The queen warmed to the idea, but the king was not buying.

Overwhelmed with gratitude for Fersen's loyalty and courage, Louis remained firm in his opposition to try a second escape. Fersen recognized the great risks of getting them all out of the palace, but felt it was worth a chance. But Louis could not bear a repeat of Varennes:

> I know that people tax me with weakness and indecision. But no one has ever been in a position such as mine. I know I missed the opportunity in July of 1789 when I should have left, and I wanted to, but Monsieur [the king's brother Provence] begged me not to leave; and the Maréchale Broglie, who was in command, replied to me, "Yes we may go to Metz, but what shall we do when we get there?" I missed the moment then, and I have never found it since. I have been abandoned by everybody.

Louis' words confirmed a man who saw himself as doomed. Having failed to convince the king to escape, Fersen took his leave of the royals. At half past nine in the evening on February 14 he left the Tuileries unnoticed, and melted into the night. How fitting that Antoinette and Fersen would last embrace each other on a day currently celebrated for undying lovers, Valentine's Day.

> "There is no dilemma compared to a deep-sea diver
> who hears the message from the ship above,
> 'Come up at once, we're sinking.'"
> *Robert Cooper*

Chapter 67

War with the Queen's Birthplace

*T*he month of March heaped more devastating news on the royals. On the first of March the Austrian emperor died unexpectedly. While not close to Leopold, Antoinette nonetheless lamented the loss of her brother at a critical juncture. The emperor's successor was his son Francis II. This nephew of the queen regarded his distant aunt as an indifferent stranger. To compound Antoinette's distress, her staunch supporter, Gustavus III of Sweden, was assassinated at a masked ball on March 16. What next, for God's sake! The Lisbon Curse seemed out of control.

All of Louis' ministers resigned on March 10 in protest to Louis' reluctance to declare war on Austria. To punish Louis for his anti-war stance, the Girondin party forced on him a cabinet of war hawks. Privately, Louis wished for war but pretended a public position for peace.

The post of foreign minister was awarded to a plucky soldier, General Charles François Dumouriez. He and the king worked well together due to their shared interest in naval matters. When he was received by the queen in a private audience, she railed against all of the anarchy and insolence that assailed the monarchs. Instead of appealing for the general's support, Antoinette dressed-down the general, decrying the intolerable conditions she had to endure daily. Antoinette was probably exasperated to have to cozy up yet again to someone she regarded with suspicion. With a frosty facade, she warned, "Monsieur, you are all powerful at present, but this is through the favor of the people who break their idols. Your existence depends upon your conduct. You must consider that neither the King nor I can accept all the innovations or the constitution. I tell you so frankly: do make the best of it."

Unlike Mirabeau and Barnave before him, this soldier did not fall under Antoinette's spell. Who would with such a snippy welcome? Dumouriez was an army guy, not an elegantly seasoned courtier. He counseled the queen that conditions would improve if she followed his advice:

> Madame, I am sorry about the painful secret Your Majesty just confided in me. I will not betray it, but I am caught between the King and the nation, and I belong to my country. Allow me to impress upon you that the King's salvation, yours and that of your august children is tied to the constitution. I would be serving you badly and him too, if I spoke to you differently. Madame, believe me, I abhor as you do anarchy and crime. But I am better placed to judge events than is Your Majesty. This is not a popular movement which will pass; it is the spontaneous resistance of the whole nation to deep-seated wrongs. The King and the nation must remain united; everything which leads to their separation will ruin them both.

Dumouriez offered a sound assessment of the political landscape, however unflattering. But Antoinette could not place her trust in the hands of a man who endorsed the emasculation of the Crown. With no chance for a rapprochement, the queen kept her sights trained on the one source of salvation, foreign forces.

One day, Dumouriez brought the new minister of the interior, Jean-Marie Roland, to be introduced to Louis. The ever-punctilious master of ceremonies, Dreux-Brézé, cringed when he caught sight of Roland. He whispered to Dumouriez that he could not introduce to the king a man who wore ribbons to fasten his shoes instead of the court mandated silver buckles. Dumouriez feigned dismay but pushed past Dreux-Brézé, and the introduction proceeded.

Louis and Roland instantly loathed each other, ribbons notwithstanding. They were always at odds, precipitating nasty conflicts in the council meetings. Roland was actually a mouthpiece for his powerful wife, Manon Roland. She presided over a salon entertaining the movers and shakers of her time. She was a strident voice for republican government even at the dawn of the Revolution. In 1789 she upbraided lukewarm sympathizers: "You are nothing but children. Your enthusiasm is like a fire of straw, and if the National Assembly does not put in action the trial of two illustrious heads [one guess whose], then you are all fucked." What a potty mouth on such a pretty hostess! She dismissed the king as a useless eunuch. And there was no limit to her disdain for the Austrian bitch.

In the Legislative Assembly war fever dominated policymaking, especially among the Girondins. They espoused war while the Jacobin faction, guided by Robespierre, resisted the war drums. Dumouriez dispatched an insulting ultimatum to the emperor in Vienna demanding the end of an armed congress and the withdrawal of imperial troops from the French border. The Austrians coolly dismissed Dumouriez's impertinence. For three tense days, Louis' council of ministers hashed out a response ending in unanimous agreement for hostilities to be launched against Austria.

On April 20, 1792, Dumouriez read a report to the deputies in the Legislative Assembly highlighting the reasons for war against Austria, foremost being the perceived subjugation of France to the Hapsburgs. Cued by the general, a listless Louis announced, "You have just heard the report. Its conclusions have been unanimously adopted by council. They conform to the wishes expressed by the Assembly. I have exhausted all means for maintaining peace. Now I come in the name of the constitution to formally propose war."

The month of May 1792 brought fresh worries to the royal family. Louis sank into a depression, more severe than any he had previously. After ten days, the king emerged from an unreachable space, only to confront another crisis. Since the war began with a series of defeats for French forces, the Girondins needed a scapegoat to calm the anxieties that wound up the people of Paris. Deputy Brissot blamed the military routs by the Austrians not on the disorganized French troops, but rather on "the Austrian committee in the Tuileries" bent on seeing the revolutionary forces defeated.

Targeted as the one betraying the country, Antoinette feared imminent arrest. The word on the street accused Antoinette of squealing the French troop movements to the Austrians; this time the rumors were true. This "Austrian Committee" within the Tuileries had to be eliminated. The queen's onetime admirer, Barnave, knew his political power had evaporated, as Crown and Legislative Assembly ignored his advice. He staunchly opposed war, convinced that such a tragedy would topple the monarchy and exacerbate the chaos that convulsed France. He sadly conceded that Louis and Antoinette welcomed war as their only route to freedom. In a last letter to the queen, Barnave expressed his disillusionment writing with foresight: "I see very little hope of success in the plan you are being made to follow. You are too far away from help now; you will be lost before it can reach you."

Feeling the heat to dissolve the monarchy, the Girondin faction was now determined to put Louis in the hot seat. Between May 27 and June 8, the Girondins passed three decrees. The first dealt with the non-juring clergy who were required to take the oath of the clergy immediately or face deportation. The second required the elimination of the king's constitutional guard, increasing his personal vulnerability. The third ordered the establishment of a camp in Paris of twenty thousand ardent recruits to the National Guard. The king's response to these three decrees would set off an explosive attack on the Crown.

Louis' ministers, in particular General Dumouriez, nearly sat on him to approve these decrees without delay, arguing that with the country at war, the people would interpret any veto by Louis as a reactionary threat. Even the queen considered the pragmatism of signing the odious decrees if for no other reason than to buy time for their deliverance.

Surprisingly, Louis planned to sign only the second decree on the abolition of his constitutional guard. He planned to veto the first decree regarding the forced deportation of all non-juring priests to the penal colony of French Guiana. Once again his religious scruples opposed a policy that would have meant certain death to thousands of priests given the dreadful sanitary conditions in the colony, not to mention the logistical nightmare of transporting them there. The king would also veto the third decree sanctioning twenty thousand armed men in Paris for eventual deployment to the warfront. Louis rightly feared that such a huge gathering of untrained military men in Paris would be hostile to his survival. He ordered they must establish their camp at a site far from Paris.

Louis met with his council and informed them of his intentions. Three ministers berated Louis, especially Roland, who fumed that "a grieving people will see in its King the friend and accomplice of conspirators." Suppressing an urge to break a chair over Roland's head, Louis fired him and two Girondin ministers on June 13, while promoting General Dumouriez to war minister. The general felt that he was now in a position to pressure Louis to sign the two outstanding decrees.

Invoking his executive powers, Louis issued his two vetoes on June 19, 1792. Immediately he was slammed as "Monsieur Veto," with demonstrations popping up within hours of news. A group of eight thousand marchers invaded the Legislative Assembly on June 20, frightening most of the deputies. Their message of intimidation ended in an uneasy standoff as the Girondin deputies directed the belligerent petitioners to take their cause to the gates of the Tuileries.

The protesters scampered off to the Tuileries, overrunning the palace grounds. The rioters wanted to force the king to reverse his vetoes and recall the three Girondin ministers. The contingent of National Guardsmen on duty passively stood by as the mob sprinted for the king's chambers. Surrounded by twelve tall, strong soldiers known as grenadiers, and several loyal courtiers, Louis awaited the onslaught, resigned to be murdered. He and his guards were no match for the wave of malodorous demonstrators swarming through the palace shouting, "Down with the Veto."

Facing this semi-deranged crowd, Louis stoically persevered. A butcher with a booming voice and the oratorical finesse of a dockworker, berated Louis to the approval of his cohorts: "Monsieur, now you listen to us, indeed you are required to listen to us. You are a treacherous rogue who has always deceived us, and you are still deceiving us. The people are tired of being your toy."

The king calmly countered, "I continue to perform what the constitution and its decrees order me to."

Throughout the terrifying standoff Louis remained unruffled, refusing to reverse his vetoes, or recall the three ousted ministers. A lady was spotted behind the king, half obscured in a window seat. The rioters assumed it was the queen and before they could lunge at her, one of the grenadiers yelled that it was the king's sister and not the queen. Antoinette and her children were trapped elsewhere in the palace.

The mob pushed all of Louis' buttons. The red cap worn by the rioters was passed to him on a pike. They instructed Louis to put it on to prove his loyalty. Too tight for his large head, one guy grabbed it and stretched it on his grubby pants. He then shoved it back to the king to don. The cap looked ridiculous when contrasted with Louis' court attire. But the spectators roared their satisfaction; the king looked like a carnival clown.

The red cap was similar to the ubiquitous tricolor. It was worn by the most hardened revolutionaries who were known as the *sans-culottes* (men who wore long trousers instead of knee breeches). The red cap made reference to ancient Rome when a slave who had won or purchased his freedom would wear a red cap to announce his new identity. Likewise, for these Parisian bottom feeders, the cap signified their freedom from the chains of the feudal past.

The palace drama continued with the rabble demanding the king drink to the health of the nation, something they had already done plenty of during the day. A glass of red wine was passed to Louis. The king took the glass, raised it high, toasting, "People of Paris, I drink to your health and that of the French people." In the meantime, some of the intruders were destroying furniture, while others took advantage of the disorder and stuffed palace trinkets into their pockets.

A slave to indecisiveness all his life, Louis was rock solid when faced with this perilous confrontation. The king's steadfastness gained him some begrudging respect from the crowd. After several hours, a few deputies of the Legislative Assembly deemed it safe to appear on the scene. In their wake, Mayor Pétion arrived, being carried by two burly guards pushing their way through the dense crowd. Upon standing before the king, the mayor confessed that he had just learned "of the situation in which you find yourself." Pegging Pétion for the phony SOB he was, Louis responded with intended irony, "I find that most remarkable, since this has been going on for hours. I have ordered that the State Apartments be opened; it may amuse the people to see them." It proved to be the solution to get the mob to disperse and end the horrible standoff. Pétion urged the good citizens of Paris to exit the palace calmly, "lest the enemies of the Revolution question their respectable intentions."

When the crowd had first flooded the palace, Antoinette tried to reach Louis' side. She must have felt that this was October 6 all over again. However, she sensed that this time the mob would finish the job. Once she had her children in her arms, they all huddled together in a secret passageway, listening to the frightening din above them where the king was trapped. The doors near their hiding place were being hacked to pieces, and the queen could hear shrieks of "Kill the Austrian." Fearing she was about to die, she fled with her children into a hallway hoping to reach the king, keeping the vow to never be separated in times of danger. Antoinette was intercepted by Chevalier Rougeville who forcefully guided her to the adjacent council room where he barricaded her and her trembling retinue into a corner behind a massive table.

Rougeville persuaded Antoinette that her presence next to Louis would incur his certain death, as he would strive to protect her from the fury of the crowd. With just a few guards, Rougeville braced himself for the approaching onslaught. Within minutes a splinter group of rioters discovered the queen's party. They pelted the "Austrian bitch" with the vilest death chants. With weapons aimed at Antoinette's throat, they demanded she affix to her hair a tricolor cockade. The queen remained outwardly calm, addressing the hostile Parisians: "You have been misled. I married the King of France, and I am the mother of the Dauphin. I am French, and I shall never again see my native land. I can only be happy or unhappy in France, and I was happy when you loved me."

This impromptu appeal no doubt saved her life, but the loathing remained entrenched. All the while, Antoinette's terrified children clung to her. For her thirteen-year-old daughter, this day of terror impacted the rest of her life. Happiness would always remain an elusive dream for this young princess. For several hours, she endured the non-stop threats hurled at her mother, expecting that the crazed crowd would kill the queen and perhaps the rest of them. Her younger brother was equally traumatized. Like his father, he was forced to put on the red cap of the sans-culottes that covered his entire face. The next morning when he awoke, the still frightened child asked his valet, "Is it still yesterday?"

At six in the evening the royal family was at last reunited. It took another two hours before the remaining stragglers vacated the building. The palace was quiet again, but evidence of the damage done during the invasion was inescapable. Meanwhile, across Paris some were celebrating the shaming of the monarchs. Mayor Pétion, who had been solicitous in the king's presence, hours later harangued supporters that "The Great Warning" should be a wake-up call to the residents of the Tuileries. Even Madame Roland, calling the shots in her salon, was rhapsodic about the queen's ordeal, exclaiming, "How I would have loved to see her long humiliation, and how much her pride had to suffer."

Following the habit of governing bodies, the Legislative Assembly launched an investigation into the events of June 20. The queen conducted the deputies through the palace to show the widespread damage. She expressed her distress that these horrifying events were robbing her children of a normal childhood. She described without resentment the emotional damage suffered by her family. Condolences were offered, but no measures were implemented to improve the safety of the royal family.

Snatching a few minutes, Antoinette sneaked off a message to Fersen after the horrible day, describing the nightmare:

I still exist, but it is by a miracle. The twentieth was a dreadful day. It is no longer against me that they are the most bitter, but against my husband's very life; they do not hide it anymore. He showed a firmness and strength that impressed them for the moment, but the dangers could once again rise at any time. Farewell. Take care of yourself for our sakes, and do not worry about us.

Worry! Even the steadfast Fersen was on the verge of cracking up, trying to figure out a way to prevent any further escalation of violence against the royal family.

> "Sometimes when I am down and nothing is going right,
> I like to take a home pregnancy test. Then I can say,
> 'Hey, at least I'm not pregnant.'"
> *Daniel Tosh*

Chapter 68

A Farewell to Crowns

*M*any people across France were outraged at the events of June 20, voicing their concerns in letters to the Legislative Assembly. The king's unexpected firmness inspired respect and admiration, reflecting the mercurial character of the Revolution. Much like a spastic stock market, one's fortunes could rise and fall unexpectedly. Mayor Pétion was suspended from his post for his botched response to the events of the day. Another casualty of June 20 was General Dumouriez. After the king refused to sign the decrees, the general resigned his post. He figured that the king's days were numbered, and Dumouriez declined the ignominy of being on the bridge of a sinking ship of State. He returned to the front lines where he could be his own boss.

Given that Lafayette considered himself the conscience of the Revolution, he deputized himself to steer it on a stable path. He hurried from the warfront on June 28 to address the Legislative deputies, many of whom felt he was about to launch a power grab. He upbraided the representatives for allowing the Revolution to run amok. He urged shuttering the radical clubs, limiting the out-of-control press and cauterizing the interference of the Parisian radicals in the work of the Legislative Assembly—all timely remedies.

Afterward, Lafayette sought out Louis with a daring plan to escort the royal family to Compiègne. There, with the combined armies of Lafayette and General Luckner, a new constitution could be drawn up, restoring some executive powers while demanding that the Austrians and Prussians withdraw to their borders. Louis, although tempted by the audacious plan, wavered in response. Even his far-right sister Elisabeth urged him to accept the offer. But incredulously, Antoinette was inflexible, blinded by her loathing of Lafayette. She pleaded with Louis, "Better to perish than be saved by Monsieur Lafayette." Ultimately, Louis sided with his wife. This proved to be the last chance at salvaging the monarchy. In the end the royals pinned their hopes on the foreign armies for rescue, a gamble they were willing to risk.

To his bitter surprise, Lafayette discovered he was vilified in the press; incapable of stirring the National Guard to his call; derided by the Legislative Assembly; and, rejected by the royal family. Disillusioned, Lafayette returned to his military command in Alsace, fearing the undoing of the new order that he had dreamed of ever since he had returned from the land of George Washington.

During the summer of 1792, some of Antoinette's close friends reached out to her. Her childhood playmates from the House of Hesse approached her with a plan to smuggle her out of France. Although grateful for their support, the queen flatly refused to abandon her place next to her family. At the end of a touching letter of thanks, Antoinette signed off tearfully: "They have taken everything away from me except my heart, which is still mine to love you. Never doubt it; it is the only unhappiness that I could not bear."

Oddly enough, an offer of succor came from an unexpected source— Necker's daughter, Madame de Staël. The famous hostess and writer proposed a plan of escape for the royal family, presented through an intermediary: "See if you can transmit this proposition. There is no time to waste. Bring me the King's answer tonight or tomorrow." The monarchs could not allow themselves to trust her because it once again required the participation of Lafayette. The royals conveyed their appreciation, affirming they felt no urgency to leave Paris. The fatalistic couple would face a final showdown with the Parisian rebels.

By mid-July the queen sensed that the endgame was fast approaching. She lived in horror that the next attack on the palace would spell the murder of her family. In frantic desperation, she wrote to Count Mercy, "Everything is lost if the rebels are not halted by fear of imminent punishment. They want the republic at any price; to achieve it they have resolved to murder the King. A manifesto must be issued making the Legislative Assembly and Paris responsible for his safety and that of his family." Forgetting the disaster of the Pillnitz Declaration of the previous year, the queen believed that threats from the united powers abroad would derail the ire of the militants in Paris from committing any further atrocities.

In response to the queen's desperate pleas, Count Fersen participated in drafting a document along with several key French émigrés. On July 25, 1792, at army headquarters situated on the French border, the Duke of Brunswick released to the press a manifesto that bore his name. The duke felt that as a military tactic it could prove harmful to the residents of the Tuileries. However, he was pressured to sign it from the royal family in Paris as well as the exiled princes. Several days later the manifesto descended on Paris with the impact of a nuclear bomb.

The Duke of Brunswick warned the people of France, and particularly the citizens of Paris, of his intentions "to put an end to the anarchy in France, to check the attacks upon the throne and the altar, to reestablish the legal power, to restore to the King the security and liberty of which he is now deprived, and to place him in a position to exercise once more the legitimate authority that belongs to him." The initial articles of the manifesto offered magnanimity as the duke insisted that the sovereigns of Austria and Prussia "have no intention of enriching themselves by conquests" and further, "they do not propose to meddle in the internal government of France, and they merely wish to deliver the King, the Queen, and the royal family from their captivity."

The tone escalated sharply with each remaining article. One article bluntly stated "Members of the National Guard who fight against us and who are taken with arms in their hands shall be treated as enemies and punished as rebels to their King." The final article was the most incendiary of all:

> The city of Paris and all its inhabitants shall be required to submit
> without delay to the King, to place that Prince in full and complete
> liberty, and to insure him the inviolability and respect which the
> law of nature and of nations demand of subjects toward sovereigns.
> If the chateau of the Tuileries is entered by force or attacked, if the
> least violence is offered to Their Majesties, and if their safety and
> liberty are not assured, then we shall inflict an ever-memorable
> vengeance by delivering over the city of Paris to military execution
> and complete destruction, and the rebels guilty of the said outrages
> to the punishment they merit.

Louis and Antoinette hoped the duke's harsh words would restrain the more militant Parisians. But some in the palace refused to sink into a bleak mood in the early days of August. Madame Elisabeth confidently exclaimed, "We are quite at ease about all of this because we can count on Monsieur Danton." No doubt, a hint that he was being bribed to exert his influence on behalf of the royals. But Danton's pattern of behavior was anything but reassuring, especially to the queen. His feelings about the fate of the royal family were murky and downright hostile if his political hide were at stake.

In a final letter to Fersen dated the first of August, 1792, Antoinette pleaded, "For the moment our main thought must be to escape dagger thrusts and to defeat plans of the conspirators who swarm around the throne. I need merely repeat that unless help arrives promptly, no one but Providence can save the King and his family." In reply, Fersen swore that the Duke of Brunswick would be in Paris within four weeks. Neither the duke nor his army would ever catch a glimpse of the city's rooftops.

The initial shock of the manifesto froze the capital, quickly followed by a blind rage. Diehard republicans welcomed the manifesto as a gift that signaled the eradication of monarchy. The Legislative Assembly was bombarded with deputations from political clubs throughout the city to oust the king and declare a republic. The reinstated Mayor Pétion appeared before the Legislative on August 3 demanding the king's abdication. The Assembly promised to discuss the matter soon.

Fearing the arrival of Brunswick's forces any day at their doorstep, revolutionaries in Paris decided to bypass the feeble legislative body by storming the Tuileries and ousting Louis. The evening of August 9 was unlike any other night in the history of court etiquette. Confusion reigned everywhere, and residents and visitors to the chateau wandered in and out of the king's bedroom. The symbolic sign of the monarchy's dissolution was the omission of the traditional *coucher* of the king. This was one night where the demands of rigid ceremony were ignored.

"It has never been so bad,
that it couldn't be worse."
Wayne Dyer

Chapter 69

It's Tits Up

*J*ust after midnight on August 10, sirens sounded all over Paris. Within the palace, the occupants flinched at this signal of an imminent attack. No one slept, and nerves were ready to snap. Marquis Mandat, in charge of the National Guard, made sensible preparations for the defense of the palace, confident that his forces could defend the chateau. With this assurance, the king snatched a few hours of sleep without bothering to undress. The palace was defended by two thousand National Guardsmen, hundreds of gendarmes, scores of devoted noblemen, and the fiercely loyal nine hundred Swiss Guards in their red uniforms.

At half past four in the morning Mandat received a summons from city hall for an urgent meeting to discuss the dicey situation. Actually, it was a trap. The existing municipal government had been overthrown, and in its place a more radical Commune assumed power. Mandat was seized and murdered as soon as he dismounted his horse. With no firm leader in command at the palace, the troops of the National Guard began to waver. Incredibly, Louis chose this moment to shut himself away with his confessor for a half hour, while Antoinette was desperate for a show of strength.

The king had not yet received a reply to the note he dashed off earlier to the Legislative Assembly requesting a deputation from that body to attend him in his chambers. The writhing deputies purposely shelved the invitation from His Majesty.

After leaving his confessor, Louis reviewed the defenders of the palace. This was one time that Louis needed to inspire loyalty: mount a horse;

make a rousing speech; and, lead his forces into combat. Instead, the king appeared in the violet satins that he had slept in, with his hair unkempt. How could anyone be inspired by this rumpled mess, plodding along inspecting his defenders? After a few lifeless salutes of "Long Live the King," Louis was bombarded with chants of "Long Live the Nation" by nearly all of the National Guard troops on duty. Louis' attendants firmly coaxed the king to withdraw inside the Tuileries. Though outwardly calm, the king's confidence was shaken by this nasty reception. He took refuge in his council chamber surrounded by anxious faces waiting for a command as Antoinette encouraged him to resist the attack.

Meanwhile Pierre Louis Roederer, the senior official of the Department of Paris, arrived at the palace after a summons from the king. Before entering the palace, he gauged that the troops on duty could no longer be counted on to defend the palace. He sought out the king but bumped into the queen first. He advocated that the royal family flee to the Legislative Assembly without delay. He definitely did not want an inscription on his tombstone to read, "Responsible for the murder of the French royal family on 10 August 1792." A nervous mess, the queen opposed such an option. She resolutely insisted, "It is time to find out who will overcome—the King and the constitution, or the rebels."

Roederer found the downtrodden Louis and urged him to seek asylum at once in the Legislative Assembly. Louis lamely protested, citing his forces could withstand an attack. Roederer estimated that the rebels were larger in number than the king believed. Antoinette heatedly interrupted, telling Roederer that the palace's defenders were strong and loyal. He reminded the queen that the National Guard troops were already fraternizing with the riled crowd. Roederer persisted that Louis make a break for the Legislative Assembly. The queen, in meltdown mode, screamed that she would prefer to be nailed to the palace walls. Roederer looked her straight in the eye and predicted that she would be responsible for the massacre of the king, her family, her faithful servants, and finally herself. She replied, with a mix of fury and sadness, "On the contrary, what would I not do to be the only victim?"

Roederer hounded the king to withdraw to the Legislative Hall. The queen, close to hysteria, implored Louis to give the palace defenders a chance. All those around the king fell silent, their gaze fixed on him for a response. Beyond the royal chambers the clash of the combatants provided a dreadful drone. One cry above all others could be deciphered: "Deposition or Death." After the longest minutes of his reign, Louis rose, faced the queen, and simply said, "Let's go; there's nothing more to be done here." With these fateful words Louis resigned himself to embrace defeat. Antoinette was crushed by this decision, but the word of the king was sacrosanct. The queen felt certain that her husband's dethronement would be guaranteed in the Legislative chamber.

At half past eight in the morning Louis and company exited the palace with just the clothes they wore—no time to snatch personal belongings from their suites. The queen consoled her ladies left behind, promising to return later. Roederer led this sad procession through the Tuileries gardens to gain access to the Legislative Assembly. The king walked alone behind Roederer, followed by his wife holding her son's hand. Typical of a child, he playfully kicked the fallen leaves. Behind them came Madame Elisabeth and Madame Royale, arm in arm, and in the rear Madame Lamballe and Madame Tourzel. Several Swiss Guards surrounded the royal family for protection along with a handful of loyal National Guardsmen. Anticipating a sinister outcome in the Assembly, tears streamed down Antoinette's face.

As they approached the entrance to the chamber, a murderous crowd barred the way, launching chilling threats to the royals. True to his character, Louis remained calm and patient. After a bit of a tussle, the royals gained access to the chamber. The king squeezed his way to the podium as the entire space became still. Louis addressed the leader of the Legislative Assembly, Acting President Vergniaud: "I come to prevent a great crime, and I believe that I could not be safer anywhere than in the midst of the representatives of the nation."

Vergniaud politely replied, "Sire, you may count on the firmness of the Legislative Assembly. Its members have sworn to die to uphold the rights of the people and the constitutional authority."

The rules of the legislative body did not allow business to be conducted in the presence of the monarch, requiring the royal family to retire to a miniscule press box about ten feet square above the president's desk. Like sitting ducks in the crosshairs, the royals could be observed as they witnessed all that occurred within their false sanctuary.

Back at the palace, the rioters demanded that the defenders lay down their arms. The stalwart Swiss refused, "We are Swiss, and the Swiss only abandon their arms with their lives." Shots were exchanged, and roughly three hundred attackers were left dead from the sharp aim of the Swiss Guards and the volunteer forces shooting from the palace windows. After the first assault, the rebels withdrew to regroup. Initially, it seemed as though the defenders might win the day. However, they were inexplicably low on ammunition and simultaneously received retreat orders from the king. When Louis had departed the palace earlier, he assumed that the offensive would not take place. No way of that happening now. The attackers wanted blood, and the Swiss Guards represented the last hateful symbol of royal protection. Inside the Legislative Assembly, Louis was alarmed to hear continued shooting. In his last act as king, Louis scribbled a note from the cramped reporter's box: "The King orders the Swiss to lay down their arms immediately, and to withdraw to their barracks. Louis."

The obedient Swiss began their orderly retreat in two stages. The first group of one hundred fifty were mowed down in a hail of gunfire as they headed for the Legislative chamber, leaving only a handful to reach safety. The remaining Swiss and royal volunteers faced a wholesale slaughter in their effort to vacate the palace. It is estimated that of the nine hundred defenders killed that hot summer morning, about six hundred were Swiss Guards. The rioters stripped them naked, mutilated their bodies, and piled the corpses in heaps to be burned. The note from the king failed to prevent the spilling of blood and became a sober summary of the ineffective command of the king. Louis, who always tried to spare the flow of blood, would now be blamed for this carnage, as well. Once in control of the palace, the attackers killed anyone who was unlucky enough not to escape, whether a nobleman or palace servant. The palace was ransacked with the wine cellars taking the first hit. After the pillage, some of the drunken rioters invaded the Legislative Hall, hauling booty from the palace that they dumped on the president's desk. From the box above, Antoinette caught sight of some of her jewelry.

For fourteen hours, the royal family was cooped up in the suffocating heat of the tiny cubicle, while the Assembly squabbled over how to cope with the volatile mess. At one point, a hungry Louis ordered food to be served. No matter what crisis Louis faced, neither his appetite nor his sleep was impacted adversely. It was probably how Louis medicated himself to cope with stress. The unruly spectators did a double take as the king devoured an entire roasted chicken, seemingly oblivious to his circumstances. While their words could barely be heard in the reporters' box, it seemed that "fat pig" was repeated often. Even Antoinette was mortified by her husband's robust appetite, but she could only turn her face away.

More than half of the deputies of the Legislative Assembly played hooky that day out of self-preservation. Those in attendance were taunted by the crowd to suspend the king. The radical members of the new Paris Commune arrived on the scene and dictated harsh terms. In vain, President Vergniaud called for order. Insults and death threats rained on the deputies for not deposing the "fat pig." Convinced they were trapped by the Commune leaders and their murderous thugs, the deputies surrendered to the calls for deposition. With a trembling voice Vergniaud read a tersely worded decision: "The Legislative Assembly decrees The Chief of the Executive Power is provisionally suspended of his functions." It took seconds to achieve a unanimous vote.

This was not enough to satisfy the shrill protesters. The terrified deputies were forced to disband their legislative body within a month in favor of a National Convention to be elected by universal male suffrage. They also capitulated to the Commune's demand that Louis and his family "be put in a state of arrest." At this point, the traumatized deputies would have turned Notre Dame into a whorehouse if it brought the proceedings to an end.

By two in the morning the turbulent session adjourned, and the perspiration-soaked royal family was escorted to an adjacent convent where they would spend the night. Practically no one slept, except for the king, who nodded off as soon as his head hit the pillow. All the while, a huge crowd screamed death threats to the confined family; no wonder sleep was a luxury. The queen bitterly wept as she paced the room, bemoaning her fate and the bad luck she had attracted during her lifetime.

Next morning the royal family was forced to return to the press box and follow the fine points of their future in the Legislative Assembly. The agenda item at hand was where to house the deposed king. One deputy suggested the Luxembourg Palace—that option was instantly squelched by the Paris Commune, citing it was too posh. The Commune insisted that the captives be taken to the austere medieval fortress of the Temple. The queen cringed in horror and whispered to Madame Tourzel that many times she had begged the king's brother Count Artois, who owned the Temple, to raze that fearful dungeon. Some deputies in the Assembly balked at such an accommodation, but the flailing weapons of the Commune's supporters cured them of their resistance. They also agreed to their dissolution as a legislative body, effective once the newly-created National Convention met. Georges Danton would serve as acting chief executive for the time being. He signed the decree ordering the transfer of the royals to the dreaded Temple.

"The people are like water and the ruler a boat.
Water can support a boat or overturn it."
Li Shimin

Chapter 70

Unspeakable Crimes

*T*he royal family and their party entered a State carriage on August 13 for the ride to the Temple. Along the way, a crowd bombarded them with familiar insults and threats. After arriving at the Temple, the detainees ate an elegant meal in the modernized portion of the building where Marie Antoinette often had passed an evening with her brother-in-law Count Artois during calmer days. Mayor Pétion was present and suggested that the royal family be allowed to stay in the more comfortable quarters of the Temple. The Commune responded with an unyielding "nyet." After dinner, the royals were herded off to the adjoining foreboding structure, causing their collective hearts to sink.

As the prisoners adapted to their Spartan surroundings, a punishing reminder of their fragile existence befell them on August 19. Commissioners from the Paris Commune entered the Temple, ordering the removal of the royals' attendants for interrogation. The Commune had created the Criminal Tribunal Court to prosecute "plotters guilty of crimes committed against the people during the day of August 10." The list of suspects included everyone in the royal family's pitiful entourage: Princess Lamballe; Madame Tourzel and her daughter, Pauline; three ladies-in-waiting, Mesdames Navarre, Thibault, and Saint Brice; and lastly two valets, Hue and Chamilly.

The queen demanded that Madame Lamballe be excluded from the list since she was a member of the royal family. Her pleas were futile; there would be no exceptions. A vague promise was offered that the captives would return. The royal family was inconsolable at the removal of these last faithful faces. The queen had to be pulled away from her clenching hold of Princess Lamballe. As they tearfully embraced in farewells, the sobbing queen implored Madame Tourzel to look after the vulnerable Lamballe. The bereft royal family barely slept a wink that night, racked with worry about their absent companions.

Rather quickly a daily rhythm governed the royal family's life. The king and his son occupied the third floor of the fortress, while the ladies were housed on the second floor. Breakfast was taken in the king's rooms and afterward, all descended to the queen's room where they would pass the remainder of the day. Even though their quarters bore no resemblance to their former residences, they were provided with a degree of physical comforts. They were outfitted with a new, but limited wardrobe. The queen's must haves included a bathtub and a harpsichord to entertain her children. Their meals were plentiful, well prepared, and served on silver plates. Slowly, each of these niceties would either diminish or disappear.

Louis and Antoinette took their children's education in hand with fixed lessons every day. To pass the tedious hours of confinement, Antoinette and Madame Elisabeth engaged in hours of needlepoint. With each stitch, Antoinette imagined foreign troops advancing closer to Paris to secure their release.

A happy outcome of the confinement was the amount of time the king and queen spent together. In their twenty-two years of marriage, never had the royal couple shared each other's company for most of the day. They discovered that they truly enjoyed these hours together, often playing card games or backgammon, while joking and teasing each other. To the guards overseeing their every move, Louis and Antoinette seemed to be a devoted married couple.

After the king's removal to the Temple, Louis' captors began addressing the king and his family by the surname, Capet. In the tenth century, the first king of France was Hugh Capet. Since Louis was reckoned to be the last, he was mockingly labeled "Louis Capet." Louis bristled at the name, "I am not Louis Capet; my ancestors bore that name, but I have never been called that." The revolutionaries were stoked that they could rattle the king with this dishonor.

The sole advantage of confinement in the Temple was the tentative security the royals felt in this gloomy structure. Even though they were tightly watched, the royals no longer feared being murdered at any moment as during their final months in the Tuileries. Antoinette's endless stream of misfortunes had taught her to adapt to new degradations with a glacial fortitude. Her focus remained unchanged—the survival of her family. It was her only thought and constant prayer.

With the royal family imprisoned, some apprehensive Parisians feared an effort by crazed aristocrats to rescue the royals or incite revolt to overturn the Revolution. Lafayette had defected to the Austrians on August 17 triggering a wave of paranoia over who could be trusted, either at home or on the front lines. Emotions flared to purge the army leadership of officers with royalist sympathies who might engineer defeats on the battlefield. Danton grabbed the rostrum in the moribund Legislative Assembly demanding stringent measures to thwart the enemies of the nation. Danton's inflammatory speech precipitated mass arrests of non-juring priests and thousands of "suspects," exceeding the capacity of the prisons.

For the moment, Danton, the unequaled opportunist among his peers, seized the public stage. He ordered house inspections to ferret out any hidden traitors, incriminating documents, or weapons that would be useful in the defense of all true patriots. The Revolution thrived like a flesh-eating plant, gathering strength by feeding on the blood of those who stood in its way. And that craving for blood was about to explode.

Rumors swirled through Paris that Verdun was about to capitulate, reigniting suspicions that aristocratic officers were responsible for orchestrated defeats. Recognizing the public panic, Danton hurried to the Legislative Hall, demanding immediate action. Using the tactic of identity politics, Danton brilliantly crystallized the "us versus them" argument. Perhaps no other speech during the Revolution precipitated a more feverish resolve to sacrifice oneself on the barricades:

> The fatherland will be saved! While one part of the people goes
> to the frontiers, another digs our defenses, and a third, armed with
> pikes, will defend our cities and towns. The tocsin that will ring
> will be no mere signal for alarm; it will sound the charge against
> the enemies of the nation. Citizens, to deflect them will require
> boldness and again boldness, and always boldness if France is to
> be saved.

Proud of his oratorical home run, Danton was nonetheless scared like all high-profile politicians. It was a moment of personal survival that demanded vengeance to boost patriotic zeal. To achieve the immediate objective of saving the targeted city of Paris from the Prussians, action was required to shore up the capital first, and not the distant battlefield. Tabloid darlings like Desmoulins, Hébert, and especially, Marat, penned rabid exhortations to rid the city's overflowing prisons of these vile enemies of the nation. Marat absolved all radicals of moral hesitation, spouting, "Let the blood of traitors flow. This is the only way to save the country." The sights of many Parisians narrowed on the suspects sitting in the prisons; these undesirables had to pay for the defeats of the French army.

The red flag of martial law was hoisted over city hall on September 2, and the tocsins began banging nonstop, signaling the green light to commence the killings. Estimates vary widely, but between 1,400 and 1,600 persons were murdered over a three-day period. The executions were particularly brutal for the non-juring priests and young seminarians. Many imprisoned courtiers were also butchered, along with the surviving members of the Swiss Guard. The slaughter morphed into a fiendish fury when innocent detainees were also hacked to pieces.

Heaps of butchered body parts formed grotesque mounds in prison courtyards. The most infamous of these ghastly murders was that of the queen's friend Princess Lamballe. The dainty lady, who could fall into a swoon over the meow of a kitten, faced the fright of her life. She was dragged from her cell and forced to disown the queen. She emphatically refused. In a rage, the wild murderers stabbed her to death and sliced off her head to be pierced on a pike; what remained of her naked torso was dragged through the streets. Her head was rushed off to a wig-maker where the terrified shop owner was compelled to style the severed head for presentation to her dissolute lover, the queen. Once Antoinette learned the identity of the "trophy" outside her windows, she slumped to the floor and could not be consoled. When the inspector of prisons rushed to city hall to implore Danton to halt the bloodbath engulfing the prisons, Danton was in no mood for moderation. He bellowed, "To hell with the prisoners! They must look after themselves."

News of the unimaginable carnage reached the capitals of Europe, unleashing a unified voice of revulsion. The highly regarded *London Times* typified the disbelief with a front-page article on September 10, 1792, sparing no words for the barbarity:

> As the affairs of France very naturally engross the whole of
> the public attention, we have made it our business to collect
> the occurrences that have happened with as much precision as
> circumstances would admit. In the history of mankind, we have
> no precedent of such wanton and disgraceful excesses. Are these
> the Rights of Man? Is this the Liberty of Human Nature? The most

savage four-footed tyrants that roam that range of the unexplored deserts of Africa, in point of tenderness, rise superior to these two-legged Parisian animals.

After the September Massacres, the Legislative Assembly on the verge of disbanding in favor of the National Convention, passed several laws aimed at pacifying the public mood. Among the decrees enacted was a law banishing from France all members of the Bourbon family. An exception was made for the person and family of the Duke of Orléans, the king's turncoat cousin, now known as Philippe Égalité. The duke's once regal ambitions went underground as even he was getting jittery, especially after the grotesque murder of his sister-in-law, Princess Lamballe. He had obviously misjudged the true sentiments of the revolutionaries. But he was in way too deep to slink away, trapped in a web woven by his own deeds.

"It is forbidden to kill.
Therefore, all murderers are punished,
unless they kill in large numbers
and to the sound of trumpets."
Voltaire

Spotlight Seven

The Days of Painful Partings

Chapter 71

Who Needs a King Anyway?

On September 20, 1792, the deputies of the newly-elected National Convention convened. They wasted no time in abolishing the monarchy and proclaiming the French Republic. With the monarchy discarded, some deputies in the Convention wanted to obliterate any reminder of royal authority. Roland, the interior minister, proposed that the Convention either sell or rent the chateau of Versailles, including other royal residences. I have to pose the questions: Was Roland's wig on too tight that day? Who could afford to lease and maintain Versailles?

Worse still, several deputies demanded the palace be razed to eradicate the memory of its former occupants. But the townspeople of Versailles marshaled their forces and descended on the Convention like a biblical pestilence. Making an intimidating case that their economic survival depended on the palace and its contents remaining untouched, they won a reprieve of sorts. The building would survive, but the contents would be sold to raise needed cash for the war effort.

From August 1793 through January 1795, a series of auctions were held to unload the contents of the royal residences, constituting the finest garage sale in history. Nothing was held back, except for select items deemed irreplaceable. Even the toys of Antoinette's children were hawked to the highest bidder. Like most yard sales, items sold for a fraction of their value—much to the delight of the shoppers. As the queen was reduced to crude furniture in her prison cell, magnificent furnishings that once belonged to her were being snapped up by savvy bargain hunters. Gouverneur Morris, the ambassador of the United States, snagged a few smart pieces of furniture for himself. Like all bargain hunters, he couldn't resist a steal, no matter the provenance.

Among the heated items argued in the Convention, the fate of the former king dominated the agenda. What to do with a deposed king? The Convention members were divided on how to resolve this issue. Any pussyfooting ambivalence evaporated on November 20 when an explosive jolt of information detonated in the Convention.

It was common knowledge throughout France that Louis pursued the unorthodox hobby of a locksmith. For years, the king had employed François Gamain as a tutor to sharpen Louis' skills. The two men spent hours in the attics at Versailles and subsequently at the Tuileries. Besides the hunt, Louis lost himself completely in this tinkering pastime. Gamain, in a lustful quest for his fifteen minutes of fame, snitched to authorities that a strongbox hidden in a safe in the Tuileries Palace might be of interest to them. Roland gained access to the contents and immediately ran off to the Convention Hall. He basked in his moment of critical importance, revealing a smoking gun that elated his ambitious wife, Madame Roland. The opened safe spilled out six hundred twenty-five documents, confirming that Louis had double-crossed the Revolution.

Deputies uncovered that Louis had corresponded with émigrés, coordinating their activities. The king had secretly negotiated with foreign powers regarding the course of the war, issuing orders to agents abroad while referring to the constitution as "absurd and detestable." And most shocking of all, he had bribed patriotic luminaries such as Mirabeau, to dilute the Revolution with the aim of derailing it and restoring his autocratic position. Also discovered were two letters from Talleyrand written after Mirabeau's death when Talleyrand wished to fill Mirabeau's shoes as adviser to the Crown. The damning discovery produced a whiplash effect in the Convention. Louis was screwed.

The overriding question was what type of punishment should be meted out to deal with Louis' treachery? The radical Convention members, especially the Jacobin faction, demanded an immediate sentencing of the king without a trial. Robespierre summed up their position neatly: "If the King is not guilty, then those who deposed him are." Many of the deputies came from a legal background, thereby dictating some form of due process. The loose cannon in the Convention, Marat, whose contrariness could make Robiespierre's blood pressure skyrocket, foamed at the mouth for a public trial. His inflamed oratory won the argument for a show trial. The Convention deputies decided on December 5 that they would serve as judge and jury of Louis XVI.

On the same day, a decree mandated that Mirabeau's remains be removed from the Pantheon and be unceremoniously dumped. In addition, all busts and portraits celebrating his patriotic fervor were to be destroyed. An arrest warrant was issued for Talleyrand who had fortuitously hightailed it to London just weeks earlier. With proof that some of the brightest stars of the Revolution had supported the king's double-dealing, delegates began questioning who else among their midst were traitors?

On December 11 Louis sensed something was afoot when he heard drums pounding outside his prison walls. Without explanation, Louis' son was removed from the king's care and led downstairs to the queen's quarters. The mayor arrived informing Louis that he was escorting him to the Convention to be arraigned for trial. An unshaven Louis, wearing an olive-green satin coat and carrying his hat, entered the Convention Hall. Piercing the solid silence in the chamber, the president boomed, "Louis, the French people accuse you of having committed a multitude of crimes in order to establish your tyranny by destroying its liberty. The Act of Crimes is going to be read to you. You may now sit down." As the thirty-five charges against the king echoed through the chamber, every eye was riveted on the sight of the former sovereign. Resembling Humpty Dumpty, the king's simple dignity left an indelible imprint on all in attendance. Even the avowed regicides were spellbound by the once almighty monarch. One deputy in particular, the king's cousin Philippe Égalité never allowed his lorgnette to stray from his relative's face.

After the charges were read, Louis was barraged with questions, answering all of them without hesitation. He often replied, "I do not recall." Sometimes the king lied to protect himself or the safety of those mentioned in the questions. When confronting the incriminating documents found in his safe, the king simply denied it was his handwriting. When rebuked for his vetoes, he firmly invoked the executive powers given to him in the constitution, a copy of which he kept in his pocket. His overall performance stirred some sympathy that supporters hoped would benefit his cause. At the end of the session the king loudly proclaimed before he exited, "I demand counsel." Although no longer the king, his natural instinct to issue orders remained intact.

The following day Louis was notified that the Convention had consented that he gather his defense team. His first choice was Guy-Jean-Baptiste

Target, the stellar attorney of Diamond Necklace fame who got all charges dismissed against Cardinal Rohan. Target declined the request, noting that he was physically indisposed for such a case. The obese Target was literally the butt of cruel jokes whenever he wobbled into public view. Rumors spread that he was petrified to defend Louis. To dispel such lies, Target penned a passionate pamphlet wherein he staunchly argued for the king's acquittal.

The Convention was deluged with requests from all over France to defend Louis, some from women, such as the outspoken Olympe de Gouges. Within three days the king had his team assembled. They included François Tronchet, at age sixty-six, one of the sharpest lawyers in France. Monsieur Tronchet had been one of the three deputies who had questioned Louis after his ignominious return from Varennes. Next came an old acquaintance of the king, the septuagenarian, Lamoignon Malesherbes, one of the most decent men in France. He had personally written to the Convention to request the opportunity to defend the king. They signed him up on the spot. The last of the trio was the youngest, the forty-six-year-old Raymond Desèze, noted for his hypnotic oratory. He would serve as the mouthpiece for the defense.

When the venerable Malesherbes met with the king in the Temple, they reminisced about the early years of his reign when Malesherbes was a minister in the king's council. Expecting a death sentence, Louis spoke with emotion regarding Malesherbes' acceptance of the task ahead: "Your sacrifice is so much the more generous as you expose your life without being able to save mine."

Malesherbes gallantly assured Louis, "It would be too easy to defend Your Majesty successfully." Louis' defense team was instructed to present their case before the Convention on December 26.

Christmas Day 1792 was a bleak holiday for the separated royal family. On that day Louis chose to write his will, the words of a man expecting the worst. The king began with a religious posture, asking God to receive his soul, but if He granted him life, Louis vowed to uphold the Church of Rome at all costs. He begged all to pray for him and he forgave "with all my heart those who have made themselves enemies, without my having given them any cause, and I pray to God to pardon them, as well as those who through false or misunderstood zeal, did me much harm." Louis' emotions escalated when he spoke of his family:

I pray God particularly to cast eyes of compassion upon my wife, my children, and my sister, who have suffered with me for so long a time, to sustain them with His mercy, if they shall lose me, and as long as they shall remain in this mortal world. I commend my children to my wife. I have never doubted her maternal tenderness for them. I enjoin her above all to make them good Christians and honest individuals; to make them view the grandeurs of this world (if they are condemned to experience them) as very dangerous and transient goods, and turn their attention toward the one solid and enduring glory, eternity. I beseech my sister to take the place of a mother, should they have the misfortune of losing theirs. I beg my wife to forgive all the pain which she suffered for me, and the sorrows which I may have caused her in the course of our union; and may she feel sure that I hold nothing against her, if she has anything with which to reproach herself. I most warmly enjoin my children that after what they owe to God, which should come first, they should remain forever united among themselves, submissive and obedient to their mother, and grateful for all the care and trouble which she has taken with them, as well as in memory of me. I beg them to regard my sister as their second mother.

Louis remained uneasy that Antoinette's destiny might soon mirror his own, acutely aware that she was the most villainized person in the kingdom. As he related to his counsel, "Poor woman; she was promised a throne, and it has ended like this."

Louis again appeared before the Convention on December 26. Raymond Desèze spoke passionately for three hours in the king's defense. His main argument claimed that under the constitution the king was immune from prosecution. He ended his stirring defense exhorting the deputies, "Frenchmen, the Revolution that inspires you has developed great virtues in you, but beware that it has not weakened the sentiment of humanity in your souls." Even Marat who had no patience for Desèze, reluctantly conceded, "Desèze read a very long speech with a great deal of art."

Louis was permitted to offer concluding remarks that highlighted his anguish of having been accused of spilling French blood:

Speaking to you for perhaps the last time, I declare to you that my conscience has nothing to reproach me with. I have never feared a public examination of my conduct; but my heart is rent at finding in the indictment the imputation that I wished to shed the blood of the people and above all the misfortunes of August 10 should be attributed to me. I confess that the manifold proofs that I have given at all times of my love for the people and the manner in which I have always conducted myself seemed to me sufficient proof that I took little heed of exposing myself to spare its blood, and to remove from me such an imputation forever.

Louis exited the Convention a broken, but impressive man.

"Man will never be free
until the last king is strangled
by the entrails of the last priest."
Denis Diderot

Chapter 72

The Year of Bouleversement

The French word *bouleversement* creates the perfect explosive sound to describe the events of 1793. The word suggests a total upheaval with no way of predicting how matters will fall into place. If the Revolution had a make-or-break year, it was definitely 1793. There were moments when the Revolution suffered huge setbacks, such that its existence perched on an abyss. These near fatal calamities were followed by magic wand victories either on the political or battle fronts, thus keeping the Revolution on life support.

The fate of the deposed king topped the Convention's agenda as a matter of urgency in January 1793. The deputies realized their legitimacy would be questioned until they resolved the unpleasant business of Louis Capet. While there was little doubt regarding the king's culpability, a formula had to be devised on how to proceed. Once the customary shouting matches abated, the deputies agreed on three resolutions to be put to a vote: the guilt or innocence of the king; a national referendum on the king's fate; and, finally, the penalty to be levied against the king. The deputies began voting on the three issues on January 15.

The first resolution concerning the king's guilt passed easily. The second resolution on holding a national referendum failed by a large margin after a rowdy fight. It is often repeated that all politics are local, and this proved true regarding the idea of holding a plebiscite. Since Louis was in Paris, militant Parisians feared that a referendum would absolve the king, an outcome that would be unacceptable to them.

The last question concerning the imposed punishment proved to be a stomach churner. First, they had to agree on how they would vote. Some of the deputies insisted on a secret ballot requiring a three-fourth's majority. This option would almost guarantee imprisonment for life or banishment. After hours of mudslinging, it was decided to proceed with a roll call vote requiring a simple majority of deputies would suffice for the death penalty. This arrangement was the least favorable for Louis' chances of escaping execution. The exhausted deputies adjourned for the showdown vote to be held the following morning.

On January 16, 1793 the visitor's gallery was packed with a spectrum of Parisian society, as well as foreign travelers and correspondents. Food concessions did a brisk business throughout the long day. As the proceedings commenced, the president of the Convention announced that 28 deputies were absent, leaving the task to 721 jurors. The spectators, jammed in the gallery, quickly did the math. The required number for a simple majority sentence was 361 votes. Immediately there arose an argument regarding the wording of the question concerning the king's sentence. After hours of contentious wrangling, the deputies settled on the question: What penalty should be inflicted on Louis Capet?

Late at night the roll call began. One by one deputies stood before their colleagues and declared their vote. Sometimes just one word was uttered— "Death." Other deputies required a phrase or two to justify their verdict. The most anticipated vote came from the king's cousin, Philippe Égalité. He approached the platform withdrawing a piece of paper from his pocket and coolly read a statement: "Preoccupied only by my duty, convinced that all those who attack the sovereignty of the people deserve death, I vote for death." Philippe's vote disgusted even those in favor of regicide in the Convention. Several days later Citizen Égalité described his untenable situation to his English mistress, the gorgeous Grace Dalrymple: "I no longer own myself; I obey what surrounds me." He soon became persona non-grata in Paris.

The American patriot, Thomas Paine, was one of two foreign nationals serving as a Convention deputy. He elegantly pleaded, through an interpreter, for the exile of the king and his family to the United States, in recognition of the king's vital support for the American Revolution. He promised deputies that Americans would reeducate Louis and his family to revere republican principles. His plea was dismissed when the scaly Marat piped up in lethal opposition.

Once the last vote was cast, it became an accountant's headache to sort them because of the stipulations attached. The final tally fell into four categories: for imprisonment or forced exile–288; for a suspended death sentence–46; for death with a delay for public discussion–26; and for immediate death with no conditions–361. With the bare majority achieved, Louis was to be executed within twenty-four hours. But in reviewing the votes, the Convention surpassed the majority for death when you added those who wanted death, but with a delay. Even if the king had received enough votes to avoid execution, there is a strong case to be made for his elimination. Extremists such as Marat and Hébert could have easily whipped up a frenzy among the Parisian militants to storm the Temple and murder Louis on the spot, and perhaps his entire family.

Though the rhetoric of some deputies sounded harsh, most of that bombast was intended for public consumption. In fact, Louis' appearance at his trial sparked genuine sympathy. Yet, for the republic to flourish, the symbol of autocratic rule had to be sacrificed. Perhaps, Robespierre best expressed the ambivalence of his fellow colleagues when he admitted, "I felt republican virtue wavering in my heart at the sight of the guilty man humiliated before the sovereign power." Now, there's a regicide with scruples.

> "Fame is a vapor, popularity an accident,
> and riches take wings. Only one thing endures,
> and that is character."
> *Horace Greeley*

Chapter 73

A Family Fractures

On Sunday morning, January 20, Louis learned of the verdict. The king notified the Convention that he required three days to prepare himself spiritually. He asked to see a priest of his own choosing and to visit with his family. He specifically requested, "I wish that the National Convention should immediately interest themselves in the future of my family and should permit them to leave their present quarters and establish themselves wherever they think fit."

The Convention tersely replied, "Louis is authorized to send for any minister of religion of his choosing and to see his family freely without witnesses. The Nation, invariably generous and just, would see to the future of his family. Just payments would be made to his creditors." The National Convention ignored the request for a respite of three days; Louis would be executed the following day. Reverend Henry Edgeworth, an Irish-born priest and the confessor of the king's sister, was summoned. Louis purposely chose a foreign clergyman, hoping the priest would be better treated by the authorities after the execution.

Around dusk a stupefied Antoinette heard the barks of the newspaper hawkers announcing Louis' fate. Shortly afterward the family was allowed to visit the king. At first, they could only weep together. Between sobs, Louis related the details of the trial to the queen, acknowledging that he was crushed by his cousin's vote for death. The choking tears of the three women and the little prince continued unabated. After an hour and a half, Louis rose and paternally signaled it was time for them to withdraw. The moans redoubled as the distraught queen implored her husband to allow them to spend the night with him. Louis firmly rejected the suggestion. Then, the queen begged to see him in the morning before he left. Sensing his family's emotional collapse, the king agreed to see them at seven in the morning. Madame Royale clasped her father and would not release him until she crumbled into a faint. After more heart-rending goodbyes, the inconsolable group was assisted from the room. Their cries echoed throughout the Temple as they returned to their quarters.

Antoinette did not undress and remained awake in the event the king summoned her. After the wrenching farewell, Louis realized he could not withstand another cruel parting the following morning lest he falter at a moment demanding solid stoicism. The solitary king sat down to a last meal with his customary appetite. By midnight he was astoundingly sound asleep.

Monday, January 21, 1793, was shrouded with fog and scattered showers. After a solid sleep, Louis was awakened at five in the morning by his faithful valet, Cléry. The king dressed and prepared for the ordeal ahead. He ate no breakfast. Louis spent an hour alone with Reverend Edgeworth and assisted the priest with the mass. After conferring with his priest, Louis charged Cléry to beg the queen's forgiveness for not seeing her as he had promised, noting the distress would be too overwhelming for both of them. He removed his wedding band and handed it to Cléry to deliver to his wife: "Tell the Queen that I do not part with this ring without pain." Along with the ring, Louis gave Cléry a small parcel that contained the royal seal for his son and lockets of hair of the members of his family. At nine in the morning the municipal officers arrived to take him to his death. After receiving a final benediction from Reverend Edgeworth, the king gave one of the guards a small package containing his will and a few personal effects that he asked to be delivered to Antoinette. He embraced Cléry, then stomped his foot and commanded, "Let's go!"

Louis was led from the Temple to a waiting green carriage. The king looked up momentarily to the shuttered windows of his family's rooms. He sighed and entered the carriage along with Reverend Edgeworth and two gendarmes. Louis XVI took his final ride through the packed streets of Paris to the place of execution guarded by thousands of troops. The unimposing killing machine had been moved the previous night to the newly-named Square of the Revolution where until just months before stood a sculpture of Louis' grandfather, Louis XV.

The mercantile life of Paris halted as the city turned out to witness this unprecedented moment in France's history. In the carriage, the king immersed himself in his prayer book. He ceased his prayers and lifted his head when he sensed that they had arrived at the scaffold. After a few minutes, Louis stepped down from the coach and immediately the executioner and his aides approached him to remove his coat and tie. The king rebuffed them and removed his three-cornered hat, brown coat, and tie. The king forcefully resisted having his hands tied, but to no avail. Earlier in the morning Louis had pinned up his hair, but the assistants undid it and cut it off. Louis slowly mounted the steep steps of the scaffold leaning on Reverend Edgeworth for steadying support. He immediately headed for the center of the scaffold but was forced to stop. From where he stood, Louis scanned a crowd of more than twenty thousand uneasy subjects squeezed into the square. The well-meaning Louis XVI, who cringed at the thought of shedding one drop of French blood, would now have his own spilled on a cruel altar of spiteful atonement.

Louis ordered the drummers to be silent, and surprisingly they obeyed. In a thunderous voice the king declared, "I die innocent of all the crimes with which I have been charged. I pardon those who have brought about my death, and I pray that the blood you are about to shed may never be required of France." Those were the last audible words from the king as the drummers were ordered to renew their drumming with vigor. Louis was grabbed, roughly strapped to the plank, and thrust forward into the neck lock, reflecting an urgency to get the job done. At twenty-two minutes after ten, the blade fell, and Louis' head plopped into the waiting basket.

Once the blade had descended, the severed head of Louis XVI was paraded around the scaffold. As the once revered face was displayed to the public, shouts of "Long Live the Nation" increased in volume. Many rushed the scaffold to dip their handkerchiefs into the spilled blood of their former king. There was no undoing the crime as a new era dawned to define France. Louis-Sébastien Mercier, a writer and member of the Convention, recorded his impressions:

> I saw the schoolboys of the Quatre-Nations throw their hats in
> the air. An executioner on the scaffold sold little packets of hair
> and the ribbon that bound them; each piece carried a fragment of
> his clothes. I saw people pass by, arm in arm, laughing, chatting
> familiarly, as if they were at a party.

Louis' remains were flung into a wicker basket and placed in the waiting red cart for the trip to the graveyard. Only the day before, the Commune of Paris had acquired a patch of land that used to be a vegetable garden for the Benedictine nuns in the parish of the Madeleine. It was here that Louis XVI's body was laid in a crude wooden coffin and buried in a hole six feet wide and deep. The municipal officials who accompanied the body recorded that he was buried without a tie, coat, and shoes. The coffin was immediately covered with quicklime before the dirt was shoveled on it. No impressive royal interment—only oblivion to send off the sixty-sixth King of France. Louis left his mark in history, not the way he wished for, but by heroically enduring it. Back at the mournful Temple, the cannon shots confirmed the crime to the prostrate Antoinette. What would happen now to the king's family?

> "… how do you like your blueeyed boy
> Mister Death"
> *e e cummings*

Chapter 74

Life without Louis

*T*wo days after the king's execution, the National Convention issued a decree justifying the king's execution, but also demanding that the nation bind itself together. The decree framed the fragile condition of the new republic and predicted a draconian response to forces aimed at its destruction.

Many voices in the Convention and the political clubs who had denounced Louis XVI as a traitor would eventually be labeled the same. The guillotine excelled at resolving any political polarization within government.

After the king's death, Antoinette requested mourning attire for herself and her family. Her precious son was now King Louis XVII of France. The three women prisoners treated the boy-king with a slightly increased reverence. The queen made a point of having her son sit at the head of the table on a cushion. On the occasion of her son's eighth birthday, the queen measured the height of her children, leaving wall markings to record their growth. The date on the wall read March 27, 1793, and noted their progress: Madame Royale, at age fourteen, was four feet, ten inches tall, and the eight-year-old king stood at three feet, two inches.

During February and March two of the queen's guards, Toulon and Lépitre, became sympathetic to the plight of the captives and hatched a plan to free them. Despite their efforts, they could not procure the needed passports which killed the chances of success. But they were confident enough to rescue the most vulnerable prisoner, the queen. Antoinette thanked them, saying, "We had a beautiful dream and that was all. I could not have any pleasure in the world if I abandoned my children." Meanwhile, she still clung to the hope that foreign troops would reach Paris or that her relatives in Vienna would ransom her family.

On March 10, 1793, the National Convention was running scared while the French army was being defeated on the front lines. Any time bad war news hit Paris, the Convention would enact a law to calm the restless population, as well as themselves. At Danton's instigation, a decree created The Revolutionary Tribunal, a court composed of a president, a public prosecutor, and a jury pool. The court was designed to convict royalists and enemies of liberty, where the defendant was considered culpable until proven innocent. Besides the Revolutionary Tribunal, the Convention also created the Committee of Public Safety, a twelve-member body composed mostly of radical Jacobins, with Robespierre as their guru. Their first task aimed their sights on the royal irritants in the Temple.

Nothing—absolutely nothing—could have prepared Marie Antoinette for what happened on July 3, 1793. This would always be the most traumatizing day of her life, and she had already experienced quite a few nightmare scenarios. As was the custom of the four prisoners, the young prince went to bed first after saying his prayers. Then, the three women engaged in mending their clothes, reading, and chatting among themselves.

Around ten in the evening, the lock on their quarters was swiftly undone, and municipal officials stomped into the room. They read a decree from the Convention ordering the removal of Louis Charles Capet from his mother, the Widow Capet. For just a moment the queen seemed incapable of comprehending the order. But as the officers advanced to snatch the still sleeping prince, the queen sprang up and threw herself on her little boy. "Never," she screamed, "never!" She would never allow such a crime. They would not dare to separate a mother from her child. They would have to kill her first.

The officers threatened physical force to carry out their orders. The boy must go with them. Clutching her now sobbing son, Antoinette was deaf to their commands to release the boy. *Oh, God no, anything, anything but this!* They tried to reason with her to ease the child's fear by allowing him to leave without further struggle. Sinking into abject pleading, Antoinette begged them to have a heart and not take her sweet son. Her pitiful pleas melted no hearts. One of the guards threatened to kill her daughter unless she relinquished the whimpering child. Any further resistance now seemed futile. Capitulating, Antoinette loosened her grip on her son and collapsed in an ocean of tears. Her daughter and sister-in-law tenderly dressed the boy, overseen by the nearly deranged mother. After heartrending embraces, the child was yanked away from his family and the doors slammed shut on the three overwrought women.

Of the many losses Antoinette had endured, the removal of her adored son nearly destroyed her. For days, she barely spoke, lost in a haze of disbelief and numbing loss. The queen admitted to Elisabeth in despair, "God himself has forsaken me! I dare no longer pray." Her precious child, the rightful king, and her hope for a better future, was beyond her loving care, guidance and protection. What made it more maddening was that the child was confined in the room one floor below—so tantalizingly near, yet totally inaccessible. Fortunately for Antoinette, her sister-in-law was rock solid in her support, coaxing Antoinette toward a tolerable degree of sanity.

On the first of August, the strategic town of Valenciennes had fallen to the European allies, making the way to Paris more certain for the foreign invaders. Terror again gripped the capital, especially among the delegates in the National Convention. Deputy Barère made an impassioned speech declaring, "The Capet family gave the enemy the audacity to advance." All the deputies chimed in agreement and hastily passed several measures. First, the Widow Capet was to be transferred to the Conciergerie prison to await trial. Next, the former king's sister Elisabeth would be deported after the sentencing of the Austrian Woman. Third, the two Capet children would remain in captivity, at reduced cost to the government. Finally, the remains of all deceased monarchs of France were to be disinterred and thrown into a common grave. The metal from the sarcophagi was to be melted down for ammunition for the patriots fighting to save the republic.

On August 2 at two in the morning, Antoinette, her daughter, and Madame Elisabeth were startled awake by loud pounding on their door, ordering them to rise and dress immediately. They faced four officers of the Paris police who notified the queen that she was being transferred to the Conciergerie prison. Her daughter's request to accompany her mother was ignored. The queen gathered a few personal keepsakes, wrapping them in a handkerchief. As a final token of motherly affection, Marie Antoinette removed her royal seal from her watch and pressed it into her daughter's hand. She embraced her daughter, urging her to remain strong, to look after her aunt, and to obey her as a mother. She tightly hugged her sister-in-law who whispered inspirational words into her ear. Without looking back, Antoinette left with the guards. While descending the dark stone steps, the queen hit her head against an overhead beam. When a guard asked if she was hurt, she responded, "No, nothing can hurt me now."

"We are healed of a suffering
only by experiencing it to the full."
Marcel Proust

Chapter 75

A Marked Woman

$\mathcal{A}$ntoinette rode in a closed carriage to the prison of the Conciergerie, once a royal residence dating from the Middle Ages. Oftentimes in the prisons, amenities and privileges were accorded to prisoners with the means to pay for them. But Antoinette was intentionally singled out to have no consideration at all. After being processed as prisoner number 280, her pitiful personal possessions were inventoried. These precious mementos were spitefully confiscated on the spot. She was allowed to keep three rings and a gold watch. Under her dress, she concealed three precious keepsakes of her son: a lock of his hair, a miniature portrait, and a tiny yellow kid glove from his toddler years. After being processed, she was led off to her cell at three in the morning. She recoiled as she took in the wasteland of her cell before the candles were withdrawn.

The light of dawn confirmed the yuck factor of her new lodgings. Antoinette inhabited a damp space, roughly eleven feet square, with a camp bed, two wicker chairs, a rickety table, and a shoddy privacy screen. There was no source of heat, candles were not provided when darkness fell, and sanitation facilities consisted of a bucket. The queen shared this confined space with two armed guards who ignored her while they smoked, swore, and played cards among themselves. She was not permitted needles to knit nor do embroidery. The hours of each day dragged by prompting the kindhearted jailers, Monsieur and Madame Richard to lend her adventure novels that she reread several times. During this solitary time, she reminisced about her once illustrious life. She never doubted that she was chosen by God to be queen, a distinction that no mortal could seize from her. Did she have any regrets or second thoughts? No doubt she wished for the opportunity to revisit some of her past actions. But second chances were not accorded in the Conciergerie.

At times, it appeared that the powerful Committee of Public Safety was fixated on a familiar theme: fifty shades of cruelty to punish the Austrian Woman. Five days after her arrival at the Conciergerie, the queen's gold watch was noticed hanging from a nail. Given to her by the empress as she left Vienna twenty-three years earlier, it was confiscated without explanation. Antoinette whimpered like a child at the loss of this cherished memento, a last link to her mother.

As for her wardrobe, it was slim pickings. The queen arrived with the clothes on her back, a black widow's dress, kind of shabby after seven months of daily wear. Fortunately, the queen's undergarments were in better condition. The prison serving girl, Rosalie Lamorlière, made sure they were freshly laundered. Antoinette dispatched a note to her daughter:

> I want to write to you, my dear child, to tell you that I am well; I am calm, and should be quite at peace if I knew that my poor child were free from anxiety. I embrace you, and your aunt too, with all my heart. Send me some silk stockings, a dimity jacket, an underskirt, and the stocking I am knitting.

The note never reached her daughter, but personal items were fetched from the Temple by Michonis, the prison inspector. Years later, the maid Rosalie recalled the delivery:

> A parcel was brought from the Temple. The Queen opened it without delay. It contained some beautiful cambric chemises, pocket handkerchiefs, some fichus, black silk stockings, a white wrapper to wear in the morning, some night caps, and several pieces of ribbon of various widths. Madame, who was quite touched at the sight of this linen, said, "From the careful way in which all these things have been arranged, I can recognize the thoughtfulness and hand of my poor sister, Elisabeth."

Adapting to her dreadful circumstances, Marie Antoinette struggled to maintain standards in her personal appearance. One of the women employed in the Conciergerie would arrange her hair every morning with some pomade, a dusting of powder, and a white ribbon. Before long, curiosity seekers bribed their way into the prison to walk past the queen's cell for a fixed stare. Even in jail, she was on public display, just like when she had first arrived at Versailles so long ago. This woman, who cherished her privacy, was destined to be robbed of it.

One day, the jailers Richards brought their son to meet the queen, hoping to cheer her. Unfortunately for Antoinette, the little fair-haired boy bore a resemblance to her imprisoned son. The queen hugged the child as though he were her own, sobbing hysterically. Wisely, the Richards knew to never repeat such a stressful scene.

When news of the queen's removal to the Conciergerie reached beyond France's borders, desperation filled the hearts of those who cherished Antoinette. Foremost was Fersen. He sought out Count Mercy to propose a rescue plan composed of chosen military men. Another brainstorm was to raise a huge ransom to bribe French authorities. Mercy dismissed both schemes as pure folly. Fersen wrote despondently, "Mercy believes that the whole royal family is doomed, and nothing can be done to save them."

A spark of hope flickered in Antoinette's heart on August 29. Michonis, the prison official, strode into her cell, accompanied by a gentleman, as was his custom. The queen never knew these strangers (often English tourists) who had bribed Michonis to see the discarded queen. During this particular visit, the queen's heart flat-lined for a brief second. She recognized the visitor. He was the Chevalier Rougeville, the man who saved her life on June 20, 1792, when the Tuileries was invaded. The queen grew agitated, but the chevalier kept his cool. He would later write that he barely recognized her as the woman he had rescued fourteen months earlier during the palace riot. The chevalier had two carnations pinned to his jacket that he nonchalantly threw behind the queen's dressing screen. The chevalier motioned to the queen to pick them up. The next moment, Rougeville and Michonis vanished from her cell. Shaking, Antoinette retrieved the carnations, finding two tiny notes inside. One spoke of the chevalier's loyalty, and the second proposed an escape plan. With no means to write a response, Antoinette took a pin from her bonnet and pricked in holes the words, *J'y vais,* roughly meaning, "Count me in."

Antoinette requested one of her guards, Gilbert, to pass the dotted piece of paper onto Michonis, and he surprisingly complied. Late at night on September 2, Michonis came to the queen's cell with an order to return her to the Temple. The subsequent details are a bit murky. Some sources reported that she had gained access to the door to the street; others indicate that Gilbert had chickened out and refused to proceed with the gambit. Regardless, the rescue was aborted, and the Chevalier Rougeville hurried to the border.

The members of the Convention saw red when they learned of the escape attempt. They launched an investigation into what became known as the Carnation Plot. Michonis was fired on the spot. The amiable Richards, husband and wife, who oversaw the care of the prisoners, were relieved of their duties. Luckily, Rosalie was allowed to retain her lowly position. In place of the Richards, a dourer couple was installed, Citizen Bault and his wife.

The Committee of Public Safety adopted two measures as a consequence of the attempt at escape. The committee decided to try Antoinette without delay. By this action, they intended to send a stern message to Antoinette's relatives who had resisted all hints of brokering a deal for her release. The second decision dealt with Antoinette's removal to an even more dreadful accommodation. In this inferior cell, she had no privacy screen to dress behind or relieve her bowels. Her fresh supply of linen was harshly curtailed. She was mortified by the vaginal blood loss that soiled her undergarments. Secretly, Rosalie would leave pieces of her own petticoat for the queen's sanitary uses. No one dared to do Antoinette's hair anymore, leaving her to arrange it herself for the first time in her life. The guards were ordered to watch her every move and discourage anyone from speaking to her. Rosalie was the only friendly face left.

In the early years of the Revolution, the queen reflected in a letter: "Tribulation makes us realize who we really are." Now at her extreme moment of political danger, emotional vulnerability, and physical deterioration, Antoinette inspired scattered admiration.

Outside of France, news of Antoinette's imminent trial panicked Fersen. Deeply distraught, he noted in his diary, "Should this trial take place, all will be lost." Fersen besieged Count Mercy to exert his influence on the Austrians to negotiate with the French authorities. Mercy roused himself, exhibiting rare emotion in a note to the emperor:

> So long as the Queen of France has not been directly threatened, we have been able to keep our silence for fear of arousing the rage of the savages around her. But now that she has been handed over to a bloody tribunal, any step that gives hope of saving her should be taken as a duty. Posterity will hardly believe that so enormous a

crime took place only a few steps away from the victorious armies of Austria, and that those armies did nothing to prevent it.

The queen's nephew, Emperor Francis II, sent no reply. Alarmed, Mercy urgently contacted the emperor's foreign minister:

> Is the Emperor going to allow the Queen to perish without even trying to save her from her executioners? I know the impossibility of taking any political step in common with the other Parties in this matter, but are there not private attentions, separate from political considerations, owed by the head of the House of Austria to the daughter of Maria Theresa who is about to mount the scaffold of her husband? Is it either to the dignity or the interest of His Majesty the Emperor to see the fate with which his august aunt is menaced and do nothing to try to deliver her from the hands of her executioners?

The response to the plaintive appeal was a stony silence. Nobody—not one soul in Antoinette's large family spread across Europe—lifted one finger to help her. Ultimately, Marie Antoinette would be written off as collateral damage.

> "Life is truly known only to those who suffer, lose, endure adversity and stumble from defeat to defeat."
> *Anaïs Nin*

Chapter 76

Buck Up, Sister

*A*s evidence for the trial was gathered, the magistrates felt they hit paydirt when Antoinette's son revealed "secrets." On October 6 Louis Charles told interrogators that his mother and aunt had met clandestinely with Lafayette, Bailly, and Pétion while in the Tuileries palace; and in the Temple, municipal guards relayed news from outside and served as couriers for smuggled notes. The clincher that amazed everyone was the revelation that his mother and aunt had sexually abused him.

The following day, the boy's sister was questioned regarding her brother's assertions in his presence. Madame Royal denied them all, confused at hearing her brother speak such trash. Next, Madame Elisabeth was interrogated before her nephew. She recoiled in disgust at her nephew's claim, yelling at him, "Oh, you little monster!" The public prosecutor, Fouquier-Tinville, contentedly smiled to uncover evidence confirming Antoinette's baseness.

In the early evening of Saturday, October 12, 1793, Antoinette had just dozed off when the heavy doors to her cell swung open. She was ordered to get dressed and follow the gendarmes. She was led through a series of corridors until she entered the former Grand Chamber of the Paris Parlement that she recognized immediately. Previously, this impressive space used to be decorated with tapestries and a painting of the Crucifixion. Now the queen saw a chamber renamed the Hall of Freedom, minus all the previous décor. All that dotted the walls were emblems of the Revolution, along with two large busts: one of Brutus, and the other of Marat. The queen was instructed to sit on a bench facing three men: Armand Herman, the president of the Tribunal; Antoine Fouquier-Tinville, the public prosecutor; and the court stenographer, Fabricius. The first two were costumed like malevolent wizards from a fantasy film, wearing all black attire with large hats sporting a turned-up front, festooned with tall black feathers. A heavy medallion hung on their chests bearing the inscription, The Law.

Antoinette was brought to this court in accordance with the laws of the republic, for a preliminary hearing in advance of her trial. The court stenographer noted that the prisoner seemed on edge. She sensed a group of people in attendance whom she could not see for lack of lighting. These unseen observers were guests of Fouquier-Tinville. They must have felt like theater patrons at a dress rehearsal.

The pre-trial interrogation, and the trial itself, would forever sparkle as the crowning achievement of Marie Antoinette's life. No matter her shortcomings and mistakes, she stepped up to the challenge and delivered one of the sharpest testimonies ever witnessed in a courtroom.

Simulating machine gun fire, Antoinette was sprayed with craftily prepared accusations intended to fluster her. Her inquisitors expected haughty, angry answers. The queen knew she had to summon a sharp mental presence and an unbreachable composure. Nicholas Herman fired off the questions.

Herman—*State your name, age, profession, birthplace, and place of abode.*

Queen —*I used to be called Marie Antoinette of Lorraine and Austria. I am about 38 years of age, widow of the King of France, and born at Vienna.*

Herman—*What was the place of your abode at the time of your arrest?*

Queen— *I had not been arrested. They came to take me from the chamber of the Legislative Assembly and conducted me to the Temple.*

Right out of the gate, Antoinette was on her mettle. She brilliantly identified herself with the title she held before her marriage, implying she was still Queen of France. She also corrected the president of the Revolutionary Tribunal, rejecting the assertion that she had been arrested. As far as she was concerned, she had been unjustly detained.

Herman attacked the queen for draining the Treasury and sending money to her brother Joseph.

> Herman—*Isn't it true that besides outrageously squandering the finances of France for the sake of your pleasures, you also sent vast sums of money to your brother, the Emperor, the fruits of the sweat of the people?*

> Queen—*Never! I recognize that this lie has often been leveled against me. I loved my husband too much to dissipate the money of our country. Furthermore, my brother didn't need any money from France.*

Herman then accused her of corresponding with the enemies of France, leading her husband by the nose, and orchestrating the flight to Varennes.

> Herman—*Wasn't it you who taught Louis Capet the art of dissimulation with which for so long he deceived the French people?*

> Queen—*Yes, the people have been cruelly deceived, but neither by my husband nor me.*

> Herman—*Well, then, who has deceived the people?*

> Queen—*By those who felt it to be in their interest. We had never deceived them.*

> Herman—*You were the principal instigator of Louis Capet's treachery. It was because of your goading he desired to leave France, and to make himself leader of those madmen who wanted to destroy their country.*

> Queen—*My husband never desired to leave France. I followed him everywhere, but if he had wanted to leave his fatherland, I would have tried to dissuade him.*

Herman castigated her for being an enemy of the people and then hit her on the sensitive matter of her son's future.

Herman—*You have never ceased wishing to destroy liberty; you wanted to reign no matter what the cost, even if you remounted the throne over the corpses of patriots.*

Queen—*We had no need to remount the throne; we were already on it. We never wished for anything but the happiness of France; if the nation were happy, we would have been content.*

Herman—*Do you think that kings are necessary for the happiness of a people?*

Queen —*An individual cannot make a decision on such a subject.*

Herman—*No doubt you regret that your son should have lost a throne on which he might have sat if the people, at last enlightened to its rights, had not destroyed that throne?*

Queen— *I shall regret nothing for my son if his country is happy.*

Herman grilled her about her secret dealings with municipal officers, as well as the infamous Carnation Plot. To Herman's irritation, Antoinette kept her cool and made him look like a fool. Finally, the peeved Herman concluded the pre-trial interrogations.

Herman—*Have you anything to add to these answers, and do you have any counsel?*

Queen—*No, I know no one.*

Herman—*Would you like the Tribunal to appoint one or two for you?*

Queen—*Yes, willingly.*

The transcript was read back to Antoinette, and she declared that it was truthful. She signed the statement and retraced her steps to her cell. After Antoinette withdrew, the two officials discussed how best to proceed during the upcoming trial, convinced that they would break her during the proceedings. Unbeknownst to the queen, the trial was purposely planned during her menstrual cycle. Officials were aware that she was losing significant blood during her cycle that weakened her considerably. With little sleep and the loss of blood, they were confident that Antoinette would not be at her best and publicly demonstrate that she was an arrogant bitch.

On the next day in the late afternoon, Antoinette's appointed defense lawyers, Messieurs Chauveau-Lagarde and Tronson Doucoudray entered her cell. The queen expressed her appreciation for their courage to defend her. They presented the eight-paged accusation that they had just received but not read. The queen was convinced it had to be a document filled with lies. The attorneys, alarmed at having zero time to prepare for the next day's trial, strongly advised Antoinette to petition the National Convention to grant her attorneys three days to prepare her defense. The queen flatly refused this odious request, citing that the deputies of the Convention had murdered her husband. The skilled lawyers countered that she owed it to the memory of her late husband and for the sake of her children to make the best defense possible. Their argument melted her abhorrence of contacting the Convention:

> Citizen President,
>
> Citizens Tronson and Lagarde, whom the Tribunal has assigned to me as defenders, tell me that they have only today been instructed on their mission that I should be judged tomorrow, and it is impossible for them to understand such a mass of documents in so short a time, or even to read them. I owe it to my children not to omit any means toward the justification of their mother. My defense asks for a delay of three days; I hope that the Convention will accord them this.

Lagarde took the letter to Fouquier-Tinville, who in turn passed it on to Robiespierre. Both men brushed aside the request. After Robiespierre's death, it was found with a cache of other documents hidden under his bed. The trial would not be delayed.

> "Women are like teabags. We don't know our
> strength until we are in hot water."
> *Eleanor Roosevelt*

Chapter 77

Day One of the Trial

At eight o'clock on Monday morning on October 14, Antoinette appeared again in court. With the daylight, she could see that it was a SRO crowd of six hundred spectators jammed into the courtroom. Every eye was glued on her to get a better view. An audible gasp spilled from the spectators when confronted with the queen's physical presence. She had been out of visual circulation for more than a year and appeared to be a ghostly figure walking into the courtroom. The newspaper, *Le Moniteur*, validated the astonished response of the crowd, noting, "the Widow Capet was prodigiously changed." She was told to take her place in an armchair. Antoinette became the prey dropped into a tank of fasting piranhas.

The trial opened with the Act of Accusation portraying Antoinette as treasonous, selfish, duplicitous, a plunderer, and worst of all, "She is so dissolute and so familiar with all crimes, that forgetting her quality as a mother, and the limits prescribed by the law of nature, she has not hesitated to prostitute herself with Louis Charles Capet, her son; and according to the confession of the latter, she has committed indecencies with him, the very name of which strikes the soul with horror."

Spasms besieged Antoinette's heart when forced to listen to these charges originating in hell. What hideous coercion did they apply to her son to make him utter such filth? Devastated by this cruelty, the queen somehow mastered a poised visage.

With the Act of Accusation introduced, President Herman fixed his eyes on the queen, bellowing, "This is what you are accused of; lend an attentive ear; you are going to hear the testimonies brought against you." The prosecution began by calling the first of forty-one witnesses, with no cross examination permitted. However, witnesses, members of the jury, and even the accused, could propose questions or interrupt whenever they chose.

The first to testify was Laurent Lecointre, the second-in-command of the National Guard deployed at Versailles in October of 1789. How he survived the Revolution is nothing short of miraculous. His unofficial title should have been "Denouncer in Chief." He never missed an opportunity to question the patriotism of accused citizens. In Antoinette's trial, he described for two hours the banquet given to the Flanders Regiment at Versailles, including other events he allegedly witnessed during the summer of 1789. When this windbag ended his account, questions were posed to the queen in an effort to trap her in a lie.

Herman—*What were the plots about surrounding the representatives of the people with bayonets, and assassinating half of them if possible?*

Queen —*I never heard of such a thing.*

Herman—*Did you have knowledge of the plans of the former Count Artois to have the National Assembly Hall burned to the ground? Having discovered the violent nature of this plan, was he not told to emigrate for fear that his behavior would become public knowledge?*

Queen—*I have never heard it said that my brother d'Artois had any such plan of which you describe. And as for his departure from France, he decided to emigrate of his own free will.*

Herman—*What use did you make of the immense sums which you had been provided with by the various finance ministers?*

Queen—*No enormous sums had ever been entrusted to me; the monies that were given to me covered the salaries of those who were employed in my household.*

Herman—*How did the family of the Polignacs, who were poor at first, grow so rich?*

Queen—*The family held offices at Court which were very lucrative.*

The next witness, Jean Baptiste Lapière, a former major of the National Guard, related his recollection of the Varennes incident. He declared that on June 20, 1791, he had heard that aristocrats planned to abduct the royal family during the night, but that notwithstanding his vigilance, he had seen nothing. Then, the prosecutor grilled the queen about the escape attempt. She answered all his questions with dignity and honesty.

The prosecutor then called the slime bucket radical, Jacques Hébert. He reported finding in the queen's prayer book a holy card depicting a flaming heart, "a counter-revolutionary emblem." Then he noted a hat found in Elisabeth Capet's room that once belonged to Louis Capet, and no doubt was given to her by a deceitful employee in the Temple. Vindictively, he related the young Capet's following admissions: Lafayette played a role in the events surrounding the flight to Varennes; news vendors were paid to shout the headline news under the prisoner's windows; and written messages were secretly passed on to the prisoners in their laundered clothing. Then came the bombshell: Hébert disclosed that he had heard that the young Capet masturbated. Hébert questioned the child how he learned such vile practices. The boy responded that both his mother and aunt taught him.

Marie Antoinette's head must have been spinning to listen to these accusations. After Hébert finished, Herman unleashed questions to the accused about unpatriotic municipal officials who assisted her during her detention in the Temple. Unexpectedly, a sensation shook the courtroom when one of the jurors interrupted the prosecutor insisting that the Widow Capet answer with respect to the physical abuse crimes against her son. This demand roused the queen from her seat, and in an emotional outburst she declared:

Queen—*I remained silent on that subject because Nature holds all such crimes in abhorrence.*

Then turning to the stunned spectators, she became animated and cried out:

Queen —*I appeal to all mothers who are present in this chamber, is such a crime possible?*

As Antoinette regained her composure, a favorable buzz arose from the public. The upstaged judge quickly called for a recess. As the courtroom emptied, the queen exited holding her head high as was her habit. One of the spectators shouted out, "Look at how arrogant she is." There was no placating this bunch of poisoned hearts.

During the recess the queen questioned her attorneys if they felt she had put too much dignity in her answers. They assured her that she was doing an admirable job. They reviewed the testimony thus far with the queen, feeling confident that the prosecution had proved nothing. Years later, Chauveau-Lagarde would write that the queen believed her acquittal was highly possible due to a lack of proof to the accusations.

At five in the evening the session resumed with Herman grilling Antoinette once again about the Varennes episode. At one particular question, Antoinette's heart skipped a beat.

Herman—*Who supplied the famous carriage you traveled in with your family?*

Queen —*A foreigner.*

Herman—*Of what nation?*

Queen —*A Swede.*

Herman—*Wasn't it Fersen who resided in Paris on the Rue de Bacq?*

Queen—*Yes.*

If the court officials had suspected any hanky-panky between the queen and Fersen, they would have seized this moment to use that evidence to destroy her image as a faithful wife and thereby cast doubt on the legitimacy of her son. Fortunately, their liaison remained a non-issue. Likewise regarding the apocryphal sound bite, "Let them eat cake," not one crumb fell from the prosecutor's lips.

Not all witnesses appeared willingly, such as Bailly, one of the early luminaries of the Revolution, and the former mayor of Paris. The opening questions immediately cast doubt on his patriotic fervor. Herman taunted him, implying that he was a secret friend of the monarchy. His appearance at the trial was a dress rehearsal for his own trial the following month.

A former maid at Versailles took the stand spouting clichéd allegations that appealed to the prejudices of the jurors and courtroom audience. It is interesting to note that the court could not cajole any other servant to testify against Antoinette; her staff generally revered her.

The motormouth maid asserted that the queen had sent money to her brother in Austria based on a conversation she had overheard. She also took credit for eavesdropping on collaborators of Count Artois hatching plots to massacre guards friendly toward the Revolution. She proudly foiled such plans. She next referred to a sensational charge that Antoinette concealed two pistols under her skirts with the purpose of assassinating the Duke of Orléans. Upon learning of this plot, the king ordered the queen to be searched and confiscated the weapons. As a punishment, Louis XVI confined Antoinette to her private apartments for a period of two weeks. Herman demanded that the queen reply to the charges.

Queen—*It is possible that I might have received an order from my husband to remain a fortnight in my apartments, but it was definitely not for the reason just mentioned.*

This answer begs amplification. It is a pity that whatever prompted Louis' order for Antoinette's confinement is not pursued in the trial. Obviously, Herman was a man of limited curiosity.

The trial dragged on with more witnesses, some of whom served as window dressing. Among them were the Richards, the former jailers at the Conciergerie. Finally, more testimony came from a guard regarding the Carnation Plot. By this time, it was eleven at night, and everyone was seeing cross-eyed. Herman adjourned the proceedings until nine the following morning. The courtroom emptied, and Antoinette was escorted back to her cell.

"Courtroom—a place where Jesus and Judas would be equals,
with the betting odds favoring Judas."
Henry Louis Mencken

Chapter 78

Day Two of the Trial

Normally, October 15 was a memorable day for Marie Antoinette, marking the name day of her mother and daughter. She must have thought of both of them during this final, grinding day of her trial. The morning session would not break for a recess until half past four in the afternoon.

The first witness of the day, Count Charles Henri Estaing, a career officer, took the stand. He expressed strong feelings against Antoinette, pointing out that she had unilaterally prevented him from receiving the honors due to him, including being made a Marshal of France for his heroic services rendered in the land of liberty, America. Furthermore, he revealed that he had warned the accused about the bad advice she received from her minions, but she disregarded his counsel.

The court wasn't swallowing this testimony, convinced that the count orchestrated the abortive attempt of the royal family to flee Versailles during the events of October 1789. Estaing recalled being present at an urgent meeting on October 5, discussing the march from Paris aimed at harming the queen. He quoted Antoinette as saying, "If the people of Paris are coming here to murder me, it is at the feet of my husband that they will find me, but I will not flee."

The queen interrupted Estaing, remarking, "Yes, that is exactly true. They prevailed upon me to leave alone because they said I was the only one in true danger."

Estaing's comments in the queen's defense were not a good move for him in the long run.

Following Estaing's testimony, Antoine Simon slithered into the courtroom. The queen now had to master her emotions at all costs. This was the man who was her son's "guardian" in the Temple prison. Goosebumps traversed her flesh on seeing him, knowing that he terrorized her son daily.

After several more testimonies, a little bundle was exhibited with fanfare in the courtroom. It held the personal items that Antoinette had gathered in a handkerchief as she was led from the Temple to the Conciergerie. The pathetic contents were displayed to the court; the queen was forced to identify her confiscated property. First to be identified were locks of hair of her husband and her children. Next was a piece of paper, full of symbols and ciphers that the prosecution was convinced had been used to communicate with supporters outside the Temple. The queen insisted it was a mathematical table to teach her son his numbers. The clerk continued with the inventory: a small case containing scissors, needles, silk and thread, a small mirror, a gold ring with locks of hair, a paper with written devotional prayers, and lastly, a miniature portrait of Madame Lamballe.

Following the piteous show-and-tell portion of the trial, more witnesses recounted events that occurred at Versailles in the summer and fall of 1789. The most significant witness called was the Marquis La Tour du Pin, a seasoned military man and former minister of war. He confessed to knowing the accused but was ignorant of the charges listed in the Act of Accusation. The court didn't believe a word he said, guaranteeing numbered days for him. President Herman aimed his next round of questions at Antoinette.

Herman—*Didn't you abuse the influence you had over your husband in asking him continually for sums of money from the public Treasury?*

Queen —*I never did so.*

Herman—*Where, then, did you get the money to build and fit out the Petit Trianon in which you gave feasts, where you were always the goddess?*

Queen —*There was a fund designated for that sole purpose.*

Herman—*This fund was quite considerable since the Petit Trianon has cost enormous sums.*

Queen—*It is possible that the Petit Trianon may have cost immense sums, maybe even more than I wished. This expense was incurred by degrees; in fact, I desire more than anyone that everybody be informed as to what has been done there.*

Herman—*Was it not at the Petit Trianon that you met the woman, La Motte?*

Queen —*I have never seen her.*

Herman—*Was she not your victim in the affair of the famous necklace?*

Queen —*How could she be, as I did not know her?*

Herman—*So you persist in denying that you ever knew her?*

Queen —*My intention is not to deny; I speak the truth, and I shall persist in doing so.*

A flurry of witnesses next appeared who described the conduct of the royal family at the Temple. One municipal employee spoke of fellow employees, Toulan and Lépitre, often coming together to the Temple. He asserted that they engaged in conversations with the prisoners. This witness declared that he saw Antoinette give Toulan a small gold box on one occasion.

Herman to the queen—*Did you ever give a gold box to Toulan?*

Queen —*No. I gave nothing, neither to Toulan nor any of the other municipal officers.*

But Antoinette *had* given Toulan a small gold box that he foolishly showed to colleagues.

Six more witnesses, mostly municipal officers, were called to testify; they were suspected of aiding and abetting the queen while imprisoned in the Temple. Like many witnesses who preceded them, they all professed ignorance of the charges leveled against the accused. Then the prosecutor rehooked his claws onto Antoinette.

Herman—*Do you still stubbornly maintain that neither Bailly nor Lafayette had anything to do with your flight on the night of June 20, 1791?*

Queen —*Yes.*

Herman—*I want to point out to you that you will find yourself in sharp disagreement with the testimony of your son.*

Queen —*It's easy to get a mere child of eight years old to repeat words that you wish to hear.*

Herman—*But we were not satisfied with just one such declaration. He repeated this fact to us several times, and it was always the same story.*

Queen—*All the more reason to believe the child was coerced; I resolutely deny the truth of those statements.*

Herman next called Jean-Baptiste Michonis to testify. Michonis stated he was a lemonade seller, a member of the Paris Commune of August 10, and a police administrator. He said that he had known the accused since August 1793 when he transferred her from the Temple to the Conciergerie. Michonis was a resourceful man and for a price arranged admittance to the Conciergerie. Any inkling that such an arrangement might be construed as a conflict of interest escaped his grasp. He tried to wiggle his way out of knowingly advancing the Carnation Plot, haplessly digging his own future grave with his testimony. However, he genuinely treated Marie Antoinette as decently as possible.

In their quest to leave no witness unheard, Herman and Fouquier-Tinville summoned Pierre-Edouard Bernier, a physician charged with the care of Antoinette's children. From the peanut gallery, stinging remarks were hurled about the royalist proclivities of Bernier. Witnesses observed that whenever the doctor approached the children of the accused he would manifest the basest servility that typified the scrapping etiquette of the former royal regime. In reply, Dr. Bernier suggested that the court did not appreciate the difference between groveling and good manners.

Finally, Herman wrapped up the long day of questioning.

Herman—*Why did you promise to raise your children in the principles of the Revolution, and yet teach them nothing but errors? For instance, you treated your son with a respect that proves you imagined him one day as the successor of the former King, his father?*

Queen—He was far too young to speak on such a subject. I placed him at the head of the table to supervise him myself with what he wanted to eat.

Herman—Have you anything to add to your defense?

Queen —Yesterday I had absolutely no idea of the witnesses to be called. Nor did I have any inkling of what they would depose against me. Not one person here has produced a shred of evidence. I finish by observing that I was only the wife of Louis XVI, and it was my duty to conform myself to his will.

Herman declared that the interrogations were completed. Fouquier-Tinville addressed the jury, reminding them of the evil conduct of the royal court and in particular, the avowed enemy of the French nation, the Austrian Woman. She was the principal instigator of all the troubles that had taken place in France, responsible for the deaths of thousands of French patriots.

After these remarks the queen's defense team pleaded its client's case. In comparison to the length of the trial, this portion was brief, spanning two hours. The attorneys knew better than to refute the witnesses called. Instead they implored the clemency of the court to spare the defendant. Their defense was met with an indifferent reception. Not one word of their argument was recorded in the court records. However, the court reporter did mention that the attorneys fulfilled their civic duty with zeal and elegance. Any doubt about the outcome?

> "Think like a queen. A queen is not afraid to fail.
> Failure is another stepping stone to greatness."
> *Oprah Winfrey*

Chapter 79

A Drum Roll, Please

*W*hen Chauveau-Lagarde sat down after his closing argument, the queen leaned over to him, expressing her thanks: "How tired you must be, Monsieur. I am deeply moved by all you have done for me." Herman overheard these words and sternly admonished the accused to keep her mouth shut. Closing in on one in the morning of October 16, Herman ordered that Antoinette be led out of the court to a waiting room.

Facing the twelve members of the jury, Herman took one hour to sum up the trial. He began, extolling, "A magnificent example is given as a gift to the entire world today. The significance of this gift will forever abide in the hearts of all of humanity. Nature and Reason, which sadly for such a long time were trampled underfoot, are now finally liberated. Equality is now and forever triumphant." He reaffirmed that all the statements presented to the court regarding the despicable behavior of Antoinette were true. He presented the following two questions for the jurors to consider regarding the sentence of the Widow Capet:

"Is Marie Antoinette convicted of having cooperated in the machinations and of having participated in intelligences with enemies of the republic?"

"Is Marie Antoinette convicted of having played a part in that plot and conspiracy to foment civil war in the republic?"

After two days and forty-one witnesses, the jury's decision boiled down to the two unproven charges. Not one word is mentioned of her reported molestation of her son, an accusation that the court magistrates wished they could have been expunged from the record. The jury filed out of the courtroom, returning an hour later with their verdict on both charges:

GUILTY

Antoinette was summoned back to the hushed courtroom. Herman intoned, "Antoinette, hear the sentence of the jury!" Fouquier-Tinville read the sentence demanding that the accused be executed in accordance with the articles of the penal code. The queen showed no visible reaction, seeming to be in a trance. Execution? How could this be? The Lisbon Curse could have supplied the answer.

Herman asked the accused, "Do you have anything to declare or do you object to the sentence of the laws demanded by the public accuser?" The best Antoinette could muster at the moment was to shake her head no. The shock of the death sentence robbed her of her voice. The courtroom was gyrating faster than an out-of-control merry-go-round. Herman ordered Antoinette be returned to her cell. The queen recollected herself and exited with her head held majestically high. She knew she was leaving the courtroom, yet she felt as though she was encased in some other person's body. In the dark passageway to her cell she momentarily faltered, telling her guard, De Busne, "I can scarcely see where to put my feet." De Busne offered her his arm for support, sparking his arrest the next day as a suspected royalist sympathizer. Paranoia was the law of the land.

"Never bend your head.
Always hold it high.
Look the world straight in the eye."
Helen Keller

Chapter 80

Time to Grab a Hanky

*A*ntoinette unsteadily reentered her cell and asked for candles, some paper, and a pen and ink. The jailer quickly complied, knowing her message would not reach the recipient, but find its way to the office of the Revolutionary Council. By this deceptive method, its leaders often learned valuable information, often compromising other traitors, or learning the location of hidden valuables that could subsidize the Revolution.

At half past four in the morning on Wednesday, October 16, 1793, a dazed Antoinette wrote to Madame Elisabeth, her stalwart sister-in-law. In this final letter, the queen exposed the brush strokes of valor, vulnerability, and utmost tenderness. Her tears forever stained the paper as she wrote her heart-rending goodbye:

> It is to you, my dear sister, that I write for the very last time. I have
> just been condemned to death, but not a shameful death because
> that is reserved only for criminals, but rather to go and join your
> brother. Innocent like him, I hope to display the same courage
> as he did up until my last breath. I am calm as anyone would be
> when there's nothing to reproach my conscience. I am suffering the
> cruelest sorrow to leave behind my two poor children; you know
> that I lived only for them, and you my sweet and tender sister, you
> who by your loyal friendship have sacrificed everything to be with
> us. My God, in what a dreadful position I must now leave you.

I have learned from the prosecuting attorney that my daughter has been separated from you. [Antoinette misunderstood the prosecutor's remarks; Madame Royale was still confined with her aunt.] Alas, the poor child, I dare not write to her because she would never receive my letter; I don't even know if this one will reach you. With utmost tenderness receive my blessings for them. I hope that one day when they are grown up, they will be reunited with you and enjoy once more your tender care. May they both always remember the lessons that I have tried ceaselessly to inspire in them: that principles and fulfilling their obligations should be the primary foundation of life, and that their mutual trust and affection for each other will be the cause of their happiness in life. May my daughter, mindful of her greater maturity, be always helpful to her brother with advice which her greater experience provides in abundance. As for my son, may he always take care of his sister's concerns and requirements which his affection for her will make easy. And finally, may they both remember that no matter what station in life they achieve, that they will never be truly happy unless they remain lovingly close to each other. I hope they learn from our example. How many times during our shared misfortunes have we found consolation in each other; and then in happy times, one can enjoy such affection twice as much. And where can one find a more tender or sincere attachment than within one's own family? Let my son never forget his father's last words which I purposely repeat to him: that he may never seek to avenge our deaths.

My dear sister, I must speak to you about something that weighs heavily upon my heart. I know how my son deeply hurt you with his testimony; please forgive him, my dear sister. Think of his young age and how easy it is to make a child say what one wants to hear, without truly comprehending the meaning of his words. I pray that the day will come when he will know better than anyone else the high price you have paid for your goodness and kindness for both him and his sister.

It remains for me to entrust to you my final thoughts. I actually wanted to write them from the very beginning of the trial, but apart from the fact that I was allowed no writing materials, events unfolded so rapidly that I never really had the time to write a word. I die in the Catholic, Apostolic, Roman religion of my ancestors in which I was brought up and always professed. Having no spiritual consolation to assist me now, and not knowing if there are still priests of my religion around here, and considering the circumstances of where I am now, I recognize the great risks any such priest would incur in seeing me. I sincerely ask God to forgive me all my sins that I have committed during my life; I hope that in His goodness, He will hear my final prayers, as well as those that I have been making for a long time. May He gladly receive my soul with His infinite mercy and kindness. I ask for the forgiveness of all those whom I have known and especially you, my dear sister, for all the hurts that I have caused you without realizing it. I forgive all my enemies the harm that they have done to me. I say farewell to my aunts, and to all of my brothers and sisters. I have had friends. The very idea of being separated from them forever and their inevitable suffering is one of the greatest regrets I have in dying. But let them know, that up until my very last breath, I was thinking of them.

Goodbye, my good and sweet sister. May this letter reach you! Always remember me. I hug you tightly with all my heart, as well as my two poor children! My God, how it is tearing me apart to leave them forever. Farewell, farewell! I must now devote myself to my spiritual needs exclusively. Since I have no freedom regarding my actions here, it is possible that they will bring me one of their sanctioned priests, but I swear here, I will not say a word to him and that I will treat him as an absolute stranger.

The letter ended abruptly with no signature, not unusual for Marie Antoinette. Imagine the words left unsaid, but suggested since the queen knew this letter would first be read by municipal officers before it ever reached Elisabeth. Above all, Antoinette affirmed that she died in her true religion. This implied that she had received the sacraments of confession and communion sometime during her incarceration at the Conciergerie. Second, she mentioned her friends, assuring them of her loving thoughts until her last breath—a reference particularly intended for Count Fersen. Next, she exhorted her children to cling to each other other, speculating that one day they would be restored to their exalted status. And most touching of all, she implored her sister-in-law to remember her. Anyone who has been incarcerated for either one night or a lifetime can identify with that bleak desolation. Finally, Antoinette ends on a defiant note, refusing to acknowledge any impostor priest. What a queen!

Antoinette summoned the jailer, requesting that he deliver her letter to Madame Elisabeth. He knew the drill, and automatically passed it on to the prosecutor. Even though Antoinette never signed the letter, the signatures of high profile honchos of the Revolution littered the bottom of the letter, acknowledging their perusal.

In her green Moroccan-bound leather prayer book, Antoinette penned the following lines to her children:

My God, have pity on me; my eyes have no more tears left to cry for you, my poor dear children; goodbye, goodbye.

The prayer book, the queen's letter to Madame Elisabeth, and a few other personal mementos belonging to the queen were later found under the bed of Robiespierre after his execution. What a twisted memorabilia collector he proved to be!

After writing her final letter and goodbyes to her children, Antoinette collapsed into sobs on her cot, an emotional and physical wreck. For three days, she had little sleep and barely anything to eat. She wept deeply, terrified at her imminent execution. She hated to leave this world especially when her children were so vulnerable to the mad caprices of their captors. She felt totally abandoned as hopelessness swamped her heart. How could she, the Queen of France, be living this grotesque nightmare? How did her life tumble into this death spiral? Why hadn't her family intervened to rescue her? Why? Why? Trembling with fear, nauseous, and physically drained, she struggled to pull herself together, knowing she had to steel herself for the ordeal ahead.

That's how the maid found her as she entered Antoinette's cell shortly after daybreak. Rosalie gently asked the queen what she required, offering to bring some warm broth that she had prepared. The queen sobbed, "I shall never need anything again, my girl; everything is over for me." But Rosalie sweetly insisted that she take some nourishment. To appease Rosalie, the queen forced down several spoonsful of bouillon.

Prohibited from wearing her black mourning dress, this demand must have brought a weak smile to Antoinette's face, considering the limitations of her wardrobe. Her only other garment was a simple white piquet dress. It was intended to be worn in the privacy of a lady's home before changing into something more appropriate for public venues. Her humorless accusers feared that her fraying widow's weeds might evoke sympathy from the impressionable throng. So white was the only option. But white symbolized innocence and martyrdom and was also the color of the Bourbon dynasty.

By wearing white, Antoinette was making a lasting imprint that the revolutionaries were too obtuse to recognize.

Antoinette dressed with Rosalie's help as the guard observed all. The queen begged him to allow her some privacy as she undressed: "I entreat you, Monsieur, in the name of decency, to allow me to change my linen without a witness." He grunted that his orders were to watch her every move. The queen sighed in resignation, trying to preserve some shred of modesty with Rosalie's body acting as a barrier. The queen gingerly removed the undergarment that was stained with blood from her hemorrhages. She stuffed it into a crack in the cell's wall. She then put on a clean undergarment followed by a white chemise and black stockings, held up with garters. Over these garments she slipped into her white dress. She finished the outfit by wrapping a white muslin fichu around her shoulders. She arranged her fair hair with gray-white traces with Rosalie's help. She carefully placed her white bonnet on her head and a ribbon on her wrist. Finally, she slipped her feet into plum-colored two-inch heels.

Marie Antoinette was unrecognizable as a queen. No gown, no makeup, no perfume, no stylish coiffure adorned with feathers, no jewels, and no royal crown—absolutely nothing! The only distinction that remained was her imperial bloodline. She was ready for her final close-up.

> "Courage is being scared to death—
> and saddling up anyway."
> *John Wayne*

Chapter 81

Surrender, Antoinette

A constitutional priest, Reverend Girard, entered the queen's cell offering his priestly services that she declined. He persisted, requesting to accompany her to the scaffold. She replied indifferently, "Do as you wish, Monsieur." She was on her knees praying when Herman, the president of the Revolutionary Council, and three associates entered. They informed her that her sentence would be read. She waved them off saying that was unnecessary. Herman ordered her to be silent and pay attention.

Suddenly, the frightening figure of the executioner, Sanson, loomed forward, commanding her to hold out her hands. Horrified to have her hands bound, Antoinette protested that her late husband did not have his bound. Hesitating, Sanson looked to Herman, who snapped at him, "Do your duty." The executioner snipped off her neatly arranged hair with large scissors. He stuffed the unevenly cut hair in his pocket and plopped the linen bonnet back onto her head.

Antoinette was led out of her cell into the courtyard. Merciful God in Heaven, where was her carriage? She knew that Louis had been taken to the guillotine in a closed carriage; she expected the same. The previous night the executioner had asked the prosecutor if he should hire a cab for the Widow Capet. The prosecutor scoffed at the idea, snorting the manure cart was good enough for the Austrian Woman.

Deaf to her pleas for a carriage, they pointed to the open cart, yanking her toward it. Terror grabbed hold of her guts. She resisted any further step, instructing the executioner to untie her hands so she could relieve herself.

Marie Antoinette, the Queen of France, was forced to squat in a corner for all to witness as she emptied her bowels. Still shaken, her hands were retied. She mounted the cart accepting the steady arm of the executioner. She sat on the rough wooden plank facing the horse but was ordered to sit with her back to the horse. Even the Revolution had its own distinct rule book of execution etiquette.

Aware of the violent nature of some revolutionaries, Antoinette feared that the mob would drag her from the cart and butcher her. She prayed to be spared that type of ending. The gates opened and the cart, hitched to two farm horses, entered the street a few minutes past eleven in the morning. The executioner and his assistant stood behind the queen while the constitutional priest sat next to her, on occasion flashing a crucifix before her face. Amazingly, she sat bolt upright for almost an hour as the cart wobbled over the cobblestones—no easy feat considering her hands were tied behind her back.

Mostly silence marked the procession to the scaffold. At the head of the cart rode a lone soldier raising his sword, signifying to the crowd to make way for the prisoner. Only on the Rue St. Honoré did the temper of the crowd turn ugly. At this location, the tough market women and their sort had gathered. These girls did not believe in holding back. The queen was battered with a torrent of threats and curses. The troops kept them from grasping at their target. Once past these harpies, an eerie stillness resumed. The crowd was stunned by the appearance of this diminished woman wearing a humble dress. It was hard to believe that she had once been so glamorous, powerful, and untouchable.

The artist and revolutionary, Jacques Louis David, cornered a sniper's view of the fallen queen as she passed below him. From a balcony window, he penciled his memorable drawing of the condemned woman. While he sketched her as a frightful crone, his unerring artist's eye nonetheless recorded her regal essence. With an economy of lines, David raised this remnant of a woman to an image that still haunts viewers today.

The shattered queen maintained a detached gaze, not registering the fixed stares. The tricolor flags of the Revolution waved from most buildings as her sendoff. Besides the occasional insults, not one word of pity was offered.

Fragmented memories vied for her flickering attention. Thoughts of her children tugged at her heart. The uncertain future of her precious son magnified her anguish. Her death would be worth the price of having her beloved child become king. And restore her honor. The image of her late husband crowded her competing thoughts. She took solace in remembering that he never wavered in his devotion to her and their children. His exemplary fortitude during his final moments now helped to bolster hers. Antoinette had to prove herself to be a worthy consort of Louis XVI. No doubt, she wistfully recalled her august mother's great hopes for her future as a queen of fair France. What a relief that her mother had not lived to see this dreadful day! Lastly, she must have wrapped her heart around the face of Fersen, her true knight, who had sacrificed so much for her. How wrenching to never see him again!

Eyewitnesses who later wrote of their recollections were in agreement on one observation. They noticed that her dulled gaze was dispelled when she caught sight of the Tuileries gardens. It was there that she had walked daily with her children to enjoy their uplifting company. How many times had her son rushed to her with flowers he had just picked from his garden! As one witness described, for a brief moment a hint of color returned to her pale white face as "she turned with an earnest and lingering look."

Arriving at the scaffold, the queen alighted from the tumbrel resisting the assistance of the phony priest. She lively mounted the steep steps, anxious for this ordeal to end. It is often repeated that her final words were addressed to the executioner. Having stepped on Sanson's foot, Antoinette uttered, "Excuse me, Sir, I did not do it on purpose." A few writers recount that her last words spoken to the executioner were, "Make haste." Most reflections were written by surviving eyewitnesses after the monarchy was restored in 1815, leaving room for conjecture. No matter what she said, the outcome remains undisputed.

The spectators nearest the scaffold could see that her legs were shaking. She could not falter at this ultimate moment of her life. With a last wistful glance toward the Tuileries, the queen was shoved against the vertical plank. A leather belt was strapped around her waist and another around her upper back, to secure her. The plank was lowered to the horizontal position and quickly slid forward. Her head hung over a waiting receptacle. In quick succession, her bonnet was snatched from her head, and her fichu was ripped off her shoulders. Her last futile gesture was an attempt at modesty to cover her bare shoulders with her bound hands.

Swifter than a bolt of lightning, the blade was released with a muted click, descending the eight feet in a mere second, simultaneously severing the royal head. From the moment she arrived at the execution site until the blade fell, the deed was over within five minutes. Like all victims before her, the head was paraded around the scaffold for all to see. Obscene gestures, curses, and shouts of "Liberty" greeted Antoinette's head in its procession around the scaffold. The Lisbon Curse had fulfilled its promise.

Daniel Strobel, an American from Charleston traveling on business in Paris, saw the execution up close. He recalled that when the head was shown, he was startled that the queen's eyes flickered and then remained wide-open with an appearance of astonishment. Her body was tossed into the waiting cart layered with straw to absorb the blood. Her head was thrown into the cart, landing between her legs where it jiggled like a puppet on a string, all the way to the cemetery of Madeleine.

The grave diggers submitted their invoice for their services. Business was brisk and profitable in 1793.

To sum up Marie Antoinette in a few phrases is not adequate. But the polarizing argument remains unchanged: Antoinette was a solid narcissist whose meddling led the monarchy to its destruction, versus the conviction that she was a maligned martyr. But her narrative is more nuanced. Certainly, she brought a sophisticated style and glamour to Versailles. She also made a lot of enemies by snubbing influential people and breaking some of the sacrosanct societal rules. She was an exemplary mother and loyal friend. Politically, she was ill-equipped to take the reins of government when faced with her husband's passivity. In the end, what truly mattered is that she tried to perform her duty as queen and consort as she understood it. She endured much to preserve a throne for her husband and son. It is safe to say that few pampered queens have undergone a more radical plunge into misfortune during their lifetime. Somehow she weathered a storm of woes that would have broken many others. Neither a leech nor a saint, she was a flawed woman with a steel-plated backbone.

Perhaps poignantly, even her overbearing, but sage mother, Empress Maria Theresa, would have felt mighty proud of her Hapsburg daughter. Seeing her daughter imperiously upright in that disgusting dung cart lurching its way to the scaffold would have overcome the mother. Certainly, the empress would have saluted her youngest archduchess through choking sobs with a hearty German equivalent of, "You go, girl."

As for the rest of Antoinette's surviving relatives, a gilded curtain shrouded the very mention of her name. Years later, when Napoleon married Marie Antoinette's grand-niece, he remarked on this imperial amnesia. He noticed that an uncomfortable silence lingered in the air any time the executed queen's name surfaced in a conversation. Guilt hid itself under the nearest satin pillow.

Antoinette's circle of intimates was beyond consolation. In England, Antoinette's friend Georgiana, Duchess of Devonshire, bemoaned her loss: "The impression of the Queen's death is always before my mind. Besides the admiration that is universally felt for her answers during her trial, her cleverness, composure, and greatness of mind blaze forth in double splendor. But the horror of making the child depose against her is what one should have hoped that the mind of man was incapable of."

Her Swedish count, drowning in a sea of sorrow, groaned, "Her suffering and death and all my feelings never leave me for a moment. I can think of nothing else." Poor Fersen never recovered.

"Say goodnight, Gracie."
George Burns

Flashback to the Present

So, the fairy tale that begins with a dewy-eyed, teenage princess about to marry her prince does not conclude with the clichéd expectation, "And they lived happily ever after." Quite the opposite, indeed. Like a Wagnerian wheel of fortune with a cast of thousands, the fade-out scene discomforts us with an indelible image of widespread loss. There are no winners among the participants in this epic struggle. Just some fortunate survivors. The guillotine plays no favorites, as aristocrats and revolutionaries are all equals when bolted to the plank under its blind blade. Amidst the scattered carnage, the severed head of the queen reigns as most the unsettling visual in the national nightmare.

From Marie Antoinette's glittering beginning to her hideous end, her life resembles a roller-coaster ride. Sometimes it is a thrill a minute, but mostly a white knuckled shriek. At the end of the twisting tracks, the coaster emerges from the threatening tunnels, gulping for the reassuring daylight. The careening ride becomes smoother as the clicking cars glide to a slow stop, crowned by a gentle jolt. With awed astonishment, we marvel at a patrician lady seated alone in the front row of the capricious cars of destiny. We cannot suppress a hushed gasp, riveted by the woman's penetrating gaze. She is none other than the tenacious, courageous, unbreakable, and resplendent …

Austrian Woman

"And to make an end is to make a beginning.
The end is where we start from."
T.S. Eliot

Long Live the Queen